Magic in Ancient Greece and Rome

Magic in Ancient Greece and Rome

Lindsay C. Watson

BLOOMSBURY ACADEMIC
LONDON • NEW YORK • OXFORD • NEW DELHI • SYDNEY

BLOOMSBURY ACADEMIC
Bloomsbury Publishing Plc
50 Bedford Square, London, WC1B 3DP, UK
1385 Broadway, New York, NY 10018, USA

BLOOMSBURY, BLOOMSBURY ACADEMIC and the Diana logo are trademarks of
Bloomsbury Publishing Plc

First published in Great Britain 2019

Copyright © Lindsay C. Watson, 2019

Lindsay C. Watson has asserted his right under the Copyright, Designs and Patents Act, 1988, to be identified as Author of this work.

For legal purposes the Preface on p. viii constitute an extension of this copyright page.

Cover image: *Circe Invidiosa* (detail), 1892. John William Waterhouse, 1849–1917.
Photo by Fine Art Images/Heritage Images/Getty Images

All rights reserved. No part of this publication may be reproduced or transmitted in any form or by any means, electronic or mechanical, including photocopying, recording, or any information storage or retrieval system, without prior permission in writing from the publishers.

Bloomsbury Publishing Plc does not have any control over, or responsibility for, any third-party websites referred to or in this book. All internet addresses given in this book were correct at the time of going to press. The author and publisher regret any inconvenience caused if addresses have changed or sites have ceased to exist, but can accept no responsibility for any such changes.

A catalogue record for this book is available from the British Library.

Library of Congress Cataloging-in-Publication Data
Names: Watson, Lindsay, 1947– author.
Title: Magic in Ancient Greece and Rome / Lindsay C. Watson.
Description: London : IB Tauris, 2019. | Includes bibliographical references and index.
Identifiers: LCCN 2018049060 (print) | LCCN 2018050032 (ebook) | ISBN 9781350108950 (epub) | ISBN 9781350108967 (epdf) | ISBN 9781788312981 (pbk.)
Subjects: LCSH: Magic, Greek. | Magic, Roman.
Classification: LCC BF1591 (ebook) | LCC BF1591 .W38 2019 (print) |
DDC 133.4/30938—dc23
LC record available at https://lccn.loc.gov/2018049060

ISBN:	HB:	978-1-7883-1297-4
	PB:	978-1-7883-1298-1
	ePDF:	978-1-3501-0896-7
	eBook:	978-1-3501-0895-0

Typeset by RefineCatch Limited, Bungay, Suffolk

To find out more about our authors and books visit www.bloomsbury.com
and sign up for our newsletters.

Contents

List of Figures	vi
Preface	vii
List of Abbreviations	ix
1 Introduction	1
2 The Violence of Amatory Magic	23
3 *Defixiones*: A Recent History	57
Appendix: did *defixiones* work?	84
4 Magic and Herbs	99
5 Animals in Magic *Patricia Watson*	127
Appendix: amulets	149
6 Fictional Witches	167
7 Human Sacrifice in Ancient Magic?	203
Bibliography	227
Index	245

Figures

1	The Louvre 'Voodoo Doll'	27
2	Leaden curse tablet from Rome (first century BCE) separating Rhodine from Faustus	57
3	Wax poppet with multiple pins (France, modern era)	75
4	The inspiration for Tolkien's ring? Ring of Silvianus	83
5	White peony	102
6	Mandrake root	116
7	Mole's foot amulet, Norfolk, England, 1890–1910	133
8	David Teniers the Younger, *An Alchemist in His Laboratory*, c. 1650	145
9	Joan's Cottage	145
10	Kylix showing Odysseus' men turned into animals by Circe (sixth century BCE)	168
11	Medea murdering one of her sons (Ixion painter, Cumae, c. 330 BCE)	171
12	Goya, *The Witches' Sabbath*, 1798	191
13	Goya, *Wizards and Witches Offering a New-Born Baby to Their Master*, 1796–8	205

Preface

The seeds of this book were sown with the award of a research grant by the University of Sydney in 2006 to study the at that time somewhat under-examined role of animals in Greek and Roman magic. For bibliographical and other help at that period thanks are owed to Malcolm Choat and Korshi Dosoo, the latter of whom has also kindly sent me a valuable pre-publication copy of a jointly authored paper on animals in Graeco-Egyptian magical usage. The project then went into abeyance for a few years while the authors concentrated their attention on literary texts, before being reactivated by a conference on the psychopathology of ancient love-magic at the University of Trondheim in 2013. This prompted me to re-examine the quite startling violence of both language and intention in the large and ever-growing corpus of Graeco-Roman erotic spells. Since then the scope and ambition of my work has enlarged greatly, originally under the aegis of I.B. Tauris, to encompass most of the main arms of Greek and Roman magic, though it by no means claims to offer complete coverage of the topic. Rather, my focus has been on challenging a number of orthodoxies where scepticism seemed in order, on discussing aspects of magic that have not been subject to the same level of study as others, and on opening up for examination areas where fresh evidence has necessarily forced a revision of earlier views: this is especially the case in Chapter 3 on curse tablets. Above all, the book seeks to stress that the magic of Antiquity was a highly pragmatic, goal-focused matter.

When my interest was first engaged by Greek and Roman magic in the late 1980s, the most significant work was in German, French and Latin, perhaps most notably Theodor Hopfner's monumental *Griechisch-Ägyptischer Offenbarungszauber*. But in the interim there has been an explosion of works written in English (or translated into that language), added to which is the continual appearance of new documentary texts in publications such as the *Oxyrhynchus Papyri* and *Zeitschrift für Papyrologie und Epigraphik*. So vast and daunting in fact has the bibliography become that the primary author realised after a time that, if he was to have any hope of finishing a book which traverses so many areas of magic, he needed to co-opt the assistance of his wife and colleague, Patricia Watson, who is responsible for Chapter 5 and has there developed many themes not touched upon in the initial research grant application mentioned above.

Much of the research for this book was done in Oxford's Sackler and Bodleian Libraries, though largely written up at home, where LW's desk is whimsically presided over by a witch-troll who used to serve as course mascot when he lectured at the University of Sydney on Greek and Roman magic.

Acknowledgements for the illustrations that feature throughout the book are provided in the captions, but particular thanks are due to Simon Costin, Director of the Museum of Witchcraft and Magic in Boscastle, Cornwall, who not only granted permission to use three of the images that feature in the book, but took photographs of each from several angles, so that we were able to choose those which best served our purposes. An especial debt of gratitude is owed to the anonymous peer reviewer of the book, who drew our attention to some important items of bibliography which we had missed and made a host of constructive suggestions for improvement, on virtually all of which we have acted. Thanks also to Steen Ress for photoshopping the image of the peony which appears in Chapter 4.

The concluding bibliography is intended to be representative, not comprehensive, in the sense that we have not included mention of all that we have read. Daniela Urbanová's *Latin Curse Tablets of The Roman Empire* (Innsbruck, 2018) unfortunately reached us too late for us to take more than cursory account of it.

Lindsay C. Watson, Oxford
September 2018

Abbreviations

Abbreviations for classical authors and works and journal titles are those listed in the fourth edition of *The Oxford Classical Dictionary* (2012) ed. S. Hornblower, A. Spawforth and E. Eidinow. For journals not listed in the *OCD*, the abbreviations of *L'Année philologique* have been used.

ANRW	Haase, W. and H. Temporini, eds. 1972–. *Aufstieg und Niedergang der römischen Welt*. Berlin.
Audollent	Audollent, A., ed. 1904. *Defixionum Tabellae*. Paris.
Betz	Betz, H.D., ed. 1992. *The Greek Magical Papyri in Translation*. 2nd edn, Chicago.
Brill's *NP*	Cancik, H. and H. Schneider, eds. 2002–10. *Brill's New Pauly: Encyclopaedia of the Ancient World*. Leiden.
CIL	*Corpus inscriptionum Latinarum*. 1863–. Berlin.
CLE	Bücheler, F. and E. Lommatzsch, eds. 1895–1926. *Carmina Latina epigraphica*. Leipzig.
DTA	Wünsch, R. 1897. *Defixionum Tabellae Atticae = Inscriptiones Graecae Volumen III Pars III, Appendix*. Berlin.
DTM	Blänsdorf, J. 2012. *Die Defixionum Tabellae des Mainzer Isis-und Mater Magna Heiligtums. Defixionum Tabellae Mogontiacenses, in Zusammenarbeit mit Pierre-Yves Lambert und Marion Witteyer*. Mainz.
Gager	Gager, J.G., ed. 1992. *Curse Tablets and Binding Spells from the Ancient World*. New York/Oxford.
Hopfner OZ 1	Hopfner, Th. 1974. *Griechisch-Ägyptischer Offenbarungszauber*, vol. 1. Amsterdam.
Kotansky Amulets	Kotansky, R.D. 1994. *Greek Magical Amulets: The Inscribed Gold, Silver, Copper and Bronze Lamellae Part 1*. Opladen.

Kropp	Kropp, A., ed. 2008. *Ein aktuelles Corpus lateinischer Fluchtafeln*. Munich.
LSJ	*Liddell and Scott, Greek-English Lexicon*, 9th edn, rev. H. Stuart Jones (1925–40); Suppl. by E.A. Barber and others (1968). Oxford.
NGCT	Jordan, D.R. 2000 [2001]. 'New Greek Curse Tablets (1985–2000)'. *GRBS* 41: 5–46.
PDM	*The Demotic Magical Papyri*, translated in Betz.
PGM	Preisendanz, K. and A. Henrichs, eds. 1973–4. *Papyri Graecae Magicae*. 2nd edn, Stuttgart.
P. Oxy.	*The Oxyrhynchus Papyri*. 1898–. London.
RE	Pauly, A., G. Wissowa et al., eds. 1893–1980. *Paulys Realencyclopädie der classischen Altertumswissenschaft*. Stuttgart.
SGD	Jordan, D.R. 1985. 'A Survey of Greek *Defixiones* Not Included in the Special Corpora'. *GRBS* 26: 151–97.
SHA	*Scriptores Historiae Augustae*.
SM	Daniel, R.W. and F. Maltomini, eds. 1990–2. *Supplementum Magicum*, Opladen.
Tomlin	Tomlin, R.S.O. 1988. *Tabellae Sulis: Roman Inscribed Tablets of Tin and Lead from the Sacred Spring at Bath*. Part 4 (The Curse Tablets) of Barry Cunliffe (ed.) *The Temple of Sulis Minerva at Bath, II: Finds from the Sacred Spring*, 59–277. Oxford.
ZPE	*Zeitschrift für Papyrologie und Epigraphik*.

1

Introduction

In academic quarters it has become almost *de rigueur* to initiate discussion of Greek and Roman magic with a host of abstract questions such as 'what do we understand by the term "magic"? Which of the various definitions on offer best captures its essence?[1] Can magic be legitimately distinguished from religion?[2] Is the convergence of magical with religious usage so close that the term "magic" should be abandoned altogether as a descriptive category in favour of hybrid labels like "magico-religious phenomena" or "unsanctioned religious activity"?[3] Should magic be studied using an emic or an etic approach?[4] Is "magic" so elusive and nebulous a phenomenon that it is better apprehended using a taxonomic method, breaking the field down into generic categories, divination, cursing, healing and so on?[5] How legitimate is it to study Graeco-Roman magic in a comparative way, adducing examples of magical praxis from societies widely separated in both time and space from those of the ancient Mediterranean?'[6]

In books on Graeco-Roman magic, questions such as these are routinely incorporated in introductory chapters surveying the development of theoretical and definitional approaches to the study of magic over the last hundred years or so. These commence with Sir James Frazer, whose monumental *The Golden Bough* in effect first announced magic as a subject of scholarly discourse, and continue through the important contributions of Malinowski, Lévy-Bruhl, Evans-Pritchard, Mauss and Tambiah, to name the most significant figures. Triggered by the issues listed above, supplementary theoretical questions also raise their heads. They include: what contribution can pragmalinguistics make to comprehending the rituals and speech-acts which informed the magic of Greek and Roman Antiquity?[7] Can cognitive theories of religion help illuminate and unpick the magical mindset of Graeco-Roman times, or assist with the contested issue of whether magic and religion are discrete phenomena?[8]

The above topics have issued in a vast and frankly daunting bibliography. They have also generated a good deal of scholarly heat. Daniel Ogden, the UK's leading authority on the magic of Greece and Rome,[9] states in the bracingly polemical preface to his 2008 monograph *Night's Black Agents: Witches, Wizards and the Dead in the Ancient World*:

> readers will be grateful and relieved to be spared the narcissistic posturings about the definition of magic in an ancient context that ritually populate the introductions to parallel books, not to mention the childish rehearsals of doxography that attend them. Their befuddled authors confuse the attempt to give final definition to an abstract concept, which is self-evidently impossible, with the delineation of a coherent core of source-material for study, which, in this case, is easy ... the combination of weak philology with arbitrary theorising has been corrosive. It has produced a wholly unsympathetic history of ancient magic that no one in antiquity could have found intelligible.

Polemical blasts have not been lacking from the other side of the ideological fence. The anthropologist Stanley Tambiah's critique of Keith Thomas's monumental 1971 *Religion and the Decline of Magic* attacks the historian for ignoring the symbolism of magic and witchcraft and for being 'insensitive to the performative features of ritual acts that are familiar to students of the linguistic philosophy of J. Austin and followers'.[10] Tambiah refers here to the distinction made by Austin between 'illocutionary' and 'perlocutionary' speech-acts, that is, between utterances that are essentially static and descriptive, and those that effect a change in attendant circumstances. A straightforward instance of a perlocutionary utterance would be when the author of a *defixio*, curse tablet, spoke the formula 'I bind X'. In the mind of the curser, the situation of the target is materially altered by the words uttered, in that he or she is thereby rendered no longer capable of autonomous action. The theory of performative utterance championed by Austin and Tambiah has been extremely influential in studies on Graeco-Roman magic, but, as C.A. Hoffman points out in a riposte to Tambiah, Thomas is in effect being attacked here for failing to privilege the analytical categories which happen to interest Tambiah; in other words Tambiah is being arbitrarily doctrinaire.[11]

The present work will not go down the theoretical path sketched above. The reasons are twofold. First, because questions of the kind catalogued there will simply not have troubled the head of, say, a wise-woman who came to purify with eggs and sulphur the house of a sick mistress or a man suffering unsettling dreams,[12] a herbal physician who attempted to heal a disease using plant derivatives culled under specific ritual protocols so as not to vitiate their curative powers, or a person who inscribed or commissioned a *defixio* with the intention of harming an enemy. Such persons had no need to meditate on the metaphysics of magic. Why so? Because individuals who engaged in magic *knew* that it worked, or fully expected it to do so. Copious examples of this belief have been assembled in the following chapter: it is worth noting here that, so deep-rooted was the faith in the power of magic that, according to the first century CE sage Apollonius of Tyana, even in cases where magic had been deployed without success, its exponents did not abandon their belief in its efficacy, but rationalised the failure by blaming themselves for some crucial procedural omission (Philostr. *Vit. Apollon. Tyan.* 7.39.1–2).

A second reason for avoiding an excess of abstraction is that, amid the thicket of theory, there is a risk of losing sight of a key fact: that magic is a profoundly pragmatic business with concrete, clearly delineated aims, no matter how diverse, be these causing someone to fall helplessly in love with you, tilting the outcome of a chariot race in your favour, silencing an opponent in court, obtaining a revelatory vision of a deity, acquiring grace and charm in the eyes of others, or even ridding an orchard of caterpillars by leading a woman who is experiencing her first menstruation, with hair and clothes unbound, three times around the garden beds and hedge.[13] To put it another way, magical acts have a sharp and exclusive focus on the end result, large or small, and all its energies are ultimately channelled towards that outcome.[14]

The present work will concentrate on aspects of Greek and Roman magic that best encapsulate the practical, goal-focused nature of ancient magic, its purpose of eliciting quite specific outcomes, a feature that remains a constant in the thousand or so years covered by this study and expresses itself in a multiplicity of ways. Some of these topics will be familiar, some less so, others are decidedly contested in the specialist literature.

Chapter 2 examines the large corpus of amatory spells, in both the *Greek Magical Papyri* (of which more below) and curse tablets. These characteristically invoke, in a manner that can only be described as solipsistic, physical and psychic torments upon the love-object, with the intention of reducing that person to a condition of utter debilitation in which they will perforce yield to the spell-caster's desire for complete sexual compliance, as the only way to be rid of their sufferings. The chapter argues against the fashionable trend to rationalise the violence of the spells by treating it as purely symbolic, or as a therapeutic retrojection of the agent's own amatory pangs back onto the party who occasions these. On the contrary, it is suggested, the violence is real, so that to speak of 'love-magic' is a complete misnomer; 'sex-magic' would be a better label. The second half of the chapter takes issue with the widely canvassed view that, when it comes to erotic magic, there is a radical disconnect between life and literature:

according to this thesis, *in reality* it is men who practise such magic, whereas in literary accounts amatory magic is portrayed as an entirely female preserve. Examination of texts ranging from the fourth century BCE to late Antiquity reveals this to be a false dichotomy. In regard to amatory magic there is ample evidence for female agency, and of women's capacity for erotic self-determination.

Chapter 3 opens by surveying the main features of *defixiones*, curse tablets, which enlist supernatural means to 'bind' or hobble the actions or well-being of others *for the benefit of the curser*. The (generally agonistic) contexts in which they are used are forensic, amatory, competitive and economic. A further, specialised category is 'prayers for justice'; these solicit divine assistance to punish persons perceived to have wronged the curser, usually in the shape of a theft. From early times *defixiones* may seek to encompass the death of an enemy: there is some reluctance to acknowledge this feature of curse tablets. The bulk of the chapter is devoted to examining the various ways in which major recent finds of *defixiones*, especially from Bath, Rome and Mainz, have altered or modified perceptions of the medium by throwing up a host of unexpected features. These include using the sanctuary of non-chthonic gods for deposition of the *defixio*, the investing of the curse-text with a patina of literary allusion, a taste for retributive violence and cruelty which exceeds that hitherto seen, the enlisting of cultic protocols to fashion individual curses, and an extreme instance of the magical principle of 'pluralising for power'. The chapter concludes with a glance at a British curse tablet which may or may not have had a part in the genesis of Tolkien's *The Lord of the Rings*.

The fourth chapter is concerned with the use of herbs in magic, an integral part of the art from its very beginnings. The magical dimension of herbs and plants is especially on view in the bizarre ritual and gestural protocols which attended their picking, the goal-focused, hands-on pragmatism of magic in the countless, often quaint-seeming curative regimes of which they form part. Botanical derivatives were fundamental to ancient therapeutics, both rational and folk-medicinal. Herbal magic proves a convenient venue for examining the thought processes and rationales that governed the collection, selection and administration of plants, in particular the key principles of magical sympathy, antipathy and contiguity. These various ideas are illustrated and analysed in some detail, as conveniently illuminating a broad swathe of magical beliefs. Here I draw particularly on the *Investigation into Plants* of Theophrastus, on the medical writers Dioscorides and the more magically inclined Marcellus Empiricus, but above all on the *Natural History* of the Elder Pliny, who is an indispensable fount of information on Greek and Roman magic, in a work which is remarkable for its blend of scepticism, polemic and credulity in regard to magic. The conclusion of the chapter draws attention to the characteristic admixture in ancient therapeutics of the pharmacologically potent with the arrantly magical, and notes that the particular medicinal properties ascribed in Antiquity to medicinal plants are sometimes confirmed by modern science; this suggests that, for all its magical overlay, the traditional medicine of Greece and Rome was at some level also based upon an empirical understanding of the therapeutic capacities of plants.

The fifth chapter offers an overview of the role of animals in magic, beginning with their medicinal use, for which an abundance of evidence is found in the *Natural History* of Pliny the Elder, in addition to the magico-medical *Cyranides* and medical treatises dating from the first to the fourth centuries CE. Emphasis is placed on the thin dividing line between folk-medicine and magic. After a brief survey of various uses of animals and their products, the question is addressed of whether a reason can in some cases be discerned for the use of a particular animal or animal part. Factors considered include the belief that some animals have intrinsic magical potency, the use in erotic magic of animals known for their sexuality, the association of an animal with the deity whose aid is requested (e.g. the donkey and Seth/Typhon), the magical principle of similarity (e.g. an animal's tooth used to cure toothache or a yellow animal as a remedy for jaundice), and the symbolic use of a black animal in invocations to chthonic deities. Some practical questions follow, such as how animals were obtained; whether parts were preserved; and when, where and by whom magic rites involving animals were carried out. The final section discusses the prominence of animal ingredients in Roman literary portraits of witches (a subject to be treated in depth in the subsequent chapter), considering the extent to which these seemingly fantastic accounts bear any relationship with actual magic practices.

Chapter 6 deals in a loosely diachronic sequence with representations of the witch in literature, beginning with the mythical figures Circe and Medea, who emerge as less malign and terrifying than their later incarnations: it continues with Theocritus' third century BCE sorceress Simaitha, whose magic rite – in anticipation of a pattern that will become common in the Roman poets – reveals an intimate familiarity on the author's part with the rituals and verbal formulae of the *defixiones* and the much later, but in terms of content tralaticious *Greek Magical Papyri*, in other words with magic as actually practised. Turning to witches in Latin and later Greek literature, I highlight a range of differences from their fictional predecessors, notably a relentless focus on self-serving, harmful ends, a malignant polyvalence and a tendency to boast extravagantly of powers which sometimes fail hopelessly when put to the test. Of a piece with this last is a tendency to ridicule the witch in one way or another. At the same time, other witches can be genuinely horrific, above all Lucan's Erictho, whose ghastly assemblage of magical stuffs surprisingly finds ready parallel in the various categories of *materia magica* deployed in real-life spells. The chapter next interrogates possible reasons why Roman literature of the late Republic and the early Empire shows such a modish fascination with the figure of the witch, and also why the fictional mage is almost invariably female, in a pattern supposedly repeated in the real-life witch persecutions of the sixteenth to eighteenth centuries, causing one expert to coin the term 'gendercide'.[15] Throughout the chapter literary witches, for all their armoury of diverse powers, are seen to be quite as focused on gratification of their desires (usually amatory) or on immediate satisfaction of their need for revenge as are the practising magicians of Antiquity. In this respect magical feats like Circe's turning Odysseus' men into swine seemingly just for the fun of it, or drawing down the moon from the heavens as a mere exhibition of magical virtuosity, stand out as exceptions.

The final chapter considers whether there is any historical basis to the many charges in Roman texts of human sacrifice, especially the sacrifice of children for either divinatory or initiatory purposes, that supposedly took place in rites that were explicitly flagged as magical, or were stigmatised as sorcerous or religiously deviant by ideological or political antagonists. A comparison of such accusations with those bandied about the so-called Satanic Panic of the late 1980s and early 1990s shows multiple points of convergence – a tendency for the charges of ritual murder and attendant atrocities to assume a similar, stereotyped form, the trading of accusation and counter-accusation, the difficulty of establishing the veracity of the charges amid a flood of exaggerations, wilful distortions and black propaganda. The crucible for such accusations in Antiquity was the widely entertained belief that secret gatherings, such as those of the Bacchists in the second century BCE or the Catilinarian conspirators in the first, deliberately overturned sacral protocols by perversely antinomian behaviour such as human sacrifice, blood-drinking and sexual free-for-alls, charges which Roman pagans readily applied to the ill-understood sacraments of the early Christians. For the pagans these alleged rituals constituted false or debased religious practice, which they equated with magic. The Christians in turn directed similar charges against heretical sects and apostates. Most of such accusations are transparently false and tendentious but, it is suggested, there remains a limited body of evidence which perhaps makes it injudicious to dismiss out of hand the possibility that human sacrifice might occasionally have occurred in perverted rituals, or to mock the naivety of scholars who are prepared to entertain the feasibility of such things having happened in exceptional cases.

In the course of this book an extensive airing has been given to most of the main sources upon which we base our knowledge of ancient magic, that is the *Greek Magical Papyri*, curse tablets, a range of prose authorities including, prominently, Pliny the Elder, and fictional accounts of witches, which, as noted, tend to mirror the activities of actual practising magicians. One further element of some importance, magical amulets,[16] receives mention at various points in the book, but to go into the topic in detail – for all the current interest in the physicality of magic – was felt to lie outside the scope of this volume.[17] This said, in the interest of completeness a brief overview of the subject has been provided in an appendix to Chapter 5, where there is frequently occasion to note the use of animal ingredients in amulets. One particular corpus of texts must however be singled out here for special attention, for reasons that will become clear below, and this is the *Greek Magical Papyri* or *PGM*.

The *Greek Magical Papyri*[18] – more accurately, the Graeco-Egyptian magical papyri – along with curse tablets (*katadesmoi* or *defixiones*) constitute our most important source of knowledge for magic as actually practised in Classical and post-Classical Antiquity. The story of their discovery and publication deserves to be told, both for its intrinsic interest and on account of the many obstacles which fate placed in the way of their appearance in printed form. For readers encountering these documents for the first time, a certain amount of orientation is also in order.

Some time before 1828, seemingly in (Egyptian) Thebes and reportedly in a tomb,[19] villagers discovered a large cache of papyri, including sizeable magic books, that constitute the core of what is now known as the *Greek Magical Papyri*. The find was of unrivalled importance for the understanding of ancient magic, quite as significant in its way as was the unearthing of the Nag Hammadi library in Upper Egypt for the history of Gnosticism.[20] The magical texts found their way into the hands of Jean d'Anastasi (1780?–1857), a key figure in the acquisition and dissemination of these documents.[21] Apparently of Armenian origin, d'Anastasi (not his real name) went to Egypt with his father, eventually establishing himself as one of the most important merchants in Alexandria. He formed close ties with the pasha there, and in 1828 was appointed Consul-General to the kingdoms of Norway and Sweden, a post that he held until his death. Sensing a profitable sideline in collecting Egyptian antiquities from the nascent interest in these on the part of European museums, d'Anastasi amassed via his agents a vast collection of such items, which he had no difficulty in exporting thanks to his friendship with the pasha and his own shipping facilities. Among the items thus exported to Europe were what came to be known as the d'Anastasi magical papyri – not all necessarily from the Theban trove[22] – which were auctioned and sold to national museums in London, Paris, Berlin and Leiden.

By 1857 the bulk of what we now think of as the Greek Magical Papyri had been housed in the great museums of Europe, but work on deciphering and interpreting them proceeded slowly, and scholars who did turn their attention to these documents worked largely in isolation from each other. By 1893 virtually all the important papyri known at that time had been published, in a range of stand-alone papers or monographs[23] of uneven quality,[24] but there remained an urgent need for a collected edition in order to put the study of these vitally important documents on a properly scientific basis. To do so was the long-cherished project of Albrecht Dieterich (1866–1908) of the University of Heidelberg. Dieterich had, however, to contend with the contemptuous attitude[25] of professional colleagues towards these late-antique documentary texts, which, in view of their often distasteful, superstitious and solipsistic character, sat very ill with the romantic, idealised view of the Greeks which then prevailed in the scholarly community. In a striking instance of the prejudice against which he had to struggle, in his first public foray into the field, in 1905, Dieterich taught a Heidelberg seminar on the magical papyri under the deliberately misleading title 'Selected Pieces from the Greek Papyri'. Work on the papyri was disrupted by the sudden death of Dieterich, at little more than forty years of age, on 6 May 1908. However, various scholars already active in the study of these texts agreed to pool their talents and collaborate on the production of a composite edition of the *PGM*. These were Dieterich's pupil Ludwig Fahz, Richard Wünsch, who assumed overall direction of the *PGM* project,[26] Adam Abt,[27] Adolf Erman and Georg Möller, who was entrusted with the substantial number of Coptic passages interspersed in this corpus of mainly Greek texts.

When the bulk of the work on *PGM* 1–4 was almost ready for publication by the German house B.G. Teubner, the First World War broke out. By the end of it, Wünsch, Abt and Möller were dead: Wünsch was killed in action on 17 May 1915, Abt died in 1918 and Möller was taken unexpectedly soon after on a trip abroad. Notwithstanding these tragic losses to the world of scholarship and the formidable costs entailed in publishing such a specialised work at a time when Germany was suffering acute economic hardship, Teubner agreed to press ahead with publication and the task of producing an edition was entrusted to Karl

Preisendanz (1883–1968), a student of Dieterich who had volunteered his services to his teacher before his death.[28] But work proceeded slowly because of the need to take account of new advances in the understanding of Graeco-Egyptian magic and the scholarly imperative of re-examining papyri 1–3, a laborious process which both yielded a host of new readings and in other instances entailed jettisoning some of those arrived at by scholars who had examined these texts before the war. But, in a heartening example of international cooperation, Preisendanz was able to enlist the services of Adolf Jacoby of Luxemburg and the great Norwegian scholar of religion and magic, Samson Eitrem of Oslo, who in 1920 had acquired in the Fayûm (and subsequently edited with detailed commentary)[29] the lengthy and important papyrus which we now know as *PGM* 36. Moreover, Preisendanz was afforded ready access to the papyri, which, as noted above, were held in various European capitals and cities. The result was the publication in 1928 of the first volume of *PGM*, containing papyri 1–6: on the final page of the preface to volume 1, Preisendanz touchingly thanks the Bibliothèque Nationale in Paris for 'having permitted him with equal graciousness both before and after the War' to study in situ the 'Great Paris Magical Papyrus' (*PGM* 4), which at 3274 lines, is by a considerable distance the largest and most important of all the *PGM*.

Volume 2 of the *PGM*, containing papyri 7–60, as well twenty Christian texts (P 1–20), some ostraka (O 1–5) and two tablets of wood (T 1–2) appeared in 1931, also under the imprint of Teubner and the editorship of Preisendanz. Volume 3, which bears a publication date of 1941 and contained papyri 61–81, a text of the hymnodic inserts in the *PGM* and, crucially, sixteen indices to the words, names and magical formulae contained in the three volumes, had advanced to the galley-proof stage, when on 4 December 1943, the Teubner factory in Leipzig was bombed and completely destroyed by Allied forces. Nearly seventy-five years later the projected volume 3 has yet to appear, though happily the galley proofs survived the bombing: as a result photocopies, including the invaluable indices, are available in major institutions such as the Sackler Library in Oxford: also, in some cases, photocopies of photocopies have found their way into private hands. Matters have also been helped by the incorporation of the *PGM* and the *Supplementum Magicum* (see below) in the *Thesaurus Linguae Graecae* database, where they can be readily searched.

When Preisendanz died at an advanced age in 1968, a revised edition was commissioned from Albert Henrichs, originally of Cologne, subsequently of Harvard. This appeared as a two-volume set in 1973–4 and contained the papyri originally intended for volume 3 (61–81), as well as the hymns and four more

Christian texts (P 21–4) and a thoroughgoing revision of the text of a number of papyri contained in the original volumes 1–2 and the ill-starred volume 3.

In a sign, however, of the frequency with which new papyri are appearing, the number of texts in the edition of the *Greek Magical Papyri in Translation* edited by Hans Dieter Betz in 1986 (second edition with updated bibliography in 1992) has grown to 130, adding forty-nine pieces to the 1973–4 revision of Preisendanz. Most of these are of brief compass, unlike the voluminous *PGM* 1–5, 7, 12, 13 and 36, which owe their length to the fact that each represents a magical recipe book containing numerous spells of diverse types. A most important departure from Preisendanz was the incorporation of four texts (*PDM* 14, the longest, 12, 61 and *PDM* Supplement) written in that form of the Egyptian language known as Demotic, *PDM* being a Latin abbreviation of what translates into English as 'The Demotic Magical Papyri': these texts are for the most part bilingual, in that (shorter) passages of Greek are interspersed with them. The Demotic spells are close, in terms of their content and theological matrix, to the *PGM* and may in some cases even be translations of Greek originals. Notwithstanding this, Preisendanz excluded them from his volumes, which contained only the Greek sections of the bilingual Greek-Demotic papyri, and in so doing obscured to a degree the polyglot character of the corpus. This, in addition to the Demotic texts, also contains sizeable portions in Old Coptic, a form of the Egyptian language in the Greek alphabet but with additional sounds taken from the Demotic and, interspersed within sections, the old Egyptian script known as Hieratic.[30] It remains the case, however, that Greek is the predominant language of the texts.

Some of the new Greek spells in Betz (nos. 82–130) are included in the important two-volume *Supplementum Magicum* of 1990–2 edited by Daniel and Maltomini. But, in contrast to nearly all of Betz 82–130, a number of the spells in *SM* are of considerable length, e.g. *SM* 45. A further difference from many of the texts published in the earlier collections is that quite a few of the spells in *SM* are *applied*: that is to say, they are charms that were deployed in real life, in the sense that the names of the person commissioning the spell and, if need be, the target[31] have been spelled out in the text: in pointed contrast, many of the texts in the earlier corpuses are *formularies* in which the notional participants are represented by an anonymous NN ('so and so'), a generic appellation which can be replaced by the name of an actual person or persons when a spell is put into practice for the benefit of a client who consults a specialist who has in his possession books of magic spells. The *SM*, which brought together in two volumes 100 texts which had previously appeared in scattered publications, was conceived of as a supplement to Preisendanz vols 1–3; but, in one more departure from Preisendanz, it included a number of texts inscribed on lead, with the justification, however, that a number of these were applied spells based more or less closely on a papyrus recipe for binding a lover, *PGM* 4.296–466.

New magical papyri continue to be published thick and fast, as a glance at successive volumes of the *Oxyrhynchus Papyri*[32] – including a major addition in *P. Oxy.* 82 (2016) – will show. Happily, the recent history of such texts has not been characterised by misfortunes such as attended earlier attempts to make them available to the world at large. It might therefore be fanciful to invoke here – notwithstanding the discovery in a tomb of the most significant texts in the *PGM* – the cinematic cliché of the Pharaoh's curse. But it was certainly the case, as we have noted, that unforeseen death and destruction stalked the early labourers in this ever-fascinating field.

The spells in the *PGM* are extremely diverse in nature. This results from the fact that, as noted above, the individual papyri in the corpus are (mostly) magical-recipe books, or fragments of recipe books; these, as one would therefore expect, contain a wide assortment of charms. For example, the fifty-seven-line *PGM* 122, following an introduction detailing its contents, 'an excerpt of incantations from the holy book called Hermes', includes four different kinds of spell: the first 'an enchantment using apples', the second a love spell that prognosticates the total surrender of the desired party and includes the startling detail 'I have devoured your liver', the third a fetching-spell for a recalcitrant beloved, and the last, in a quite different register, a headache charm. And the diversity is naturally much greater in the longer papyri, running to hundreds if not thousands of lines, which form the core of the *PGM*. Betz xi–xxii provides a table of all the spells, labelled according to type, which were known up to 1986 (the second edition of 1992 added no new texts). It may however be helpful to signal here the most common classes of spell.

At the head of the list, in terms both of statistical frequency and the total number of lines that they occupy in the corpus, come various categories of love spell – fetching spells (*agōgai*), erotic binding spells (*philtrokatadesmoi*), separation spells (*diakopoi*), philtres to be drunk (*potismata*), spells employing fire to kindle burning passion (*empura*), penis ointments to compel a woman's fidelity, and finally erotic spells of unspecified type.[33] Other common types of spell are amulets to ward off illness, charms for a direct vision of a deity or a dream oracle, sundry other divinatory procedures, especially ones using a lamp or some form of vessel, spells to cause insomnia, and charms to restrain anger in others.

Even the most cursory perusal of the *Greek Magical Papyri* will reveal that the title is something of a misnomer. The spells were written down in Greek Egypt, and they reveal Egyptian religious and cultural influences on every page, making 'Graeco-Egyptian' a far more accurate label. A list of indigenous Egyptian elements in the *PGM* includes: the levelling of threats against deities (a peculiarly Egyptian phenomenon) and threats of cosmic disorder by magicians should the divine powers fail to comply with their demands; the invocation of divine figures by their secret names and the conviction that knowledge of these granted power over the gods; the use of hymns in magico-religious contexts and especially the inclusion in the *PGM*'s hymnodic sections of extremely lengthy lists of a deity's names; the predominance of solar and Osirian themes; the self-identification of the magician with a deity; the drawing on the papyri of representations of Egyptian deities such as the dwarf-god Bes, likewise of characteristically Egyptian theriomorphic gods such as Seth or else bizarre, demonic human-animal hybrids which are also common in Graeco-Egyptian amulets; the invocation of indigenous Egyptian deities such as Re (Helios), Isis and Osiris, or of Greek deities in heavily Egyptianised form; the animation of figurines for supernatural purposes; false accusations of ritual improprieties on the part of an individual (*diabolai*), in order to animate the wrath of a god or goddess against them; various uses in charms of animals native to Egypt such as the crocodile or the ibis; the marked belief in the power of the written word (whence the term hieroglyphics, 'sacred carvings'); grandiose claims for the effectiveness of spells; the use in rites of what the papyri call 'deified' animals, that is ones that have been ritually sacrificed.[34]

In addition to the foregoing, David Frankfurter has argued in a number of influential publications[35] that the *PGM*, the MSS of which date mostly to the third to fifth centuries CE, reflect above all the Egyptian priestly milieu of the later Roman Empire; as they faced growing social and economic hardship due to the religious and gubernatorial constraints imposed upon them by the central Roman government, the Egyptian priests became increasingly uncoupled from their traditional locus of sacral activity, the temple and its scriptorium, and to a degree reinvented themselves as independent magical specialists who conformed to the Greek and Roman stereotype of the Egyptian sorcerer-priest:[36] at the same time, they were still able to trade upon their time-honoured standing as priests and as literate individuals in a largely illiterate society to dispense 'magical' advice coloured by traditional religious forms and protocols; advice which, however, increasingly gravitated towards the solution of intensely personal crises, especially affairs of the heart. It was from this reconstituted sacral ambience, Frankfurter argues, that the *PGM* emanated.

The above opens up a notoriously vexed problem. Are we to believe, with Bonner, that 'the magic of the Greek papyri is predominantly Egyptian',[37] with Frankfurter that the spells in the *PGM* are firmly anchored in the traditional operations of the Egyptian temple priests (not however perceived by them as magic),[38] or even with Ritner that the ritual matrix of the *PGM* is almost exclusively Egyptian?[39] Or should we hold, with other Egyptologists, Geraldine Pinch and Janet Johnson,[40] that the *PGM* are an amalgam of Greek and Egyptian magical practices? The issue is deeply contentious and inherently complicated by discipline-based biases: Egyptologists will naturally privilege in their analyses manifestly Egyptian content, while Classicists have at times been guilty of treating the *PGM* as providing exactly the same evidential basis for Graeco-Roman magic as practices indigenous to those two cultures.

For all the demonstrably Egyptian input summarised above, it would be injudicious to downplay or minimise Greek input into the *PGM*. There are many reasons to think so. Even if, as Frankfurter claims, not much weight should be attached to the fact that the bulk of the spells are written in Greek,[41] there remains a solid core of Greek magico-ritual practice in the *PGM*. As discussed in Chapter 3, Greece had a native tradition of *katadesmoi*, binding spells, stretching back to the sixth century BCE, and many of the spells in the *PGM* figure themselves precisely as *katadesmoi*, or, if amatory binding spells, as *philtrokatadesmoi*, erotic binding spells. *Katadesmoi* routinely availed themselves of so-called persuasive analogy, such as in a sixth/fifth century BCE text from Sicily[42] or a third century BCE judicial *katadesmos* from Attica (*DTA* 105) 'just as this lead [on which the curse tablet is inscribed] is cold and passionless, in the same way also let the words and deeds and tongue of those inscribed here be cold and passionless'. The same process of reasoning from analogy (first seen in Hom. *Il.* 3.298–301) is often replicated in the formulae of the *PGM*, for example 36.340–1 'as you [myrrh] burn, so will you also burn her [with love]'; indeed, it is pervasive in Graeco-Roman magic of every kind. Early curse tablets or ritual curses also made extensive use of 'voodoo dolls', and the manipulation or symbolic maltreatment of figurines is a prominent feature of spells in the *PGM*, although in this case Egyptian usage may also have had a part to play. In sum, a number of key ideas already enshrined in early *katadesmoi* may be shared with the *PGM*, but are unquestionably indigenous to Greece.

It was remarked above that a very large number of the spells in the *PGM* are amatory. In an important analysis, Faraone (1999) has shown that there is a long-standing Greek tradition whereby love is envisaged as a violent, physically invasive force that strikes, burns, whips and tortures its victims, rendering them ill and enfeebled, and has cogently argued that there is a direct line of descent from this conceptualisation of *Eros* to the startlingly violent and sadistic love spells of the *PGM*; these, as discussed in Chapter 2, seek to reduce the target to a condition of such corporeal and mental anguish that she (less commonly he) has no choice but to yield to the overtures of the spell-caster. An excerpt from the fetching-spell *PGM* 36.333–60 gives a sample of the manner:

> go into every place and seek out her, NN, and open her right side and enter like thunder, like lightning, like a burning flame, and make her thin, pale, weak, limp, incapable of action in any part of her body, until she leaps forth and comes to me

But in addition to the evident similarity of ethos between the early Greek material which he adduces and the violent tone of the amatory spells in the *PGM*, Faraone's argument looks the more appealing because this level of aggression, as Pinch notes, is something new in Egypt.[43]

As we saw, Frankfurter tied his insistence on the Egyptian colour of the *PGM* to their provenance in the priestly ambience of late-antique Egypt. This is, however, to gloss over to some extent the transmission history of the papyri. To be sure, our physical copies of the magical papyri belong mostly to late Antiquity, but it has long been recognised that these are descendants of copies going back perhaps hundreds of years[44] – as indeed one might expect of works that are mostly not 'applied', the product of events anchored to a specific time and place, but instead recipes or formularies of a wholly generic character. Preisendanz indeed believed that some portions of the *PGM* may have originated in the third or second century BCE, and pointed out that the earliest papyrus in *PGM* volumes 1–2, no.16 (first century CE), foreshadows in many respects the contents of papyri written many centuries later.[45] And with the publication in the late 1970s of two erotic spells on papyrus dating respectively to the first century BCE and the Augustan period (27 BCE–14 CE), *PGM* 117 and 122 (= SM 72), *spells that in their mechanics and conjurations anticipate at every turn amatory charms on papyrus inscribed several hundred years later*, it becomes indisputable that the ideas in question were already in circulation some time before the Common Era.

But can one push these ideas further back in time? Here it will be helpful to consider a number of the key features of erotic magic contained in *PGM* 117 and 122, all of which, to repeat the key point, routinely appear in later papyrus love spells. Briefly, these are as follows: in 117, the request that the (female) target leave her house and come to the operator, (?) that she 'forget' her husband in favour of the spell-caster, the technical term *telein*, 'fulfil a spell', the use of *ousia*, magical material[46] in the shape of two strands of hair as a symbolic stand-in for the target, the command to a divine agency to 'fetch' the beloved, finally an invocation to a 'dreadful' immortal, probably Hecate.[47] *PGM* 122, which contains three separate amatory spells, offers the first documentary instance, in column 2, of an *agōgē*, fetching-spell, used by a woman against a man; the rite is also to take place at night (2.1–3), as is usual with magic procedures; in column 1, we find the familiar wish that the target 'go mad for love of me', as well as a threefold repetition of the rite. Additionally, in *PGM* 122 there are four occurrences of the formulaic 'bring to perfection this perfect spell', a conjuration which, as Faraone (1992) has shown, is centuries older than *PGM* 122.[48]

I have focused on the just-catalogued ideas for a specific reason. Every single one of them is represented in the account by the third century BCE Greek poet Theocritus of a love spell hatched by a sorceress, Simaitha, in the hope of recovering the affections of a lover who has deserted her. If we now add to this the fact that various other of Simaitha's sorcerous procedures are amply attested in Greek magical texts which are considerably earlier than the third century BCE but equally have a significant presence in the *PGM* (see Chapter 6), it is tempting to accede to Faraone's view that there is a continuous tradition of Greek love-magic stretching from the pre-Classical period to the erotic formularies of the late Empire: in other words, the verbal and ritual mechanics of love-magic depicted in Theocritus' poem represent an authentically Greek strain of love-magic which became embedded in and is amply reflected by the later erotic spells of the *PGM*. For what it is worth, the Elder Pliny (*HN* 28.19) seems to regard the conjurations of Simaitha as representing a belief system and magical processes which were indigenous to Greece, and had already assumed a ritually stabilised form by Theocritus' day.

It is implicit in the argument just advanced that the protocols of Greek love-magic at least were translated to their new homeland by the Hellenic colonisers of Egypt, or simply became established there by a process of cultural interplay between the two countries, to reappear on Egyptian soil. But not all the traffic was one way. Far from it. It seems likely for example that some of the magico-medicinal remedies attributed by the first century CE Roman writer Pliny the Elder to (nebulous) *Magi* and a pseudonymous Democritus come from the *Cheiromekta* of the second-century BCE iatromagical writer Bolus of Mendes, a learned Egyptian who wrote in Greek.[49] And this is one part of a larger pattern. Books of magic, such as those famously mentioned in Acts of the Apostles 19.17–19, circulated freely in the ancient Mediterranean World,[50] some of them explicitly designated Egyptian.[51] *PGM* 1.42–195, 'the spell of the sacred scribe Pnouthis for acquiring a <demonic> assistant', a characteristically Egyptian rite found a number of times in the *PGM*, speaks (line 47) of the prescriptions for this procedure which are supposedly preserved in 'countless books'. The Latin poet Horace's witchy antagonist Canidia is said to possess 'books that have the capacity to detach and draw down the stars from the sky' (*Epod.* 17.4–5), a feat which is not only ascribed to sorceresses in literary texts, but is also one of the processes which the just-mentioned spell of Pnouthis claims to be able to impart to the magical practitioner (*PGM* 1.124).

In a previous publication I have argued that two of the most important accounts in Latin of a witch and her doings, Horace's *Epodes* 5 and 17 (30s BCE), show a clear affinity with the magical beliefs and ritual mechanisms that we find in the *PGM*. The first of these texts deals with the sorceress Canidia's plan to starve to death a kidnapped boy and afterwards cut out his desiccated liver in order to fashion from it a potent love philtre, the second with the attempt of Canidia to punish Horace for versified attacks on her by inflicting upon him intolerable physical and psychic suffering. Again and again in these poems we encounter details that have multiple parallels in the *PGM*, as well as in curse tablets, which in their later realisations exhibit profound overlaps with the *PGM*. Two examples among very many are the enlisting of divine anger against the magic practitioner's enemy (5.51–4), or the figuring of the witch as riding in triumph on Horace's shoulders (17.74). It is hard to believe that these correspondences do not arise from an acquaintance on Horace's part with the magic books of which we spoke above.

The same process of assimilation from magic volumes can be discerned in the Latin poet Lucan's account in book 6 of his *Pharsalia* (mid-first century CE) of his superwitch Erictho. Once again there are multiple overlaps with the *PGM*, not least in a lengthy disquisition (533–68) on Erictho's acquisition of the magically potent *ousia* of the dead. But one detail stands out as indisputably deriving from Egyptian sources: this is Erictho's threat, when they prove initially unresponsive to her magical demands, to inflict monstrous cosmic disorder upon the gods, a distinctively Egyptian idea, as remarked above. Her words at 742–4:

> upon you, worst of the world's rulers (Pluto), I shall send the Sun's rays, breaking open your caverns, and you will be assaulted by sudden daylight

could be lifted straight from a manual in the *PGM*, as we can see by comparing 62.29–32:

> if ... the apparition of the god delays, <say> 'open up, open up, Olympus; open up, Hades; open up Abyss. Let the darkness be dispelled by command of the highest god and let the holy light come forth from the infinite into the abyss'

None of the above is meant to suggest that indigenous magical beliefs are lacking from the two Latin poetic accounts of witchcraft. Indeed Horace flags the fact that he is taking account of both sides of the magical coin by subtle allusions to the native belief that the Marsians, an old Italic tribe, had the ability to split snakes and had a further range of magical powers (17.29, 5.76). What we see here in miniature and in literary garb is the domestication in Roman soil of supernatural concepts inherited from Egypt, or rather the beginnings of the extension of the frontiers of magic that is such a pronounced feature of documentary magical texts, both the *PGM* and curse tablets, under the Roman Empire. In these we find a sometimes bewildering agglomeration of Graeco-Roman and Egyptian sacro-magical beliefs, supplemented by an accretion of material from other Oriental cultures, Jewish not least.

To summarise: in the light of all that has been said in the preceding pages, it seems injudicious either to overplay or artificially insulate from external influences the Greekness of the *PGM*, or conversely to see them as wholly Egyptian in genesis. By the time of the early Roman Empire there was plainly a two-way traffic in ideas between the Graeco-Roman and Egyptian worlds, so that, instead of privileging one particular cultural currency or another, it is better to speak of the 'internationalisation' of magic, or of a 'pan-Mediterranean' tradition of magic limited only by the borders of the known world.

Notes

1. E.g. Ritner (1993), 3–28; Graf (1997), 14–19; Hoffman (2002); Stratton (2007), 1–38; Sørensen (2007), 9–30; Collins (2008), 1–26.
2. E.g. Aune (1980), 1510–16 (a useful synopsis); Phillips (1986); Versnel (1991b); García Teijeiro (1993); Fowler (1995); Stratton (2007), 4–15.
3. See Hoffmann (2002), 188–9. Versnel (1991b) points out that rejection of the term will prove unworkable: however defined, something conveniently called magic had an ontological existence. Indeed scholars (Graf, Stratton, Sørensen, Collins) continue unabashedly to use the term in the titles of their books: cf. Kraemer (2011), 245 n.7.
4. An 'emic' approach means studying a given phenomenon from within the society in question (as Malinowski did with the Trobriand Islanders, or Evans-Pritchard with the Nigerian Azande), 'etic'; from the perspective of someone external to that society. In the case of ancient magic an emic stance entails immersing oneself culturally in the pertinent societies, an admirable project, towards which Graf (1997, 18–19) implicitly edges, but one ultimately doomed to fail (Hoffmann (2002), 189–91).

The main proponent of the etic approach is Versnel (1991b), seconded by Bremmer (1999), 10–12.
5 Smith (1995).
6 E.g. Collins (2008), 26. Frazer (1917) treats the approach as a given.
7 A good account of the matter in Kropp (2010). Further Urbanová (2018), 72–6. See also below on Austin and Tambiah.
8 See Sørensen (2007), not a work for the beginner, Kraemer (2011), 22–5.
9 In saying this I by no means downplay the many important contributions of Richard Gordon of the University of East Anglia and latterly of Erfurt. However Daniel Ogden is the author of four substantial books on aspects of Greek and Roman magic, as well as a major piece dealing with curse tablets.
10 Tambiah (1990), 23–4. The work of the social anthropologist Tambiah is perhaps most familiar to students of ancient magic in the shape of his important essay on the magical power of words (Tambiah 1968).
11 Hoffmann (2002), 180–1.
12 Ov. *Ars* 2.329–30, Mart. 7.54.
13 The last example comes from the first century CE agronomical writer Columella 10.357–68. The procedure is explicitly designated magical (358) and indeed contains many magical elements – the absence of bindings which might inhibit the flow of occult forces, the ritual number three, the lustration (sacral perambulation) of the orchard, the belief in the destructive power of the menses (Lennon 2010).
14 See Mauss (1972), 63; Malinowski (1974), 38 'in the magical act the underlying idea and aim is always clear, straightforward and definite'. The focus on specific goals is one of the ways in which scholars seek to distinguish magic from religion, in that, it is claimed, 'religious activities tend [by contrast] to be regarded as ends in themselves' (Aune 1980, 1512). The distinction has some validity, but, as Fowler (1995), 12 noted, religious rites can be goal-oriented too.
15 Briggs (1996), 8, debunking the entrenched but ill-founded belief that in the European witch persecutions of the sixteenth to eighteenth centuries the victims were nearly always female.
16 'In the broadest sense of the word, an amulet is any object which by its contact or its close proximity to the person who owns it, or to any possession of his, exerts power for his good, either by keeping evil from him and his property, or by endowing him with positive advantages'. Bonner (1946), 26.
17 My reasoning was that there exist admirable specialised studies of the topic (bibliographical references in Chapter 5 n.140), to which I had nothing material to add, and further that amulets, broadly speaking, tend to supplement our understanding of ancient magic, rather than opening up new horizons (though it could be that the ongoing and comprehensive work of Christopher Faraone on the topic might alter the picture somewhat).

18 See Preisendanz-Henrichs vol. 1 (1973), v–xii; Betz, xli–iv; Brashear (1995), 3398–3412.
19 Brashear (1995), 3405 suggests possible reasons for the placement in a tomb; 'it is conceivable that they were hidden <in the tomb> for safe keeping in time of peril [posed by the fourth century CE Roman government's hostile attitude to magicians]. Another possible motive may have been to conceal the texts from curious and profane eyes. Still a third, is that the books might have been placed in the tomb in an act of concern for the deceased'.
20 See S. Martin (2010), 9–13.
21 Dawson (1949), 158–60.
22 Brashear (1995), 3403–4. The issue of which of the magical papyri discovered in the nineteenth century and subsequently associated with d'Anastasi came from the Theban cache has proved controversial: see the painstaking study of Dosoo (2016), who settles for ten.
23 Preisendanz-Henrichs (1973), viii.
24 Brashear (1995), 3407.
25 Cf. Preisendanz (1950), 223–6; Betz, xlii; Brashear (1995), 3399, 3410; Dosoo (2016), 271–3. The giant of German Classical scholarship, Wilamowitz, damned the work of Dieterich and others interested in the *PGM* as '*Botokudenphilologie*', the Botocudo being a now extinct tribe of eastern Brazil.
26 Wünsch had already published *DTA* (1897) and *Sethianische Verfluchungstafeln* ('curse tablets') *aus Rom* (Berlin, 1898).
27 Whose *Die Apologie des Apuleius* (1908) remains of great importance for students of ancient magic.
28 Preisendanz-Henrichs (1973), viii.
29 Eitrem (1925a).
30 See Johnson (1992), lv–vii; Pachoumi (2017), 3.
31 In the case of aggressive love spells, which represent about a quarter of the corpus.
32 Oxyrhynchus, a town about 160 km south-south-west of Cairo, is the site of the richest haul of papyri ever discovered, decipherment of which continues to this day. The results are published, at a rate roughly of one a year, in successive volumes of the *Oxyrhynchus Papyri*. See Parsons (2007), Chapters 1 and 2.
33 Some of the multiple ways in which a woman's erotic attention could be magically captured are vividly summed up in the conclusion to item no. 52 in Kotansky Amulets (= Gager no. 125) 'protect Alexandra whom Zoe bore' . . . 'in order that you [hostile forces] may not hurt or defile or bewitch/use magic drugs upon her, either via a kiss or osculation [by kissing as a form of social greeting] or a chance meeting, or through food or drink ['a reference to poisoning, erotic love potions or both' Kotansky] or in bed or via intercourse, nor by a glance/the Evil Eye nor [by magical use of] her clothing'.

34 Threats: Ritner (1993), 22; Brashear (1995), 3394; Pinch (2006), 73–5; Wortmann (1968), 92–3; with Martinez (1991), 69–73 for the rationale. Secret names: Brashear (1995), 3392; Pinch (2006), 163. Hymns/hymnodic lists of divine epithets: Bortolani (2016), 26–36, 42–4; Solar and Osirian themes: Bortolani (2016), 45. Self-identification of the officiant with the deity: Brashear (1995), 3392; Pinch (2006), 140. Drawings of gods: Pinch (2006), 163. Images of Seth and of human-animal hybrids: e.g. *PGM* 12.449–52, *PGM* 36, Bonner (1946), 33. Egyptian deities invoked, or Egyptian gods in Greek guise: Frankfurter (1998), 229; Pinch (2006), 164. Figurines animated: Pinch (2006), 96. *Diabolai*: Ritner (1993), 173; Pinch (2006), 93–4. Use of native animals: *PGM* 1.247, 7.300, 13.321, 13.1065–6. Power of writing: Frankfurter (1994). Grandiose claims: Ritner (1993), 105; Brashear (1995), 3394; Pinch (2006), 62, 116, 140. 'Deification' of animals: Pinch (2006), 163.

35 See especially Frankfurter (1997 and 1998), 198–237, echoed by e.g. Pollard (2013), 14 n.39, Bortolani (2016), 19 and Pachoumi (2017), 4.

36 For a selection of such figures see Ogden (2002a), 52–60, 136–40.

37 Bonner (1950), 22.

38 See Ritner (1993), passim, especially 242 'within the *Egyptian* world view there is no distinction between magician and priest, spell and prayer, nor ultimately between religion and magic'; Frankfurter (1997), 131. As Smith (1995), 18 notes, '"Magic" . . . is almost always a third-person attribution rather than a first-person self-designation'.

39 Ritner (1993), 99 'one of many indications of the inherently *traditional Egyptian* basis of most *PGM* . . . ritual' et passim.

40 'The Graeco-Egyptian Papyri belong to an international school of magic, but many of the techniques featured in the spells find precedents in earlier Egyptian magic', Pinch (2006), 163; Janet H. Johnson in Betz (1992), lvii 'one must . . . be leery of overstating the Greek case and attributing *too much* [my italics] to Greek influence'.

41 Frankfurter (1997), 118–19.

42 *SGD* 99 (text and translation in Eidinow (2007), 427–8). Further early examples of the so-called *similia similibus* formula in Eidinow (2007), 150.

43 Pinch (2006), 163, though she qualifies this with the rider '<such aggression> may simply be finding open expression in private written magic for the first time'.

44 For clear textual and artefactual evidence that the spells in the *PGM* were largely put together from formularies, transmitted over long centuries, see Nock (1972b), 177–80; Jordan (1988); Brashear (1995), 3412–19, 3459–60; Brooten (1996), 88–9; Faraone (1999), 4–5; LiDonnici (2003), 141; also Hull (1974), 20–7 for a good synthesis of the matter.

45 Preisendanz (1950), 230–4.

46 On *ousia* see Chapter 2 n.6.

47 In addition, we have in *PGM* 117 the earliest occurrences in a documentary love spell of ideas which are commonplace in the later erotic hexes of the *PGM*: the

'joining of black to black' as a formulaic circumlocution for intercourse, the infliction of pain and suffering on the beloved until she cooperates, and the invoking of insomnia upon the target to ensure the same end.

48 Note also in col. 2.14–15 the earliest appearance of the demand, ubiquitous in the amatory spells of the *PGM*, that all quotidian activities, drinking, eating, sleeping and so on, should be suspended by the victim in favour of an exclusive erotic focus on the operator.

49 See Dickie (2001), 117–22.

50 Suet. *Aug.* 31 (over two thousand books of prophetic writings burned by Augustus), Paulus *Sententiae* 5.23.18, Ammian. Marcell. 29.1.41, Brown (1970), 34 'sorcery ... was an art consigned to great books ... knowledge of sorcery techniques could be widespread among the literate people that the historian meets', Watson (2003), on Hor. *Epod.* 17.4–5 (bibliography), Bremmer (2015), 252–64.

51 [Democritus] *Physica et Mystica* 2 p. 42, 21 Berthelot, Thessalus of Tralles *De Virtutibus Herbarum* 6 Friedrich, Plut. *De Iside et Osiride* 375f, Lucian, *Philops.* 31 a great number of Egyptian books on exorcising ghosts.

2

The Violence of Amatory Magic

In 1992 William Brashear published a lengthy piece on a Graeco-Egyptian magical ensemble of unknown provenance which had been acquired ten years earlier by the Museum of Egyptian Antiquities in Munich. The ensemble consisted of a small clay pot with a lid, two wax figurines embracing each other, and a papyrus written in Greek containing an elaborate erotic spell, in which one Priskos demands the assistance of various supernatural powers in constraining Isis, daughter of Auei, to fall passionately and irresistibly in love with him. The figurines were enfolded in the papyrus, and the whole was placed in the pot, whose lid was then sealed and remained so until the 1980s. In its physical details (lidded and sealed pot, figurines of wax wrapped in a Greek love-spell inscribed on papyrus) the ensemble was virtually identical to one held in Cologne[1] and discussed by Dierk Wortmann some twenty-five years earlier as item number 4 in a famous paper which examined thirteen newly discovered magical texts, of which nos. 1–4 were amatory (Wortmann (1968)). The resemblances between the two ensembles did not end there. The text of the Munich spell exhibits significant overlaps with Wortmann no. 4 (as well as occasional parallels with his nos. 1–3),[2] making it clear that the authors of both the Munich spell and Wortmann no. 4 were drawing on a common source, viz. a book of magical spells or formularies of the kind that, it has long been recognised, were regularly used by ancient experts in magic. These formularies provided the magician with a broad template for a spell, which he could then adapt to the specific needs and circumstances of the individual client.[3]

The text of the Munich spell begins as follows:

> I bind you [the target of the spell] with the indissoluble fetters of chthonic Fate and mighty Necessity to love me, Priskos, whom Annous bore. I conjure you, the daemons who lie here and who pass your time here and the daemons here who died by violence.[4] I conjure you by the unconquerable god *iao barbathiao bremai chermari*, rouse yourselves, you daemons who lie here, and seek Isis, whom Auei bore, and bring her to me, Priskos, whom Annous bore,[5] in a state of frantic passion

and fleshy love, unable to get sleep the whole night and day long ... with passion and love for me, Priskos, whom Annous bore. For I have bound her brain and heart and her hands and her guts and her genitals to love me, Priskos, whom Annous bore. But if you [the daemons enacting the spell] disobey me and do not accomplish what I tell you, the sun will not set beneath the earth and Hades and the cosmos will be no more. But if you bring Isis, whom Auei bore, whose magical stuff (*ousia*) this is,[6] from every place and every house and every street to me, Priskos, whom Annous bore, in a state of frantic passion and fleshy love, I will give you Osiris *Nophrioph* the brother of Isis[7] and he draws cold water and will refresh your souls (1–20).[8]

After further conjurations of the demonic agents enacting the spell, including the instruction to bring Isis 'burning and tortured to Priskos ... in state of frantic love and passion' (32–4), the spell concludes

[daemons] seize Isis whom Auei bore, whose magical stuff you have, and bind her with indissoluble strong adamantine fetters in frantic passion and fleshy love, and let her glue thigh to thigh and lip to lip in sexual intercourse with me, Priskos, whom Annous bore, and let her not be fucked by any other man except by me alone, Priskos, whom Annous bore. Bring her ... Isis, whom Auei bore, [bring] the spell to fulfilment, now, at once, at once (48–56).[9]

Rather less elaborate, but similar in intent, is a Greek erotic *defixio* first published some twenty years ago (Jordan (1999a)). Inscribed on lead, the usual medium for curse tablets, it is accompanied in the left quadrant by a drawing in partly theriomorphic form of Seth-Typhon, the evil genius, so to speak, of the Egyptian pantheon. It reads:

I conjure you, Daemon,[10] by the great god *Erekisephthe Araracharara Ephthesiker[?e]* (further magical names/words of power).... Kleopatrion, (?) daughter of Patrakinos, bring Tereous, whom Apia bore, to me, Didymos, whom Taipiam bore, burning up, aflame, tortured in her soul, her mind, her woman's parts, until she comes to me Didymos, whom Taipiam bore, and glues her lips to my lips, her hair to my hair, her belly to my belly, her wee black [pubic hair] to my wee black,[11] until I accomplish my intercourse and <join> my male genitals with her female genitals. Now, immediately (twice).

There are many interesting aspects to the above spells, including the typically Egyptian practice of threatening the spirits of the dead and the gods (see Chapter 1) and the piling up of strings of words of power in order to increase the efficacy of the charm. But what concerns us here is the aggressive physicality of the spells, their sheer psychic and bodily invasiveness, the brutal, indeed solipsistic subjugation of the victim to the spell-caster's desires ('I have bound her brain and heart and her hands and her guts and her genitals to love me' . . . 'let her not be fucked by any other man except by me alone' . . . 'bring Tereous to me, burning up, aflame, tortured in her soul, her mind, her woman's parts' . . . 'glues her wee black to my wee black, until I accomplish my intercourse and <join> my male genitals with her female genitals').

Students of ancient magic have often remarked upon the extreme violence and cruelty directed at the targets of the love-spells in the *Greek Magical Papyri* (*PGM*), as well as those Greek and Latin 'binding spells' (Gk. *katadesmoi*, Latin *defixiones*) which are amatory in intent.[12] The purpose of such texts is to induce in the victim an irresistible passion for the spell-caster (LiDonnici (1998); Ficheux (2006), 290, 292–3), an intention frequently expressed in even more graphic and brutal terms than above. This brutality is most marked in the so-called *agōgai*, 'fetching spells', of the *PGM*, which seek to bring the object of desire to the bed of the person commissioning the love-spell, and there to keep her or him in a state of erotic subjection or slavery – usually in perpetuity.[13] One example of such viciousness, which it is hard to reconcile with our modern notions of love, can be found in the 'fetching spell over myrrh which is burned as an offering' (*PGM* 4.1496–595). This includes the instructions to the agent enacting the spell

> do not enter through <the target's> eyes or through her side, or through her nails or even through her navel or through her frame, but through her 'soul'.[14] *And remain in her heart and burn her guts, her breast, her liver, her breath, her bones, her marrow, until she comes to me NN, loving me, and until she fulfils all my wishes . . . inflame her and turn her guts inside out, drain out her blood drop by drop (ekstaxon autēs to haima).*

Later in the same corpus (*PGM* 36.134–60), an injunction to the magician's supernatural assistants runs

> cause her . . . to be sleepless . . . hungry, thirsty, not finding sleep, to love me . . . passionately with passion in her guts until she comes and glues her female pudenda to my male one. But if she wishes to fall asleep, *spread under her prickly leather scourges (sittubas akanthinas)*[15] *and thorns upon her temples*, so that she may nod agreement to a courtesan's love.

We equally read in *PGM* O2 – a separation spell or *diakopos* intended to direct the affections of a woman away from her current partner and towards the spell-caster – the injunction 'burn, inflame the "soul" of Allous, her female parts, her limbs, until she leaves the house of Apollonius, send Allous to bed with fever, with unceasing illness, so that Allous cannot eat and Allous loses her senses'. Spells such as we are discussing routinely speak of the victim being 'tortured' (*basanizomenē/-os*) in both body and spirit.[16] The most striking instance of such 'torture' in Greek and Roman love-spells occurs in the *philtrokatadesmos thaumastos*, 'wondrous spell for binding a lover' at *PGM* 4.296–466. One of its procedures involves making a doll of wax or clay to represent the female target of the *katadesmos* and piercing the doll while pronouncing a magic formula. The relevant instructions run:

> take 13 copper needles and stick one in the brain <of the doll> while saying 'I am piercing your brain, NN' – and stick 2 in the ears and 2 in the eyes and 1 in the mouth and 2 in the midriff and 1 in the hands and 2 in the pudenda and 2 in the soles, saying each time – 'I am piecing such and such a member of her, NN, so that she may remember no one but me, NN, alone'.

In empirical confirmation of the startling violence of this rite, a female figurine pierced with thirteen needles precisely according to the specifications of the *philtrokatadesmos thaumastos* was discovered in the 1970s.[17] Now on display in the Louvre, it invariably crops up whenever the viciousness of Greek and Roman erotic magic is discussed.

Faced with such sadism towards the love-object, scholars of ancient magic have responded in multiple ways. In an influential paper dating to 1991, J.J. Winkler adopted a psychoanalytical approach to the unsettling brutality of the erotic spells. The extreme physical and mental sufferings called down in the erotic magical papyri and amatory *defixiones* upon the targets of love-spells, Winkler contends, at base stem from the profound distress and anguish experienced by upper-class males who have been gripped by feelings of pain, madness and erotic yearnings against which they are helpless,[18] and which drastically undermine their sense of emotional autonomy: feelings which, *in an act of fictitious transference which simultaneously operates as a form of emotional catharsis*,[19] the lovers *project back* onto the persons responsible for inspiring these pangs of unreciprocated love, displacing onto these the very bodily and psychic torments to which the practitioners were previously subject. In addition, the sheer animus displayed towards their targets also reflects a powerful hostility on the part of the practitioners towards the females who inspired extremes of desire but declined to respond in kind.[20]

It is implicit in Winkler's approach that the violence directed at the targets of the love-spells remains at the level of the word i.e. is not meant to be realised in any *physical* way. Others – John G. Gager,[21] Bernadette Brooten,[22] Fritz Graf,[23] Daniel Ogden,[24] Geraldine Pinch,[25] Daniela Colomo,[26] Derek Collins[27] and Daniela Urbanová[28] – go much further and deny outright that the love-spells

Fig. 1 The Louvre 'Voodoo Doll'. © Marie-Lan Nguyen / Wikimedia Commons / CC-BY 2.5.

show any intention of maiming, wounding or harming their victim – no matter how violent their *language*. On the other side of the fence are ranged H.S. Versnel and Lynn LiDonnici;[29] these argue, in their different ways, that the love-spells *do* have the purpose of physically disabling and injuring their targets,[30] to the point that these will be susceptible to the advances of the spell-caster, as the only possible means of alleviating their symptoms: for the core message of the spells is 'let her suffer, until she comes to me'. In the same camp, broadly speaking, is

Christopher Faraone who apparently treats the 'transitory violence' of *agōgē* spells as real (Faraone (1999), 55–69 especially) and believes that a supplementary purpose of the Louvre doll (viz. in addition to binding the victim) was 'most likely' to hurt the female target by persuasive analogy.³¹ At the same time, however, he speaks of *agōgē* spells as 'at least at the *symbolic level* (my italics) ... designed to move a woman from the home of one man to that of another'³² and regards the violence of these as shadowing or embodying the traditional pattern of abduction marriage or 'bridal theft', the forcible carrying off of a bride by her suitor: an analogy so strained as to damage his overall case regarding the element of violence in the spells under consideration.³³

To sum up the argument thus far, a majority of specialists in ancient magic contend, either implicitly or explicitly, that the amatory spells do not propose actual bodily violence against the love-object, while a few countervailing voices assert that the verbal cruelty of the spells is meant to be actualised in real physical hurt to the target. In what follows I set out a case for the second, less popular position, at the same time suggesting that scholarly attempts to rationalise the violence of the love-spells not only sweep some unpalatable facts under the carpet, but fall victim to methodological shortcomings.

I begin with Winkler's neo-Freudian/social constructionist approach, because it is repeatedly cited with approbation even by those who do not accept its basic premise.³⁴ This, readers will recall, is predicated on the notion that the authors of the love-spells are undergoing agonies of unanswered love from which they seek to free themselves by retrojecting these agonies back onto the persons who originally inspired them. But if this is so, we should surely expect to hear much in the papyri and the *defixiones* of the authors' feelings of helpless passion and resultant animus towards the unresponsive love-object. In fact, however, our texts are almost completely silent on that score. I have been able to find only three Greek or Roman instances where the spell-caster actually gives voice to such feelings.³⁵ The first is *PGM* 4.1405–12 (from a formulary however, rather than an applied spell), where the text mentions the 'tears and bitter groans' of the person utilising the spell, how he is 'beset with the torments [of love]' and 'suffering at heart on account of NN woman, impious and ungodly'. The second is *PGM* 17a.6–8, where Hermeias begs Anubis to 'make Tigerous cease from her arrogance, calculation and shamefulness'. Last – and rather more tame – is *SM* 49.63–4 and 77–9 'Matrōna, whom Theodorus has in mind'.³⁶ One might profitably contrast here Sappho's *Hymn to Aphrodite* (frg. 1 Lobel-Page) and Theocritus *Idyll* 2, in both of which the apparatus of love magic is extensively deployed³⁷ *and in which the practitioner articulates in the most explicit way the sense of longing which she is attempting to replicate in a recalcitrant lover.* And the almost complete absence from the erotic papyri and amatory *defixiones* of indications that the instigators of these spells are suffering the acute amatory distress which Winkler's approach assumes is thrown vividly into relief if one compares the late but tralaticious Coptic love-spell of Cyprian of Antioch,[38] where Cyprian expresses in the most unambiguous terms the physical and mental agonies provoked in him by the abject failure of his sex-magic to attract a Christian virgin. The relevant portion of the text reads:

> everything has changed in my soul: everything has changed in my person. My heart has grown bitter. I have grown pale. My flesh shudders; the hair of my head stands on end. I am all afire. I have lain down to rest, but I could not sleep; I have risen, but I found no relief. I have eaten and drunk in sighing and groaning. I have found no rest either in soul or in spirit for being overwhelmed by desire. My wisdom has deserted me; my strength has been sapped. All contrivance has been brought to naught. Yet I am Cyprian, the great magician ... but all this did me no good with a virgin named Justina.[39]

In the absence of clear markers of emotional distress such as we find here, Winkler's thesis, in sum, seems to rest on an argument largely from silence.

Those who deny that the love-spells mean to visit physical harm on their targets tend to focus on the *philtrokatadesmos thaumastos* at *PGM* 4.296–466 which, as noted above, involved piercing a doll with thirteen needles so that, in the words of the incantation (328–9), the victim 'may remember no one but me' viz. the spell-caster. It is pointed out quite rightly in regard to these words, that 'the will of the victim <is to> be bound to the practitioner's wishes, <rather than> that ... she be physically disabled or injured'.[40] But by fixating on the *philtrokatadesmos thaumastos* and its physical correlate, the Louvre doll, the apologists risk erecting the non-violence allegedly found there into a global principle of love-spells, and shunt aside a lot of evidence that these do genuinely mean to injure and inflict hurt upon the desired party. Representative instances which surely point in this direction include *PGM* 4.1425–31, part of a fetching spell, 'give heed to me and rouse her, NN, on this night and from her eyelids *remove sweet sleep, and cause her hateful care and fearful pain,* cause her to follow after my footsteps and to my wishes give her a willingness, until she does what I command of her'; *PGM* 4.2909–15 'bring NN ... to my bed of love, driven forcibly by frenzied passion, *by violent goads*'; *P. Oxy.* 4468 (late first century CE), col. 1.28–9 'shatter and make bloodless NN, daughter of NN'; *PGM* 36.355–60 'go into every place and seek out her, NN, and open her right side and enter like thunder, like lightning, like a burning flame, *and make her thin, pale, weak, limp, incapable of action in any part of her body* until she leaps forth and comes to me'. Of particular note here is a fetching spell at *PGM* 4.2485ff., 'go to her ... and take away her sleep and put a burning heat in her soul, punishment[41] and frenzied passion in her thoughts ... and attract her here to me', before adding, in very short order, that the same procedure can be used to make the female subject *ill* or, alternatively, to *kill* her. In view of such a striking juxtaposition – by no means unique[42] – it would seem difficult to deny that the pangs conjured against the unfortunate woman whose sexual compliance is the primary aim of the spell are meant to be felt by her in a very *physical* way.

Returning now to the *philtrokatadesmos thaumastos*, I wonder how unequivocal, as is claimed, is the evidence that the piercing of the doll there is *not* intended to induce pain in the subject whom it represents imagistically.[43] Not only does another section of the same spell overtly visit violence upon the target ('drag her by the hair, by her heart, by her soul ... to me etc.': 375–81),[44] but given that in a non-amatory spell, *PGM* 124.1–43, a waxen image is maltreated by having needles stuck into its eyes with the declared intention of causing illness in the human subject, it seems methodologically questionable to rule out or discount a similar intention for the virtually identical procedure in the *philtrokatadesmos thaumastos*.[45] Also of note for the possibility that the piercing of a doll may be intended to cause pain is a late tale involving one Theophilus, who suffered incurable agonies in hands and feet, until he discovered an image of himself pierced with four nails, one for each hand and each foot. When the nails were pulled out the pain disappeared forthwith from the affected limb.[46]

Moving on to a fresh point, it is well known that love was conceived of in Antiquity as a disease with tangible physical symptoms (Winkler (1991), 222–3), a psychosomatic illness that could be diagnosed by a sufficiently alert doctor. The best-known instance of this involved the royal physician Erasistratos, who correctly analysed the cause of prince Antiochus' sickness as unfulfilled love for his stepmother Stratonice.[47] The pathology of lovesickness canonically involved loss of interest in food and drink and, as Galen *in Hipp. prog.* 1.4.18 (Kühn 18b.18) put it, 'growing gaunt or pale or losing sleep or even getting fevers for reasons of love'. But it is precisely such symptoms that the authors of love-spells typically invoke upon their targets, as in the following instances, which are merely three among many: 'let Vettia ... have me alone in her thoughts, *out of her mind (insaniens), sleepless, let her burn, let her freeze* (i.e. suffer the heat and chills of fever),[48] *let Vettia burn* ... with love and desire for me' (Kropp 11.2/1/4, Audollent 266), 'attract to me, NN, her, NN, *aflame, fevered (puroumenē)* ... *hungry, thirsty, not finding sleep*, loving me, whom NN bore, until she comes and glues her female pudenda to my male one, immediately, quickly, quickly' (*PGM* 36.110–14), or '*let her not even be able to eat or to drink or to get sleep ever or to enjoy good health or to have rest in her soul or mind as she yearns for Ailourion*, whom his mother Kopria bore, until Kopria[49] ... *inflamed*, and comes to Ailourion' (*SM* 48.9–11). Given that, as noted, love was perceived as a *physical* illness, and given the homology between the characteristic symptoms of lovesickness and the physical and psychic discomforts invoked upon the targets of the love-spells – in particular the recurrent motifs of sleep deprivation and erotic burning/fever[50] – it seems counterintuitive not to treat the latter as intended to assault the victim with real bodily and mental pain: the intention being to reduce the desired person to such a state of corporeal and mental debilitation that they will yield to the spell-caster's desires, as the only recourse in order to be quit of their symptoms.

There is a further reason to take the sufferings called down upon the targets of aggressive love-spells as real, and not, as some would have it, as figurative, or as mere signifiers of the spell-caster's anguish. It is that such spells, whether inscribed on papyrus or lead, the preferred medium for *defixiones*, are a subcategory of binding spell (*katadesmos*),[51] and that, in binding spells, bodily as well as mental tortures are standardly visited upon the parties at whom they are aimed (see next chapter). In non-amatory binding spells the sufferings most commonly invoked are burning and fever, the wasting away of the victim's flesh, insomnia, inability to eat or drink, the compromising of health, the targeting of various body parts, generalised physical 'torture' and, often, death in one form or another. But with the exception of the last item, these are essentially the same sufferings as are invoked upon the targets of love-spells. These generic resemblances can be conveniently illustrated by comparing the catalogue of symptoms in four binding spells, the first two non-amatory, the third and fourth amatory. The first is a *defixio* from Pagans Hill in the UK against a family of thieves 'do not permit them good health or drinking or eating or sleeping ... until they make good my loss'.[52] The second is a commercial curse from Rome (Kropp 1.4.4/4, Audollent 140) which reads in part 'hand over to death the baker Praeseticius, the son of Aselle, who lives in the ninth region, where he can be seen to ply his trade ... *and if perchance he treats you* [the divine executor of the spell] *with contempt* [i.e. if you do not succeed in killing him] *may he suffer fevers, chills, bodily tortures, pallor, sweats, shiverings by day and night*'. The third instance is an amatory spell at *SM* 46, including the details 'bind Heronous, whom Ptolemais bore, to me Posidonius ... so that Heronous may not be able to eat, to drink, be content, have strength, enjoy good health, sleep apart from me

Posidonius' (ll. 8–12).⁵³ The fourth and last instance comes from a male-targeting erotic *defixio* commissioned by one Septima (Audollent 270), of which lines 15–21 run 'make Sextilius, the son of Dionysia, not get sleep, but let him burn with love and desire for me, let his spirit and heart burn, let all the limbs of the whole body of Sextilius be consumed'. One could pursue at infinitely greater length the commonalities between on the one hand, the love-spells of the *PGM* and amatory *defixiones* and, on the other, *defixiones* of various different kinds, but my point can be summed up briefly as follows. Given that other types of binding spells, as all agree, seek to visit physical hurt on their victims,⁵⁴ does it not smack of special pleading to deny the same intention to one particular kind of binding charm, the love-spell?

There remains one argument that tells powerfully against those who would ameliorate or downplay the violence which, I have been arguing, characterises Greek and Roman love-spells. It depends upon the fact that in Antiquity magic, not least binding magic – of which love-spells represent one class – was very widely held to be highly effective, and in an intensely physical way. The evidence for this belief is legion.⁵⁵ Plato complains that the rich are persuaded that incantations can be used to injure (*blaptein*) their enemies, who in turn are convinced that they are being harmed by these spells (*Leg.* 933a–b: cf. *Resp.* 364b–c), the Elder Pliny remarks 'there is no one who does not fear being cursed (*defigi*) with imprecations' and reports a popular belief that asphodel planted before the gate of a country house, wards off 'the damaging effects of sorcery' (*HN* 28.19, 21.108); numerous inscriptions commemorate persons thought to have been killed or harmed by malevolent/binding magic (*defixi*),⁵⁶ amulets⁵⁷ or spells might be tailored specifically to offer protection against the hurt inflicted by curse tablets or antisocial magic (e.g. *PGM* 13.803 asks for 'health which no magic can harm'),⁵⁸ and we know of several binding spells which counter an earlier *defixio* considered to have wrought material injury to the authors of the counter-charms.⁵⁹ The most familiar instance of the deep-rooted belief that binding magic could inflict palpable physical harm involves the circumstances surrounding the death of the imperial prince Germanicus. As Tacitus (*Ann.* 2.69) describes it, after the prince's death 'there were found, unearthed from the floor and walls of his house, relics of human bodies, spells and binding curses (*devotiones*) and the name of Germanicus inscribed on lead tablets, half-burned ashes, smeared with gore and other instruments of harm by which it is believed that human souls are devoted to the powers of the Underworld'. The key phrase in Tacitus' account – which captures to perfection the procedures and formulations attendant upon the deposition of *defixiones* – is the last one, 'by which it is believed that human souls are devoted to the powers of the Underworld'.

The point to take away from all this is that binding magic, like Graeco-Roman magic in general, was seen by both practitioners and targets as pragmatic, goal-directed and as eminently capable of having a direct physical effect upon the target of the spell – as the cataloguing in *defixiones* of body parts to be 'bound', a ubiquitous feature of such spells, clearly suggests. It is surely then a perversion of the whole ethos of binding spells to argue, with Winkler and co., *that the purpose of amatory defixiones was to effect a psychic release for the individual in the grip of love, rather than work by any possible means on the affections of the spell's target*. Nor is it much better to argue, with others, that the violence of language in the love-spells is merely symbolic or metaphorical,[60] for this again flies in the face of the intense goal- and body-directedness of the love-spells, a focus encapsulated in stock formulations such as 'until she comes and glues her lips to my lips, her hair to my hair, her pubic hair to my pubic hair, until I accomplish my sexual intercourse and <join> my male genitals with her female genitals'.[61]

To conclude this section of the chapter, what are we to make of those who, in the face of the evidence to the contrary, rationalise or deny the violence of ancient amatory *incantamenta*? I have a suspicion that the reluctance of scholars to believe that the love-spells of Rome and Graeco-Roman Egypt actually sought to inflict harm on the love-object – as the texts, I am arguing, unequivocally suggest – arises out of a misguided romanticism[62] which is anachronistic to say the least (I am reminded here of the view of Eduard Fraenkel, the former Corpus Professor of Latin at Oxford, that the so-called Helen episode of *Aeneid* 2, found only in a scholiast to Virgil but missing from the main MSS of the poet, could not be authentic because Virgil would never have made his virtuous Aeneas entertain the deplorable idea of killing Helen, as he does in these lines).[63] But we are not dealing, in the spells, with love as we understand it, or even with love as explored in the pages of Greek and Roman poetry, but rather with a self-serving sex-magic *in which violence is naturally at home*.[64] The language of the spells bespeaks an egotistic, ruthless disregard for the love-objects, talking, as they routinely do, of 'torturing, whipping, burning and enslaving' the targets[65] 'causing them to swoon' from physical distress (*PGM* 19a51–3, 61.16), or of being constrained to obey the wishes of the spell-caster 'whether she will or not'.[66] In the final analysis, the sufferings of the victim are almost entirely directed towards the carnal satisfaction of the spell-caster's desires, as in this concluding expression from a Carthaginian *defixio*, 'bring her to me so that she can satisfy my desires', which is preceded by the even more explicit *coge illa[m] m[ec]un coitus facere*, 'compel her to have sex with me'.[67] All this discloses purposes to which sentimental feelings, sympathy with the victim's plight or romantic notions of emotional reciprocation appear entirely alien.[68] To speak of love magic here is, in short, a misnomer: we are dealing with a highly purposive and self-serving type of erotic gratification, as the often strikingly explicit written and visual language of the spells attests. Examples include a jealousy-inspired 'binding' of a woman 'in her own genitals' (a *defixio* from Tebessa in Roman North Africa);[69] another North African *defixio* which seeks to win *four* women for one man (*SGD* pp. 186–7); the frequent targeting of the so-called 'vaginal soul' in the fetching spells of the *PGM*;[70] graphic language such as 'bring her to him in a state of humility and subjection, while he beholds her strip naked all the time, as his desire mingles with hers, as he sleeps with her and she never satiates him';[71] magical *charaktēres* accompanying a love-spell which seek by way of visual reinforcement to depict a penis entering a vagina;[72] the two instances noted earlier of waxen dolls enfolded in erotic embrace which enact imagistically the purpose of the papyrus love-spells in which they were originally enclosed;[73] and, finally, the oft-used formulations of the type already mentioned in the previous paragraph, such as 'let her come and glue her female organ/her pubic hair to his male organ/his pubic hair' and so on. In such a context as this, is it surely difficult to credit that the violence conjured up against the mostly female victims is merely symbolic or no more than a kind of psychological release-valve, as Winkler and his disciples would have it.

In his important monograph of 1999 on ancient Greek love magic, Christopher Faraone contends that the amatory spells of Classical Antiquity divide neatly along gender lines. On the one hand, there are what he calls *erōs*-inducing spells, utilised almost exclusively by men against women, and marked by a conspicuous violence of tone: such spells aimed to torture their victims with sleeplessness, fever and madness until they came to the door of the practitioner and submitted perforce to his desires. This class of procedure is best represented by the erotic binding or fetching spells (*philtrokatadesmoi*, *agōgai*) discussed *in extenso* above.[74] Distinct from these were *philia* spells, much less aggressive in character than the former, and practised primarily by women,[75] often in a distinctly surreptitious manner. The basic purpose of *philia* spells was essentially to restore or to maintain affection in an already existing relationship. The best-known instance of this type of spell is Deianeira's (ultimately disastrous) attempt to recover Herakles' love, after he has succumbed to passion for his captive Iolē, by using a *kēlētērion*, 'charm', against him.[76]

Faraone's dichotomising of ancient love-spells according to the sex of the practitioner is ultimately grounded in his application to them of what he calls a 'misandrist model ... according to which men must burn and torture women'.[77] In this reading, the men who commission *erōs* spells project onto their female targets the burning desire and madness typical of male lovers, *erastai*, in an attempt to overcome the females' innate modesty: for, in marked contrast to the misogynist perception of women as intrinsically lascivious and body-driven so widely canvassed in ancient literature, the women of love-spells are seen as naturally 'moderate and chaste',[78] self-controlled and sedate, domestically minded, 'reluctant to have intercourse' (Faraone (1999), 166). In marked counterpoint to *erōs* spells, the *philia* spells that women employ are far less violent in nature, and in fact aim at taming and subduing the angry and passionate temperaments of their '"naturally" wild husbands', who are intrinsically inclined to stray in the sexual arena (Faraone (1999), 128). In a further elaboration of this account, Faraone argues that 'gender is socially constructed in the world of love magic' (1999, 146). Hence when females, anomalously, employ *erōs*-magic, they are adopting an aggressively masculine persona,[79] a fact which is best explained by regarding them as prostitutes, who cannot afford to feel a natural female reserve in relation to matters erotic.

Faraone's thesis has met with widespread approbation.[80] His gendering of ancient love-spells, with its markedly structuralist flavour, has hardly ever been subjected to serious scrutiny – for all that its sheer neatness arouses disquiet.[81] It is nevertheless problematical on a number of fronts.

In the first place, the author is guilty of terminological imprecision. In attempting to distinguish *erōs* spells from *philia* spells, he skates over the fact that in the love charms of the *PMG* and amatory *defixiones* – if not necessarily elsewhere – *erōs* and *philia* are often employed interchangeably.[82] A good illustration of this is found in Brashear (1992): here we read at ll. 7–8 *axate autēn pros eme ... epi erōti manikō kai philia hedonikē*, 'bring her to me in a condition of mad *erōs* and [sexual] pleasure-driven *philia*':[83] (cf. 18), an expression which subsequently resurfaces as *epi philia manikē kai erōti hēdonikō*, 'in a condition of mad *philia* and pleasure-driven *erōs*' (34), suggesting that the phrases in question, in particular the two nouns, are synonymous in sense.[84] And there are numerous other instances in the documentary magical texts where *erōs* and *philia* or the cognate verbs *eran* and *philein*, are coupled in such a way as to make it apparent that no meaningful semantic distinction between them is intended, e.g. *SM* 45.36 *heina katadēsate moi Euphēmian, emoi Theōni, philia kai erōti*, 'so that you can bind for me, Theon, Euphēmia, with *philia* and *erōs*' (similarly 42.55), 47.27 *philousan me, erōsan mou*, 'loving me, desiring me' (similarly 45.48).[85] Nor is this synonymity of *erōs* and *philia* and its cognates a late phenomenon: in an *erōs*-spell of the Augustan period, *SM* 72 (122 Betz), we encounter the phrase *mainoito ep emēi philotēti*, 'may she be mad with *philia* for me' (col. 1.11–12), where, as the context shows, *philotēs*, the poetic equivalent of *philia*, is to all intents and purposes equivalent to *erōs*.[86] To enfeeble Faraone's case still further, there are a number of (fetching) spells that seek to engender *philia*, according to him a less carnal concept than *erōs*, in a female target, but then couple this purpose with the specification that the woman should seek *sunousia*, 'sexual intercourse', with the male operator, e.g. *PGM* 19a54 'but let [Karōsa] come melting with *erōs* and *philia* and *sunousia*, 'desire for intercourse'.[87] In addition to all this, as Dickie (2000, 583) notes, *philtra*, 'love-charms/love potions', the use of which Faraone ties closely to his category of *philia* spells,[88] can be used to produce *erōs*, for example in Eur. *Hel.* 1104. A particularly clear instance of such convergence is the *philtron epaineton*, 'commendable love charm', at *PGM* 61.1–38, which summons its female victim by inflicting upon her exactly the same symptoms of swooning, disorientation, erotic burning, loss of appetite for food and drink etc. as are called down upon the targets of *erōs* spells. The same convergence is seen in a recently published charm boasting the title *philtron* which aims to 'fetch' one party to another,[89] in other words functions as an *agōgē*, which is, according to Faraone, an archetypal form of *erōs* spell. In sum, the terminological and semantic distinction which Faraone erects between his two types of spell must be called seriously into question.

More troublesome still is a second difficulty with Faraone's division of love-spells according to the sex of the operator. The problem is that he heavily underplays the fact that spells of the *erōs* type, supposedly an almost exclusively male preserve, were also extensively deployed by women.[90] The evidence for this is considerable. For example, 'an *agōgē*, an excellent fire spell' at *PGM* 36.69–101 is advertised as 'fetching men to women and women to men and making maidens to leap forth from their homes',[91] while a similar claim is made for another *agōgē* at *PGM* 13.238–9, 'it fetches a woman to a man and a man to a woman, in wondrous fashion'. Another spell, *PGM* 12.14–95, a rite for acquiring Erōs as an assistant, reads at lines 61–2 'cause all men and all women to turn to love me, the man NN (or the woman NN)',[92] while *PGM* 19b1–3 is a formulary specifically for 'bringing him, NN, to her, NN', and a formulaic inscription in Kotansky Amulet no. 40 reads 'give her charm ... especially in regard to him before whom she herself desires this'.

In addition, individual *agōgē* spells can oscillate confusingly in specifying the sex of the target, who may be at one moment male, at another female, which means that the sex of the practitioner is left equally indeterminate: but the presumption must be that, in the case of a male victim, the person undertaking the spell is female.[93] To illustrate such imprecision in specifying the gender of the parties involved, it is useful to consider the *agōgē* known as 'The Sword of Dardanos' (*PGM* 4.1716–1870).[94] Here the victim to be fetched to the house of the individual commissioning the spell is twice designated as male, but the text then continues 'turn the soul of NN woman towards me, NN man, so that she loves me, so that she desires me, so that she gives me what is in her hands. Let her tell me what is in her own soul', before concluding with instructions for a procedure at the house door of the target who is identified three further times as female.[95] In a similar piece of confusion, 'Pitys' Spell of Attraction' (*PGM* 4.2006–2125) instructs the supernatural helper as follows: 'I say to you, chthonic daemon, for whom the magical material of this female (of this male) has been embodied on this night: proceed to where this female (or this male) resides', before continuing, without a break, 'and bring *her* to me' (2087–91). An even more startling instance of gender slippage occurs in the second column of a somewhat damaged erotic formulary belonging to the Augustan era (*SM* 72.2.1–25 = *PGM* 122 col. 2). In the initial lines the practitioner is instructed to 'lift his hands to the stars' and 'to anoint his face with myrrh', the sex of the referent being established by the application to him of the masculine participles *aras* and *labōn*. But the anointing of the face with myrrh is something that would more naturally be done by a woman (cf. Dickie (2000), 567), and that impression is reinforced when lines 6–8 cite a mythical precedent for the use of myrrh in an erotic context, in the shape of the goddess Isis, who anointed herself (*chreisamenē*) with this substance 'when she went into the embrace of her own brother Osiris'. Next, Isis is enjoined to wake up the target, 'him, NN, or her, NN' (7). Then, in a further muddying of the biological waters, the text speaks of 'him, NN' (11), of how 'I run, but he flees me' (12) and of 'fetching him, NN' (21: cf. 22): hence the spell, in pointed contrast to its opening, appears to conclude with an indisputable focus on female agency.[96] As Dickie puts it, 'the simplest explanation for this type of confusion is that recipes for spells tend to be written in the masculine gender even when [as here] they would most appropriately be used by a woman.'[97] To this tendency to lability in specifying the sex of the agent may be now added a slightly different instance of gender indeterminacy. This is found in the recently published *P. Oxy.* 5304 col. 2–9. Here the scribe appears to assume that the client will be a woman aiming to attract a man, but then hedges his bets by two interlinear additions which also allow for a male operative and a female target,[98] one more proof that erotic biding spells and *agōgai* need not be sex-specific in terms of their operator.[99]

A similar picture of the accessibility to women of *erōs* spells and of their readiness to avail themselves of these emerges if one compares the number of applied[100] spells of that type used by females with those commissioned by men. On a rough reckoning there are eight applied *erōs* spells issued by females (two of them homoerotic), as against thirty-three male-authored ones.[101] In other words, just over one-fifth of the applied spells come from women, hardly 'an insignificant number',[102] if one considers the various constraints that may have inhibited female use of such spells;[103] and the proportion in question looks all the more meaningful when we consider that three pairs and one triad of the male spells each have the same target.[104] To illustrate such – conspicuously aggressive – *erōs* spells commissioned by women I cite two (not *in toto*). The first is *PGM* 16 (first century CE),

> I adjure you, daemon of the dead by Adōnaios Sabaōth ... make Sarapion, whom Pasametra bore, to waste away and his flesh to melt from passion for Dioskorous, whom[105] Tikoi bore. Brand his heart, cause it to melt, and suck out his blood because of love and passion (*philia, erōti*) and pain, until Sarapion, whom Pasametra bore, comes to Dioskorous, whom Tikoi bore, and does all that is pleasing to me and continues loving me, until he comes to Hades.[106]

The second instance, Audollent 271, comes from Hadrumetum in Roman North Africa:

> I conjure you, daemonic spirit who lies here, by the holy name Aōth Abaōth ... to bring and yoke Urbanus, whom Urbana bore, to Domitiana, whom Candida bore, impassioned, tortured, sleepless with desire and passion for her, so that he may bring her to his house to be his mate ... bring, yoke Urbanus, whom Urbana bore, to Domitiana, impassioned, maddened, tortured with love and passion and desire for Domitiana, whom Candida bore, yoke them in marriage and passion, living together for the whole time of their lives, make him, in his passion, to be subject to her just like a slave, desiring no other woman or maiden, but Domitiana alone, whom Candida bore, to have her as his mate for all the period of their lives. Now, now, quickly, quickly.

Here we meet precisely the same themes of erotic domination in perpetuity, wasting of flesh, sleeplessness, torture, madness, irresistible passion and solipsistic insistence upon satisfaction of the spell-caster's desires as characterise male-authored *agōgai*.[107]

Now it is impossible to determine with any exactitude the mindset of the women who used *erōs* spells, based as they were on formularies.[108] At the same time, we should not make the mistake of supposing that the inscribing of erotic *defixiones* patterned on such formularies was a passionless, mechanical procedure. Since the *PGM* regularly prescribe that the client 'write' or 'recite' the text being employed, this could hardly be done without some attendant infusion of emotion, and the same surely goes for the process of depositing an amatory *defixio* in a location giving access to the supernatural agents who would enact it. Nor did the impassioned, sadistic language of the erotic formularies come out of thin air: at some level it must correspond to and reflect the actual feelings of the parties commissioning the spells.[109] My point is that, at a very minimum, the female users of *erōs* spells undoubtedly knew what they were about, both pragmatically and emotionally, in the general sense of *taking active, indeed, violent, steps to assert and secure their amatory futures*, to the extent of enforcing total erotic subjugation on the desired male. Faraone's taxonomy of ancient erotic spells, which characterises male amatory magic as aggressive and passionate, but female amatory magic as primarily reactive and mollifying must surely be called into question here.

In fact, the pattern whereby women show a forceful, even militant, determination to exert control over their amatory destinies by magical means sets in very early. In a fourth-century BCE *defixio* from Pella in Macedonia a woman possibly called Phila[110] 'binds' the marriage of Dionysophōn to Thetima, or any other women, in order to secure Dionysophōn for herself in perpetuity, Thetima being dismissed with the curse 'may she perish evilly'. It is interesting that the Pella text is contemporary with the earliest surviving *defixio*, also from Macedonia, that seeks to enforce the sexual submission of a woman to a man,[111] suggesting that *both* sexes were at this period beginning to harness *defixiones* to influence beneficially their amatory or conjugal lives. *DTA* 78 from Attica, also of the fourth century, binds 'Aristokydes and the women who let themselves be seen by him. Let him not ever "marry" another woman or youth'. This could be the work of a *hetaira* who, whether for reasons of love or financial security (or a combination of both), wanted Aristokydes for herself;[112] it could also come from a jealous wife or fiancée anxious to stop extramarital amours on a spouse's part ('marry', *gamein*, being euphemistic for 'have sex with').[113] A marital or quasi-marital situation seems more secure in Audollent no. 5, one of a series of thirteen *defixiones* datable to the second or first century BCE found in the temple of Demeter at Knidos in Caria, a region of Asia Minor. In this text, which combines a *defixio* of amatory import with a prayer for justice,[114] a woman called Prosodion dedicates to Demeter and the Maiden and the gods at Demeter's side whoever is taking away the husband of Prosodion <the husband of Prosodion>, Nakōn, from his children. Do not let Demeter nor any of the gods at Demeter's side be merciful to her, whoever receives from Nakōn, to the detriment of Prosodion, but let Prosodion be blessed and her children in every way. And any other woman who receives from Nakōn the husband of Prosodion, to the detriment of Prosodion. Do not let her meet with a merciful Demeter, nor the gods by Demeter's side, but let there be blessings for Prosodion and her children in every way.

Now the three female-authored *defixiones* just discussed are not *erōs* spells, hence not, in Faraone's terms, instances of women practising aggressive male-style magic in the defiance of his stereotype of female sexual passivity. Rather, they are relationship spells, whereby the women in question seek to insulate themselves magically against all possible rivals and to monopolise and control the affections of a given man. But there is in these spells none of the docility and submissiveness which Faraone, in his rather monolithic view of women's erotic magic, imputes to his female practitioners. Indeed the Pella *defixio* ('let evil Thetima perish evilly') and the Knidian text resonate with a sense of assertiveness and a determination to right wrongs that sits ill with Faraone's taxonomy of ancient erotic spells, which sees male amatory magic as stamped by aggression and a determination to win at all costs, but female amatory magic as gentler and emollient.[115] To offer one further example of how urgent and assertive female magic can be once we move outside the restrictive parameters of Faraone's *erōs* spells, I refer to a Greek separation spell (*diakopos*)[116] from Rome, which reads '<a spell> to produce hatred, in order that Eros may hate Felicissima and be hated by her'.[117] The initial focus on the male, Eros, and his feelings makes it almost certain that the *defigens* is a female who wants Eros for herself and hence Felicissima out of the way. But in its directness of tone this is no different from a second separation spell, from Oxyrhynchus in Egypt[118] in which the practitioner is beyond question a male with an erotic interest in the female target: 'separate Allous from Apollonius, her man. Give to Allous arrogance, hatred, disagreeableness, until she quits the house of Apollonius'. Aggressive magic in order to load the amatory dice firmly in one's favour was not, in sum, primarily a prerogative of the male sex.

The conclusion to be drawn from the evidence amassed above is that our documentary sources (*PGM*, *SM*, *defixiones* inscribed on lead/other media) made ample allowance for the use of highly purposeful and goal-focused erotic magic by women, no inhibition being felt in this regard. In fact, far from it being the case, as often alleged, that in documentary texts men practise aggressive love magic, whereas in fiction it is women who do so,[119] the testimonia just discussed if anything provide confirmation that the violent and compulsive love magic of literary figures such as Theocritus' Simaitha, Horace's Canidia or Apuleius' Pamphile,[120] have their correlate in real life.[121]

I turn now to the contentious issue of the status of the females targeted in the *erōs* spells of the Graeco-Egyptian papyri and late Empire *defixiones* upon which Faraone bases so much of his analysis: a question which is inextricably bound up with the perceived purpose of such spells. For Winkler, Graf and Faraone, the intended victims of *erōs* spells are usually or often respectable maidens, watched over solicitously by family and neighbours, 'young women ... usually living in their natal home' (Faraone (1999), 28), the targets of young men of social standing seeking to make an advantageous match and determined to do so by instilling in the former via their spells an irresistible passion that will have the desired effect of prising them away from their guardians.[122]

This reading rests mainly on the wish, repeatedly encountered in both the formularies of the *PMG* and applied *erōs* spells, that the relationship thereby established should last in perpetuity,[123] from which it is inferred that a (socially desirable) marriage is in question. The case cannot withstand scrutiny.[124]

In the first place, the wish for the permanence of the relationship often occurs in a very sexually charged context, as in *PGM* 4.400–5 'so that you may bring the woman, NN, to me and glue head to head and join lips to lips and glue belly to belly and bring thigh close to thigh and fit together black with black and she carry out her own sex acts with me for all eternity' or *SM* 38.9–13 'so that Theodotis ... may bring thigh close to thigh and genitals to genitals for intercourse for all the time of her life', making it look as though what is sought is not marriage until parted by death, but sex – indeed total sexual compliance[125] – on tap for the foreseeable future.

Second, the formularies and applied spells contain expressions like 'let her not be fucked by any man except me alone' (Brashear (1992), lines 52–3), 'let her not be fucked nor buggered (*mē binēthētō, mē pugisthētō*) nor do anything for the pleasure of another man unless with me alone' (*PGM* 4.352–4, *SM* 47.8–9, 48.8–9) or 'let her not be fucked nor buggered nor fellate nor do anything for the pleasure of another man, except for me' (*SM* 46.9–10), which hardly sounds like the sort of language appropriate to blushing virgins,[126] but is better suited to females who are known to be sexually available. Particularly noteworthy is the incorporation in the above prohibitions of the detail 'let her not fellate' (*SM* 46.9, *SM* 49.22, 38.5), since this activity was thought to be a speciality of prostitutes (Krenkel (2006), 210–12, 215).

The same inference about erotic availability and the status of the women in question can be drawn from exclusionary injunctions in *erōs* spells like 'if she lies abed with any other man in her lap, let her thrust him away' (*PGM* 4.2740–1), 'if she has another man in her lap, let her put him off and forget and hate him' (*SM* 45.49–50),[127] and the particular formulation of the forgetting motif so common in erotic spells which sees the woman enjoined to forget her own husband/man (*PGM* 19a53, 61.30) or other men in general (Kropp 11.2/1/4 = Audollent 266), along with her family. Further, *agōgai* sometimes feature an instruction to the daemon enacting the spell in the form 'go to every place, house and street and fetch her to me/bind her' (*PGM* 4.348–50, 36.355, *SM* 46.7–8) or 'make her leap forth from every place and every house to me' (*SM* 42.17, 45.46–7); but, in a telling amplification of this stock formulation, *SM* 49.19 and 50.19 add the detail 'go to every tavern (*kapēlion*)' – precisely the sort of establishment where prostitutes were to be found.[128] A final piece of evidence for the status of the women in female-targeting erotic spells is the expression quoted earlier from the *agōgē PGM* 36.134–60, 'so that she may nod agreement to a courtesan's love' or, in Dickie's paraphrase (2000, 571), 'so that she may to consent to love the man as would a woman available for sex'. It is hard to fault his conclusion (ibid.): 'my suspicion is that we can see here the market at which the erotic spells in the formularies were mainly directed: young men who wanted to monopolise the sexual activities of the kind of woman with whom they would not have considered entering into a formal contractual relationship'.

An examination of the late Antique erotic spells and amatory *defixiones* on which Winkler, Graf and Faraone largely[129] base their view that the male authors of such spells were aiming at marriage has suggested that this view cannot hold water, and that the men in question had in mind, rather, a longevity of carnal enjoyment based on the total submission and exclusive availability of the woman in question. We should however be careful of applying 'a one size fits all' approach. For all that there are multiple continuities, as Faraone (1999) and Petropoulos (1988) have shown, between early Greek erotic magic and that of the late imperial material, the cultural matrix of the early Greek spells is very different from that of late Roman Egypt,[130] the influence of indigenous Egyptian practice on the imperial spells is beyond question, even if its extent is disputed, and the limited evidence we have for real-life amatory spells in Greece of the later Classical and Hellenistic eras involves relationship crises, not, as in the *agōgai*, wresting away by violence the object of the spell-caster's affections. So not only are the circumstances of the two different, but the situations which threw up the former are often uncertain and capable of being reconstructed in different ways, as Eidinow (2007) well shows. It may well be that some of these earlier texts did aim to expropriate for a male agent the sexual attentions of a *hetaira*, but to go beyond that would be injudicious, as is, I have argued, the wrapping up of male-authored and female-authored spells in watertight compartments, dismissing the possibility of confluence between the two.

Notes

1 The only difference being the fact that, unlike the Munich ensemble, the Cologne ensemble additionally featured a sheet of blank papyrus which enclosed the spell, evidently for protective purposes.
2 No. 4: Wortmann (1968), 85–102 = *SM* 45, no. 101 in Betz's translation of the *PMG*. For nos. 1–3 = *SM* 49–51, all aimed at a woman named Matrōna, see Wortmann, 57–84.
3 For evidence that the love-spells/spells in the *PMG* (and the *defixiones* too) were mostly put together from formularies, which could be tailored to individual purposes by insertion of the name of both agent and target when the spell was put into practice, see Chapter 1 n.44.
4 It seems clear from the text that the ensemble was deposited in a graveyard (though not in a grave, as was the practice with leaden curse tablets, *defixiones*): cf. Wortmann (1968), 85. For the use of the spirits of the violently dead to execute malign spells see Chapter 3.
5 It is usual in Greek and Roman love-spells to identify both agent and target matrilineally, in contrast to the usual practice in those societies. Curbera (1999) explores possible reasons.
6 *Ousia* is material such as hair (as in *SM* 49.20–1 and 50.21–2; cf. Jordan (1985), 251) acquired from the target of a spell, by working upon which, the magician believed, its one-time possessor would be adversely affected by the process known as magical 'sympathy': see Eitrem (1925a), 51–2; Hopfner OZ 1.§643–79; Gager 16–18; Brashear (1992), 94; Fountoulakis (1999): the last three list instances where the *ousia* of a target has been preserved along with the relevant spell.
7 Isis here is the goddess, not the homonymous target of the spell.
8 Osiris was closely associated/identified with the waters of the Nile, while the dead in the Underworld were thought to suffer from parching thirst (Deonna (1939)): their souls will be relieved by a revivifying draught from Osiris/Nile-water, Wortmann (1968), 93–5.

9 Papyrus spells and *defixiones* routinely conclude with formulations such as this demanding immediate fulfilment of the magician's purposes: cf. Watson on Hor. *Epod.* 5.53–4 and Jordan (1996), 119.
10 'The word here no doubt with the sense *nekudaimōn*, "ghost", into or near whose grave or sarcophagus the lead tablet would have been placed' Jordan (1999a), 166.
11 The use of the diminutive form *melanion* ('wee black') in place of *melan* ('black'), the standard term for the pubic hair in stock formulations such as this, seems to be unparalleled. For another departure from the usual pattern, cf. *P. Oxy.* 4673.28–9, where the 'white' pubic hair of an older man is apparently to be joined to the 'black' of a younger woman.
12 For comments on the violence of love-spells see e.g. Winkler (1991), 216, 231; Versnel (1998), 252, 253, 267; Ficheux (2006), 290, 295.
13 Cf. Kropp 11.1.1/17 = Audollent 231, *usque ad diem mortis suae* [Kropp 11.2.1/5 = Audollent 267], *PGM* 7.914 'she will love you for all the time of her life', 11c, 16, 61.17–18, *SM* 39.17, 46.24–6, *P.Oxy.* 4672.15. Exceptions: *SM* 37 Tab. B (five months), 45.36–7 (ten months): see Winkler (1991), 232 n.108.
14 On this euphemism for 'vagina' see n.70 infra.
15 Different translations of the Greek phrase here are offered by Preisendanz, Eitrem 1925a (who reads *stoibas* for *sittubas*) and Mastrocinque (2014a), 31, but all are agreed that the victim's flesh is to be punctured by prickles or thorns. Betz's 'knotted leather scourges' is inaccurate.
16 *PGM* 4.1414, 36.201, *SM* 42.16, 37, 60, Brashear (1992), line 33, Audollent 271.14, 41–2.
17 Cf. Kambitsis (1976). The text of the love-spell accompanying the doll is most readily accessible as *SM* 47.
18 See Graf (1997), 189 for acceptance of Winkler's view that erotic magic stems from a deep emotional crisis, also Pinch (2006), 124, who posits that the aggressive tone of the love-spells emanating from Egypt may partly be explained by the perception of a woman's capacity to throw a man into sexual turmoil as akin to sorcery.
19 See Faraone (1999), 83 for other proponents of the view that the love-spells serve a therapeutic or cathartic purpose, adding Meyer and Smith (1999), 148 and Fountoulakis (1999).
20 Thus Winkler (1991), 216 ('the performer's own sense of victimisation by a power he is helpless to control'), an idea developed in some detail by Versnel (1998), 263–4, who, in support of the idea that the targets of the spells *wrong* the writer by not responding to his overtures, points to cases where *kolasis*, 'punishment' or *timōriai*, 'penalties' are invoked upon the targets of love-spells. There is, it is true, some (less than secure) evidence in documentary erotic spells for a lover feeling, or affecting to believe, that he has been treated unjustly by an unresponsive target – see, in addition to Versnel, *P. Oxy.* 5304, with the remarks of the editor Maltomini ad loc.

– however, Versnel fails to mention the fact that on several occasions when such language is applied to the victims of love-spells, it is in the context of a *diabolē*, an invented charge of ritual violations designed to recruit the assistance of a supernatural agent in inflicting upon the target the harm which the practitioner wishes upon her. In other words, the 'punishment' to be suffered by the target is not necessarily, *pace* Versnel, for amatory maltreatment of the spell-caster, but for a fictitious offence against a deity: see Eitrem (1925b).

21 Gager 24 argues that amatory *defixiones* did not seek to do harm to their targets. At p. 81, he remarks of the Louvre figurine pierced with thirteen needles (see above) '<its> explicit goal is not to harm the target but to constrain her' (cf. ibid. 15): further, in regard to the violent language of the spell instructing how to fashion the figurine (*PGM* 4.296–466) and that of the love-spells more generally, this, he says, 'is deeply symbolic and will simply not allow an overly literal interpretation'.

22 Brooten (1996), while offering a thoroughgoing critique of Winkler's and Gager's spells-as-therapy approach (96–103), agrees with them (101) that 'we must be cautious of interpreting the <Louvre> figurine and the spells too literally'.

23 Graf (1997), 140 'the performer has no intention to maim or wound the victim', 145 'sorcerers did not wish to wound the victim's members in the same way that they pierced the members of a figurine'. In an unnoticed piece of self-contradiction, however, he contends p. 144 that the targeting of various bodily parts in erotic spells reverses an Egyptian rite of healing whereby the individual members of the body were entrusted to the care of specific divinities. But the logical implication of any such reversal is surely that harm is intended to the limbs and organs in question!

24 Ogden (1999), 37, 66, 73.

25 Pinch (2006), 90 'the infliction of physical harm was not the main intention of the Louvre figurine'.

26 Colomo (2007), 117 'ovviamente il tutto (*sc.* the violence of the *agōgē* and the *philtrokatadesmos*) è da intendersi nella chiave metaforica propria della magia simpatetica'.

27 Collins (2008), 89 'erotic magic demands that the will of the victim be bound to the practitioner's wishes, not that he or she be physically disabled'. Note also Tavenner (1942), 27–32, who appears unsure whether fire imagery and the use of fire in love-spells is intended to generate real or metaphorical burning in its targets.

28 Urbanová (2018), 52 'in the amatory context of <*PGM* 4.296–466>' the piercing of the figurine 'denotes only a temporary restriction of the victim's mental and bodily faculties. The one who performs the love-curse ritual longs for his beloved, and as such he does not want to hurt her'.

29 LiDonnici (1998), Versnel (1998) 265 'the immediate aim <of erotic spells on papyrus and lead> is not to bind … but to hurt: the victim must suffer through torture, pains, illness, very often fever or fire' and 247–67 *passim*.

30 Versnel (1998), 258–64 holds that the violence of the spells is prompted by the competing forces of *odi et amo*, and by a feeling that the love-object has wronged the agent by being immune to his overtures (but see n.20 supra). LiDonnici (also 1998), noting that the erotic spells regularly invoke fever upon the target, sees this as a means of weakening the humoral and psychological equilibrium of the victim in order to make them responsive to *erōs*. See especially p. 88 'fever or generalised heating could affect the other bodily systems that might in turn weaken control and rationality to an extent sufficient to lead the object or victim to respond favourably to the spell-caster's advances or even to seek him out, appearing to do so independently'.

31 Faraone (1999), 42. Note also here Hor. *Sat.* 1.8, where, in a clear echo of the rite at *PGM* 4.296–446, a female doll manipulates punitively a smaller, presumably male one (Faraone (1999), 51–2). In this rite the latter 'stood in a suppliant pose, as if about to perish in the manner of a slave' (32–3) – a clear indicator of physical hurt intended by analogical means for the individual represented by the smaller doll.

32 Faraone (1999), 69, followed by Mastrocinque (2014a), 26.

33 Faraone's bridal theft model is accepted by M. Martin (2010), 132, but the only real point of contact, so far as I can see, between abduction marriage and *agōgē* spells is that both involve the forced relocation of a woman from one house to another. As Eidinow (2007), 208 n.18 puts it, 'the spells frequently ask that a woman come to a man, an idea which seems to negate the violent invasion of a household which bridal theft seems to require and, more practically, demands that the target not be a secluded, sheltered young female' – a situation which bridal theft presupposes. Nor is there much common ground between the burning, sleeplessness, whipping and tortures standardly invoked upon the targets of *agōgai* until they come to the spell-caster, and the momentary violence attendant on the forcible removal of a girl from her natal home. Moreover, the assimilation of *agōgai* to abduction marriage obscures the fact that the formularies make ample provision for the employment of the former by women against men. Finally, it is far from clear that the majority of such spells aimed at marriage: see further below on the last two points. In general on abduction marriage see Evans-Grubbs (1989), who, inter alia, points out that the violence which is a feature of abduction marriage is often pretend rather than real, when the bride's family colludes in her removal in order to save face.

34 For admiring voices see Gager 81–2; Martinez (1995), 354–5; Johnston (1995a), 179 n.3; LiDonnici (1998), 82 n.65 and 92; Eidinow (2007), 208; Rynearson (2009), 351–5; Versnel (1998), 257–8, but with reservations.

35 The *defixio* from Pella seeking to inhibit the 'marriage of Dionysophōn' to another woman is, as Voutiras (1998) 50–1, 55, 57 and 72 noted, unusual in that the *defigens* openly gives voice to her feelings; but, as he also showed, her motives are almost certainly financial – viz. the desire to secure her position as Dionysophōn's consort – not amatory.

36 Pachoumi (2012), 81–4 cites expressions like 'the ungodly one' and calls for 'bitter retribution' and the like as indicative of a sense, on the part of a lover, of having been wronged by a would-be beloved. But these come from slander spells falsely accusing an *inamorata* of having perpetrated sacral violations (see n.20 supra), and certainly do not prove in themselves that the agent is cherishing feelings of resentment towards the other party. Nor, given the formulaic nature of the spells in which such expressions occur, need we even assume that a relationship of any kind between the two has even begun. It may be simply that the man's eye has fallen on the woman and he, suspecting that she may prove unresponsive, resorts to a magical shortcut.

37 Sappho: see Cameron (1939) and Petropoulos (1993). Theocritus: see e.g. the commentary of Gow ad loc. and García Teijeiro (1999).

38 On this spell and its background see Ogden (2008), 87–90.

39 Quoted from Meyer and Smith (1999), 154.

40 Collins (2008), 89. Similarly Gager 81; Graf (1997), 140; Ogden (1999), 66; Urbanová (2018), 52. Versnel (1998), 253 undermines this point by noting that the spell which accompanies the piercing-ritual contains some extremely violent language such as 'drag her by the hair, the heart and soul etc.'; also, in response to Gager's observation 'the penetration of the female figurine by needles probably carries sexual meaning as well' queries why this suggestion should be permissible, but the proposition 'the penetration of the female figurine by needles probably carries sadistic meaning should be *anathema* [to Gager]'.

41 For the context in which the term 'punishment' is used here, see n.20.

42 Cf. *PGM* 4.2441–52 'a spell of attraction ... it attracts those who are uncontrollable (? resistant to erotic magic) ... it inflicts illness excellently and destroys powerfully ... it attracted in one hour, it made someone sick in two hours, it destroyed in seven hours'. A similar conjunction of love-and-sickness-inducing effects in *PGM* 12.376–81 and 64.1–12, also in an inscriptional postscript (Bonner (1950), 118) to an amulet which functioned as an *agōgē* (as amulets not infrequently did). The postscript, evidently added after the original spell had failed, read 'either bring him or put him to bed with an illness'.

43 In fact, as Ficheux (2006), 291 suggests, the piercing of the figurine's eyes with needles probably signifies the infliction of sleeplessness – an affliction often invoked in love-spells – upon the target symbolised by the doll (cf. *PGM* 4.2943–66, a 'love spell of attraction through wakefulness', which involves sticking needles into the eyes of the image of a little dog). If Ficheux is correct, the victim of the *philtrokatadesmos thaumastos* does after all suffer palpable physical symptoms as a result of the piercing of her imagistic surrogate. It is worth adding that spells to inflict sleeplessness could assume a very sinister aspect: *Cyranides* 1.5 Kaimakis attests to a belief that malign magic could bring about death from insomnia.

44 Compare for such violence *PGM* 7.887–90 'draw her by her hair, by her feet, in fear, seeing phantoms, sleepless on account of her passion for me and her love for me ... until she comes' and *P. Oxy.* 4674.13–15 'haul her forcibly (*ekspason*) out of her house enflamed in her guts, her entrails'.

45 Note also *DTM* 21, which contains only the name of the target, where however the *defigens* signalled his intention by roughly moulding a figure in clay and piercing it with eight needles, and furthermore by breaking the figure in two: in this case the intention was not merely to harm the target, but to kill him. Also relevant: an Olbian *defixio* featuring a portrait of a dagger inserted into the victim's throat as well as a circular graffito, above each letter of which are depicted three needles evidently designed to reinforce the harmful effects of the curse (Lebedev (1996)). Cf. also *PGM* 5.70–95, a spell against a thief, which prescribes striking the image of an eye with a hammer (*PGM* vol. 1 Abbildung 5). As long as the striking of the painted image continues, the eye of the thief will be struck and swell up.

46 Sophronius, *Account of the Miracles of Saints Cyrus and John* (Migne *PG* 87.3, cols. 3541–8), quoted by Gager 262–3. Graf (1997), 142 dismisses this evidence for no good reason.

47 Plut. *Demetr.* 38, App. *Syr.* 59–61, Lucian, *Dea Syr.* 17–18: cf. *Icar.* 15.

48 Gk. *rigopurētion PGM* 7.211 etc., Plin. *HN* 23.92 *febres cum horrore uenientes*.

49 The name of both Ailourion's mother and of the target is Kopria, which may say something about the social milieu in which the spell is cast, since so-called copronyms seem at least in some cases to indicate that the possessors of these names had been picked up as foundlings from the dung heap (Gk. *kopria*) or were descended from such (Pomeroy (1986)).

50 See, in addition to LiDonnici *passim*, Martinez (1995), 354.

51 Note particularly the combinations *axon kai katadēson . . . tēn deina*, 'fetch and bind the woman, NN' (*PGM* 4.350–1) and *axon, katadēson Matrōan*, 'fetch, bind Matrōna' (*SM* 49.19).

52 Kropp 3.18/1. Almost identical curse formulations at 3.22/29 and 3.23/1. The applicability of the sleep-deprivation motif across all categories of *defixio* is neatly illustrated by its use against a *uenator* in the arena (Kropp 11.1.1/25 = Audollent 250.4–5), as well as the horses of an opposing faction in the circus at Hadrumetum (Kropp 11.2.1/25 = Audollent 289.16)! The motif of bodily and psychic 'tortures' (Greek *basanizein*, Latin *cruciare, concruciare*) similarly is found in nearly all categories of curse: cf. Versnel (1998), 227–64.

53 Further instances of sleep deprivation in erotic spells: *PGM* 4.357–8; 7.888; Audollent 271.67; *SM* 45.6, 45–6; 47.10–11; 48.9–10, 23; 49.25–6, 77; 50.25–7, 55–6, Brashear (1992), line 9 with n. ad loc., Wortmann (1968), 71–2, 74–5. Inability to eat or drink: *PGM* 4.356; *SM* 46.20–1; 47.10, 20–1; 48.9, 23; 50.55–7.

54 It is sometimes argued that early Athenian curse tablets seek merely to compromise or impair the operation of their targets' faculties, especially their organs of speech, but already by the fourth-century BCE *defixiones* are found invoking illness and/or death upon their targets: cf. *DTA* 93, 98, 102, 103 and Voutiras (1998), all reproduced in Eidinow (2007).
55 See in addition to the instances cited below Bonner (1932); Gager 45, 120–1, 153–4, 176, 218–42; Ritner (1993), 189–90 ('voodoo death'); Graf (1997), 58–9, 195; Dickie (2001), 57, 77, 244; Kiernan (2003); Collins (2008), 76.
56 Cf. *CIL* 6.3.19747, 8.2756 *carminibus defi/xa iacuit per tempora mul/ta* (alii *muta*), *ut eius spiritus ui/ extorqueretur quam/ naturae redderetur*, 'hexed by spells she lay sick for a long period, so that her spirit was violently torn from her rather than rendered up by a natural process', 11.4639 (*defixa* l. 8), Graf (1997) 163 n.140 and (2007).
57 On amulets see appendix to Chapter 5, with the definition by Bonner quoted there.
58 Cf. Ogden (1999), 51, Kotansky Amulets no. 40 = Gager no. 125, Kropp 11.1.1/25 = Audollent 250A 'mighty spirit, may you ... nullify' (fatally) every remedy and every phylactery and every protective measure' of which the beast fighter at whom the *defixio* is directed avails himself, *PGM* 4.2158–60 'whenever someone thinks he has been magically bound', he should utilise as an amulet a *lamella* inscribed with Homeric verses, 4.2176–7, 8.32–4, 36.221–3, 36.178–87 (a charm to break spells), Bonner (1950), 117, a phylactery against a *katadesmos*.
59 *DTA* 46, Jordan (1999b), 117 (*antikatadesmeuō*, 'I bind reciprocally'); Sherwood Fox (1912) text 1 (Plotius) 38–43 with commentary ad loc.; Gager no. 107.
60 Thus Gager n.21 supra. Similarly Brashear (1992), 100 'fire, heat and burning and so on are often used metaphorically in the magical papyri to signify desire'. See also Faraone quoted supra with n.32.
61 *P. Duk.* inv. 230.25–30. For numerous parallels, see Jordan (1999a), 169 and the text supra.
62 Gager 83 and Ogden (1999), 66 use the term 'romantic' to characterise Audollent 271, in which Domitiana seeks to be united in marriage with Urbanus 'for all the period of their lives', glossing over the unsettling fact that the *defixio* seeks to 'make him, in his passion, to be subject to her just like a slave'. Gager 83 n.24 regards in the same light the fourth-century BCE *defixio* from Pella (Voutiras (1998)), in which a woman expresses the wish to marry Dionysophōn and to grow old with him – but concludes with the imprecation that Thetimē, her main rival for Dionysophōn's affections 'should perish evilly': hardly romantic stuff in our terms! On the vexed issue of what kind of relationship is envisaged by the lifelong union regularly wished for in love-spells, see Ogden (1999), 66, and the discussion below.
63 Personal communication from Robin Nisbet, the next but one occupant after Fraenkel of the Corpus Chair. A detailed account of the problems associated with the Helen episode in Goold (1970).

64 This is particularly the case if, as Dickie (2000) argues, the ambience in which love magic flourished was primarily that of female prostitution or sexually available women – a context in which, as literary accounts amply demonstrate, violence is not far to seek.

65 See for a representative sample of such language Versnel (1998), 247–52, Ficheux (2006) and n.16 supra. Erotic slavery of a woman to a man: *PGM* 4.383, 7.611, 17a.17–21, *SM* 38.10, 46.26, 47.26–7; of a man to a woman, Audollent 271.43–4.

66 Jordan (2006), line 20 (from a *katadesmos* to bring a woman to a man).

67 *Mihi conferre ad meum desiderium*, Kropp 11.1.1/16 = Audollent 230A11–12. Similarly, 'and that she may grant me all that she has' (*SM* 51.5) surely with Wortmann (1968), 84 means 'give all that she has to offer sexually' and not, with the translators of *SM*, 'grant me all her possessions'. I also find it difficult to attribute, with Jordan (1999a), 161, an economic rather than an erotic motive to similar language at *PGM* 17a16–25, quoted n.125 below, where only a single phrase, 'with hands full', suggests an interest in material as opposed to sexual concerns. The same goes for two of three passages, *SM* 39, Audollent 230 (see above) and *PGM* 4.1806, cited by Faraone (1999), 85 as evidence of 'an active interest in the dowry and property that such a woman [the target of an *agōgē*] might bring with her', the exception being *PGM* 4.1806, 'in order that she may give me what is in her hands'.

68 As Ficheux (2006), 302 aptly notes, the love-spells have little interest in female sexual pleasure. I have found only one clear exception to this, *PGM* 17a20–1 'serving both my desire and her own unhesitatingly and without shame'. Winkler (1991), 233 detects in three passages of the *PGM* an awareness of female pleasure, but it seems to me that this is only mentioned in so far as it subserves the desire of the male agent constraining the woman to have sex. The same goes for *PGM* 4.352–3 'may she do nothing for pleasure with another man, except for me alone', where Martinez (1991), 58 also sees a suggestion of the woman's erotic fulfilment.

69 *AE* 1967.551, Roesch (1966–7), 234. Another view of the matter in Eidinow (2007), 351 and 434–5 (text and translation).

70 The idea, first advanced by Ganszyniec (*non uidi*), that in frequently encountered expressions like 'drag her <to me> by her hair, by her heart, by her *psuchē*' (*PGM* 4.377–8), *psuchē*, literally 'soul', is slang for 'vagina' has attracted much support, on the grounds that 'drag her by her hair, heart and *psuchē*' suggests that the 'dragging' is effected by holding onto something tangible: see Preisendanz, who translated 'Natur' *sc.* genitals in *PGM* ibid.; Bonner (1950), 118–19; Martinez (1991), 11 n.49; Betz, glossary s.v. 'soul'; Gager 111 etc.; Graf (1997), 141; Faraone (1999), 45 n.23, 50 n.48; and Dickie (2001), 120 n.100. The vaginal soul has been attacked as a 'myth' by Smith (2004), who argues for the meaning 'chest' or 'heart', particularly in passages where an animal's organ is to be deposited on a sleeping woman's chest in order to make her disclose the name of her lover. But in a Latin instance of the identical

procedure, Damigeron-Euax *De Lapidibus* 67, which reads *si uiuenti cor contuleris et dormienti mulieri super pectinem posueris, si cum alio uiro coit, dicet per somnum*, ' if you harvest the heart from a living <hoopoe> and put it on the *pecten* of a slumbering woman, she will tell you in her sleep if she is having sex with another man', *pecten*, despite Smith's attempt to deny this (210 n.37) must mean 'pudenda', as the term often does. None of this is to deny that in other passages such as 'bind her and her mind and her *psuchē* (NGCT no. 79), *psuchē* can only mean 'soul', without any sexual implication.

71 From the erotic spell of Cyprian of Antioch in Meyer and Smith (1999), 156–7.
72 *SM* 38, with Gager 109. I also wonder whether the magic words attending the very sexually explicit *PGM* 17a are intended by their shape to represent a vagina surrounded by pubic hair.
73 Illustration of the Cologne *symplēgma* in Gager fig. 14.
74 Also included by Faraone under this rubric are the *iunx* (wryneck spell), *agrupnētikon* (insomnia-inducing spell), 'voodoo doll' and apple-throwing spell.
75 Or by males in a position of social inferiority to the target of the spell.
76 See Sophocles *Trachiniae*, with the discussion by Faraone (1999), 110–19 of how such love charms often go wrong, with fatal effects.
77 Faraone (1999), 166–9. The seeds of this idea are found in Winkler (1991).
78 Cf. *PGM* 10.20–1 'may the woman, NN, fall in love with me upon seeing me, and may she never ... resist me because of modesty'.
79 Conversely, according to Faraone, when males employ *philia* magic, generally to influence in their favour the affections of their social superiors, they are assuming a feminising, submissive stance more appropriate to women.
80 See the reviews by Brakke (2000); Frankfurter (2000); Kedletz (2000); Ogden (2000); Hubbard (2001); Bonnet (2002); Phillips (2003); Rives (2003); and Veenman (2003).
81 An exception is the brief but cogent addendum to Dickie (2000), 582–3, to which now add Pachoumi (2013), who does not address in any detail Faraone's division of love-spells into the *erōs* and *philia* type, but successfully challenge his and others' related belief that the targets of the aggressive type of spell were in the main closeted virgins, and the goal of the spells marriage. Much of what Pachoumi says is already in Dickie (2000), but she does helpfully and additionally bring into play the category of separation spells, and usefully provides a comprehensive list of amatory and separation spells, both formulaic and applied, as it stood in 2013.
82 In keeping with his schema, Faraone is determined at all costs to downplay or deny any sexual component to the verb *philein*, 'to love' and to minimise the semantic confluence in Greek love-spells between *erōs* and *philia*, likewise the frequency of this phenomenon (29, 97 n.2, 110, 118 n.75). He even goes so far as to render *philotēs* ('the poetic equivalent of *philia*' 110) in the Homeric expression for having sex, *migēnai en philotēti* by 'to lie with <him> *affectionately*': see rather LSJ s.v.

83 The noun *hēdonē* and the related adjective *hēdonikos* routinely refer to sexual pleasure.
84 Martinez (1991), 63 on *SM* 48.12 treats *erōs* and *philia* as synonyms in passages such as the preceding, noting the tendency in spells to intensify by accumulation of synonyms.
85 Numerous other examples of these terms juxtaposed in the *PMG* and *defixiones* in such a way as to elide the distinctions in sense which elsewhere pertain between *erōs* and *philia* can be found in Brashear (1979) 273 on *SM* 72 col.1.24–5, Martinez (1991), previous n., Dickie (2000), 583.
86 Already in Homer *philotēs* is closely connected with sexual desire, as LSJ note. See n.82 supra.
87 Cf. *PGM* 17a8 and 15, and *P. Oxy.* 4672.4–8 'take away her sleep until she, leaping vigorously forth comes to me, NN, son of NN, loving (*philousa me*) and feeling affection for me *and seeking out sexual intercourse (sunousia) with me*', ibid. 11–14.
88 Faraone (1999), 25 and 28.
89 *P. Oxy.* 5305 (2016), col. 4, ll. 1 and 14.
90 Surviving instances of female-authored *erōs* spells 'are perhaps an insignificant number' Faraone 149; 'males . . . did have a monopoly of sorts over spells used to induce erotic infatuation' 96. Veenman (2003), 220 rightly objects 'Faraone tends to belittle the erotic magic spells actually written by women'.
91 The language is similar to that of an anonymous epigram, *AP* 5.205.1–2, 'the *iunx* [see Chapter 6 n.9] of Niko, that knows how to draw (*helkein*) a man from across the sea and maidens (*paidas*) from their chambers'. A different view of *paidas* ('youths') in Faraone (1999), 151–2.
92 Lines 67–70 repeat the same message in expanded form, with similar imprecision as to the sex of the person operating the spell.
93 The inverse of course equally applies, that a female target presupposes a male agent – though the sex of the victim cannot invariably give a clue to the sex of the operator, since a small number of homoerotic spell exist: see Faraone (1999), 147–8. See also n.101 below.
94 On 'swords', a generic term for a magical formula to be inscribed or pronounced in erotic spells, see Mastrocinque (2014a), 32–3 and Kotansky Amulets, no. 62, a tiny gold *lamella* featuring the image of sword, accompanied by a text which invokes erotic madness on a female target, an idea amply paralleled in the *PGM*.
95 Further instances of such confusion over the gender of the target in Dickie (2000), 567 with n.15.
96 Faraone (1999), 140–1 treats ll. 9–25 *tout court* as a male homoerotic spell, but at 105 regards ll. 1–8 as a spell designed to 'bring charm to a woman in the eyes of her husband or lover'. He does so apparently on the basis that the initial incantation breaks off at line 8. But line 9 begins a hymnal incantation to the rising sun (Betz ad loc.), which gels

with the details in ll. 1–3, 'raising your hands to the stars ... you look towards the sun', while Brashear (1979), 273 makes a compelling case for regarding 1–25 as a whole, divided into three sections (1–3, 4–8, 9–25). In other words, it is unnecessary with Faraone to split 1–8 and 9–27 into two distinct procedures. In any event, Faraone simply does not address the difficulties caused by the confusion of genders.

97   Dickie (2000), 567. Note also here a further instance of gender-confusion in the *agōgē* spell *PGM* 78, which commences 'it brings a woman to a man and likewise makes them steadfast and faithful' but later continues with the formulation 'I shall burn up the soul of him, NN, to cause desire for her, NN'. Also of note: a formulaic old Coptic and Greek *agōgē* at *PGM* 4.94–153 which seems in different sections of the text to act on behalf of females and males, an oscillation between genders summed up in the prescription at 144–5 'say these things on behalf of women. But when you are acting against women, speak conversely so as to arouse the females towards the males'.

98   In *P. Oxy.* 82 (2016). On the indeterminacy of the gender of agent and victim, see the comment p. 57 of the editor, Maltomini.

99   For some further examples of scribal imprecision in identifying the respective sex of target and operator in amatory spells of the documentary type, see Pachoumi (2013), 301–3.

100 For applied spells, spells used in real life by a named individual, as opposed to mere recipes, see Chapter 1 and n.3 supra.

101 Female-authored *erōs* spells: *PGM* 15, 16, 32 (Lesbian), 39, 68, *SM* 42 (Lesbian), Audollent 271, Kropp 11.2.1/8 = Audollent 270. To this may be added an amulet inscribed on the reverse side with the words 'bring Achillas, whom [masculine relative pronoun] Serapias bore, to Dionysias, whom [feminine relative pronoun] Serapias bore' (Bonner (1950), 117). In addition, Brooten (1996), 95–6 makes a strong case for regarding *SM* 37 as a Lesbian spell, as against the editors Daniel and Maltomini, who emend the text to produce a male agent targeting a female (a procedure followed by Pachoumi (2013), 300). I can see no reason to speculate, with Pachoumi (2013), that Audollent 103 (no. 119 in her list) is a female-authored, male-targeting amatory *defixio*. Indeed it is probably not a *defixio* at all: Kropp (2008) omits it entirely.

102 Faraone (1999), 149.

103 Dickie (2000), 573 suggests a number of factors. Cf. also Winkler (1991), 228.

104 Respectively Kropp 11.2.1/2 and /3 (Audollent 264–5), Kropp 11.2.1/5 and /6 (Audollent 267–8), Kropp 11.2.1/7 and /33 (Audollent 269 and 304) and *SM* 49–51.

105 The sex of Dioscorous is put beyond question by the application to her of the female relative pronoun *hēn*.

106 Text of *PGM* 16.10–18. The same formulation is repeated nine times in the course of the spell, with minimal changes except for the names of the divine assistants

107 In regarding Audollent 271 as an exceptional case of an amatory spell that seeks to bring two parties together in love and marriage, Pachoumi – who rightly concludes that the primary purpose of amatory spells was sexual gratification (2013: 308–14) – seems to me to seriously understate the unpleasant insistence on erotic domination and sexual slavery which characterises the spell, which has nothing romantic about it, but rather a strong air of pragmatism, like the Pella *defixio* discussed below.

108 Eidinow (2007), 219 n.70 '<the formularies> are unlikely to provide much of a guide to the state of mind of the individual who commissioned the spell'. Cf. Graf (1997), 146–7 for a denial that the formularies allowed for 'a discharge of erotic frustrations'.

109 I borrow the preceding points from Versnel (1998), 255–6.

110 The name of the woman responsible for the *defixio* is missing from the text. 'Phila' is supplied exempli gratia by Voutiras (1998), 11–12, on the grounds that the name is known in Macedonia from the fourth century BCE and fits well into the available space.

111 From Acanthus. Text: Jordan (1999b), 122; Eidinow (2007), 452–3. Discussion: Eidinow 213–14.

112 As seems to be the case in Audollent 86, which should be consulted in the improved version by Ziebarth, reproduced in Eidinow (2007), 402. In this text, dated no later than the Hellenistic period, 'Zois, the Eretrian woman' is consigned to earth and Hermes and cursed in such sexually suggestive terms as to make it likely that the *defixio* originates from a fellow prostitute jealous of the pulling-power of a rival. For some late Roman-period examples of prostitutes trying magically to interfere with the business of professional rivals, see Jordan (1985), nos. 7–9.

113 For these alternative possibilities, see Eidinow (2007), 216. For *gamein*, 'copulate with' see Voutiras (1998), 55–7, 117–18.

114 On prayers for justice see Chapter 3.

115 See the schema in Faraone (1999), 28.

116 Faraone (1999), 18 explicitly excludes such spells from discussion.

117 Bevilacqua (1997). Date: late third century CE (*SGD* no. 129).

118 *PGM* O [ostrakon] 2. Date: second century CE.

119 For this view, see particularly Winkler (1991), 227–8, Graf (1997), 185–90 and Stratton (2007), 79–80. The dichotomy is questioned as artificial by Pachoumi (2013), 298–304 on the grounds that, in the amatory spells of the *PGM*, the flexibility and pervasiveness of the noun *deina*, which only becomes sex-specific once a male or female definite article is appended, allows for the utilisation of such spells by women as well as men.

120 Theocr. *Idyll* 2, Hor. *Sat.* 1.8, *Epod.* 5, Apul. *Met.* 2.5, 3.15–16.
121 That literary descriptions of magic, love magic prominently included, correspond in many respects to actual usage is widely accepted: see e.g. Faraone (1999), 38. See further Chapter 6.
122 See Winkler (1991), 232–3 'in fact the agent in at least some of these cases [*agōgai* and *philtrokatadesmoi*] seems to be aiming at the bondage (*sic*) of marriage or its equivalent' and 233 'in fact *agōgai* are aimed as a rule at women and maidens, who are constantly guarded and watched by their own families and by all the neighbours'; Graf (1997), 186 'what is sought in our texts [erotic binding spells and rites of attraction] is almost always permanent union, that is marriage'; Faraone (1999), 86 'extant erotic spells ... could be used by males either for sexual conquest or to advance their social position by arranging profitable marriages for themselves'; cf. id. 92, the aim of spells to induce *erōs* is 'sex and sometimes marriage'. Faraone's assimilation of *agōgē* spells to the process of abduction marriage (see n.33 supra) also appears predicated on the idea that the object of the former was marriage.
123 E.g. 'let the woman, NN, love me for all her time on earth' (*PGM* 36.288), 'for all time' (*SM* 39.17), 'with unceasing passion' (*SM* 41.12–13), 'make <Heronous> inseparable from me until death, so that I may have Heronous ... subject to me for the entire time of my life' (*SM* 46.25–6), further Martinez (1995), 359 n.82 and n.13 supra. In a further point, Martinez (1991), 57 notes that the forbidding of sexual activities in formulaic expressions such as 'so that she may not be fucked or buggered by any other man but me' (see discussion of these phrases below) is 'reminiscent of the style of marriage contracts, where the forbidden activities are specifically sexual' (naturally not so crudely expressed); he does not however pronounce on the nature of the relationship envisaged by the spells which use such language.
124 For some of the points made below on the status of the female victims of erotic spells, see also Pachoumi (2013), 304–8.
125 See n.65 supra. That 'enslavement' of the target means total sexual compliance with the man's wishes is made particularly clear by *PGM* 17a16–25 'until she comes whipped by you, lusting after me, with hands full, with a generous soul bestowing on me herself and all she has, and fulfilling what is fitting for women in regard to men and serving both my desire and her own unhesitatingly and without shame, glueing thigh to thigh and belly to belly and her black to my black in a manner most pleasant ... bring me Titerous, whom Sophia bore, to me, Hermeias, whom Hermione bore, immediately immediately, quickly quickly, driven by your lash'.
126 *Binein*, 'fuck', and *pugizein*, 'bugger', 'belong to the lower register of the Greek language' (Bain (1991), 51) and are blunt and coarse in tone (Bain 54–62 and 67–70 respectively). The somewhat bowdlerising translations of Martinez (1991), 30–1

and Winkler (1991), 231 illegitimately downplay the verbal explicitness and crude physicality of the context.
127 Cf. *PGM* 4. 2759–60 'and hating all the race of men and women except me'.
128 Cf. Pachoumi (2013), 308, Wortmann (1968), 71 'No doubt used with the pregnant sense of a *casa meritoria* (viz. a brothel). Matrōna [the target of *SM* 49 and 50] was probably of dubious reputation or, more likely, the author of the formulary had composed it in precisely such a form as to cover all possible situations'.
129 Faraone (1999), in keeping with his synchronic approach to the erotic magic of Antiquity, also adduces a number of literary texts of the classical period in which different forms of erotic magic initiated or utilised by males succeed in overcoming a female target's resistance to love and marriage.
130 E.g. Dickie (2000), 571–3.

3

Defixiones: A Recent History

In an oft-quoted formulation, David Jordan, the undisputed American expert in the field, defined the subject of this chapter[1] as follows: '*defixiones*, more commonly known as curse tablets, are inscribed pieces of lead, usually in the form of small, thin sheets, intended to influence, by supernatural means, the actions or welfare of persons or animals[2] against their will' (*SGD* p. 151). This purpose is captured in their Greek name, *katadesmoi*, from the verb *katadein*, 'to bind down': cf. *DTA* 45 'I bind down [*katadeō*] Evander in a bond of lead'.[3] The tablets are however generally referred to by their Latin title, *defixiones*, a term derived from the verb *defigere*.[4] This literally means 'to stick in, implant', reflecting the practice of piercing the curse tablet, after folding it, with nails,[5] thereby symbolically immobilising or binding the victim's capacity for autonomous action[6] – an analogical procedure which is very common in early Attic curse tablets, but tails off somewhat in later texts (Ogden (1999), 14; NGCT p. 5). The interest of these brief, often startlingly violent documents lies not least in the fact that they give us direct access to one particular aspect of the ancient mindset, unmediated by the often emollient filters of literature; for magic can only be perceived as effective if deeply embedded in a culture's way of thinking.

Fig. 2 Leaden curse tablet from Rome (first century BCE) separating Rhodine from Faustus (= Audollent no. 139).

By way of orientation and to give readers unfamiliar with these documents a feel for their ethos and content, it will be helpful to quote at the outset two randomly chosen instances of *defixiones*, one Greek, one Latin. The Greek example, dating to the fourth century BCE, was unearthed in 2003 in a Classical cemetery just outside the quondam Athenian Long Walls, but has just recently been published for the first time (Lamont (2015)). Commercial in character, it is vividly illustrative of the fierce rivalries that could exist between competing practitioners of the same trade, frequently issuing in vicious curses, as here. It reads:

> Chthonian Hekatē, Chthonian Artemis, Chthonian Hermes, look with hate upon Phanagoras and Demētrios and their tavern[7] and their property and their possessions. I will bind my enemy Demētrios and Phanagoras in gore and in ashes[8] with all the dead. Nor will the next four-year cycle release you <from the curse>.[9] In such a bond will I bind you, Demētrios, as strong as is possible, and I will hammer into your tongue a *kunōtos*.[10]

Our Latin exemplar (Kropp 3.22/34) belongs to a much later period (second or third century CE), and comes from the other side of the world from Athens, from Uley in Gloucestershire. Its purpose this time is the punishment of a thief and the hoped-for restitution of the stolen property. The text is fragmentary, but its tenor and import clear:

> I entrust to you <Mercury> ... the person who cheated me of those *denarii*[11] which he owed to me .... <may the guilty parties be> half-naked, toothless, tremulous, gouty, without pity from anyone ... <let him/them bring the stolen goods> to the shrine and treasury of the most powerful god.

Defixiones are essentially a Greek invention:[12] our earliest examples date to the beginning of the fifth or perhaps the close of the sixth century BCE and come from the Greek colony of Selinous in Sicily (Graf (1997), 173; Ogden (1999), 4). The use of *defixiones* soon spread from there to Athens and other parts of the Greek mainland[13] and was subsequently taken up by the Italian tribes and by the Romans, who in turn exported it to their overseas territories: in fact one of the earliest known *defixiones* written in Latin comes not from Rome, but from Spain, one of Rome's first colonies.[14] By the time of the Roman Empire *defixiones* have become internationalised, in the sense that they are found all over the Mediterranean basin, as well as the very furthest confines of Roman influence (Britain in the west, Syria and the Black Sea region in the east, Egypt and Nubia in the south): but they are internationalised also in that examples from the imperial era are often heavily infused by syncretism, incorporating elements of Hebrew, Near Eastern and especially Egyptian religion and mysticism in a giddying blend. Partly as a result of this theological inclusiveness, many of the later *defixiones*, such as the numerous curse tablets from Carthage and Hadrumetum in Roman North Africa, are long and elaborate (Hull (1974), 10; Gager 6–7); they also feature such rhetorical devices as repetition, pleonasm, rhythm and metre in order to enhance the incantatory potency of the words.[15] This stands in stark contrast to early Attic exemplars, which may consist of no more than a simple list of persons to be hexed.[16] An additional factor contributing to the length of *defixiones* from the late Roman period was the incorporation of magical *charaktēres*,[17] unintelligible letter shapes, and series of vowels or strings of peculiar sounding words, so-called *uoces magicae*. These were believed to enhance the efficacy of the spell (Frankfurter (1994), 199–205), or at least to work on the credulity of persons commissioning *defixiones* from professionals,[18] who seem to have been responsible for creating the majority of our curse tablets, though it is clear that many also were fashioned by amateurs possessed of differing levels of literacy (Ogden (1999), 54–60). The *uoces magicae* need not concern us here, first, because they are largely unintelligible or of contested interpretation in the limited number of cases where scholarly attempts have been made to unpick them;[19] second, because the fundamental ethos of *defixiones* remained essentially unchanged by these verbose inclusions. The ancestor of *uoces magicae* was the so-called *Ephesia grammata*, 'Ephesian letters', which we know to have been in circulation from the fourth century BCE onwards: they could be used for defensive as well as aggressive purposes. Originally a mere six in number, *askion, kataskion, lix, tetrax, damnameneus, aisia* (or *-on*), the *Ephesia grammata* spawned a veritable arsenal of hocus pocus.[20] Many of the *defixiones* bulked out by the incorporation of such material, or by drawings of human, animal, divine and demonic figures accompanying the text,[21] belong to the third century CE or later, and in fact the practice of inscribing curse tablets continued past the collapse of the Roman Empire in the west: it seems to have died out somewhere between the sixth and eighth centuries CE.[22]

An integral part of the cursing process was the deposition of the *defixio*, normally below ground. There were various sites for this.[23] The most important were graves – many *defixiones* have been unearthed in the extramural Athenian burial site, the *Kerameikos* – or a body of water (Martin (2007)). *PGM* 7.451–2 prescribes the burying of a *defixio* after its manufacture 'either in a river or land or the sea or a stream'[24] or a coffin or a well'.[25] Other possibilities were the sanctuaries of chthonic deities (hence for example the curse tablets found long ago in the temple precinct of Demeter at Knidos in Asia Minor and more recently in the sanctuary of Demeter and Kore at Corinth),[26] different localities having associations with death/the dead, for instance a battlefield (Ogden (1999), 17), and, lastly, non-chthonic sanctuaries, such as the quondam temple complex of Isis and Magna Mater at Mainz. The dominant idea underlying the deposition of the *defixiones* was that these should be brought into proximity with the subterranean world and the supernatural beings that held sway there, in order that they could implement the harmful wishes expressed in the curse; hence a preference, statistically speaking, for depositing the tablets in graves (probably the first locations to be used when *defixiones* originally came into being); sometimes indeed the tablet was placed in the right hand of the corpse.[27] In a number of early *defixiones*,[28] the mere act of burying in a grave a tablet bearing the names of the persons to be hexed, without an attached verb stating that these had been 'bound down' or the like, apparently sufficed, along with ritual procedures attendant on the deposition of the tablet, an integral and crucially important part of the whole process,[29] to convey to the powers below the object of the curse.[30] Alternatively the victims might be explicitly 'delivered', 'handed over', 'dedicated to', 'registered with' or 'entrusted to'[31] infernal deities such as Demeter, Persephone, Pluto, Hecate or Hermes, so that these could influence adversely the actions and circumstances of the persons thus targeted. In another possible script, Hermes or other chthonic deities might be enjoined to 'constrain' (*katechein*) the target (Wünsch *DTA* index V Dc). In later, more elaborate formulations, the assistance of the occupants of a tomb, the spirits of the dead or *nekudaimones*, is co-opted: these were enjoined or compelled verbally, as an integral part of the *defixio*, to execute the spell which the tablet contained.[32] Occasionally too the *defixio* was conceived of as an 'epistle' to the powers of the Underworld, in the expectation that they would act upon its contents:[33] additionally, so-called 'prayers for justice', a special category of *defixio* (see immediately below) were often explicitly phrased as a letter, though in this instance directed to Olympian as well as chthonic deities (Versnel (2002a), 62, (1991), 68). In the case of fulfilment of a *defixio* by *nekudaimones*, the preference was for harnessing the spirits of those who had died prematurely (*aōroi*) or by violence (*biaiothanatoi*), since such persons were believed to tarry about their graves, making them easy of access for the *defigens* (the curser), and also to entertain feelings of malignity towards the living[34] which comported neatly with the ethos of the spells whose enacting spirits they became.[35] But equally, as implied above, the divine agent charged with executing the curse might be a major deity of the nether regions, as for example in Audollent 38.29–32 'Gē [the goddess Earth] of the Underworld ... I conjure you by your name to effect this business and to keep safe for me this binding spell [*sc.* in the ground] and to make it effective'. Finally, as the recently discovered Mainz *defixiones* have most surprisingly demonstrated, the deities whose aid was solicited in curse tablets need have no connection with the Underworld – a connection which had hitherto been regarded by specialists as almost mandatory.

As a brief encapsulation of their nature and purpose, Jordan's definition of *defixiones*, quoted at the beginning of this chapter, remains, broadly speaking, as valid today as it was in 1985.[36] But in the thirty years and more since Jordan wrote there have been various significant developments in our understanding of curse tablets, of which several may be singled out here. The first involves the discovery and publication of several large caches of *defixiones*, from Roman Bath, from the *fons* of Anna Perenna in Rome, from Mainz and from Corinth. These have thrown up some real surprises and necessitated a revaluation of received ideas about the contents and scope of curse tablets. A number of these will be discussed in detail below: it suffices for the moment merely to flag their emergence. A second matter of note is the rediscovery of most of the 220 texts published at Berlin in 1897 by Richard Wünsch under the heading *Defixionum Tabellae Atticae*.[37] It had been thought that the originals, which until the Second World War were kept in Berlin's Antikensammlung, had been lost. But it now transpires that, after being removed from the Museum as bombing of the city intensified, to one of two anti-aircraft blockhouses at the Berlin Zoo, they were subsequently transported to Moscow or Leningrad after the Russian capture of the Reichstag in 1945, and only returned to the German Democratic Republic in 1958, whereupon they disappeared into a storage room of the Pergamon Museum. Re-emerging after the fall of the Berlin Wall, they are now in the process of being re-edited – with, importantly, notable improvements to Wünsch's text.[38] Since this is work still in progress, nothing more will be said of it here.

The next two developments involve theoretical advances. The first of these is the now widely accepted view that the social context of many curse tablets, particularly the early ones, is agonistic (Faraone (1991)); that is, they arise in a situation of contestation or rivalry. Thus for example some of the numerous Attic judicial *defixiones* are equally as concerned, it may be argued, with the working out of elite political enmities as with the outcome of a trial in prospect (Faraone (1991), 16). Similarly, the obscure and vexed *SGD* 91 from Gela in Sicily, dated by Jordan to the mid-fifth century BCE, seems to be an attempt by one Apelles, on behalf of an admired or loved *chorēgos*, Eunikos, to curse with ineffectuality (*ateleia*) all other *chorēgoi* who may come up against the latter in a dramatic festival.³⁹ As for the numerous *defixiones* from the late Roman Empire seeking magically to nobble the horses and drivers belonging to factions other than that favoured by the *defigens*, the context of these is self-evidently agonistic, at times indeed violently so. On the other hand, it is important not to import the agonistic paradigm into all situations covered by *defixiones*.⁴⁰ It will not work, for example, with many of the amatory *defixiones*, where frequently the object is simply to hijack the emotions of the party targeted and no rival is in question.⁴¹

The second major theoretical development to emerge since Jordan wrote is Versnel's identification of a category of marginal *defixiones* or 'prayers for justice', as he termed these in a seminal paper of 1991 which has come to command almost universal assent.⁴² In it, he identified seven elements to be found in such para-*defixiones*, as they might be styled, which in Versnel's view differentiate these from curse tablets of a more traditional type. The key distinction is that all such texts are animated by, and give voice to, a sense of having been wronged in some fashion or other. They are reactive, rather than pre-emptive like many *defixiones*,⁴³ and their ethos may be conveniently summed up in a phrase from one such text, 'I ask this [for divine help], being wronged and not initiating wrongdoing'.⁴⁴ Also of importance is the supplicatory tone adopted in addressing deities, as opposed to the more compulsive tenor of *defixiones*, and self-identification by the operator, something which is very rare in curse tablets.⁴⁵ At the same time, these prayers for justice remain in the hinterland of more conventional *defixiones* (Ogden (1999), 38), not least by the ferocity of the punishments which the operators invoke upon the parties⁴⁶ – frequently unidentified – whom they perceive to have done them wrong.

Versnel's widely accepted identification of a fresh category has had important ramifications for the classification of *defixiones* by type. In his 1904 collection of *defixiones* Audollent listed five different types of curse tablet:

1. Litigation curses, whereby one tried to muzzle or place on the losing side one's adversaries in a trial, a form especially associated with Attic texts of the fifth and fourth centuries BCE and the political rivalries of the times – often worked out in proxy form in the courts – though by no means confined to that period.
2. Amatory curses, under which head he included not just spells to inspire passion, but also relationship curses involving a situation of amatory competition,⁴⁷ as well as two curses apparently against a rival prostitute (68–9) calling for lack of success in both her business and her personal relationships.⁴⁸

3. Agonistic or competitive curses against rival factions in the circus or opponents in the arena, essentially a phenomenon of the later Roman Empire, to which we may add curses against athletes and curses arising from dramaturgical rivalries, two types not included by Audollent under the rubric of competitive curses.[49]
4. Curses against economic competitors, usually known nowadays as trade curses, a type which has received increasing scholarly emphasis over the course of the twentieth century.[50]
5. An amorphous class directed 'against thieves, calumniators and ill-sayers'.

This fifth category has effectively been replaced by Versnel's prayers for justice, a designation reflecting the fact that very many texts of this kind are concerned with recovering from thieves property stolen from the curser, notably the large tranche of *defixiones* from Bath and Uley in the UK, as well as a number of tablets in the Mainz hoard, all discovered long after Audollent wrote. To sum up, scholars now more or less standardly speak of judicial, erotic, competitive and trade curses, along with prayers for justice (e.g. M. Martin (2010), 35; Urbanová (2018), 20). Under the second of these heads it is convenient, with Dickie (2000, 565) to lump not only curses designed to manipulate the passions of another (fetching spells, erotic binding spells and separation spells, where the separation is explicitly or implicitly engineered for the erotic benefit of the *defigens*), but also relationship spells, whereby an individual seeks to protect from external threats an established union, without there being necessarily any great sexual passion involved.[51]

As touched on above, a key factor that has greatly altered the landscape of *defixio* studies is a host of new finds, both Greek and Latin, that have given a radically expanded idea of the potentialities of the form, in terms of its ethos, levels of sophistication, typology and localised variations. To put it another way, the horizons of curse tablets have turned out to be infinitely wider than could have been gleaned from the turn of the nineteenth century – though still invaluable – collections of Wünsch (*Defixionum Tabellae Atticae*, 1897) and Audollent (*Defixionum Tabellae Quotquot Innotuerunt . . . praeter Atticas*, 1904): as was only to be expected when the combined number of texts in these two path-breaking volumes was 525, whereas now we have roughly 600 Latin curse tablets and almost double that number of Greek ones (Blänsdorf (2008b), 68), a total that continues to increase as new texts come to light.[52] At the most basic level, the new discoveries have thrown up curses invoking specific sufferings of a type not hitherto seen in *defixiones*, which tend to be predictable and broad-brushed in terms of the punishments that they call down upon their targets.[53] I cite here two instances, one Greek, one Latin (more will be encountered below). The Greek text, from Corinth, dating to the late first or early second century CE, calls down on one Karpimē Babbia, weaver of garlands, 'monthly destruction', that is, continuous infertility, while conversely soliciting fertility for the *defigens* (Stroud (2013), nos. 125–6). The theme appears unique among *defixiones* thus far found, though there is a parallel of sorts in the *PGM*.[54] The Latin example, from the *fons* of Anna Perenna, curses with blindness in both left and right eyes the *arbiter* Sura, seemingly to prevent him from exercising his sight in a judgement from which the *defigens* anticipates adverse consequences.[55] While eyes are often included in lists of bodily parts targeted in curse tablets, and blindness called down, for example, upon charioteers in circus *defixiones*, this appears to be the only instance to date where eyes are the sole focus of attack.[56]

The texts just cited come from two of the four recently discovered *defixio* hoards that were listed earlier. Notwithstanding important new accretions on the Greek side, it seems fair to say that overall the most exciting and substantial additions to the corpus over the last twenty-five years or so have been in Latin, in particular the large tranche of tablets from Aquae Sulis (Roman Bath), the thirty-four from the combined temple of Isis and Magna Mater in Mainz, and the remarkable magical ensemble, discussed at the close of the chapter, which was discovered in the *fons* of Anna Perenna in Rome; localities sufficiently far apart as neatly to illustrate the spread of *defixiones* in the imperial period throughout the whole of the Roman world.

Some of the new discoveries have turned up most unexpected material. A case in point is a stand-alone *defixio* of a particularly complex and unusual type unearthed relatively few years ago in a tomb in the neighbourhood of Rome's via Ostiense. Written in Latin, it can be dated on palaeographical and archaeological grounds to the first century CE (Bevilacqua (2006–7), 328–9, 304). In literal translation it reads:[57]

Side A
Father Dis, divine Proserpina, Hounds of Orcus,[58] infernal Burners,[59] Bonebreakers, Ghosts, Furies, Spirits of Madness, Birds of the night, Harpy birds,[60] Ortygian birds, Virga, the Chimaera,[61] Geryones,[62] Sirens, Circe, the Giants, the Sphinx, he beseeches you and requests, asks you, powers of the infernal deities, you whose names are written above: that that Caecilia Prima, or whatever other name she goes under,[63] you, father Dis, should send her below and assail her with terrible pangs, carry her off to your home. Divine Proserpina, may you bring it

about that that Caecilia Prima, or whatever other name she goes under, you send her below, take the blood from her veins, steal from that Caecilia Prima her flesh, the heat of her mind from that Caecilia Prima. Hounds of Orcus, Three-headed Creatures of Orcus, may you consume that Caecilia Prima's liver and lungs, may you tear and rend her heart and veins, entrails, limbs, marrow, may you snatch away the eyes of that Caecilia Prima[64] and you, infernal Burners, may you burn the eyes of that Caecilia Prima, her stomach, heart, lungs, fat, may you burn and scorch all the other limbs of that Caecilia Prima, you, and let her not be able to live or enjoy good health, and may you carry off that Caecilia Prima to yourselves, hand over those parts of her to the infernal bone-breakers, you, let them break the bones of that Caecilia Prima, let them consume her marrow, let them tear apart her liver and lungs, and may you, infernal Bone-Breakers, deliver over that Caecilia Prima to Aurora, sister of Orcus. Aurora, sister of Orcus, may you take away sleep and slumber from that Caecilia Prima, may you inflict on her madness, pangs, stupefaction, a distressed brow (?)[65]... up to the time when Caecilia Prima dies, perishes, wastes away; then may you, Aurora, sister of Orcinus, deliver over that Caecilia Prima to the infernal Ghosts and Furies ... may you [plural] inflict upon that Caecilia Prima fear, frights, pangs.

Side B (fragmentary)

Stupefaction and madness and all ... let them bring about, the same ... who for herself ... let her get, immoral behaviour ... that Caecilia Prima ... let her always have. Immoral behaviour, that that Caecilia Prima may be oppressed, crushed by her enemies, consumed [by illness] and not ... Birds of the night, Harpy birds, you, may you consume the heart of that Caecilia Prima, her hands, all her intestines,[66] may you inflict upon all ... of that Caecilia Prima anguished thoughts (?), daily, tertian and quartan fevers, until the time when you wrest away the life of that ... Virga, of the infernal deities ... you [singular], may you bring it about that of that Caecilia Prima, whom you are quite subduing, lashing, burning, scorching among those persons in the Underworld who have done all kinds of wickedness and crimes in the world above,[67] that even so you, Virga, burn, scorch, lash, subdue that Caecilia Prima until you carry her off dead to you, just like persons upon a shore who have lost all their possessions.[68] Himaera[69] ... may you sink your teeth into Caecilia Prima ... so that she never becomes healthy ... her ... may you [Caecilia Prima] swell up just like a drum, and may she die from terrible pangs until she perishes that you carry off ... never ... that Caecilia Prima you should scorch ... let her be dead ... Geryones, Sirens, Circe the daughter of the Sun, just as Minerva with her tunic (*tunica*) alone[70] ... them, the Sirens, female monsters, detained men with their songs and Circe with her deadly drugs the companions of Ulysses ... may you ... that Caecilia Prima with the same evils, the same pangs you 'help' Caecilia, and may you her life and spirit ... take away, may you deliver to the infernal ... father Dis, divine Proserpina and Virga, he beseeches you who charges you in this matter[71] your [plural] ... shrine ... her ... may you bring to perfection of the perfect ....

As is true of many *defixiones* (Ogden (1999), 26; Eidinow (2007), 8, 196; M. Martin (2010), 139), the exact circumstances which produced the curses are unclear. It seems however a fair inference that the via Ostiense text represents the revenge of a spurned or cuckolded lover. The male who penned it[72] twice complains of Caecilia Prima's *turpidines* (B3, 5), a noun which in its more usual form *turpitudo* (plural *turpitudines*) frequently refers to sexual immorality; furthermore, the *defigens* appears to include the target among those who have done all kinds of wrongs (*scelera*) in the eyes of the gods (B15–16), thinking perhaps of infidelity,[73] while the prominence afforded to the agency of Aurora (A25–32) in punishing Caecilia may reflect, in a manner suited to the putative context of the *defixio*, the connexion of that goddess with love affairs which went disastrously or fatally wrong, as well as her jealous disposition towards lovers seen in dawn-songs such as Ov. *Am.* 1.13.[74] If this analysis is correct, then our *defixio* finds a ready parallel in two other curse tablets, one Latin, one Greek. The first is a *defixio* discovered in 1999 at Gross-Gerau near Mainz which desires that one Priscilla should die (*pereat*), apparently because she has married someone other than the author of the curse: see Scholz and Kropp (2004). In the same vein is a long (?) second century BCE *defixio* from Lilybaeum (*SGD* 109; Eidinow (2007), 430–2) in which the 'beautiful' Prima Allia is consigned as a gift to Hermes of the Underworld, 'buried below in Hades', with the request that the god 'scrape her off' – probably the would-be revenge of a rejected lover.[75]

What is striking or novel about the via Ostiense curse tablet? The first is that it is populated by a host of hellish creatures who belong as much to the realm of literature and myth[76] as to the normally pragmatic and tightly focused arena of *defixiones*. The opening lines of Side A inevitably recall the 'the monstrous shapes of wild beasts in different forms, Centaurs ... and Scyllas of double shape and hundred-handed Briareus, Gorgons and Harpies and the beast of Lerna [the Hydra] hissing fearsomely and the Chimaera armed with flames and the ghostly triple-bodied form' which in Virgil's *Aeneid* (6.285–9) are clustered at the entrance to the Halls of Hades.[77] Indeed, four of Virgil's monsters reappear in the opening lines of the *defixio*: the Harpies, the Chimaera, Geryon, Virgil's 'ghostly triple-bodied form', and the Giants (who stand in for Virgil's Briareus: he, though not strictly one of the Giants, is closely akin to these as equally the offspring of *Gaia*, Earth, and of monstrous size).[78] Other beings in the curse tablet too have an impeccable literary-mythical pedigree – the Hounds of Orcus,[79] the Birds of the night (= *striges*),[80] the Ortygian birds,[81] Circe (cf. Side B29, Hom. *Ody.* 10), the Sphinx,[82] and the Sirens, who are referred to at B28 in terms which may echo Ovid,[83] while the infernal Burners, the *Ossufragae*, 'Bone-breakers' and *Virga* ('Rod') are surely creatures of pure invention.[84] One is reminded of the fantastical, demonic 'forge destroyers, Smasher and Crasher and Unquenchable and Ill-Moulder and Spoiler of Unfired Pots'[85] whom, in the so-called *Oven*, an epigram preserved in the fictional 'Herodotean' *Life of Homer*, the itinerant beggar-rhapsode Homer threatens to invoke against some potters should they renege on their promise to reward him with earthenware for singing songs to them (7–10). Intriguingly, after promising that these will chomp up the pots as if in a horse's jaws (13–14), should the potters go back on their word, the poet continues 'come hither too Circe, daughter of the Sun (cf. the *defixio* Side B26), mistress of charms, throw in savage drugs, and harm them and their products. And come hither also Chiron, bringing many Centaurs, those who escaped Heracles' clutches and those who were slain' (15–18).[86] It is not suggested that, in addition to the borrowings from Virgil and possibly Ovid, the author of our *defixio* also drew upon an obscure Greek poem from around 500 BCE.[87] Yet there is about the *defixio* and the *Oven* a rich vein of literary inventiveness in regard to the punitive and the demonic which draws the two together despite the very different circumstances of their genesis and drastic difference of ethos, sophisticated humour in the first case and, it seems, bitter hostility in the second.

It is not just the pronounced literary flavour of the *defixio*, its expropriation of the fabled inhabitants of the mythic Underworld, that give pause for thought. It also follows directly from this feature that the supernatural agents of destruction invoked in the curse tablet are radically different from those normally called upon in *defixiones*. In the initial three lines an appeal for assistance is made to no less than eighteen personages, whose aid is then systematically called upon in the course of the *defixio* – scrupulously maintaining the order in which they were first introduced – to torture Caecilia Prima, before dragging her off to Hades. Of these only Dis [Pluto], Proserpina, the Furies and, to a lesser extent, the Hounds of Orcus have a recognised role in *defixiones* as executors of the curse. There is in fact a great predictability in these texts about the divine agents of retribution. In seeking to explain the presence of Aurora, otherwise unknown to *defixiones*, who pops up unexpectedly in Side A25 as a further *vendicatrice*, Bevilacqua (2009 and 2010) invokes the parallel of two other female figures, Leucothea and Althaea, who, uniquely for curse tablets, occur in *SGD* 170 (Eidinow (2007), 436–7) and Audollent 41 respectively. Bevilacqua's argument that the mythic history of all three makes them eminently suitable to be agents of punishment is persuasive, but for present purposes it is more important to note that Leucothea and Althaea are the odd women out *in otherwise highly conventional listings of divine fulfillers of a curse*: that is, Hermes, Hecate, Pluto, Persephone, Artemis, Demeter, the heroes and Praxidika (a vengeance-dealing goddess) – all labelled 'Chthonian' – in *SGD* 170; Kore (= Persephone), Hecate, Selene (the Moon goddess), Gē, and Einodia (an *altera ego* for Hecate) in Audollent 41. If we add in the Erinyes (Furies), the abovementioned *nekudaimones* and perhaps Kronos we have an almost complete listing of the divine powers whose aid is standardly invoked in curse tablets, which – until the arrival of the syncretism noted above – almost never admit exceptions to the essentially Greek infernal pantheon which is charged by the *defigentes*, 'cursers', with visiting punishment on their targets.[88] But here the 'usual suspects', Dis, Proserpina and the Furies are swamped by a plethora of unfamiliar agents of destruction based in myth, a situation without parallel in any other *defixiones* unearthed up till now.

To the extent that almost all of the entities invoked in the via Ostiense *defixio* are chthonic, the text does conform to the just-noted pattern whereby *defigentes* call upon the powers of the Underworld to execute their curses.[89] But not all the agents of destruction here (Circe, the Bone-breakers) are self-evidently infernal, and the old certainty that, prior to the importation of Eastern deities from the mid-second century CE onward, *defixiones* as a matter of course relied upon the agency of chthonic powers has been further eroded by the discovery of the Mainz *defixiones*, along with a curse-text from Gross-Gerau nearby. For in these Magna Mater and Attis are appealed to for assistance without being conceived of as in any sense infernal (*DTM* p. 88). Of these documents, more below.

There is a third, cautionary point to be made apropos the via Ostiense text. It has often been assumed that *defixiones* flourished mainly in the humblest strands of society. There are certainly reasons to think so. The first is the prevalence of errors of orthography and grammar in a large number of texts, testimony to a poor level of education: Kropp 3.17/1 is but one example among many.[90] A second is the fact that *defixiones* are often levelled by slaves,[91] aimed at persons explicitly designated as slaves,[92] or who bear names which are evidently servile,[93] clear indications of the ambience in which curse tablets were traded. A further clue comes from the professions of those who are defixed in situations of rivalry or hostility. Audollent 52 and *SGD* 11 (Eidinow (2007), 408), for example, each curse a brothel-keeper, one of a number of texts which belong to the rivalry-riven, low-life ambience of prostitution,[94] while others again are aimed at persons whose occupations were regarded as banausic.[95]

This said, the striking level of literacy on display in the via Ostiense text, with its unexpected allusions to the *Aeneid* and the *Odyssey* and obtrusive patina of mythological erudition, serves notice that *defixiones* were not just a preserve of the lower classes.[96] There is in fact a considerable body of evidence that points in the same direction. A recently rediscovered and re-edited text from Bologna appears to offer the first instance of a curse against a Roman senator (Sánchez Natalías (2012)), one of a small but significant number of Latin instances where persons of distinction are targeted, the most notable case being that of Germanicus:[97] here the importance of the victims is surely indicative of similar social status on the part of the *defigentes*. It has already been noted that Athenian courtroom disputes could be a venue for the playing out of rivalries among the political elite (cf. Curbera (2016), 109), while *SGD* 67, from the fourth century BCE, targets 'a priest and an operative of Artemis', persons, one assumes, of some account and hence a likely pointer in turn to the standing of the person who felt provoked to level curses at them. A survey of tablets from North Africa offers indications that some of their authors may have been middle- or upper-class (Mura (1994)). Kropp 1.7./4/1 turns on an inheritance dispute involving a *pupillus*, that is a boy not having yet attained the age of majority and accordingly unable to own property in his own right, who had been left an inheritance by a deceased father. The existence of the property dispute, which is in fact the occasion for a number of *defixiones*, and the fact that the boy curses the villains at his own expense (*meo sumptu defigo*) might suggest that we are dealing with a family of at least some substance. To top off the third point to which the via Ostiense curses gave rise, a number of the Mainz *defixiones*, as Blänsdorf in his 2012 edition repeatedly emphasises, show familiarity with rhetorical techniques, Roman legal terminology and traditional prayer forms, as well as educated hands[98] and an avoidance of linguistic vulgarisms. This leads the editor to conclude that the texts in question must have emanated from members of the middle or even upper echelons of the town (Blänsdorf (2010c), 164, *DTM* p. 110 *et passim*). In other words, a further warning against the widely canvassed assumption that *defixiones* were essentially the preserve of the lowest classes of society.

A fourth and final factor which must strike a reader of the via Ostiense *defixio* is its sheer ferocity. To be sure, curses hexing the individual limbs (and mind) of an enemy's body had been a feature of *katadesmoi* from the very beginning, growing in comprehensiveness over the years (Versnel (1998), 224 n.21). Moreover Riess (2012, 164–234), adducing both semantic and sociocultural data, has made a powerful case for the idea that Attic curse tablets of the fourth century BCE contain a great deal more violence, implicit and in some cases explicit, than has been generally realised. But in these (often early) instances the organs in question are usually 'bound', that is, rendered immobile or ineffectual, as for example in judicial curses paralysing an opponent's organs of speech, or circus *defixiones* of later times interfering with the eyesight of the drivers of rival teams. Not so in the present case, which is an example of what Versnel (1998) calls 'anatomical curses', that is, curses where hurt is consciously directed towards the body of another, as opposed to 'functional curses' where, as in the two instances just cited, the purpose is to put out of action the pertinent organs and senses in a specific situation of contestation. There is nothing out of the ordinary about the infliction of pain in curses of the anatomical type. That said, the sadistic relish with which the *defigens* dwells upon the torments in store for Caecilia Prima in this unusually long *defixio* practically trumps any texts in this vein which have come to light up till now. Caecilia is to be emptied of blood,[99] her innards are to be rent, and her sight is to be 'snatched away'; then, in a piece of overkill, her eyes are also to be burnt, along with her heart, lungs, fat and 'all the other limbs of Caecilia Prima', and her bones are to be broken along with her liver and lungs, on which the Hounds of Orcus have earlier been enjoined to feast. At the end of the column, Aurora is detailed to compound the physical tortures by inflicting upon Caecilia Prima mental ones, sleeplessness, madness and a host of fears. All this in Side A, before the assault is resumed in Side B with a second wave of attacks by *striges*, Harpies, Virga, and no doubt other parties catalogued in A lines 1–3 who have unfortunately disappeared from the damaged parts of B. To top it off, Caecilia is to become like a shipwrecked individual, stripped of clothing and possessions (18–19) and to swell up like a drum, possibly a reference to dropsy (22), before being subject to the 'friendly'[100] but lethal ministrations of Geryones, Sirens and Circe.

To illustrate further the extremes to which anatomical curses can go, I cite another long, notably savage *defixio*, also from Rome, dating to the first century BCE, which formed part of a major study more than a century ago. The text runs:[101]

> Goodly beautiful Proserpina, wife of Pluto, or Salvia, if I ought rather to so call you, may you take away the health, the body, the complexion, the strength, the capacities of Plotius. May you deliver him to Pluto your husband. Let him not be able to avoid this by his devices. May you deliver him to quartan, tertian, daily fever, so that they can fight, and fight to a conclusion with him. Let them overcome him, conquer him until they snatch away his life. Accordingly I hand over this victim [viz. Plotius] to you, Proserpina, or Acherusian, if I ought rather

to so to call you. May you summon and send to me the three-headed dog [Cerberus] to tear out the heart of Plotius. May you promise that you will give to him three victims – dates, figs, a black pig – before the month of March if he accomplishes this. These things, Proserpina Salvia, I will give to you when you put me in possession of my wishes. I give to you the head of Plotius, slave of Avonia. Proserpina Salvia, I give to you the brow of Plotius. Proserpina Salvia, I give to you the eyebrows of Plotius.[102] Proserpina Salvia, I give to you the eyelids of Plotius. Proserpina Salvia, I give to you the nostrils, lips, ears, nose, tongue, teeth of Plotius, so that Plotius cannot say what pains him: his neck, his shoulders, his arms, his fingers, so that he cannot help himself at all: his breast, his liver, his heart, his lungs, so that he cannot make sense of what pains him: his innards, his belly, his navel, his sides, so that he cannot sleep soundly: his *uiscum sacrum* (his urogenital region), so that he cannot pass urine: his buttocks, his anus, his thighs, his knees, his legs, his shin-bones, his feet, his ankles, his soles, his toes, his toenails, so that he cannot stand by his own strength. Whether more or less shall have been written, in what manner he has according to the laws of magic composed any curse and entrusted it to writing [see Sherwood Fox ad loc.], in the same way I deliver Plotius to you, entrust him to you that you may deliver him, entrust him [*sc.* to all the ills specified above] in the month of February. Let him perish miserably, let him end miserably, let him most miserably be destroyed. May you hand him over, deliver him so that he cannot look upon, see or contemplate a single month more.

There are a number of points about this *defixio* that command our attention. The first is the palpable wish to inflict maximum pain and suffering upon the victim, a purpose captured in the twofold repetition of the Latin verb *dolere*, 'to feel physical hurt', in the text. There are numerous *defixiones* of this sadistic type, which tend to increase in frequency in the later period. Some of the more striking or colourful instances, both Greek and Roman, include: *DTM* 2.11–14 'just as he, who committed a criminal act regarding that money, watches the blood of the *galli*, *magali* and devotees of Bellona <dripping onto the ground>, so may they watch his end' (i.e. his public execution); *DTM* 5.8–10 'that he may see himself dying in every part of his body except for his eyes'; 'burst his veins' (Sánchez Natalías (2012), text line 21), an extremely violent death; *SGD* 21 'cut the hearts of the thieves';[103] 'I chop <Saturnina> completely into pieces' (Roesch (1966–7), first century BCE); *SGD* 114 (Gager no. 116) Side B '<I bind> Valeria Arsinoē, the criminal, sickness, the bitch, putrefaction', where 'sickness' and especially 'putrefaction' are evidently not terms of abuse like 'criminal', but notably unpleasant afflictions wished on Valeria Arsinoē in a curse that exhibits feelings of intense animosity. Finally, there is the wish 'so that worms, cancer, an infestation of worms may enter his hands, head, feet, enter his limbs and marrow' in a recently discovered *defixio* from Gross-Gerau (Blänsdorf (2007), ll. 9–12); what is particularly striking about this last curse is that punishments involving the peculiarly horrible fate of being consumed from within by worms or the like is, in the literary tradition, associated with crimes or misdeeds of the most egregious sort (Blänsdorf (2012), 60–1). Yet here the identical sanction is called down upon the head of a thief, as in two further cases where a robber is similarly defixed[104] – a fine example of the disproportion which often prevails in *defixiones* between the relative triviality of the original crime[105] and the ferocity of the curses which it provokes. None of the above however approaches in its detailed and lingering cruelty the via Ostiense *defixio* – or, as we shall see, certain of the more violent Mainz texts.

A second point of note common to the two lengthy *defixiones* quoted above, and a host of other curse tablets besides, is the detailed listing of the body parts to be affected by the curse. Sometimes the catalogue of such parts is quite circumscribed, especially in instances dating to the Classical period, such as *DTA* 87 (fourth century BCE) 'I bind ... their souls, hands, tongues, feet and minds', but very often an effect of comprehensiveness is aimed at. This may be done by providing an extensive catalogue of bodily limbs and organs to be targeted, as in the two long Latin curses translated above or Audollent 135: an alternative method is to use compendious expressions such as 'all the 365 limbs of the body' (Versnel (1998), 224 n.21), 'their souls and works and them in their entirety' (*DTA* 77, fourth–second century BCE?), 'and any other part of the body there may be' (Audollent 42, first–second century CE) or 'from the head to the tips of the toenails'.[106] Different explanations, of varying plausibility, have been offered for such anatomical inclusiveness. The first is a tendency on the part of magical texts to a fullness and particularity of expression that can express itself in redundancy or over-specificity, as in *SGD* 164 'silence and subdue and crush and bewitch and enslave and catch and enchant'. A second theory (Gordon (1999), 263–4) proposes that catalogues of body parts such as those under consideration, and long lists more generally, are intended to create an irresistible rhetorical pressure that invests these with ineluctable power and authority. Another suggestion is that by tabulating all the bodily parts to be attacked the curser can imaginatively and vindictively dismember the body of his enemy (Gordon (1999), 268–9). The argument that an enhanced emphasis in the later *katadesmoi* on inflicting pain throughout the body mirrors the increasing cruelty of punishments and of society more broadly under the Roman Empire[107] is too general to be of much use: conversely, too circumscribed to be helpful in explaining the many inventories of body parts met in curses of an non-amatory type is the interesting suggestion of Versnel (1998, 258–62) that when – in a seemingly counter-intuitive move – specific organs of a desired individual are singled out in erotic *defixiones* for torture, this represents a malign inversion of the catalogues of corporeal charms so beloved of Near Eastern and Graeco-Roman poetry.

A third point of importance, again shared by the two long Roman *defixiones*, is the unequivocal wish on the curser's part that his enemy should die (cf. 'carry her off dead to you'; 'let him perish miserably, let him end miserably, let him most miserably be destroyed'). I emphasise this because there has been some considerable reluctance on the part of scholars – Riess notably excepted[108] – to recognise the desire for the extermination of the target as an integral function of many *defixiones*,[109] early as well as late; while for his part Versnel (1998, 237 et passim, 2002a, 48–50) sees the wish that the target suffer all kinds of afflictions or death as a particular characteristic of prayers for justice. A death-dealing tendency is however pervasive in *defixiones* from the start, a phenomenon that can best be illustrated by the sheer variety and number of the formulae used in curse tablets to call for the elimination of an enemy, by no means all of them prayers for justice and often lacking any expressed motivation.[110] They include the political curse Ziebarth (1934), no. 1A–B = Gager no. 56 'I bind, I bury deeply, I cause to vanish from mankind' (350–325 BCE); the multipurpose *katadesmos DTA* 55 = Gager no. 64 'all these I bind down in lead and in wax and in water/wine ... to destruction and to bad reputation ... and in tombs' (fourth century BCE); a trade curse, *DTA* 75 = Gager no. 65 'may Rhodion perish along with his workshop' (fourth century BCE); Audollent 84 Side A 'may Pythokritos[111] drag evil and wretched Zōpyros down below and may Pythokritos drag down evil and wretched Nikoklea' (second century BCE); Kropp 1.1.2/3 'kill him, dispatch, slay, choke Porcellus and wicked Silla his wife'; Kropp 1.4.4/15 'Spirits of the Dead, I entrust to you [my enemies], that they may perish'; Kropp 1.9.1/1 'may you pursue him so that he miserably wastes away until he dies' (prayer for justice); Kropp 3/19/3 'that he should shed his blood up to the day when he dies ... let him die ... let him be killed by the god' (prayer for justice); Kropp 4.31/1 (Audollent 111) 'that they arrive at Pluto's halls and be gone from here to Proserpina' (judicial); Kropp 5.1.4/7 (Audollent 100) 'names given, laid in evidence, dispatched to the powers below, so that these may snatch them away by violence' (amatory rivalry); Kropp 6.1/1 'Juno of the Underworld, summon at once the person whose name is inscribed below and hand him over to the ghosts'; Kropp 11.1.1/14 (Audollent 228) 'I entreat you, whose realm is the regions below.

I entrust to you Iulia Faustilla ... that you may carry her off at once and keep her there among your host'; Audollent 16 frg. 11 'turn him into a corpse' (a driver for a rival circus faction); Audollent 155 A52-8 'put him on a bed of punishment to be punished, to leave life by an evil death within five days, quickly', B4-8 'we hand over to you this impious and lawless and accursed Kardēlos ... so that you confine and restrain and hand him over to the Chthonian One in the house of those below in Tartarus ... thoroughly chill him, make him as frost, make him waste away, shrink him to nothingness' (prayer for justice); 'make <Philostrata> disappear' (on account of malfeasance in performance of her duties as priestess of Aphrodite);[112] 'that you deprive him of life in public view' (prayer for justice, Tomlin (2010), 258-60); *SGD* 163 'cast him into suffering and death and headaches, quickly, now' (see Jordan ad loc., Lifshitz (1970), 81-3). Lastly here we might mention *DTM* 21, the text of which contains only the name of the target. But the lethal intent of the whole is clearly indicated by the roughly moulded clay figurine with which the tablet was found. This was pierced by eight nails, had an erect phallus (which possibly indicates an erotic motive), and was broken at the waist and deposited in such a way that one half lay supine, the other prone – a clear prognostication of an agonising death.

What conclusions can be drawn from the foregoing list, which could be expanded almost indefinitely? The first is that we should by no means attempt to sanitise or underplay the lethal intent of many *defixiones*, an intention which is by no means confined to any particular category of curse tablet (and surfaces, too, in amulets with a *defixio*-like character).[113] The second is that the desire to exterminate an enemy is of a piece with the various spells in the *PGM* conjuring illness and/or death on someone (*kataklitika*),[114] as well as the wish for the premature death of an offender that is so pervasive in Greek and Roman curses other than *defixiones* (Watson (1991), 30-8). The third is that some of the *defixiones* calling down death on an enemy, such as the two long Roman instances quoted above, or *SGD* nos. 109 and 114, have a vicious particularity that put it beyond question that intense passion and anger underlie them: which is not to say that such feelings may not also infuse *defixiones* composed using formularies or the assistance of specialists in *katadesmoi* like those Plato refers to (*Rep.* 364c). This is certainly the case with, for example, Audollent 1-13 (cf. Gager no. 89) and 155-8, where, for all their highly formulaic character, the hurt and animus of the operators clearly shines through. Hence the attempt of Graf (1997, 146-7) to deny an emotional dimension to the inscribing of *defixiones* cannot stand, particularly when we consider that the mere act of doing so – in conjunction with the attendant rituals – may have served in part as a release valve for the

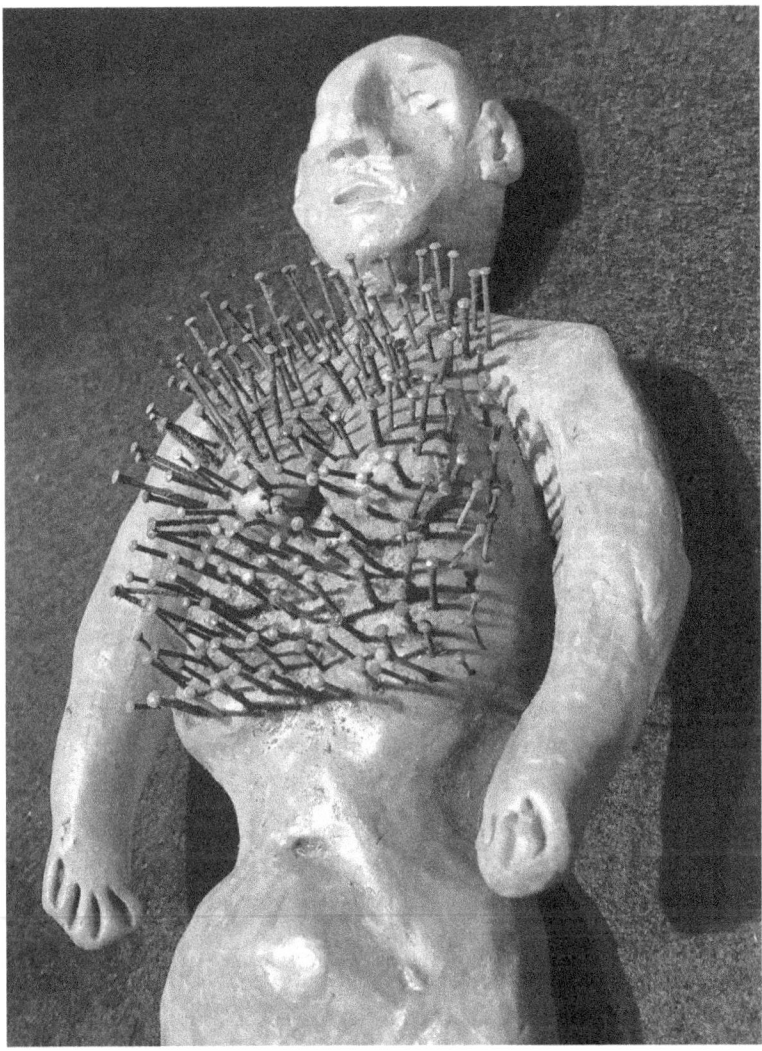

Fig. 3 Wax poppet with multiple pins (France, modern era). © The Museum of Witchcraft and Magic, Boscastle, Cornwall.

venting of a powerful sense of animus. As Ogden (2008, 140–4) rightly observes, a number of *defixiones* where a personal voice is clearly to be heard offer unmediated access to the deeply experienced feelings of the curser, magic of a hostile kind such as curses being characteristically underpinned by negative emotions such as resentment, hatred and anger (Malinowski (1974), 71–3). The fourth point is simply this: that when the authors of *defixiones* 'deliver', 'hand over' or 'consign' their enemies to the infernal powers, they mean exactly what they say, that the parties in question should die.[115] This is not at all the same thing as exhorting Hermes for example to 'restrain' someone or binding someone 'before' (*pros*)[116] Hekate, Pluto or Proserpina (cf. *DTA* 101ff.).

Returning now to the via Ostiense curse tablet, there is one further feature to which I would draw attention. It is that the curse concludes (Side B35) with the words *perficiatis perfectae*, 'may you bring to completion ... of the perfect' which – notwithstanding uncertainties caused by the damaged condition of the text in ll. 34–5 – must surely be a Latin rendering of the similarly alliterative appeal to a deity with which Greek operators regularly concluded a magic spell, *telei telean epaoidēn*, 'bring to perfection [this] perfect spell'; such a formulation for example rounds off the erotic binding spell *SM* 45.[117] The point may seem a small one, but has important ramifications. It is but one instance of the commonalities which can exist between *defixiones* notwithstanding linguistic, locational and chronological distance. This is a phenomenon that Tomlin identified in the 1980s, apropos of *defixiones* against thieves from both Britain and the Iberian peninsula,[118] and which Versnel (1991a and 1985) has traced in relation to prayers for justice, as well as in the formula 'may he [the target of a *defixio*] not be able to sacrifice' (and thereby make a god propitious), which is found in both Greek and Latin curses; in connection with the latter he has uncovered striking overlaps between Greek exemplars and multiple instances belonging to the Latin west, Spain and most particularly the UK – 'similarities', as he puts it, 'so striking as to make spontaneous [i.e. independent] development far less likely' (Versnel (1991a), 91). In other words, we have in *perficiatis perfectae* a particular example of the internationalisation of Greek and Roman magic, which may be traced inter alia to the peregrinations of itinerant magicians, the availability of books of magic in all quarters of the Roman world, or, as in the case of the prayers for justice in the southern part of England, to the permanent settlement in that country of soldiers from far-flung regions who elected to stay there once their term of service had run out.

We turn now to the remarkable haul of thirty-four tablets found in the double sanctuary of Isis and Magna Mater in the centre of Mainz (ancient Moguntiacum), which was discovered during 1999 in the course of digging operations preparatory to the building of a car park for a projected shopping mall: a find which, along with the recently published Corinthian texts, and the hoards from Bath and Uley, reminds us of the perceived efficacy of depositing curse tablets in temple contexts, as well as the more familiar graves, wells and the like. The texts, most of which were found in a sacrificial firepit adjacent to the temple, belong roughly to the years between the last third of the first and the beginning of the second century CE (Blänsdorf (2008a), 50, (2010c), 143). The earliest and most securely dated group of Latin *defixiones* thus far unearthed, they offer many surprises and unusual details, suggesting, as do the via Ostiense *defixio* and recent discoveries more generally, that curse tablets were by no means as routinised as might previously have been thought.[119] One novelty was the throwing of the tablets into the sacrificial fire at the end of the cursing ritual, a piece of *Analogie-Zauber*, analogical magic, whose purpose is spelled out in three texts (10–12), e.g. *DTM* 11 'so may their [the enemies'] limbs melt as this lead tablet will melt, in order that their end may come to pass'.[120] The texts which can be read (or partially read)[121] are those that survived the melting process. Written by different hands, of varying levels of sophistication and length, employing highly personal, indeed idiosyncratic language and concepts, the *defixiones* are manifestly not the work of professional magicians or scribes (Blänsdorf (2008a), 59, (2010c), 147). Some of the longer texts are of exceptional interest. Of these I discuss *exempli gratia* one of the most intriguing, *DTM* 6.

In tentative translation[122] it runs

> I deposit[123] in this tablet Quintus, who has turned away from me (or 'is my enemy'),[124] who (?) brings himself to a bad end, both with his principles and <those of> his life. Just as the priests of Magna Mater (*galli*) or those of Bellona (*Bellonariue*) have lopped (*absciderunt*) or thoroughly wounded themselves, so may his credibility, reputation and capacities be cut away. Neither are these reckoned among humankind (*nec in numero hominum sunt*: i.e. are held to be of no account), and let him similarly not be reckoned. Just as he has cheated me, so, hallowed Magna Mater, even so from him have you also got back everything (*sic illi . . . et relegisti cuncta*).[125] Just as the tree will dry up in your sanctuary, so may for him his reputation, credibility, good fortune and capacities dry up. I entrust to you, Lord Attis, the task of exacting punishment from him on my behalf (*ut me uindices ab eo*), <the task of bringing about> before a year is out his degrading, evil end (1–10)
>
> He/she denounces his name to the wives. Should any useful thing be done, so should he be useful[126] to us with his body. You will shudder to be cursed (11–15).

Despite various uncertainties about this *defixio* due to the lacunose condition of the tablet and the difficulty of knowing precisely what its author(s) had in mind by certain words or expressions, the general outlines of the situation are clear enough: Quintus has 'cheated' or 'defrauded' (*fraudem fecit*) the *defigens*, who, appealing to Magna Mater, in whose sanctuary the *defixio* is deposited (*depono*), curses the target with loss of financial standing ('Kredit' Blänsdorf

(2012), 104) and good name. He then entrusts to Attis, the consort of Magna Mater, the punishment (*uindices*) of Quintus, in the shape of a wretched end and death within the year. In other words, the *defixio* is of the prayer for justice type, an identification to which *uindicare*, 'avenge/punish' is a clear pointer,[127] as is the wish for the death of the offending party – a remarkably consistent feature of such prayers, which are nearly always motivated, as here, by theft or misappropriation of property. A second party, squeezing in ll. 11–15 in the left margin at 90 degrees to the main text, possibly in order to avoid writing on the back (Blänsdorf (2012), 103–4, 97) then appealed in addition to the dual agency of Magna Mater and Isis, assuming that it is to these that 'wives', *maritabus*, ll. 11–12, refer:[128] but the general thrust of these verses is the same, 'body' (*corpore* 14) encompassing the wished-for death of Quintus (Blänsdorf ad loc.).

There are a number of highly anomalous features in this text. In the first place, the divine agents charged with execution of the *defixio* are not mentioned, as is usually the case, at the outset, but only appear midway and at the end. Far more striking is the formulation of the curses by means of a series of 'persuasive analogies'[129] that draw specifically on the cultic practice of Magna Mater and the closely associated figure of Ma-Bellona, another ecstatic goddess of Eastern origin, as well as Attis. In the same way as the priests (*galli*) of Magna Mater lopped their penises in a ritual gesture of self-castration (*absciderunt*) which mimicked the self-emasculation of her follower Attis,[130] or the devotees of Ma-Bellona (*Bellonari*) hacked their flesh in a state of inspired frenzy (*conciderunt*), so the good name of Quintus is to be 'lopped' (3–4). As castrates, the *galli* were held in utter contempt,[131] a fate which is likewise to overtake Quintus (4–5); in effect, to become a non-person (4–5). Next follows an even more specific ritual detail. Just as the pine tree, the symbol of Attis, brought to the temple (*sancto*) of Magna Mater on 22 March by the *dendrophori*, 'tree-bearers',[132] would in time dry up (*siccabit*), so should Quintus' reputation, credibility, good fortune and capacities dry up and wither away (7–8). Such expropriation of specific details of cultic practice as a vehicle for a *defixio* appears unparalleled. It seems that we are dealing with a localised form of *defixio* which enlists by means of both prayer and analogy the agency of deities (Magna Mater, Attis, possibly Isis) who hardly feature elsewhere in curse tablets;[133] they are presumably deployed here because the importance of their cult in the Mainz region overrode the fact that, having no obvious connections to the Underworld, they are not the sort of gods to whom one would naturally turn for assistance in inscribing a curse. Normally, however, when the deities asked to execute a curse show a distinctly local colour they are indigenous to the area in question – and not, as with Magna Mater, major, supranational divinities in their own right. The usual pattern is to find a purely native god or goddess addressed, like Domna Fons (2.2.4/1: Itálica in Spain: cf. Tomlin (2010), 253–8) or the Celtic deities Moltinus (Kropp 7.5/1: Wilten near Innsbruck),[134] Niskus[135] and Maponus,[136] or alternatively some such figure conflated by syncretism with a Greek or Roman divinity, for example dea Ataecina Turibrigensis ['of Turibriga'] Proserpina (Kropp 2.3.1/1 = Audollent 122: Mérida in Spain) or dea Sulis Minerva, who features in many of the Bath curse tablets.

There is more to be said on the subject of the analogies discussed above. In addition to three instances already noted, there are two further persuasive analogies in *DTM* 6, the first (5–7) featuring one of the canonical markers of such *similia similibus* (as these are also called), the correlated terms *quomodo*, 'just as'... *sic*, 'even so', the second (12–15) flagged by the presence of comparative *sic*, 13. That makes a total of five analogies in a text of only fifteen lines (indeed the bulk of the *defixio* is occupied by these). In fact one of the most striking features of the Mainz *defixiones* is the quite remarkable density of the analogies which they employ as a vector for their curses,[137] a considerable number of them involving graphic allusions to self-mutilation by the *galli*,[138] as well as references to other dimensions of the Magna Mater cult.[139]

To be sure, *similia similibus* formulae became established early in *katadesmoi* as a way of underscoring the potency of the text,[140] appearing in such forms as *DTA* 67 (fourth or third century BCE) 'just as these words are cold and written backwards,[141] in the same way may the words of Kratēs be cold and backwards and those of the informers with them and the judges',[142] Audollent 25.16–18, 'just as you [*nekudaimones*] are unburied and dumb and voiceless and without a tongue ... so may my <courtroom> adversaries be voiceless, dumb and without a tongue', or the brief but drastic Kropp 1.5.4/1 'just as he is deserted by them, so may she be deserted in her cunt'. But cases where analogies subsume, as in *DTM* 6, the bulk of the *defixio*, or merely extend over a long section of text, as in a number of the Mainz tablets, have up till now been extremely rare.[143] For density of analogical material perhaps only Audollent 221[144] and the diptych Audollent 111–12 (= Kropp 4.3.1/1–2) can compete with the Mainz *defixiones*. I quote the latter.

> I give notice [to the powers of the Underworld] regarding the persons written below, Lentinus and Tasgillus, so that they may arrive at Pluto's halls and be gone from here to Proserpina. Just as this puppy harmed no one, so ... may they be unable to win this lawsuit. Just as the mother of this puppy was unable to defend it [evidently from sacrifice by the operator in a piece of persuasive analogy paralleled in another *defixio*],[145] so may their advocates be unable to defend

them, so may those enemies of mine be turned away [*auersos*] from this lawsuit [viz. ineffectual]. Just as this puppy is turned away and cannot rise, so may they too be unable to do so. May they be pierced through just like it.¹⁴⁶ Just as in this grave monument [the deposition site for the *defixio*] all living creatures have fallen silent and cannot rise, may they [magic words] concealed of the mind removed.

The analogies in Audollent 111–12 exhibit an essential coherence, keyed as they are to a single unifying, purposive concept, the respective incapacity of the puppy/its mother and the *defigens*' legal opponents to defend themselves. But such a neat fit is not always the case: the conceptual links which *defixiones* forge between analogy and desiderated outcome can at times be surprisingly tenuous. Instances are not far to seek, e.g. 'just as we do not know you [the inhabitant of a tomb where a *defixio* has been deposited], so Eupolis and Dionysios, Makareus, Aristokratēs and Dēmopolis, Kōmaios, Hermagoras are presenting themselves [in court] to do a terrible thing'¹⁴⁷ and 'such weight as this tablet of lead has, so should Eudēmus experience your [the infernal powers'] anger' (*defixio* from Carnuntum, Egger (1962)). In neither of these two texts is there an identifiable *tertium comparationis*. At times it might seem then that it mattered little to the *defigens* if the link between vehicle and tenor was intolerably weak. The mere fact of coining a persuasive analogy was felt to be per se efficacious: any comparand would serve.¹⁴⁸ And yet the tightly focused, cultic specificity of the analogies in the Mainz haul must serve as a caution – though even here the analogies are not without their incoherences (*DTM* 1.3–5 and 2.9–11).

Perhaps then it is safest to say that, for whatever reason – overwhelming passion of various kinds, inept adaptation of a formulaic template, a desire for punitive overkill, a level of education insufficient to inculcate the virtues of a structured argument – logic is not always at a premium in the world of *defixiones*. Nowhere is this better on display than in – to borrow Tomlin's felicitous phrase (p. 72) – 'the multiplication of mutually exclusive alternatives'. Some examples: *DTM* 5.6–8 'give <Liberalis> an evil death, so long as he lives' and Kropp 3.2/10 (Tomlin no. 10),¹⁴⁹ which invokes upon a thief 'utter' death, insomnia and childlessness 'until he returns my cloak to the temple of that deity', or a curse found in Kempten (Cambanodunum) in 1953, where the *Mutae Tacitae* (roughly the Spirits of Silence) are appealed to make mute one Quartus, 'like a bird fascinated by a basilisk', in other words to render him dumb in court proceedings, before appending the logically superfluous, but presumably hate-inspired coda 'let Quartus be thrust down to the Erinyes [Furies] and Orcus' (Egger (1963), 247–53).

Up to this point we have mentioned only tangentially the magical ensemble discovered in 1999 in the holding tank of the fountain of Anna Perenna in Rome, partly because it is more significant for the artefacts it contains than for inscribed curses, the primary concern of this chapter. In the words of its excavator Anna Piranomonte 'finds in the cistern [of the goddess] include 549 coins, 74 oil lamps, 22 randomly scattered *defixiones*, 18 cylindrical containers made of lead sheet, some containing poppets (anthropomorphic figurines), 3 containers made of clay [and] a large copper-alloy pot or bucket (*caccabus*)'.[150] Although there is nothing unusual about the offering of lamps to water deities (Piranomonte (2010), 202), what is striking is that six of the seventy-four had small, carefully rolled up *defixiones* inserted into their spouts – a notably unusual method of ritual deposition for curse-texts. Arguably, however, the most surprising aspect of the find was the enclosing of 'voodoo dolls' in some of the containers, since this was a practice hitherto associated in the main with Classical Athens of the fifth and fourth centuries BCE, thought to have ceased by the third century BCE (Németh (2013)). Yet now we have the same procedure reappearing across a vast gap in both time and space, in a Roman cache dating to the fourth century CE.

All of the lead containers consist of three cylinders that fit inside each other, somewhat in the manner of Russian dolls. Of particular note is inv. 475549, an illustrative study in a magical principle which has been aptly called 'pluralising for power'. This item was made of three canisters of the type just noted, hermetically sealed with resin. Of these the innermost contained a poppet (voodoo doll) fashioned of some organic matter. The doll was partially enclosed by a sheet of lead, through which had been driven two nails in a position corresponding to the figurine's midriff and lower legs. In addition, the sheet was inscribed with magical *charaktēres* and Greek letters, including the letter Θ, most likely intended to stand for Greek *thanatos*, 'death'. To summarise then, the doll that represents the target of the spell has been enfolded in a lead tablet, itself located in the innermost cylinder, the figurine has been systematically disfigured and its will symbolically nullified by the act of piercing with nails, it bears the sign of death, it has been hexed by the *charaktēres*, it has been firmly sealed off from the world of the living by resin and then, to the accompaniment of verbal curses, immersed in the cistern of Anna Perenna from which it could not readily be recovered (it was widely believed that a *defixio* remained operative unless brought to light). An extreme case certainly, but still an encapsulation of the belief that when it comes to magic, the more procedures were multiplied, the better. In the mind of the *defigens* of inv. 475549, all possibility of escape for his or her victim had surely been foreclosed.[151]

By way of conclusion to this survey, it is worth lingering, on account of the intrinsic interest of the story as well as certain characteristic features, over a famous British prayer for justice that enlisted the help of the Celtic god Nodens. Discovered during the early nineteenth century in the ruins of the god's temple at Lydney Park (Gloucestershire), Kropp 3.15/1 = Audollent 106, it runs:

> To the god Nodens. Silvianus has lost his ring. He has given half <of its value> to Nodens. May you not permit good health to any one in the group to which Senicianus belongs[152] until he brings <the ring> to the temple of Nodens

As has often been noted, it is typical of prayers for justice involving thievery, as this class of curse so often does, that the *defigens* should dedicate a portion of the value of the stolen object to a deity who is charged with its recovery,[153] the god being asked to effect the latter by inflicting punishment on the guilty party or parties. Also characteristic of British *defixiones*, almost all of which, in cases where a discernible motive survives, are prayers for justice resulting from a theft, is the request that the deity should withdraw the good health, *sanitas*, of the thieves, the curse often taking the form of a wish that the culprit pay for his or her crime 'with their blood' (*per sanguinem, sanguine suo*), in other words, with the loss of their physical well-being or – frequently – death (Tomlin, 67). In the case of Silvianus' ring it appears that the appeal for justice was unsuccessful. This at least is the intriguing possibility raised by the discovery by a ploughman in 1786, some thirty miles from Lydney, of a valuable ten-sided gold ring, datable to the same period as the just-quoted curse, bearing the legend 'Senicianus, may you live in God'; a motto which superseded theologically a seemingly earlier bust of Venus on the ring's bezel. It is tempting to hypothesise that Silvianus had his ring stolen by Senicianus, who then proclaimed his Christian affiliations over the pagan ones of Silvianus, and in a sense his 'ownership' of the ring; and that Silvianus, suspecting the identity of the culprit, in turn had his prayer for justice inscribed and deposited in Nodens' temple. Supposition this must however remain,[154] as must the equally alluring speculation that J.R.R. Tolkien, author of *The Hobbit* and *The Lord of the Rings*, but in his professional life a distinguished expert in Anglo-Saxon literature, got to know of the putative history of Silvianus' ring and its rediscovery when he was consulted for advice by Mortimer and Tessa Wheeler, the archaeologists who excavated the Lydney temple site in the late 1920s. He may also have learned of it through contact with R.G. Collingwood, the noted authority on Roman inscriptions who was a Fellow of the same Oxford college as Tolkien, and was likewise consulted by the Wheelers.[155] Tolkien enthusiasts have seized on the fact that the motifs of a curse, a ring, and the theft of a ring are shared by the history of Silvianus and *The Hobbit*, at which Tolkien was at work in 1928–9. It has been posited that, along with more obvious sources such as the *Niebelungenlied*, the former may have played its part in the genesis of Tolkien's mythical ring.

Charming though these speculations are, they involve a chain of reasoning fashioned more in self-persuasion than certainty. As such, they serve, however, as a fitting coda to this chapter on *defixiones*, since these too, notwithstanding the impressive body of evidence that people believed in the efficacy of the medium and of magic more generally, must surely at times have been conceived more in hope and in the interest of a psychologically comforting belief that one was *doing* something to right an existing or imminent wrong, than in any well-founded sense that the *defixio* would actually produce the desired outcome.

Fig. 4 The inspiration for Tolkien's ring? Ring of Silvianus, Wikimedia Commons/ CC-BY 2.0.

Appendix: did *defixiones* work?

A number of scholars have thought so.[156] That they were *believed* to work, at any rate, is clear from a number of factors: the ubiquity and longevity of the practice (which lasted for over a thousand years); the very real fear that people manifested of them; the various stratagems devised to counter their effects; the fact that in notorious cases where orators 'dried up' unexpectedly in court, they were able with a degree of credibility to claim to have been the victims of a well-established type of *defixio*, which sought to bind the tongues of forensic opponents.[157]

But *how* were *defixiones* thought to work? Above all, by enlisting successfully the agency of supernatural powers. In pre-Empire *defixiones* these tend to be the chthonic deities of the Greek pantheon, to whom, as noted above, the victims were 'delivered, handed over, registered with', and the like, in the expectation that the gods would act upon the appeals and injunctions contained in the tablets. In the specialised case of 'prayers for justice', gods both infernal and Olympian were appealed to in their *specific* capacity as upholders of justice,[158] an interest in maintaining which is attested in the so-called 'confession inscriptions', wherein malefactors publicly confessed their wrongdoings and the signal punishments that the gods had exacted from them and their families in retribution for their crimes.[159] Moreover, in British *defixiones*, which are almost exclusively of the 'prayer for justice' type, tangible and sometimes substantial rewards are regularly offered to the deities as an extra incentive to help.

In later texts there is, as remarked earlier, a pronounced tendency to co-opt the assistance of the *nekudaimones*, the spirits of the dead persons – supposedly inimical to the living and hence willing to be enlisted as agents – in whose grave the curse tablet was deposited; an example is *SM* 45 (Gager no. 30) '*nekudaimones* and *aōroi* ... rouse yourself and seek out Euphemia ... let her not be able to sleep etc.' In such cases the *nekudaimones* might act on their own, or alternatively under the aegis of more powerful entities, as in Audollent 271 (Gager no. 36). In instances where *defixiones* were figured as letters, the *nekudaimōn* seems to have functioned as an emissary to convey the message to the subterranean deities for their attention.

But what of the not inconsiderable number of curse-texts where no spirits are invoked or no verbs of binding are present, leaving us with no more than a sequence of names in the accusative case? In such cases the *defigens* seems to have assumed that the rites and prayers attendant upon deposition of the *defixio* made his or her intention clear to the powers whom he or she required to enact them, and that before the list of names was mentally to be supplied the verb 'I bind'. Other explanations of how *defixiones* were thought to function take us into more modern territory. Faraone for example has spoken of a 'direct binding formula', such as 'I bind X with a leaden bond' (*DTA* 34), as an instance of so-called 'performative speech', whereby the utterance itself actualises the import of the words, brings its intent into reality.[160] Lest this seem too abstract a formulation, it is important to remember that words were widely believed to have a magical, incantatory force, as we see for example in Gorgias's rhetorical showpiece *Helen*.

In other cases, recourse was had to what is now styled 'persuasive analogy'. This might assume a largely verbal form, e.g. 'and just as this corpse lies useless, so may all the words and deeds of Theodora be useless in regard to Charias' (Audollent 68 = Gager no. 22), or the words may be combined with a ritual action, as in Audollent 222A and B 'just as I have ripped the tongue from a living cockerel and it can no longer give voice, so may my courtroom opponents be likewise dumb and voiceless'. At other times the curse may be symbolically reinforced by dolls or figurines which enacted by their posture (hands behind back, twisting into contorted positions etc.) the torturous fate desired for the target; or the inscribing of the curse tablet in retrograde form may represent imagistically the backwards movement of his fortunes which is wished upon the target (e.g. *DTA* 109 = Gager no. 61). Or again, it has been suggested, the appearance of some tablets, when rolled up, as long, narrow strips of lead may make of them 'speaking objects' which symbolise the magical *desmoi* or *katadesmoi*, 'bonds, chains', which were meant to bind or immobilise the target.[161] In all of the above the theoretical language may be of the present, but, as we have seen (and will see further below), the *similia similibus* principle which is operative in each and every one of them is so integral to all aspects of ancient magic that a belief in its efficacy, when harnessed to malign intent in the *defixiones*, can scarcely be in doubt.

It is important to note that the procedures catalogued above more often than not operated in combination with one another, rather than in stand-alone form, reflecting the magical principle of 'pluralising for power'. To conclude, a word on what we may be called the psychosomatic dimension of *defixiones*. It has been suggested that psychic mechanisms – a belief in the power of *defixiones*, an awareness that they might have been cursed (alternatively the knowledge that they had been hexed),[162] a guilty conscience in the case of the thieves who are so often the object of British *defixiones* – might have affected adversely the physical well-being of the targets.[163] In particular, it has been posited that such mental unease may have brought about precisely that sleeplessness which is so often enjoined upon enemies in *defixiones*, especially if the victim knew that the terms of the curse involved denial of sleep.[164] This seems a reasonable proposition, especially since it is well-documented – in societies other than ancient Greece and Rome – that an awareness of having been cursed can lead to the illness, even death of the subject of the curse. Caution, however, seems in order when it is further proposed that the physical afflictions invoked in curse tablets – paralysis of the limbs, loss of sight, loss of mental faculties and so on – are consonant with recognised psychosomatic disorders such as lethargy, mental disorientation and so on. For it is hard to swallow what seems implicit in this argument; that the choice of bodily and mental symptoms for inclusion in curse tablets has been *determined* by an awareness *avant la lettre* of the possible physical manifestations in an individual of mental terrors experienced by him. And in any case, in the North African circus *defixiones* the same afflictions, blindness, loss of limb-power and so on, are called down upon the horses of rival factions, which can hardly be said to have been suffering from psychosomatic disorders caused by mental angst!

Notes

1 It is not my purpose here to give a detailed account of *defixiones*, for which see Gager 3–41; Ogden (1999), 1–90; Eidinow (2007), Chapters 7–12; and Urbanová (2018), who, despite the title of her book, makes frequent reference to Greek, not just Latin *defixiones*; also Graf (1997), 118–74. Instead I explore some recent developments in the study of *defixiones*, discuss some areas of contention, and in particular seek to draw out an enhanced picture of the medium with the aid of some recently discovered texts.

2 Referring in particular to the numerous North African *defixiones* against charioteers and their horses.

3 Identical language in NGCT 79. On 'bind down' see further Eidinow (2007), 141.

4 Although *defixio* has become the accepted scholarly term for curse tablets, the noun is only found in a bilingual gloss. The verb *defigere* does however occur in some British curse tablets (Ogden (1999), 5), in the expression *deuotum defictum* (for *defixum*) in *DTM* 4.10, and in a new *defixio* from Verona published by Sánchez Natalías (2016), who lists earlier occurrences.

5 For example, *SGD* 82 was 'folded horizontally six times, then pierced with a nail' (Jordan ad loc.).

6 Ogden (1999), 14, Audollent 49.16–17 (*c.* 300 BCE) 'all these I bind down, make to disappear, inter, nail down'. For clear evidence that the act of piercing something

had inhibiting force, see *DTA* 97. It is also relevant that nails were a symbol of the goddess Necessity (Watson (1991), 195–6), an entity often invoked to reinforce the constraining effect of binding spells.
7. The commonest targets of commercial *defixiones* are rival innkeepers: details in Lamont (2015), 164–5, 172.
8. The expression 'in gore and in ashes' is a formula lifted directly from some of the bloodiest parts of Homer, and hence indicative of the animus which drives the present *defixio*, as it does many others: see below on this.
9. An elaborate way of saying that curse will never be lifted (see Lamont (2015)), a standard idea in *defixiones*: cf. Voutiras (1998), 40.
10. This rare Greek word, like Latin *canis*, seems to refer to the lowest throw of the dice (Lamont (2015), 170), a reminder that taverns were venues for gambling (and prostitution), as well as drinking.
11. The *denarius* is a unit of coinage.
12. Riess (2012), 223. This is not to rule out some degree of Middle Eastern influence on their genesis: cf. Ogden (1999), 79–81; M. Martin (2010), 13–15.
13. For another possible scenario, see Graf (1997), 173.
14. Kropp 2.2.2/1, from the second half of the first century BCE: cf. Versnel (1998), 236 n.46. Urbanová (2018), 34 dates Kropp 1.5.4/1 and 10.1/1, respectively from Pompeii and Delos, to the second half of the second century BCE, describing them as 'the two oldest Latin curse tablets', without however specifying her criteria for dating. Well before that, however, curse tablets were being written in Italy in both Oscan and Etruscan, establishing the dissemination of Greek magical practices among the people of the Italian peninsula as early as the third century BCE (Dickie (2001), 128–9). On the Oscan tablets see now Murano (2012).
15. Gager 13–14, Riess (2012), 185–6. Metre: O'Connell (2017).
16. Later tablets can however also assume such a form, e.g. some of the *defixiones* from Roman Bath (Aquae Sulis) or Mainz (*DTM*).
17. Bibliography on these by F. Maltomini at *P. Oxy.* 5304 (2016), 62.
18. Hence the tart remarks of St Jerome *Epist.* 75.3.1 (Migne *Patrologia Latina* 22.637) 'Armagil, Barbelos, Abraxas, Balsamus and the ridiculous Leusibora and the like, more monstrosities than names, which, in order to stir up the feelings of ignorant types and pathetic women <the magicians> draw as if from Jewish sources, terrifying all those simple souls by the alien sound, in order that they may be the more awestruck by what they don't understand'.
19. For scholarly scepticism about the possibility of interpreting magical formulae, see Blänsdorf (2010a), 225; similarly Bonner (1950), 68 and 117, but note now McDonald (2016) for a contrary view. In general on *uoces magicae* see Martinez (1991) passim, who derives them from Hebrew, Egyptian and Aramaic; Frankfurter (1994), 199–205; Brashear (1995), 3429–38; and Gager 5–9, who, referring to

Tambiah (1968), makes the significant point that their incomprehensibility was no bar to their supposed efficacy, rather the reverse.

20 See McCown (1923); and Bernabé (2013), who argues that the meaningless *Ephesia grammata* developed from originally meaningful words in early hexametric inscriptions. An exception to the pattern of unintelligibility is *damnameneus*, which clearly reflects its origin in the Greek verb *damaō*, 'to subdue'. Occurring in Audollent 267 and *SGD* 145 and 147, the term sits neatly with the whole ethos of *defixiones*.

21 Broadly speaking, these images represent the victims of the *defixio* in a situation of restraint/torture, or the supernatural beings charged with executing the curse. For illustrations see Gager. The pictorial dimension of the *defixiones* adds supplementary potency to the curses (Jendza (2013)).

22 Ogden (1999), 5 with bibliography; Eidinow (2007), 141. Riess (2012), 164 extends the life-cycle 'well into the late Byzantine and Ottoman periods'.

23 Cf. Jordan (1985), 207; Watson (1991), 196–7; Ogden (1999), 15–18, the last two with further bibliography.

24 Where lived the water nymphs who were requested to enact the *defixio*, as in curse-text no. 7 from the Anna Perenna magical ensemble in Rome. One of the 'Sethian' *defixiones* from Rome, if correctly emended by Jordan (1980), appeals to 'you watery nymphs of the Underworld, who dwell in this place'. In the imperial period there seems to have been a marked preference for depositing *defixiones* in sacred springs (M. Martin (2010), 27).

25 For deposition in wells see Jordan (1985).

26 Knidos: Audollent nos. 1–13, with Gager no. 89, pp. 188–90; Ogden (1999), 15. Corinth: Stroud (2013).

27 Voutiras (1998), 97; Riess (2012), 213 n.244 (also Ritner (1993), 178–9). The idea seems to have been that the dead person should personally convey the *defixio* to the Underworld for implementation there.

28 Also in a few later instances of so-called 'onomastic' curses, curses bearing only the name or names of persons to be hexed: cf. Bounegru and Németh (2013).

29 Gager 20; Riess (2012), 177–83; Lamont (2015), 172–3.

30 Sometimes indeed *defixiones* were left uninscribed, presumably by persons unable to write who assumed that the gods who were to enact their curses could divine the authors' intentions.

31 For the various Greek and Latin terms used to deliver the targeted persons to the supernatural entities charged with implementing *defixiones*, see Audollent, lvii–viii; Ogden (1999), 26; Jeanneret (1917), 79; Faraone (1991); Riess (2012), 208–10; with Kropp (2010) for suggested modifications of Faraone's schema.

32 Also in these later *defixiones* we find the names of Oriental, Jewish and Egyptian deities such as Iaō, El, Nepthō, Ereschigal and Serapis, e.g. Audollent 271.1–4.

33 E.g. *DTA* 102 and 103; Kropp 6/2/1; Graf (1997), 130–1 with n.40; Versnel (2002a), 60.
34 *PGM* 4.2732, part of a violent love spell, enlists the aid of heroes who died untimely 'who have animosity in their hearts', a phrase which may, however, be corrupt.
35 See Tupet (1976), 12; Martinez (1991), 48–9; Johnston (1999), 77–80; Ogden (1999), 16–17, 22 and (2008), 52; Riess (2012), 179–80. The widely accepted view that the prematurely dead readily lent their services to *defigentes* because of hostility to the living is challenged by Baills-Talbi and Dasen (2008).
36 The impression given in the quoted words that curse tablets were invariably made of lead does, however, require modification (as Jordan (1981) and NGCT, 5–6, was aware). Although lead was by far the most common medium, there is evidence for the use of other less robust materials e.g. *DTA* 55.16–17 'all these I bind down in lead and in wax and in water/wine'; see also Eidinow (2007), 285 n.5; Ogden (1999), 10–11. The reasons for the predominance of lead were both practical and symbolic: cf. Martinez (1991), 2–6; Watson (1991), 194–5; Ogden (1999), 11–13; Urbanová (2018), 36–7; and Tomlin (1988), 81–2, who cautions, however, that pure lead is hardly ever found among the Bath tablets. Graf (1997), 133 questions scholarly claims that the choice of lead for *defixiones* had from the beginning some symbolic force.
37 Of the 220 texts included by Wünsch in *DTA*, fourteen had already appeared in publications by other scholars. Of the remaining 206, the 179 which are known to have been in Berlin before the war have been recovered. The fate of the missing tablets is unknown.
38 This account of the disappearance and rediscovery of the texts is based on Curbera (2012). Curbera (2015a) offers new versions of seven texts which featured in *DTA*.
39 Discussed by Eidinow (2007), 157–63. M. Martin (2010), 93 notes that choregic contests seem to furnish the earliest venue for *defixiones* with an agonistic character.
40 Eidinow (2012).
41 Winkler (1991) conjured up for the erotic *defixiones* and love spells of the *PGM* a situation in which well-born young men were competing for enhanced social prestige by capturing in marriage the hands of highly closeted virgins, a hypothesis too far: see Chapter 2.
42 The main criticisms have come from M. Martin (2010), 67–8; Riess (2012), 192–6; Gordon (2013), 266–9 and (2014), 783–4; and above all Dreher (2012). Urbanová (2018), while not unaware (p. 88) that some have found the idea of prayers for justice as a discrete category problematical, distinguishes sharply between regular *defixiones* (forensic, amatory etc.: see immediately below in the text), which she styles 'curses', and prayers for justice.
43 See Faraone (1991), 15 with n.67 for the point that judicial curses in particular were written before the conclusion of a trial with the intention of influencing its outcome. Similarly M. Martin (2010), 47. *Defixiones* aimed at fixing the outcome of a chariot

race or a gladiatorial contest were self-evidently also pre-emptive. So too the amatory *DTA* 78.
44 NGCT 23. Cf. Elderkin (1936), tablet 3.2–4; and *DTA* 98.6–7 and 102a6–9 for similar language.
45 Reasons for this: Versnel (1991a), 62. Exceptions to the rule of non-disclosure of identity by the *defigens* include *SGD* 162, a recently published Spanish judicial *defixio* of the first century BCE (Stylow (2012)) and the amatory tablets Audollent 270–1, *SM* 38 and 46–51, where it was presumably crucial to specify to the *di agentes* beyond possibility of error who was to be brought to whom.
46 As Gordon (2014), 784 points out, it is something of a paradox that the fiercest and most venomous attacks on the target are levelled in so-called prayers for justice, rather than the notionally more malign 'straight' *defixiones*.
47 E.g. Audollent 85 = Gager no. 20, Audollent 198, which also has characteristics of the prayer for justice: see ll. 38–40 (infidelity towards the curser).
48 For spells of this type see e.g. Jordan (1985) nos. 7–9.
49 Although present in his corpus, no. 110 = Gager no. 16. The theatrical type was known to Wünsch: see *DTA* 34 and 45. On competitive curses see Tremel (2004).
50 Neatly exemplified by a phrase in *SGD* 88, 'these people are registered for misfortune (*duspragiai*) in their profit': Cf. Eidinow (2007), 425.
51 A category which largely overlaps with Faraone's *philia* spells, discussed in Chapter 2.
52 An exhaustive database of Greek and Roman curse tablets is found in the online *Thesaurus Defixionum Magdeburgensis* (details in the Bibliography).
53 E.g. curses aimed at inflicting suffering on the various limbs of the body, a very common type, or the wish often met in the Bath *defixiones* that a thief cannot pay for his crime 'except by the shedding of his blood'.
54 *PGM* 62.76–106, containing the details 'let the genitals and womb of X be open and let there be bleeding night and day', discussed by Aubert (1989), 428–35. See also Faraone (2009).
55 Anna Perenna cache text no. 7, discussed by Blänsdorf (2010a) 221–7 and Faraone (2010).
56 A *defixio* from Saguntum does however curse the eye, along with the bosom and strength, of an individual who has misappropriated some money (Corell (2000)), improved by Tomlin (2010), 265–8.
57 The translation aims at preserving the halting and repetitious character of the original. Incoherences and gaps in the translation of Side B are due to the badly damaged condition of the text.
58 'Hounds of Orcus' here and 'Hounds of Orcus, Three-headed creatures of Orcus' Side A11–12 refer to the triple-headed Hell-Hound Cerberus, charged with guarding the entrance to the Underworld. Cerberus is invoked in many other *defixiones*, most notably in Kropp 1.7.2/1 ('deliver <my enemies> to your three-headed and two-headed

hounds, so that they can rip away their heads, thoughts and hearts') where, as here, he is pluralised. Dogs are infernal creatures: Gow (1965) on Theocr. *Id.* 2.12; Burriss (1935).

59 Latin *ustores*. Burning was one of the punishments traditionally meted out in Hades to sinners. Bevilacqua (2006–7) ad loc. translates 'cremators', on the basis that *ustor* is the term for a slave charged with cremating corpses. But it is not clear why such individuals should exercise the same function in the Underworld, after corpses had already been disposed of in the upper world, most commonly by incineration.

60 The Harpies, whose name means 'the Snatchers', were birds with the faces of maidens (Verg. *Aen.* 3.216) of Stygian origin (ibid. 215, 252), who carried off or befouled the food of the blind king Phineus. Chthonic beings like these often had birdlike characteristics (Watson (2003), on Hor. *Epod.* 5.92–3).

61 A monster killed by Bellerophōn which 'was a lion in front, a snake behind and a goat (*chimaira*) in the middle, and breathed out from her jaws the terrible might of blazing fire' Hom. *Il.* 6.181–2.

62 Geryones or Geryon was a three-headed, six-armed and six-legged monstrous herdsman who lived in the far west. He was killed by Heracles and his cattle taken as one of the hero's Labours. See Davies and Finglass (2014), 230–43.

63 An inclusive type of formula common in *defixiones*, intended to cover all possible bases when specifying the target or the deity whose aid was being invoked. Parallels in Bevilacqua (2006–7) ad loc.

64 For eyes targeted in *defixiones*, see Bevilacqua (2006–7) ad loc. and the Anna Perenna text (no. 7) discussed above.

65 Latin *malam frontem*. The *frons*, brow, was thought of in Antiquity as manifesting a person's feelings, often feelings of distress (Watson (2003) on Hor. *Epod.* 13.5). Something of the sort seems to be the sense here. Bevilacqua renders 'a foolish mind', comparing *malam mentem*, 'madness', in *DTM* 5.6.

66 In Ovid's account *Fasti* 6. 130–68 of the *striges*, vampiric birdlike creatures related to the Harpies, these are said (137) to 'rend the intestines' of newborns.

67 Latin *ad superos*; cf. Verg. *Aen.* 6.481–2 *hic multum fleti ad superos belloque caduci/ Dardanidae*, 'here (Aeneas was met by) Trojans who were much bewailed in the world above when they fell in war'.

68 Shipwreck is a frequent theme of literary curses.

69 The 'h' of Himaera stands for the initial chi (χ) of Chimaera (cf. Ximaera A3).

70 Bevilacqua's explanation of *tunica* as equivalent to the *chitōn*, 'tunic' put about Odysseus by the goddess in order to disguise him as a mendicant makes no sense. The context of B27–31 (and the parallel analogies in 28–9) demands some much more harmful action. *Tunica* is puzzling. Perhaps a reference to Minerva's aegis, inter alia conceived of as a breastplate (*RE* 1.971 s.v.) – a possible meaning of *tunica* – with which she terrified her enemies (Verg. *Aen.* 8.435 *aegidaque horriferam*)?

71 *[H]oc/ mandatum dedit* Side B33–4. *Mandare* in prayers for justice, as Versnel (1991a), 83 shows, signifies 'assign, entrust' to the divine powers the task of executing the operator's pleas, as expressed in the curse.
72 Cf. Side B33 'there appeals to you (the infernal powers) he who....'
73 For *scelus* of amatory betrayal, see Pichon (1966), s.v. Cf. the expression *iniurium fas* employed of amatory treachery in Side A3 of the Gross-Gerau *defixio* discussed directly below in the text.
74 Cf. Bevilacqua (2006–7), 327 and id. 2009.
75 Not so lethal in intent, but in the same vein, i.e. the curse of a rejected lover, is the first of five *defixiones* from the Kerameikos discussed by Curbera (2016). It runs 'we bind down Glykera the wife of Dion before the gods of the Underworld, so that she may be punished and her marriage come to nothing. We bind down Dion's wife Glykera before Hermes Eriounios, the Chthonian: her cunt, her self-wilfulness, her debauchery and everything of the miscreant Glykera'.
76 The closest parallel to the *defixio*'s list which I have been able to find in another documentary magical text is *PGM* 4.1400–2, 'to the Fates (*Moirai*), Powers of Compulsion, Malignities, Plague, Envy and those who died prematurely, or by violence'.
77 A number of the creatures in Virgil's account do not normally feature in chthonic myth. The author of the *defixio* may consciously have followed Virgil's lead by placing in the Underworld various monsters, the Sphinx, Circe and so on, not usually associated with the infernal regions.
78 Briareus was the most prominent of the three Hundred-Handers, monstrous creatures born to *Gaia* and *Ouranos* (Hes. *Theog.* 147–53). There was a tendency in later literature to run together the various monstrous broods of *Gaia*. Indeed Briareus appears in Callim. *H. Del.* 142–3 as one of the Giants imprisoned under Mount Etna.
79 Admittedly found in other *defixiones* (n.58), but the template here is entirely literary.
80 For the *striges* see n.66 supra.
81 The 'Ortygiae' of the text, following mention of two species of fabulous bird, ought to mean 'Ortygian birds', that is to say, quails, Gk. *ortyges*, which derived their name from Apollo's sacred island of Ortygia, first mentioned in Hom. *Ody.* 5.121–4, 15.404, and better known as Delos, whither quails migrated annually. But it is hard to see how these inoffensive little birds fit the violent context (albeit Pliny *HN* 10.64–9 ascribes to them some sinister aspects). Bevilacqua ad loc. suggests that *Ortygiae* are some unidentified type of bird of prey.
82 A hybrid being with the body of an animal, usually a lion, and a female head. Of Egyptian and Mesopotamian origin, the sphinx is best known in a Classical context as preying on the Thebans until disposed of by Oedipus.
83 The Sirens were, as Ov. *Ars* 3.311–12 puts it, 'monsters of the sea, who with their tuneful voices detained ships no matter how fast they sped', *monstra maris Sirenes*

erant quae uoce canora/ quamlibet admissas detinuere rates: cf. Side B28 *monstrinae Sirenidae cantibus homines detinebant*. Pliny *HN* 10.136, discussing fabulous birds, says of the Sirens that when people charmed by their song are sunk in a deep sleep, they tear them to pieces (*lacerent*), a detail which sits well with the violent nature of the creatures invoked in Side A1ff., where the Sirens are first mentioned in our text.

84 Bevilacqua (2006–7) ad loc. and (2010), 81 thinks the reference in *Ossufragae* is to the homonymous bird of prey, 'probably the lammergeyer or bearded vulture' (*OLD*), but the context seems to demand some more fantastical creature. *Virga* is presumably the rod or staff of Mercury with which he 'calls forth pale shades from Orcus and sends down others to grim Tartarus' (Verg. *Aen.* 4.242–3), but its personification here as an instrument of punishment is unique. For *ustores*, see n.59 supra.

85 'Töpferdämonen', in the elegant formulation of Markwald (1986), 241. A popular superstition may underlie the invention of these creatures. According to Plin. *HN* 28.19 'many believe that pottery can be smashed by incantations'.

86 'Herodotean' *Life of Homer* Chapter 32. Text as in Merkelbach and West (1967), 155–6, except that I read *Amaktos* and *Asbestos* in l. 9.

87 For the dating see Gager 155 n.13.

88 Two additions to the isolated instances already noted are Tethys (Audollent 68), Cacus (Kropp 7.5/1) and Palaemon (NGCT 14), on whom see Eidinow (2007), 148 n.45.

89 That is, in instances where divine assistance is invoked in a *defixio*, which is by no means always the case.

90 Cf. also e.g. *SGD* 20 and NGCT 66. See further Watson (1991), 198 n.33.

91 E.g. Corell (2000) line 3 (= Kropp 2.1.3/3) is aimed at *Heracla conseruus meus*, 'Heracles my fellow-slave'. In a Cordoban curse tablet (Kropp 2.2.3/1) the *defigens* is *Dionysia Den<t>atiai ancilla* ('maidservant'):

92 E.g. *SGD* 118, Kropp 1.4.3/1, 1.5.3/2 (Audollent 199), 2.2.3/3, 3.2/9 (Tomlin no. 9), 11.1.1/2 (Audollent 216).

93 E.g. Kropp 1.5.6/1, 1.7.1/1, 2.1.1/1, 4.2.1/1, 11.1.1/1 (Audollent 215).

94 Cf. *DTA* 68, 75 and 87, and *SGD* 11, which talk of 'workshops', a euphemism for brothels, or 'inns', venues for prostitution. Cf. also Audollent 86 with Eidinow (2007), 217–18, Jordan (1999b), no. 3 Side A, pp. 120–3, and, from a later period, Jordan (1985), texts 8 and 9. Wünsch (1909), 37–41 discussed a curse tablet (= NGCT 84) where one Pleitōria seeks to inhibit Clōdia Valeria Sōphrosyne, an *ergastillaria*, from sending her to an *ergastillum*, normally a place where delinquent slaves were sent, but conceivably here signifying a brothel: for the wish to avoid this fate, cf. Antiphon 1, with Faraone (1999), 114.

95 Cf. *SGD* 48; a seamstress *SGD* 72; a greengrocer *SGD* 167 s.v. 'Antioch', NGCT 109.

96 M. Martin (2010), 35–6, adducing instances of upper-class targets, rightly dismisses the view of Bernand (1991), 30–4 and others (ap. Gordon (2009), 209 n.1) that

'magic is the language of the marginal'. Note again Pliny's remark (*HN* 30.19) 'there is no one who does not fear being cursed (*defigi*) with imprecations'.
97 For Germanicus see Chapter 2. Other cases: three judicial curses from Ampurias in Spain (Kropp 2.1.1/2–4) aimed a *procurator Augusti* and two imperial legates, Sánchez Natalías (2012), 144 n.9.
98 Similarly the majority of the Roman-era *defixiones* from well 5 in the Athenian agora published by Jordan (1985) show an elegant and fluent scribal hand.
99 For the motif, cf. the formulary *P. Oxy.* 4468.6 and 28–9 (probably an amatory spell), also 'let their strength dry up' in a *defixio* from Saguntum discussed by Tomlin (2010), 264–8.
100 For the irony, cf. Kropp 1.4.4/3 (Audollent 139), Kropp 6/2/1 and now Sánchez Natalías (2014).
101 Text of Sherwood Fox (1912), no. 1 (pp. 17–19), supplemented from the four other parallel texts in the cache, which are all composed using the same formulary. Also available as Kropp 1.4.4/8.
102 For the unusual detail of a curse on eyebrows – a marker of the inclusiveness of bodily curses – cf. *DTA* 89a10 = Curbera (2015a), item 3, A15.
103 See also the discussion of Jordan (1980), 64–5.
104 *DTM* 1.31–4 and Kropp 3.2/76 (Tomlin no. 97) 'in order that [the thief or any complicit individual] may be pierced in his blood, his eyes and all his limbs, or have all his innards quite eaten up'.
105 As Scholz (2011) notes, in the numerous Latin *defixiones* that deal with theft, inheritance disputes and the like, it is never a matter of capital offences, but of small-scale criminality. In my 1991 volume *Arae* I identified a mismatch between the often insignificant nature of a given offence and the ferocity and sheer volume of the imprecations which the misdeed evoked as a peculiar marker of the literary imprecations of the Hellenistic age; but fresh discoveries of curse tablets and the scholarship since then have persuaded me that the mismatch is characteristic of *defixiones* too.
106 *SGD* 58 (first century BCE–first century CE) = Eidinow (2007), 418–19, but see also Versnel (1998), 233 for improved readings.
107 See particularly MacMullen (1986). Further bibliography in Versnel (1998), 227 n.26.
108 Riess (2012), 164–234. See also Ripat (2014), 341, 356 n.7.
109 For such reluctance see Faraone (1991), 9–10, 20, 26 n.38 *et alibi* (details in Riess (2012), 189 n.124); Versnel (1991a), 61, (2002a), 47; Voutiras (1998), 37 n.82; Ogden (1999), 73 and 22; Eidinow (2007), 151–2. Graf (1997), 159 and 217 attempts to rationalise as non-lethal two *defixiones* with evident deadly intent. M. Martin (2010), 142 also underplays the frequency with which *defixiones* invoke destruction upon their targets. In similar vein, Gager 22 cautions against reading

literally the various ills called down upon the victims of curses. By contrast, Kropp (2010), in renaming as a 'request formula' Faraone's 'prayer formula' of 1991 (viz. prayer as one means of soliciting supernatural assistance for the practitioner), identifies a sub-category of request calling for the target's death (365-7).

110 In the examples which follow I append the reason for the curse, where evident.

111 Evidently the name of the name of the person in whose tomb the *defixio* has been deposited. For similar naming of the dead person whose grave serves as a repository for a *defixio*, cf. Audollent 43, Voutiras (1998), line 2.

112 Elderkin (1936), tablet 2, col. 1.21-2.

113 Item no. 151 in Bonner (1950) carries the message 'as the [mythical] Memnon, son of the goddess of the Dawn lies dead, so may also Antipater, son of Philippa'. More graphically still, some of Bonner's magical gems show figures either undergoing mutilation (e.g. with blood jetting from neck and wrists), or being mutilated by some demonic figure – evidently a pictorial conjuration of what the amulet-wearer desires for an enemy or an antagonist, such as a rival charioteer.

114 A few *defixiones* flag themselves as *kataklitika*, by using an imperative form of the verbs *klinein/kataklinein*, 'to send a person to bed with an illness', or by self-designation as a *euchē kataklitikē*, 'a curse to send someone to bed with an illness'. In at least three cases (*SGD* 146, 163; NGCT 51) the injunction to cause illness is followed by one enjoining death for the target. See further Gaffino (2002).

115 A possible exception to the broader pattern is *SGD* 136, which contains the expression 'I destroy Saturnina for all time through madness'. But usually when someone is 'destroyed' by a curse (*apollumi, apolluō*), this signifies death.

116 For the various connotations of *pros* in defixiones, see Riess (2012), 208-10.

117 See Brashear (1979), 268 for instances, further *P. Oxy.* 4468. verso col. 2.9-10, Faraone (1992), 321-2, (2000), 202-9.

118 See Tomlin (2010), 246-7 et passim.

119 Blänsdorf (2008a), 51-2 offers an excellent synthesis of the novel features of the Mainz *defixiones*.

120 Blänsdorf (2008a), 61-2. The same analogy in *DTM* 10 and 12; possibly also in *DTM* 7 p. 110

121 Roughly one-fifth of *DTM* 2, for example, has been lost to the fire. Along with the readable tablets were found many lumps of molten lead, evidently texts which had been fully destroyed by the sacrificial fire, as the operators intended (Blänsdorf (2010c), 156-7).

122 Latin text: *Quintum in hac tabula depon[o] auersum/ se suisque rationibus uitaeque male consum/mantem. ita ut galli Bellonariue absciderunt concide/runtue se, sic illi abscissa sit fides fama faculit[a]s. nec illi/ in numero hominum sunt, neque ille sit. q[u]omodo et ille/ mihi fraudem fecit, sic illi, sancta Mater Magn[a] et relegis[ti]/ cuncta. ita ut arbor siccabit se in sancto, sic et illi siccet/ fama fides fortuna faculitas.*

*tibi commendo, Attihi d(o)mine,/ ut me uindices ab eo, ut intra annum uertente[m]
... exitum/ illius uilem malum* (1–10) *ponit nom(en) huius mari/tabus I si agatur
ulla/ res utilis, sic ille nobis/ utilis sit suo corpore./ sacrari horrebis* (11–15)

123 A Latin equivalent of the *katatithenai* or *parakatatithenai* of Greek *defixiones*.
124 The meaning of *auersum* is contested. Blänsdorf ad loc. explains 'who has turned against himself', Faraone and Kropp (2010), 356, invoking the fact that *Quinti nomen* appears upside down in line 7, and the use of compounds of *uertere* in other *defixiones* to refer to upside down or retrograde writing which is meant to suggest analogically the inversion or retrogression of the target's affairs, take line 1 as a syntactical unit and translate 'I set Quintus down in this tablet *auersum*'.
125 *Relegisti* is puzzling. One expects a present subjunctive *relegas* with optative force, to parallel *sit* 4, *sit* 5 and *siccet* 7 (Blänsdorf (2010c), 162 seems to recognise this when he paraphrases 'just as Quintus committed fraud, so is Magna Mater to deceive him'). Urbanová (2018), 90–1 and 125 reads *relegis*, but translates this as an imperative, 'take everything away from him'. The general sense is evidently that the goddess is to recover on behalf of the aggrieved party what was stolen.
126 Ironic? For instances of irony in *defixiones* cf. the via Ostiense curse tablet Side B31 and n.100 supra.
127 For instances of *uindicare* with this sense in *defixiones* see Tomlin on his no. 35, line 4 and id. (2018), pp. 196 and 284. For similar language in Greek prayers for justice, cf. Audollent 42 B10–12 'we enrol them for punishments and penalty and retribution', *SGD* 58A3, B3 'punish [an unidentified thief]'.
128 The two goddesses had Attis and Osiris respectively as their consorts.
129 That is, the notion that by the process of describing verbally a given situation or executing a given action, the corresponding result will be produced in the target of a spell. The term is grounded in so-called pragmalinguistics, and is based on J.L. Austin's theory of performative speech. A clear exposition of the theory in Kropp (2010). See also Chapter 1.
130 Cf. *DTM* 2.5–6 *quomodo / galli se secant et praecidunt uirilia sua*, 'just as the Galli cut themselves and lop off the genitals', Watson and Watson (2014), on Juv. 6. 514–15.
131 Cf. Watson (2003), on Hor. *Epod.* 9.13–14; Vermaseren (1977), 96.
132 On this practice and the connection with Attis, the *genius dendrofororum* (*CIL* 8.7956), see *RE* 5.216 and Blänsdorf on *DTM* 6.7.
133 The *DTM* represent the first time Magna Mater is invoked in a curse-text. The Priscilla-*defixio* from Gross-Gerau near Mainz appeals for help to *Deum maxime Atthis Tyranne* (Scholz and Kropp (2004)). The only other *defixio* I have found where Attis' assistance is asked for is Kropp 2.3.2/1, also a prayer for justice, from Alcácer do Sal in Portugal. Two Latin *defixiones* (Kropp 2.2.1/1 and 4.1.3/16) asks for help from Isis, the co-occupant of the Mainz sanctuary.

134 On Moltinus see *RE* 16.29 s.v.
135 'Possibly a Celtic water-deity' (Tomlin (2018), 364–5), who features on a *defixio* from the Hamble estuary.
136 In a tablet from Chamalières: see M. Martin (2010), 30, with bibliography.
137 Three, possibly four in *DTM* 1, four in the truncated no. 2, two in no. 3, one in no. 4, three in no. 7, two in no. 10, one in no. 11, two in no. 12, one in no. 15, one in no. 22.
138 *DTM* 1.6-8, 2.5-7, 9-14, 10.3-5, 12.6-8.
139 In addition to the analogies invoking ritual self-castration, note the mention of other aspects of Magna Mater's cult, the deposition of sacred objects in the shrine *DTM* 1.8–10, the *cistas penetrales DTM* 5.6 (where the severed genitals of Attis were supposedly kept), *benedictum DTM* 2.4, *megaro DTM* 4.2 and *Atthis tyranne DTM* 5.1–2, on all of which see Blänsdorf (2012) ad loc.
140 See e.g. Audollent pp. 491–2 for a list of examples from his volume, Faraone (1991), 6–9, Eidinow (2007), 150–1.
141 On such retrograde writing (i.e. writing from right to left instead of left to right), a common practice in Attic *defixiones*, see Faraone (1991), 7–8. Cf. also a retrograde curse tablet from Cologne, 'as this is written in the wrong order, so may your affairs go wrong' (Blänsdorf (2010c), 150) and n.124 supra.
142 Similar analogies in other early *defixiones*, *DTA* 105, 106, 107 (fourth or third century BCE) *SGD* 40 (probably fifth or fourth century BCE).
143 Exceptions in addition to those mentioned immediately below in the text: Audollent 139 (two analogies comprising twelve out of eighteen lines); Audollent 222A and B (three analogies in thirteen out of twenty-five lines).
144 Four instances, occupying the whole text, three effectively identical in wording.
145 Audollent 222A and B, where the tongue is torn from a living cockerel in order to impose silence in courtroom opponents and probably also Stylow (2012), where the phrase 'just as a frog is silent without its tongue, so may Marcellus be dumb and silent ... against Licinius Gallus' probably implies the excision of the frog's tongue, notwithstanding the editor's scepticism: cf. Plin. *HN* 32.49, which prescribes 'the extraction of its tongue from a living frog', as noted by Kruschwitz (2016), who takes issue with Stylow.
146 In the case of the targets symbolically, in the case of the puppy literally.
147 Bravo (1987), a curse table from Olbia Pontica on the Black Sea. Jordan (1997) offers a revised text and posits that the inconsequentiality results from the inept use of a formulary.
148 'In the process of association anything goes, as long as there is the tiniest shred of similarity' Versnel (2002b), 128. Along the same lines Gordon (2015), 164–5 stresses, in regard to the malign use of voodoo dolls, that it is the intentionality of the practitioner that is important, making it unnecessary that the doll resemble its prototype.
149 Similarly Kropp 3.22/16.

150 Piranomonte (2010), 196, who goes on to explain in the body of her article the magical significance of these various artefacts. For magical aspects of the Anna Perenna hoard additional to those discussed here, see Gordon (2015), 161–3.
151 In general on the interdependence and mutually reinforcing effects of the magic techniques in the Anna Perenna hoard, see Blänsdorf (2010b), 55.
152 For this translation of *inter quibus nomen Seniciani* see Versnel (1991a), 84 with his n.122.
153 See e.g. Tomlin, 63–5. Clear examples of a portion of the value of the stolen items being promised to the god tasked with recovery are found in e.g. Kropp 3.14/6 and 3.18/1 'to the god Mercury... three thousand *denarii*, of which I give half to you', 3.19/1 and 2, 3.22/3. The amount vowed would be paid out to the deity if the stolen goods were returned.
154 Gager, discussing this curse (his no. 99) quotes P. Corby Finney to the effect that 'the name of Senicianus is not altogether rare in Christian circles of this period' and hence could refer to another homonymous individual. Tomlin (2018), 342–3 is likewise sceptical about the purported Silvianus–Senicianus connection. For a further occurrence of the name Senicianus in a theft-related prayer for justice aimed at a 'gentile or Christian' culprit, see Kropp 3.2/77 (from Bath = Tomlin no. 98).
155 On all this see Goodchild (1953); Forest-Hill and Horton (2014); also *The Guardian* Tuesday 2 April and *The Independent* Wednesday 3 April 2013, the last three of which feature excellent photographs of the ring. The ring went on public display in 2013, apparently for the first time, at The Vyne, a National Trust property in Hampshire.
156 Notably Tomlin (1988), 101–5 and Kiernan (2003).
157 Cf. Cic. *Brut.* 217, Gager 120–1.
158 'The *defixio* is... an expression of the determination that the mills of <divine justice> shall be induced to grind, and pretty quick too' Gordon (2013), 264.
159 Versnel (1991a).
160 Faraone (1991).
161 Curbera (2015b), 100.
162 In curses of the 'prayer for justice' type, which comprise the majority of British *defixiones*, the curse is a public affair, in contrast to *defixiones* in the other categories, which are usually – though not exclusively – constructed in secret (and in any case exposed to the risk that someone might divulge their existence to the victim).
163 See n.156 supra, Gager 21–3.
164 Kiernan (2003).

4

Magic and Herbs

More than a hundred years ago H. Hubert stated 'the employment of plants and drugs drawn from plants appears to be one of the principal parts of ancient magic'.[1] Unlike many of the opinions of earlier scholars in the field that have undergone modification thanks to the appearance of new material or conceptual advances in our understanding of the subject, Hubert's verdict on the significance of botanical substances for Graeco-Roman magic has broadly speaking stood the test of time. It is the purpose of this chapter to investigate, under a number of heads and at times in some considerable detail, the various reasons for Hubert's judgement.

The use of potent herbs and plants lay squarely in the domain of magic: indeed the fourth-century BCE botanical writer Theophrastus in his *Enquiry into Plants* (9.19.2–3) and the first-century CE compendiarist Pliny in his *Natural History* (24.156–67) record certain plants which were widely believed to possess magical powers, such as spontaneously catching fire, making lions and other wild beasts torpid and unthreatening, causing uncontrollable laughter and assisting in the procreation of handsome and good children, a sort of herbal eugenics.[2] It was upon powerful herbs that the first literary sorceresses, Circe and Medea, relied for their witchy concoctions; and it is in a nod to their archetypal status as mistresses of mysterious plant-lore (e.g. Plin. *HN* 25.10–11) that Theocritus' third century BCE sorceress Simaitha is made to say '<Moon> make these drugs (*pharmaka*) of mine as powerful as those of Circe and Medea' (*Id.* 2.15–16). There was even a magical plant known as 'Circe's root',[3] and the especial magical potency ascribed to plants from Pontus and the Caucasus region[4] is partly a reflection of the fact that Medea came from there. In Ovid's *Metamorphoses* book 7 Medea appeals to 'the Earth, you who furnish sorcerers with powerful herbs' (196) before mounting her dragonmobile, which transports her to remote mountain tops and river banks where she culls the herbs, roots and grasses that she requires to magically rejuvenate Aesōn, the aged father of her husband Jason. A little before take-off she had boasted of her ability to draw down the moon from the sky (207–8), a standard witchy marvel which, Pliny tells us (*HN* 25.10), was popularly believed to be effected by *ueneficiis et herbis*, 'by charms and magic herbs'.

The word that Homer and Theocritus use to describe Circe's and Medea's magical preparations is *pharmaka*, a slippery term which can mean 'drugs' (whether beneficial or noxious), 'medicines', and 'magic potions' or 'philtres'. *Pharmaka* are composed in the main of plant derivatives, as is made clear by Homer in two passages of the *Odyssey*. In the first he describes as follows the provenance of the distress-relieving *nēpenthes* served by Helen to the Greeks at Sparta, 'such cunning drugs as these (*pharmaka mētioenta*) had the daughter of Zeus, beneficial ones, which had been given to her by Polydamna, the wife of Thōn, a woman of Egypt, where the grain-giving earth bears the greatest amount of drugs, many that are good when mixed, and many that are harmful' (*Ody.* 4.227–30). The second passage involves the famous *mōlu*, 'moly' which Hermes gives Odysseus as a magical prophylactic against Circe's transformative concoction (see immediately below); 'so saying, Argēiphontes gave me the drug (*pharmakon*), pulling it from the ground, and showed me its nature. At its root it was black, but its flower was milk-white. The gods call it moly; it is difficult for mortal men to dig up, but for the gods everything is possible' (*Ody.* 10.302–6).[5] Moly, incidentally, is the ancestor of a number of plants believed to have the capacity to ward off malign magic.[6]

Circe's use of herbs to transform Odysseus' men into swine (Hom. *Ody.* 10.233–43), and the sinister if vexed botanical term *hupotamnon* in the mid-sixth-century BCE *Homeric Hymn to Demeter* offer early evidence of an awareness that plants and herbs could be used for malign magical purposes as well as beneficial ones.[7] The word *hupotamnon* appears to refer to the cutting of herbs at their base for magical ends, and in fact one of the synonyms for 'sorcerer' was *rhizotomos* or 'root-cutter', the root being sometimes regarded as the most potent part of a plant.[8] Indeed Sophocles in his lost fifth century BCE tragedy *The Root-Cutters* (*Rhizotomoi*) described Medea gathering magical herbs and their sap in the following terms, 'she, keeping her gaze averted behind her hand,[9] received in bronze casks the cloudy juice that dripped from the cutting ... and the covered baskets concealed the roots' cuttings' (frg. 534 Radt), before adding further details that equally belong to sacro-magical practice: that Medea was naked as she harvested the herbs,[10] employed a bronze sickle for the purpose,[11] and uttered ritual cries.

Over and above what has just been said, the nexus between magic and botanical derivatives is affirmed by the broad-based appellations for 'witch', *pharmakis* and its synonym *uenefica*, derived respectively from Greek *pharmakon* and Latin *uenenum*. *Venenum* originally meant 'love-charm', in an etymological reflection of the original Italic conception of Venus as the goddess of growing plants, but comes to mean more generally 'drug', whether of a benign or maleficent type, 'poison' and 'magic spell, charm', a meaning of which Greek *pharmakon* is equally susceptible.

I have purposely left till last the feature that, more than any other, places herbs and plants firmly in the domain of magic. This is the elaborate sacro-magical ritual concerned with picking or cutting these, so-called *botanēarsis*. A particularly striking example of such plant-gathering, heavily infused with magical lore as we shall see, is the bizarre account of culling the peony – a flower with the imprimatur of the Magi, no less (Plin. *HN* 24.160) – which is given by the second–third century CE Greek writer Aelian in his *On the Characteristics of Animals* 14.27:

> There is a plant named *Cynospastos* ['Torn away by a dog'] which is also called *Aglaophōtis* [one of the many names for the peony]. By day it escapes notice among the other plants and can scarcely be seen, but by night it becomes visible and stands out, like a star. For it is fiery in character and like flame. Therefore men plant some mark beside its roots, before departing. Unless they marked it in this way, they could not remember either the colour or even the appearance of the plant. But when night has passed they come, and observing the mark which they left and recognising it, they are able to guess that this is the precise plant which they need ... but they do not pull up this plant in person, otherwise they would be sorry indeed. Accordingly, no one either digs round the plant or pulls it up, since, they say, the man who first, through ignorance of the peony's nature, touched it, died in short order. So they bring a young dog that has not been given food for some days and is mad with hunger, and attaching to it a very strong rope, and fastening the other end in noose-form securely to the stalk of the peony at its base from as far away as they can, they then put before the dog a great deal of cooked meat which emits a savoury smell. Then the dog, ablaze with hunger and tormented by the smell, dashes at the meat placed before it, and in rushing forward pulls up the plant, roots and all. But when the sun sees the roots,[12] the dog dies on the spot. They bury it in the self-same place, and after performing some mysterious rites and honouring the corpse of the dog on the basis that it had died on their behalf, they then make bold to touch the aforesaid plant and carry it home. It is useful, it is said, for many purposes. Among other things, they say that it cures the sickness with which the moon is reputed to afflict men [epilepsy] and the disease of the eyes which, when moisture has flooded them and congealed, deprives victims of their sight [cataracts].

Fig. 5 White peony. Photograph by Patricia Watson.

An amusing tale, to be sure, but not without interest. Above all it encapsulates a superstitious belief that plants were invested with mysterious powers: in the peony's case these express themselves in a diurnal near-invisibility which mutates into nocturnal luminescence (hence its alternative name *Aglaophōtis*, 'Bright Light'),[13] and in the far more unsettling capacity to kill any living creature that pulls it up by the roots. The idea that, by virtue of their occult potency, plants can be dangerous, even lethal to pluck is a common one (already hinted at in the *Homeric Hymn to Demeter*'s account of the rape of Persephone as she attempted to pick a miraculous narcissus):[14] hence the need for plant-gatherers to take various precautionary measures such as apotropaic spitting,[15] giving a verbal assurance to the plant that it is being culled for a genuine curative purpose,[16] making a propitiatory offering to the earth,[17] asking the gods for permission to pluck a plant,[18] or, as here, harvesting it at a safe distance[19] and using an animal surrogate to do the uprooting.[20] The idea that a rite, in the present case the ritualised plucking of the peony, can unleash dangerous forces that can rebound upon a practitioner sits squarely in the domain of magic. It is seen, for example, in Simaitha's instruction to her maid to 'sound the gong at once' when the sinister goddess Hecate manifests herself in response to Simaitha's conjuration (Theocr. *Id.* 2.36), as well in the numerous prescriptions in the *PGM* for *phulaktēria*, 'protective mechanisms' that the magician must adopt in order to preserve himself from harm by the powers which he seeks to utilise.[21] A final point of note is Aelian's closing remark that the peony supposedly cures epilepsy, 'which comes from the moon', Gk. *selēnē* – a connection captured in one of the Greek names for the disease, *selēniasmos*, literally 'the moon-affliction'.[22] The underlying rationale for this is the conviction, met again and again in connection with the magic of herbs, that items belonging to the microcosm – plants, but also stones and animate creatures – were linked to the macrocosm, that is the gods, the sun and the moon, the planets and astronomical phenomena such as the zodiacal signs, by an invisible nexus or filament (Gk. *seira*) known as cosmic sympathy.[23] This idea is encapsulated in the notion that plants should be plucked when the sun was in the zodiacal sign that corresponded to them, or according to certain planetary conjunctions, pivotal times such as the solstice or equinox, and the influence of the stars more generally (Thessalus of Tralles *De uirtutibus herbarum* 27–8 Friedrich; Delatte (1961), 64–8); it is equally seen in the *PGM*'s listing of the 'seven flowers of the seven stars' viz. planets (13.23–5) and in the naming of the plant *bēsata* after the god Bēs (Hopfner OZ 1.§500). In much the same way, since epilepsy is allegedly caused by the moon, it seemed perfectly logical that its botanical congener should be able to heal it by harnessing the peony's lunar connections in a benign, rather than damaging way – a case of like curing like, an instance of what has come to be known as the 'doctrine of signatures'.

Why, one might ask, should one go to so much trouble, risk danger to life and limb, in order to pick the peony? The answer is provided by the conclusion of the quoted passage – the plant's supposed capacity to cure epilepsy, in a word, its medicinal value.[24] Ancient medicine depended heavily on the curative properties of plants, that is to say their fruits, extracted juice, flowers, leaves, roots, grasses and seeds (Theophr. *HP* 9.8.1, Plin. *HN* 24.178–83): hence Pliny can speak of *periti herbarum medici*, 'physicians skilled in the use of herbs' (*HN* 25.27) as a given and state *HN* 21.116 'there is abundant use in medicine of flowers and perfumes generally'.[25] The importance of plant-lore in Greek and Roman medicine is attested by Theophrastus in his *Enquiry into Plants* (9.8–9.20) and Pliny in his *Natural History* (books 20–27), who both treat *in extenso* the pharmacological and therapeutic properties of plants, but above all by Dioscorides, who devotes the bulk of his important *Materials of Medicine* (first century CE) to these matters. Pliny states that '<most medical authorities> believe that there is nothing that cannot be achieved by the agency of plants' (*HN* 25.15),[26] emphasises their great importance in the history of medicine (*HN* 26.10–11), and, in discussing them in *HN* 20–27, even singles out as unusual those plants that do not have therapeutic powers (*HN* 24.83, 27.142). That ancient medicine leaned heavily on plant derivatives is of course unsurprising. What may, however, surprise is the extent to which the nowadays discrete categories of medicine and magic – especially herb-based magic – are closely interwoven in Antiquity.

The interfusion of magic and medicine is present from the beginning of the literary record. According to Pindar (*Pyth.* 3.47–53), Asclepius, the god of medicine, healed men by a combination of potions, drugs, surgery *and incantations*.[27] The name of Medea, sorceress *par excellence*, is connected etymologically with Latin *mederi*, to heal, and *medicus*, 'physician'. This helps to explain why, in some lesser-known versions of her myth, she is reported to have rejuvenated with magic herbs not only her father-in-law Aesōn, but also Jason and the nurses of Dionysus, and likewise to have cured Heracles of the madness inflicted on him by his stepmother Hera (Martin (2005), 129–35). Later, Pliny is quite clear that magic arose first from medicine (*HN* 30.2) and the great medical authority Galen (second century CE) excoriated one Pamphilus for his six-book work on the properties of plants, in which 'Pamphilus turned to old wives' tales and various bits of nonsensical magical charlatanry that came from the Egyptians, along with certain incantations which persons picking the plants utter. He also uses the plants for amulets and other acts of sorcery'. Such practices, Galen continues, have nothing to do with the art of medicine, and are of no use whatsoever to those who are seriously interested in prosecuting the physician's craft (Gal. 11.782–4 Kühn).[28] But in robustly excluding the work of Pamphilus and his like from rational medicine, Galen is by implication conceding that such ideas bulk large in the practice of other physicians; figures such as the important practitioner Asclepiades, whose wholly unfounded success as a doctor was due in large measure, Pliny claims, to his reliance on *magicae uanitates*, empty magical sophistries (*HN* 26.18).

This chapter has so far argued, first, that botanical derivatives are integral alike to the activities of fabled sorceresses and to hands-on magic in the shape of folk-medicine, second, that there is a profound blending of medicine and magic in Classical Antiquity which has little or no correlate in modern medicine, and in particular that the confluence between magic and medicine is crystallised in the distinctly superstition-ridden practice of *botanēarsis*, the ritualised harvesting of plants and the elaborate gestures and speech-acts mobilised in the process.

Botanēarsis rituals are common alike to fictional accounts of witches like Medea and Circe gathering herbs for malign ends and the pages of writers on botanical matters like Pliny, Theophrastus and Dioscorides (albeit less expansive in the former). Since the topic of *botanēarsis* will recur throughout the chapter, it will be helpful to give at the outset a brief outline of the ideas that underlay it.[29] Like philosophers and physicians, magicians believed in the idea of cosmic sympathy, that is, in the existence of real but intangible interconnections between everything in the cosmos, including the divine and the microcosmic – plants included. In particular, as in the case of the peony, it was thought that certain plants were under the control of the gods or astral forces and that their virtues, hidden from the profane,[30] could be unlocked by those versed in their secrets, that is by magicians or persons practising a home-grown medical magic. Now plants were regarded as 'the hands of the gods', as the distinguished medical theorist Herophilus put it,[31] a gift of nature for the healing of mankind as Pliny phrased it (*HN* 24.1). Both physicians and magicians utilised plants for curative purposes. But whereas doctors put illnesses down to physiological causes or deficiencies in daily regimen, magicians viewed these as sent by the gods to punish men for their faults and misdeeds. For purposes of healing illnesses, magicians therefore proceeded in a two-pronged fashion: first, by mobilising for their own purposes the supernatural powers vested in the particular plants whose celestial affinities they had divined and, second, by constraining the divinities to turn aside the bad influence that they exercised on human health. But, in order to effect both ends, it was necessary to carry out a number of precise ritual procedures, both speech-based and gestural, such as reciting certain prayers[32] or describing a circle around the plant to be picked, which had the effect of both placating and constraining the supernatural powers, both humble and celestial, whose aid was invoked, and hence inducing these to do the magician's curative will. And this, in essence, is the origin of the *botanēarsis* rituals which pervade the pages of the herbalists.

Some years ago, Anthony Preus (1988, 78) observed '*pharmaka*, "medicines" in the sense in which that term is used in connection with folk "medicine men", cannot readily be separated from the belief structure within which they are administered'. By 'belief structure' he meant both the rituals involved in the harvesting of a plant and the thought processes involved in supplying this to the patient, including, most importantly, the factors determining the choice of a particular plant to treat a given disease.

This brings us to the matters that will occupy the rest of the chapter. My first concern will be with what used to be styled, in now out of fashion Frazerian terminology, 'the laws of magic'. These so-called laws are essentially a construction of modern theorists, but they reflect first principles that inform at the most fundamental level magical operations of every kind, no matter whether real or fictional. They are examined here because, as Hopfner (1928, 319) noted, the use of plants and herbs in magic represents arguably the best vehicle for unpicking such ideas, so ubiquitous are they in the botanical arm of magic, above all in folk-medicinal procedures.

A second topic for discussion in the latter part of the chapter is the magically coloured rationales that attended the use of plants for therapeutic purposes, in particular the preservation of their curative powers by attendant protocols on the part of the *rhizotomos*. These include avoidance of bodily pollution, the use of stylised gestures, taking care not to compromise the plant's magic powers after uprooting by allowing it to touch the ground,[33] the observance of propitious times for gathering the plant, and prayer or other modes of utterance – all of which feed directly into the often highly elaborate collection rituals, *botanēarseis*, a single instance of which has already been discussed, and which will be subject to further examination below. In investigating the above two topics I draw mainly on prose sources, Theophrastus' *Enquiry into Plants*, Dioscorides' *The Materials of Medicine*, Marcellus Empiricus, a late Latin writer on medicine and above all on the Elder Pliny, who is a fount of information on the use of plants and herbs in an incontrovertibly magical setting.[34]

A third concern is more strictly botanical and scientific in nature. It is to examine the degree to which, beneath the carapace of magic and superstition that was so characteristic of Greek and Roman folk-medicine, a core of sound pharmacological sense may have lurked. The procedure here will be to collate the alleged therapeutic capacities of plants widely used in the medicinal magic of Antiquity with what is known nowadays about their phytochemical properties, in the hope of discovering to what extent Greek and Roman medicinal procedures making use of these plants could have been based on empirical knowledge. Here – to anticipate – a pattern will be discerned whereby the pharmacologically effective is sometimes twinned with procedures that are arrantly magical and, to a rationalist cast of mind, nonsensical.

In his famous work *A General Theory of Magic* Marcel Mauss divided the laws of magic into the law of similarity, the law of contiguity and the law of contrariety or opposition.³⁵ Ultimately all three principles of Mauss are based on the overarching idea of 'sympathy' (Gk. *sumpatheia*, literally 'feeling as one'), a concept with an impeccable Greek pedigree, subscribed to by nearly all Greek physicians (Edelstein (1967), 232), but nowadays out of favour in certain quarters as a critical term,³⁶ partly because tainted by association with its use by the classicist and anthropologist Sir James Frazer in *The Golden Bough*, whose imperialist and colonialist mentality made him free with unfortunate language like 'cunning and malignant savages'. The essence of sympathy (to pursue further an idea discussed above) is the conviction that by nature there exist real or potential interconnections between everything in the universe – be this animal, vegetable, mineral or immaterial in character – whereby one entity operates spontaneously³⁷ on its congener, or can be induced to do so by an action triggering that association. A straightforward instance of this would be the idea that the plant *lysimachia*, because its two elements are composed of Greek *machē*, 'a fight' and *luein*, 'to loosen', served to check the quarrelling of the members of a team of oxen (Plin. *HN* 25.72). The inverse, or rather the corollary of sympathy was the belief that there equally exists a natural enmity or 'antipathy' between certain substances,³⁸ so that they cannot endure to be brought into proximity with each other without material damage to at least one (Plin. *HN* 24.1-2), or, alternatively, cancel each other out, as in the tags 'these poisons are mutually antipathetic, as are many other substances' (Plin. *HN* 21.153) and 'one poison is overcome by another' (Marcell. Empir. 36.70). The essence of antipathy is neatly encapsulated in a remark of *Cyranides* 5.9 Kaimakis, 'the plant known as the violet is *cold* by nature. It checks *inflamed* boils'.³⁹

I will say no more of antipathy, as perhaps less illuminating overall of sympathy, in the broad sense, than its other two realisations, the law of similarity and the law of contiguity. The law of similarity expresses itself in two forms; like produces like, and like acts upon a (pre-existing) like, in particular, curing like.⁴⁰ Albeit not drawn from the world of plants, one instance of the law of similars is worth mentioning here, as particularly revealing of the underlying idea. This is the widespread ancient custom of averting the Evil Eye by using the image of an eye to turn aside the Eye's baneful gaze,⁴¹ a usage still seen in the practice of painting an apotropaic eye on the prow of Greek fishing vessels. The law of similarity, or the 'doctrine of signatures' as some prefer to call it, can work in a large and diverse number of ways (Tavenner (1916), 113–22), but, as regards botanical pharmacology, the main homologies involve the colour, the appearance and the names of plants. In all three cases, the effect is assumed to be automatic, but we should also however distinguish a particular application of the law as it applies to plants, whereby some contingent action on the part of an operative mimics a desired outcome (Mauss (1972), 72); in other words we have here a subset of our old friend persuasive analogy. It should additionally be noted that in such magico-medical therapies as will occupy us here, more than one type of sympathy may often be at work.

Examples of chromatically based sympathy include the heliochryse, literally 'sun-gold', whose tightly bunched cluster of yellow flowers suggested the colour of urine, so that it could be regarded as diuretic (Plin. *HN* 21.168) or, when taken with wine, as a remedy for difficulty in passing urine (Dioscor. *MM* 4.57). The famously black heartwood of the ebony tree dispels dimness of vision (*skotos* or *caligo*, literally 'darkness'), according to Dioscorides *MM* 1.98 and Pliny *HN* 24.89, who describes its powers as 'a great marvel'; the mulberry, with its rich dark-coloured fruit and juice, 'miraculously' stops the flow of blood from a range of bodily orifices (Plin. *HN* 23.137–8; *Cyranides* 1.12 Kaimakis).[42] The first of these instances obviously involves like producing or evoking like, the latter two like curing like.

Now for matters of appearance. The *orchis* plant has two roots, of unequal size, resembling human testicles, of which 'the larger makes a person more functional for intercourse, the smaller harms and prevents it' according to Theophrastus *HP* 9.18.3, which provokes the comment (ibid. 4) 'it is absurd that both effects should be caused by one and the same nature (*sc.* of the plant)'.[43] In turn Dioscorides *MM* 3.126 states 'about the *orchis* it is said that the larger root when eaten by males produces male children, while the lesser root if eaten by females produces female children. It is additionally claimed that the women of Thessaly give the tender shoot with goat's milk <to their men>, as inciting sexual intercourse, but the dry root to check and put an end to intercourse'. Although the two accounts differ in detail, they both rest on the shared inference that, because of its shape, the *orchis* is of great potency in the sexual arena, an instance of like generating like – an inference seconded by the name of the plant, for *orchis* is also Greek for 'testicle'. Along the same lines is what Pliny *HN* 22.20 reports, not without anti-Magian polemic, about a variety of the *erynge* plant, 'the root of which looks like the genital organs of one sex or the other ... if the male variety comes into the possession of men, they become lovable in women's eyes. This is why, they say, Sappho fell in love with Phaon of Lesbos', i.e. acted in defiance of her own sexual orientation because of the analogically suggestive power of the root. Again, in a somewhat bizarre twelvemonth preventative for eye pain, Marcellus Empiricus 8.27 recommends boring through cherry stones while making a vow not to eat cherries for a year. The analogy here, which strains logic,[44] rests on the resemblance of the bored-through stone to the human eyeball, and the proviso to abstain from cherries for the duration of the spell presumably on the basis that this would be tantamount to eating one's own eyes! More straightforwardly, since the stem of the *soncos*, sow-thistle, streams, when broken, with a milky juice, a decoction of the stem was believed to stimulate milk production in wet-nurses (Plin. *HN* 22.88–9). Or, lastly, 'to treat warts that spread under the skin and warts that have a neck, at the time of the new moon some people touch each excrescence with one chickpea after another, then tie up in a linen cloth the chickpeas, which they bid you throw away behind you, *on the grounds that the warts will thereby fall off*' (Dioscor. *MM* 2.104: cf. Plin. *HN* 22.149). There is a host of magical ideas collectively at work here, but for present purposes it suffices to note that at the core of the procedure lies the physical resemblance of a chickpea, with its round, cleft shape, to a wart.

Turning now to the law of similars involving plant names, which is by some distance the most important of the three types of similarity under discussion here, the main principle at work is *nomen omen*, in particular the idea that the etymology of a word indicated the therapeutic or physiological effects to be expected of it. Thus *polythrix* ('with much hair') 'strengthens and causes to grow more thickly hair that tends to fall out' (Plin. *HN* 25.132), *katananke*, a kind of vetch, is used in compulsive love-charms (Dioscor. *MM* 4.131; Plin. *HN* 27.57; *PGM* 36.370) because its name is also a compound of the noun *ananke*, 'compulsion', a cardinal idea in ancient magic of a sinister kind.[45] The *reseda* plant 'relieves' (*resedat*) diseases when combined with an alliterative incantation (Plin. *HN* 27.131). In all these cases the underlying idea is that the name of a given entity is a hypostatisation of its essential quality, an idea that goes back to Plato's dialogue *Cratylus* (fourth century BCE). In other cases involving name magic, it is not only the name per se but additionally the plant's associations that lead to inferences regarding its properties. An instance is the *agnos* tree, whose unaspirated name is suggestive of Greek *hagnos*, 'chaste', and which was supposedly so called because the Athenian matrons used its leaves for bedding during the period of ritual abstinence from sex for the three-day festival of the Thesmophoria (Dioscor. *MM* 1.103; Pliny *HN* 24.59); in the light of these dual considerations the *agnos* supposedly inhibits sexual desire, according to Pliny at least (ibid. 62). Similarly the *hēmionion*, 'mule plant' (Gk. *hēmionos*, 'mule'), greatly beloved as food by these animals, seems to owe its purported capacity to make women infertile (Theophr. *HP* 9.18.7) alike to its name and to its association with a creature known for sterility. Why, however, *chelidonia*, celandine, which seems to derive its name from the fact of its blossoming when the swallow (Gk. *chelidōn*) arrives and withering when it departs, should have the capacity to restore the sight of swallow chicks if someone blinds them (Dioscor. *MM* 2.180), or even 'gouges out' their eyes (Plin. *HN* 25.89) must remain opaque, as must the rationale behind the use of many other substances harnessed for curative purposes in folk-medicinal settings!

One caution is necessary in connection with sympathy residing in names. This is a version of the familiar chicken and egg conundrum. Dioscorides (*MM* 3.4) and Pliny (*HN* 25.95) confidently assert that *aristolochia* is so named because it is excellent (Gk. *aristos*) for lying in and giving birth (Gk. *lochos*); Pliny (*HN* 24.29) similarly claims that the ground pine, *abiga*, 'got its name from causing abortions' (*abigere*).[46] Conversely, Pliny (*HN* 22.39) states that the plant *scorpio*, 'which is effective against scorpions', derived its name from the physical resemblance of its seeds to the tail of the creature,[47] while one Apollodorus names a plant *aeschynomenē*, 'the shy one',[48] because it contracts its leaves upon the approach of a hand (Plin. *HN* 24.167). In practice, however, it can often be difficult to determine whether a given name has been assigned to a plant on the basis of observable properties possessed by it, i.e. on empirical grounds (as seems to be the case with the psychotropic and hallucinogenic plants detailed by Pliny *HN* 24.163–5), or whether on the other hand the properties thus attributed to it represent an extrapolation from a pre-existing name.[49]

As noted, the therapeutic action of a plant may be reinforced by persuasive analogy, that is, by a mimetic gesture or action intended to elicit analogically a desired end. A striking instance is Pliny *HN* 24.171, 'if the plants that spring up in a sieve that has been discarded on a cross-path are plucked and attached as an amulet to women who are pregnant, they hasten delivery'. Here the expulsion of the baby and the afterbirth from the parturient's body are thought to be encouraged by the loosely comparable process of uprooting the plants from the sieve in which they are growing, as well as by the sieve's express function of letting liquid distil through it. It is also relevant that the sieve was a symbol of Artemis-Hecate, goddess of childbirth (*PGM* 4.2304, 2284), so that several factors are operative at once. Another example of persuasive analogy twinned with the use of a plant comes in Plin. *HN* 22.71, according to whom some claim that the drying up of asphodel root suspended in smoke produces a comparable drying up of scrofulous swellings: Marcellus Empiricus 15.82 says much the same thing of vervain root,[50] adding that, in the event that payment is deemed insufficient by the practitioner, the cure can be reversed and the swelling made to recrudesce by throwing the root into water, an effect also attainable, Pliny cautions, by replanting the healing herb (*HN* 21.144, 25.174, 26.24). A more complex case also involving persuasive analogy involves the magico-medical regime for curing superficial abscesses using a poultice of *uerbascum* (mullein) pounded with its root. This is recorded by Pliny at *HN* 26.92-3, who reports

> those with experience have declared that it makes a great deal of difference [to the cure] if **a maiden** (*uirgo*) who is **naked**[51] and **fasting**[52] lays the poultice on the patient – **who should also be fasting** – and **touching him** with **hand upturned**, says '**Apollo states that a disease cannot grow worse in someone if a naked maiden quenches its effects** and **with her hand inverted** as above **says the formula three times**, and *both parties spit* on the ground **three times**'.

There is a veritable thicket of magico-religious usages here, which for information's sake I have emboldened, but for the moment the relevant detail is the action of spitting. Spitting is a recognised gesture of aversion,[53] but its purpose here, as at Plin *HN* 27.131 and an old rustic charm for relieving pain in the feet recorded by Varro *RR* 1.27, is quite specific: that by imitative magic the disease should quit the body of the patient much as the spittle is ejected from his mouth, and further be transferred to and be retained by the ground in place of the sufferer.

So much for the law of similarity and its congener persuasive analogy. In regard to the magic of plants, Mauss's second law, that of contiguity, is less important than in other fields of magical operation, such as that of amulets (see appendix to Chapter 5), whose use is entirely predicated on the idea of contiguity. Contiguity literally means 'touch', from the Latin verb *contingere*; it was believed that the mysterious powers embodied in the amulet were transferred by physical contact to the person who wore the amulet or otherwise attached it to his body (Ducourthial (2003), 182). Along the same lines, medico-magical writers such as Marcellus Empiricus regularly prescribe cures involving the transmission of a disease from a human patient into an animal surrogate by some form of physical touching;[54] in fact disease transference involving contiguity much more often involves an animal than a plant. But instances of the latter do exist. For example, according to the medical authority Herophilus, certain plants are perhaps beneficial even if merely trodden upon (Plin. *HN* 25.15),[55] while 'if one touches a painful tooth with *senecio* [a plant of the daisy family] three times ... and replaces the plant in the location <from which it was dug up> so that it stays alive, they say that the tooth will never give pain thereafter' i.e. the toothache is magically relocated into the *senecio* (Plin. *HN* 25.167). A more complex and intriguing instance involves the medicinal use of maidenhair, *adiantum*, literally 'unwetted'.[56] According to Pliny (*HN* 22.65), 'the leaves, steeped in the urine of a pre-pubertal boy, pounded with saltpetre and smeared on the belly of women are said to prevent it from becoming wrinkled (*rugosus*)'. This brief folk-remedy against stretch-marks (Latin *rugae*) is replete with magical details. The central idea is that application of a boy's urine, steeped in maidenhair, will by a process of magical transference ensure that the skin of a postpartum belly remains as smooth that of the young boy who emits it. Urine is used as the medium to achieve this effect because it was thought to be charged with the life-force of the person who voids it, a mysterious potency which was harnessed in beneficial magic for a whole variety of ends:[57] Pliny, at the beginning of the chapters that he devotes to the curative powers of the liquid (*HN* 28.65-7) states 'our authorities attribute to urine also great power, not only natural but also supernatural'. Moreover, in such curative procedures it is often specified, as in *HN* 22.65, that the urine should be that of a boy who has not yet reached puberty (*puer impubes*),[58] that is, a boy who has not yet had sexual intercourse; the Latin expression corresponds to Greek *pais aphthoros*, 'a virgin boy', literally 'a boy who is sexually uncorrupted',[59] whose use is often mandated in various recipes in the *PGM*.[60] In other words, the combined potency of the *adiantum* and the urine with which it is infused is compounded by the chastity of the boy who voided it: as one aspect of the sacral purity required in transactions with the divine,[61] virginity or, at the minimum temporary abstention from intercourse, was a common requirement in both religious and magical usage, one of many instances where the rituals of the two fields intersect.

Two observations flow from the last few paragraphs. The first is that the rationales, thought processes and affinities at work in the processes detailed above are, broadly speaking, perspicuous. To be sure, the cautious Theophrastus condemns as 'overblown', 'superfluous and far-fetched', 'unreasonable' (*HP* 9.8.5-8) some of the precautionary operations and ritual acts prescribed by the *rhizotomoi* for the *botanēarsis* of the peony, black hellebore and other plants. Certainly too the reasoning that underlies the use of a particular agent, whether botanical or not, to cure a disease can often be wholly obscure;[62] hence Pliny's well-known fulminations, 'for quartan fevers the Magi bid one attach as an amulet the excrement of a cat along with the claw of a horned owl ... who, pray, came up with this idea? What kind of combination is this? Why choose the claw of a horned owl rather than anything else?' (*HN* 28.228-9). But, for all this, instinctually formulated 'laws' based on the transference by contiguity of powers from one entity to another, or upon readily observable similarities, whether of shape, colour or name, make perfectly good sense in straightforward naturalistic terms. Similarly, the notion seen in *botanēarsis* that the corruption of a disease can effectively be countered by the agency of a person who is ritually pure (through fasting, virginity or sexual abstinence) has a readily comprehensible logic of its own, as do other of the ritual directives attendant on that process. Accordingly, we need have little truck with the claims of earlier scholars such as that magic is impervious to reason and observation,[63] that it is 'prelogical', pre-empirical, and mired in mysticism,[64] or 'naive'.[65] Much better to hold, with Malinowski – despite his sometimes deploying terminology like 'an obscure and confused concatenation of ideas' or 'a coefficient of weirdness' in magical speech[66] – that magic is profoundly pragmatic, clear and straightforward in its aims,[67] and works inferentially from a system of signs, to which end '<it>is . . . governed by a theory, by a system of principles which dictate the manner in which the act has to be performed in order to be effective . . . there are a number of general principles which govern <magic spells, rites and substances>'.[68] A conclusion which, despite the profound cultural and historical differences, is just as valid for the ancient Greeks and Romans as for Malinowski's Melanesian subjects of study.

A further point to call for attention is that a number of the procedures outlined above, such as those involving plants growing in a sieve or the application of a poultice made from mullein, are multistranded. Success is ensured by bringing into play simultaneously a plethora of magical beliefs. The same process of what one might call magical superfetation can be seen in the underscoring by attendant protocols, as mentioned above, of the magical plants subjected to ritual *botanēarsis*, to which topic – the second of the three to be addressed in the latter part of the chapter – we must now return.

Of particular interest is the account of the plucking of the *hiera botanē*, Greek for 'sacred plant', given by Pliny *HN* 25.106–7;

> the Magi at any rate say crazy things about this plant: that persons smeared with it gain their wishes, banish fevers, win friendships for themselves and cure every disease without exception. It must be gathered they say, about the rising of the Dog-Star, in such a way that neither the moon or sun see this, with propitiatory offerings of honeycombs and honey being made beforehand to the Earth: that a circle must be traced about it with iron and it should then be pulled up with the left hand and held aloft: that leaves, stem and root must be dried separately in the shade.

Pliny begins here with a broadside against one his favourite targets, the fraudulent assertions of the Magi, a term which, from the Hellenistic period onwards, seems to designate peripatetic sorcerers or peddlers of magic having only limited resemblance to the dignified members of a Persian priestly class who were the original referents of the title (see e.g. Bremmer (1999)). It should be noted however that, in characteristically confusing fashion, Pliny sometimes records other *botanēarseis* of an arrantly magical character (e.g. *HN* 21.42, 25.50) or attributes fantastical powers to a plant (e.g. *HN* 24.154) without in any way casting doubt on their validity or legitimacy by adding the qualifier 'according to the Magi' or 'they say that', as he does elsewhere – but with no particular consistency (see further Chapter 5 on this point). The several quite distinct uses to which the *hiera botanē* can be put (banishing fevers, winning friends etc.) are reminiscent of nothing so much as the polyvalent spells of the *PGM*, and the magical colour is even more pronounced in the individual details of the *botanēarsis*. The prescription that *hiera botanē* should be plucked around the time when the Dog Star rises (late July) smacks of the magical principle of cosmic sympathy, and the mysterious notion that a plant could be more potent if picked at a certain time.[69] It may also be related to the febrifugal properties of the plant, since the Dog Star ushered in the hottest and unhealthiest season of the year in the ancient Mediterranean, when malaria was particularly rife. The injunctions that neither the moon nor the sun should see the harvesting, and that it should be done with the left hand are a clear acknowledgement that the *botanēarsis* represents a magically driven, sacrilegious violation of Mother Earth – hence the need for a preliminary, propitiatory offering to her – and an impious, larcenous assault upon the plant itself and its immanent spirit (Delatte (1961), 53). For both moon and sun were all-seeing, especially when it came to evil or irreligious deeds, including magically coloured ones,[70] while the left hand was used for dirty work, especially theft, whether magical or not.[71] As Pliny puts it in connection with the *selago* plant, northern fir moss (*HN* 24.103), 'it is picked without an iron blade, with the right hand extended under the tunic and *through the arm-hole where the left hand projects, as if the gatherer were thieving*' – an elaborate procedure for deceiving the plant, which is assumed to be sentient of the fact that the left hand, not the right, was used for *botanēarsis*.[72] As for the circle to be traced around the *hiera botanē* prior to culling, this is a classic of magic. The describing of a circle around a figure or name inscribed upon writing material,[73] or as here around a living organism, was thought to have a confining or inhibiting effect on the entity thus enclosed. Bizarre though it may seem, the effect of the circle was to serve as a containment field to prevent the *hiera botanē* from escaping – as the deadly plant named *barras* supposedly did when attempts were made to pluck it (Joseph. *BJ* 7.181)[74] – and as scorpions and snakes were prevented from doing when circumscribed with a distillation of certain herbs (Plin. *HN* 22.60, 25.101). Finally, the iron used to draw the circle. Although bronze is the metal standardly used in magical ceremonies,[75] as in the Sophoclean fragment quoted above, there is plenty of evidence for the use of iron and other substances as well, as in a further plant-gathering ceremony at Plin. *HN* 25.107 and numerous other magical contexts too.[76]

To the instances of a *botanēarsis*-rite already quoted I append a further, formulaic instance from the *PGM*, 4.286–95:

> *Botanēarsis*. Use it before sunrise. The spell to be spoken is 'I pick you, NN plant, with my five-fingered hand, I, NN, and I bring you to me, so that you may be operative for me for a certain purpose. I adjure you by the undefiled name of the god. If you do not heed me, the earth which bore you will never ever again be watered in life, if I fail in this procedure ... accomplish for me this perfect charm'

This text adds relatively little to what we have already learned about plant-gathering rituals, but two points of importance may nonetheless be underlined. First, it confirms that the plant subject to *botanēarsis* is treated as a sentient, quasi-divine entity or as having an indwelling *daimōn*, albeit of a very minor type,[77] – to the extent that it is threatened with punitive actions in the event of non-compliance with the magician's wishes, as, under Egyptian influence, supernatural powers routinely are in the *PGM*.[78] Ultimately, it is precisely this 'animistic' construction of plants (to use an old-fashioned term) that underpins the perceived necessity for all kinds of magico-religious rituals in gathering them, and the reason why Theophrastus says (*HP* 9.8.7) that 'it is perhaps not unreasonable that one should be bidden <by the *rhizotomoi*> to pray while cutting a plant'.[79] Second, and just as important is the provenance of the text, namely a handbook for practising magicians. For although literary texts often picture fictional or mythical witches gathering herbs for their spells, these, at least in texts of the Roman period, typically derive from far-flung locales or places with a pronounced magical pedigree such as Thessaly or Egypt,[80] and it is on the exoticism and the difficulty of capture of these ingredients, rather than the details of the collection procedure, that the emphasis falls. The situation is quite different in regard to *botanēarsis* as described in notionally more sober texts. On the one hand, there is a wealth of magically infused detail on the actual process of plant-gathering that has only limited parallels in surviving fictional texts at least,[81] but on the other hand the pronounced magical dimension, as Dioscorides and Pliny clearly show, is in the final analysis subservient to the pragmatic, decidedly unshowy business of effecting a successful therapeutic outcome, and – the key difference – doing so by means of commonly available plants and herbs (Plin. *HN* 24.4–5): this is exactly as one would expect of lore that is essentially folk-based, handed down through the generations. To put it another way, while magic herbs are integral both to literary portraits of witchcraft and to folk-medicinal pharmacology, when it comes to the provenance of the herbs and the physical culling of these there is little overlap between the florid world of imaginative literature and the goal-orientated purposefulness of prose handbooks: hence, as already implied, it is to the latter that we must primarily look if we want to understand herbalism and its magical dimensions.

Notwithstanding what was said in the last paragraph, it is not to be supposed that fictional accounts of plant-gathering cannot on occasion cast oblique

Fig. 6 Mandrake root. © The Museum of Witchcraft and Magic, Boscastle, Cornwall.

illumination on actual practice. Two examples help to establish the case. Witches in literature are often seen culling their ingredients from remote mountainous locations, because magic herbs were believed to flourish particularly there.[82] But the judicious Dioscorides,[83] who is careful to qualify mention of magical properties ascribed to plants with a sceptical 'they say that', offers it as a fact that plants growing on exposed mountainsides are indeed more potent than those found in low-lying places (MM *praef.* 6). A second intriguing point was advanced by Anne-Marie Tupet in a major paper published after her regrettably early death.[84] Noting that witches in poetry frequently pluck their magic herbs from graveyards,[85] she observed that plants belonging to the Solanaceae family, of which the most important are mandrake (Gk. *mandragoras*), henbane (Gk. *huoscuamos*), belladonna (Gk. *struchnos*), and datura, delight in soils rich in nitrates, that is in places copiously enriched by human and animal detritus such as cemeteries. Now while the poets admittedly do not detail the names of the plants thus culled, it is the case that these four solanaceous plants attracted the detailed attention of ancient pharmacological writers for their pronounced soporific or psychoactive properties, and that they equally have a notable magical pedigree, especially the first two. Mandrake in particular has a long-established and still-vibrant association with magic.[86] Its alternative name was *Circaea*, 'Circe's plant',[87] it was used for love-charms,[88] perhaps because of its resemblance to the human body, and the method of harvesting it, as reported by the *rhizotomoi*, was profoundly magical; 'it is said that one should draw a circle three times around the mandrake with a sword and cut it with one's gaze turned towards the west; and at the cutting of the second piece one should dance round it in a circle and say as many things as possible about matters sexual' (Theophr. *HP* 9.8.8: cf. Plin. *HN* 25.148); the last detail reaffirms the plant's reputation as an aphrodisiac and promoter of fertility. In sum, it does not seem far-fetched to suppose that beneath literary accounts of witches foraging in graveyards for magical herbs, a substratum of folk-belief and even pharmacological fact may reside.

This brings us the third of the topics to concern us in the latter part of the chapter, the possible pharmacological efficacy of plants used in magic spells. We begin with a remarkable formulaic recipe at *PGM* 36.320–32, apparently addressed to any male[89] who wishes his wife or partner not to become pregnant:

> a contraceptive, the only one in the world [i.e. the only one that can be guaranteed to work]. Take bittervetch seeds, as many as you want to match the number of years you wish not to conceive. Steep them in the menses of a woman who is menstruating, let her steep them in her own genitals, and take a living frog and throw the bittervetch seeds into its mouth, so that it swallows them, and release

the frog alive at the place where you caught it. And taking a seed of henbane steep it in mare's milk, and taking nasal mucus (alternatively 'slime') from a cow, along with grains of barley, attach these to a piece of deerskin and on the outside bind it with the skin of a mule and attach it as an amulet when the moon is waning and in a female sign of the Zodiac on a day of Kronos or Hermes. Mix in also with the barley grains wax from the ear of a mule.

This whole spell is replete with magical concepts, even if the rationale for certain details – at least in terms of their presumptive contraceptive effect[90] – is less than clear. But the overall thought pattern appears to be as follows. The seeds and grains symbolise the generative principle, which is to be nullified by the procedures prescribed in the text (the number magic involving the seeds is self-explanatory). The menstrual flow of the female subject represents both her potential fertility and the temporary interruption of this due to her time of the month. The potential for her to become pregnant is transferred by contagious magic, using menses-doctored henbane seeds, to a frog (itself an icon of fecundity), which carries this off with it when released alive. The mare's milk perhaps stands for the suppression of fertility in the female while lactating. The muleskin and the wax from a mule's ear harness by contagion the association with sterility for which the mule was proverbial (the latter detail reappears in another contraceptive recipe from the Hermetic text known as the *Cyranides*, which offers a wealth of information on the amuletic use of animal and botanical ingredients).[91] The attachment of the amulet under a waning moon reflects the fact that the moon regulates the female cycle,[92] and hence a woman's fertility, which, like everything in nature, experiences growth or diminution according to whether the moon is waxing or waning, the latter being in point here.

If I have lingered over the bricolage of magical effects in *PGM* 36.320–32 it is because their sheer density makes it all the more surprising that, as John Scarborough (1991, 158) noted, 'sandwiched within are two pharmacologically potent herbs, bittervetch ... and henbane'. Scarborough gives an overview of the effects of each upon the body, but does not identify the fact that, included amid the admittedly legion medicinal properties attributed in Antiquity to each, are a number of gynaecological import. Vetch (Gk. *orobos*, Latin *uicia*), according to Hippocratic sources, was useful for fomenting the womb if ulcerated or unfruitful (!), and for controlling dysmenorrhea,[93] while Dioscorides *MM* 4.68 states that a preparation made from the first extract of the henbane's juice and dry seeds is helpful if applied to the region around the uterus, and that the seeds were good for female bleeding and other kinds of haemorrhage. Of course, neither the bittervetch nor the henbane is applied as a fomentation to, or ingested by, the female subject here, as it would be in a regular medicinal procedure; the first drug forms part of piece of contagious magic, while the function of the second is basically amuletic. But it does not seem to be stretching a point to suppose that at some rudimentary level the writer of *PGM* 36.320–32 was aware of the two plants' powers to minister to female complaints.

In a lengthy article published in 1978 John Scarborough surveyed the plants, some sixty of them, discussed in the section of Theophrastus' *Enquiry into Plants* which is devoted to medical botany (9.8–9.20), and came to the conclusion that many of them do possess the pharmaceutical powers there attributed to them and that they are frequently helpful in treating the particular complaints for which Theophrastus prescribed their use; he further noted that some of them are still employed, or were until recently employed in modern medicine, both for the same purposes as were detailed by Theophrastus, and others besides.[94] In other words, the *rhizotomoi* and *pharmakopōlai*, drug sellers, from whom Theophrastus procured so much of his information for his *Enquiry into Plants* book 9[95] were aware empirically of the pharmacological effects of plants, evidently because, as Pliny *HN* 25.16 says, they were country dwellers 'who actually lived among the plants' and indeed, according to Pliny, illiterate, so that much of the plant-lore must have been transmitted orally.

Now the recipes given by Theophrastus are simple and straightforward: generally speaking he restricts himself to describing the appearance of a given plant, followed by its various therapeutic properties; as we have seen, he pours scorn on the elaborate collection rituals observed by the *rhizotomoi*. Much the same pattern is observed by Dioscorides in the herbal portions of the *Materia Medica*, who, if he reports phytotherapeutic effects of dubious or magical import, tends to relegate them to the end of each entry, prefacing it with 'some say that' or the like, in order to indicate scepticism. Very different is the procedure of Pliny (and later authorities such as Marcellus Empiricus). First, his recipes are often complex, multi-substance affairs. Second, in many of his herbals, he freely incorporates the superstitious harvesting procedures of the *rhizotomoi* without necessarily giving them subsidiary billing or expressing reserve about their validity, as does Theophrastus.

This said, Pliny's indiscriminacy and eclecticism should not occlude the fact that a considerable number of his herbals make medical sense. Take for example his account of the mallow, *moloche agria*, in *HN* 20.29

> it is a cure for ulcers, and broken cartilages and bones. Its leaves drunk in water move the bowels: they keep away serpents and, smeared on the skin, heal the

stings of bees, wasps, and hornets. Its root pulled up before sunrise is wrapped in wool of the colour which they call 'natural', taken besides from a sheep that has borne a ewe lamb, and they bind it to scrofulous sores even when they have suppurated. Some think that when it is used for this last purpose the root should be dug up with a gold implement, care being taken that the root should not touch the ground.

In among what a modern might describe as a confection of superstitious nonsense there nonetheless resides a kernel of therapeutic sense. Mallow is good for constipation (it was famed for this in the laxative-obsessed society of Rome) and used topically, is indeed good for treating skin inflammations, ulceration, and stings and bites – exactly as Pliny, and before him Dioscorides (*MM* 2.118), say.[96]

Another interesting case involves the *hiera botanē*, vervain. As we saw above, Pliny scoffs at as 'crazy' the claims made by the Magi for its beneficial effects as well as the protocols that they prescribe for gathering it. Certainly their assertion that those who have been rubbed all over with it gain their wishes and win friends is transparent nonsense; but not so their championing of its effectiveness against fever, a property also recognised by Dioscorides, not without a dash of superstition.[97] As Tobyn, Denham and Whitelegg have noted, vervain is good for respiratory ailments, colds and fevers, tightness of the chest and whooping cough.[98] They also show that, among other medicinal plants discussed by Pliny, agrimony, burdock, artemisia, elecampane and peony – the last of these long used in Chinese herbal medicine for its anti-inflammatory and analgesic properties[99] – exhibit a number of the curative effects imputed to them by the author, as do further plants treated by Pliny and other medical writers, but not included in Tobyn's and his colleagues' survey of thirty or so plants with a longstanding herbal history.[100] In sum, for all the patina of superstition that shrouds Pliny's books on medical botany, he is not necessarily dealing in pharmacological chimeras: rather, at its heart may often lie a good deal of empirically derived, practical and commonsensical herbal lore.

This chapter has ranged over a good deal of diverse territory, so it may be helpful to restate some of its more important conclusions. They include: the centrality of herbs alike to literary accounts of witchcraft and to scientific or para-scientific works on plant-lore; the fact that *pharmaka*, whether benign or malign in nature, are largely compounded of plants; the fundamental importance of plants to medicine, in particular to folk-medicine; the profound interpenetration of medicine and magic in Antiquity; the doctrine of cosmic sympathy as it relates to the therapeutic use of plants; the magic-inspired belief structure underpinning the use of plant derivatives, including the so-called laws of magic – similarity, contiguity and antipathy; the relative clarity of these overall principles, as opposed to the obscurity which frequently shrouds the choice of particular plant-agents or procedures in individual cases; the confused and inconsistent stance of Pliny, our most important source on the magic of plants, regarding magical activities and magico-medical prescriptions; the elaborate rituals and protocols involved in *botanēarsis*; the homeliness and ready accessibility for the most part of the therapeutic plants mentioned by Pliny and other herbalists, in contrast to the typically exotic and, in real terms, impractical character of those gathered by sorceresses in fiction; the multistranded nature of later herbal regimes; the presence, within the most unlikely-seeming prescriptions, of pharmacologically sound notions whose validity is confirmed by modern phytochemistry: the inferences that this last observation allows us to draw for the empirical basis of much of ancient folk-medicine; finally, the privileging in medicinal magic of the purely pragmatic aim of curing the patient, for all the attendant paraphernalia of sacro-magic ritual.

Notes

1 Hubert (1904), 1498: cf. 1506 'the attention of <Greek and Roman> magicians is directed above all to plants', where, however, his 'directed above all' appears something of an overstatement. For a convenient listing of plants discussed in Latin writings on herbs in a variety of contexts, with cross-references to Greek authorities, see André (1985).
2 Further examples of plants with inherently marvellous capacities in Gordon (2015), 148–9.
3 Roscher (1890), 144.
4 E.g. Verg. *Ecl.* 8.95–6, Claud. *In Ruf.* 1.151–3: cf. Theophr. *HP* 9.15.1 (Latium, where Circe dwelt, is especially rich in herbal *pharmaka*).
5 The intersection of *pharmaka* with botanical substances is reaffirmed by a much later source, a scholion to Aristophanes *Clouds* 749, which states that the proliferation of magical plants in Thessaly is owed to the fact that, when Medea was fleeing after the crimes that she had committed in that land, in her haste she dropped her chest containing *pharmaka*, and from these 'grew up' Thessaly's famed magical herbs.
6 E.g. the peony as described in the anonymous second–third century CE Greek poem *De uiribus herbarum* (ed. Heitsch no. 64) 164–5 'it is able to avert the evil arts of wicked sorceresses and the tribes of men who have the Evil Eye'. Similar claims

7   are made for the bouphthalmos (ibid. 132) and the chrysanthemos (ibid. 215–16). See further Plin. *HN* 20.101, 21.108, 24.116, 25.130, Hopfner OZ 1.§521.
7   Hom. *Hymn Dem.* 228–9 with Richardson ad loc. For the mythology surrounding the discovery of botanical medicine, see Delatte (1961), 7–9.
8   E.g. Plin. *HN* 24.107, 111, 115, *Orphic Lithika* 410 'the magical power of the root'. For *rhizotomoi* and other terms for plant-gatherers, see Delatte (1961), 23–6.
9   Medea's gesture reflects the widespread prohibition on looking upon magical or uncanny things with the naked eye, lest one come to harm (cf. n.71); but the aversion of her gaze also reflects an unwillingness to gaze directly upon the plant-gathering, which could be construed as a sinful act: see below on this.
10 See n.51 on ritual nakedness. Delatte (1961), 14–21 adduces a number of Minoan and Mycenaean rings in which partially or completely naked female figures, with hair unbound, are seen to pluck or uproot plants and herbs, considering them early evidence of the elaborate rituals attaching to plant-gathering.
11 On the use of bronze implements in magic, see n.76 below.
12 That is to say, the plant is uprooted before sunrise, a common prescription (Delatte (1961), 50–4), but the death of the dog only supervenes once the sun sees the evidence of the act.
13 The peony's nocturnal brightness and diurnal invisibility results from its sympathetic connexion with the moon. Conversely, a species of lotus on the Euphrates which is connected by sympathy with the sun submerges its head and flower into the depths of the river by night, only re-emerging at sunrise (Plin. *HN* 13.108–9, Hopfner OZ 1.§517).
14 Cf. Plin. *HN* 25.50, 25.69, 25.78, 27.85, 30.18; Tzetzes on Lycophron *Alexandra* 679–80 (whoever pulls up completely the root of the plant known to Homer as *mōlu* dies immediately). Theophrastus' and Pliny's account of the peony confirms that picking the plant was popularly thought dangerous, though the risk is different from that in Aelian, blinding by a woodpecker or anal prolapse (*HP* 9.8.6, *HN* 25.29, 27.85). The Greek poem *De uiribus herbarum* (ed. Heitsch) 157–8 prescribes that the peony should be picked 'before the sun travels over its boundless circuit', otherwise the gods will 'damage the picker's mind and wits'. On the dangers of plant-picking see also Delatte (1961), 88 and 91.
15 Cf. Plin. *HN* 27.131. On the apotropaic and curative power of human saliva see Nicholson (1897); Gow (1965) on Theocr. *Id.* 6.39.
16 Cf. Plin. *HN* 21.143, 21.176, 22.38 (the name of the patient and the identity of his parents to be spoken), 23.103, 24.133, Marcell. Empir. 14.65, *PGM* 4.288–90.
17 Plin. *HN* 21.42, 25.107; Delatte (1961), 150–1.
18 Cf. Theophr. *HP* 9.8.8; Dioscor. *MM* 4.162.4; Plin. *HN* 25.50.
19 For another instance of this see Plin. *HN* 25.78.
20 According to a late source (Delatte (1961), 185–6, Hardy and Totelin (2016), 46–7, with illustration), mandrake is uprooted using the same canine strategy as with the

peony. The plant *huoskuamos* (henbane) is also pulled up in much the same way as the peony, the animal surrogate being here a bird, whose life is not, however, forfeit in the process (Ael. *NA* 9.32).

21 For such apotropaic measures specifically in regard to plant-gathering see Delatte (1961), 88–117.
22 For the moon and epilepsy see Dedo (1904), 3. The various different names for the peony reflect its connection with the moon (Hopfner *OZ* 1.§507).
23 On the sympathetic relationship between plants and the cosmic powers see Hopfner (1928), 321–5 and especially id. *OZ* 1.§464–551. See also the discussion below.
24 The peony was supposedly named after Paeon, the healer in the Homeric poems (Isid. *Orig.* 17.9.48).
25 'Perfumes' includes medicinal unguents and plasters (*kataplasmata*) made from plants.
26 *Cyranides* 1.4 Kaimakis puts it even more strongly: a plant 'is able to effect by its own power what no man could accomplish'.
27 Similarly Ael. *NA* 2.18. For the curative powers of herbs and incantations see also Plat. *Charm.* 155e ff.
28 Galen, however, is not above using curative regimes that appear incontestably magical (admittedly not involving plants), while excusing this in a distinctly Jesuitical way (Muth (1954), 129–43; Keyser (1997), especially 188–91).
29 In what follows I am guided by the discussion of Ducourthial (2003), 94–8.
30 Cf. *PGM* 12.401–44, a list of mostly botanical aliases for plants whereby the scribes of the Egyptian temples conceal their herbal lore from the masses, who do not understand such matters.
31 Galen 12.967 Kühn.
32 Prayers while gathering a plant, McEnerney (1983); Hardy and Totelin (2016), 24.
33 Cf. Plin. *HN* 21.147, 25.171, Marcell. Empir. 1.68 'lest the power of the remedy [in this case small stones] be lessened by contact with the ground'.
34 Delatte (1961), 27–33 lists the ancient writers, both lost and surviving, on the subject of herbalism.
35 Mauss (1972), 64–73.
36 Faraone (1999), 42; Fountoulakis (1999), 201 n.34 with further bibliography. Keyser (1997); Ducourthial (2003); Ogden (2008), 98; and Collins (2008) among others find the term unproblematic.
37 For the idea of a substance acting autonomously, cf. Dioscor. *MM* 3.134 on the *asplēnos* plant, 'it seems to have contraceptive powers *in its own right*', Plin. *HN* 27.34. Similarly Theophr. *HP* 9.8.1 'for some of the juices derived from roots have independently and of themselves many and varied powers'.
38 For *antipathia* see e.g. Plin. *HN* 20.1, 28, 24.67 (*erica* has a miraculous antipathy to the human spleen) so as to cure it if diseased. The related verb *antipaschein*, 'be antipathetic to' appears in *Cyranides* 5ε p. 302 Kaimakis.

39 Other instances of the principle: see Keyser (1997), 190.
40 The principle of like curing like is neatly captured in Marcell. Empir. 14.26, *uua uuam emendat*, 'the grape cures the (swollen) uvula', the homology involving both identity of nomenclature (*uua* signifies both grape and uvula) and the physical resemblance of the uvula to a grape.
41 For this means of averting the Eye, see Tafel III to Jahn (1855), still a valuable resource on the Evil Eye; Dasen (2015), 182–3.
42 For other instances of sympathetic effects based on similarity of colour see on haematite and galactite in the appendix to Chapter 5.
43 In fact botanical or magical substances are often said to be capable of diametrically opposite effects.
44 One might rather have expected the creation of a pseudo-eyeball in the cherry stone by boring into it to have caused a piercing pain in the eye.
45 Schreckenberg (1964), 135–9. A further consideration is that, according to Pliny ibid., 'as <*katanankē*> withers it crumples up into the shape of the claws of a dead kite', in other words 'it hooks its victim by imitative magic' (W.H.S. Jones ad loc.).
46 Cf. Plin. *HN* 24.95, the *alysson*, 'non-madness', plant got its name because persons bitten by a rabid dog do not develop hydrophobia if they wear it as an amulet.
47 An identical assertion apropos of *scorpiuron* (scorpion's tail') by Plin. *HN* 22.60; cf. also 25.122.
48 From Gk. *aischunomai*, 'feel a sense of modesty before someone'.
49 The difficulty is touched upon by Stannard (1982), 15 and Lloyd (1983), 133.
50 For a similar procedure see also Marcell. Empir. 23.68.
51 In general on ritual nakedness see Heckenbach (1911); Pease (1935), on Verg. *Aen.* 4. 509 and 518. Instances in a specifically magico-herbal context: Soph. frg. 534 Radt; Plin. *HN* 23.110; Ov. *Met.* 7.182–3; further Delatte (1961), 79–81.
52 Food, like sex, was regarded as an impermissible pollutant prior to a magical or religious rite. For other instances of this injunction in connection with *botanēarsis*, see Plin. *HN* 24.181, 26.91; Marcell. Empir. 25.11; Delatte (1961), 83.
53 Cf. n.15 supra.
54 For example, he recommends (12.24) that a person suffering from pain in the teeth should spit into the mouth of a frog, thus freeing himself from the toothache and transferring it to the frog.
55 Conversely, according to Dioscor. *MM* 2.164, 'they say that should a woman who is pregnant step over cyclamen root, she miscarries'.
56 The name comes from the fact that moisture does not stay on the plant's leaves (Plin. *HN* 22.62; Gow (1965) on Theocr. *Id.* 13.41).
57 Muth (1968), 1293–4 and 1296–1300. Less common is the use of urine in anti-social magic (ibid. 1294–6).
58 Examples in Muth (1968), 1297–9.

59 Although I translate *puer* and *pais* as 'boy', the possibility of a reference to a 'child' of either sex cannot be excluded, since both words can also bear that meaning.
60 Discussion, with bibliography, of magic involving sexual chastity in Watson (2003) on Hor. *Epod.* 5.13; add Plin. *HN* 22.27 (the root of the tribulus plant is to be gathered 'in chastity and purity').
61 In general see Fehrle (1910), 43–64.
62 A particularly egregious instance at Marcell. Empir. 15.9.
63 Malinowski (1974), 19 cites Preuss, Marett, Hubert and Mauss for this view.
64 So Lévy-Bruhl, as cited by Malinowski (1974), 25.
65 Bonner (1950), 72–3, who does however qualify the adjective with a following 'reasoning'.
66 Malinowski (2002), 338, (1935), 213–50.
67 Malinowski (1974) 38 et passim.
68 Malinowski (1974), 86.
69 Cf. Plin. *HN* 25.145; Costa on Sen. *Med.* 728–9.
70 For the sun, see West on Hes. *Works and Days* 267; for the moon, cf. Hor. *Epod.* 5.49–52, *Sat.*1.8.36 (the moon deliberately hides behind tall tombs to avoid witnessing the sorcerous doings of Canidia and Sagana).
71 See Ellis on Catull. 12.1; Brashear (1991), 43. The idea that *botanēarsis* constituted a religious violation is also seen in Sophocles frg. 534 Radt quoted above (Medea shields her gaze during the process), and in the Magian recommendation (Plin. *HN* 21.176) that *parthenium* should be gathered while not looking backwards, a standard prescription when dealing with potentially inimical forces in magical or religious rites: see Gow (1965) on Theocr. *Id.* 24.96.
72 See the note of W.H.S. Jones in the Loeb edn. of Pliny's *Historia Naturalis* ad loc.
73 Cf. *PGM* 4.2016, 2048, 5.304–69, 7.467–77, also 7.299 'rings or binding spells'.
74 'It tries to withdraw and does not stop until someone pours over it a woman's urine or menstrual blood'.
75 See Pease (1935) on Verg. *Aen.* 4.513; Faraone (1991), 8 n.35.
76 See Plin *HN* 10.152; Faraone and Obbink (1991), index s.v. 'iron'; and Tupet (1976), 40–4 for a persuasive argument that no intrinsic magical virtue attaches to bronze.
77 This idea is particularly to the fore in the other *botanēarsis* ritual in the *PGM*, 4.2967–3006, where the person pulling up the plant directs, at the moment of picking, a lengthy invocation 'to the *daimōn* to whom the plant is dedicated'. In general on the belief that plants had immanent demonic powers that had to be approached in the manner of a superior being, see Hopfner OZ 1.§482, especially ad fin.
78 See Chapter 1.
79 For the supposed divinity of plants see Edelstein (1967), 231.
80 E.g. Hor. *Epod.* 5.61–8; Sen. *Med.* 706–30.
81 An exception is Soph. frg. 534 Radt quoted above in the text.

82 E.g. Ap. Rhod. 3.851–3; Schol. Theocr. *Id.* 2.15; Verg. *Aen.* 7.758; Ov. *Met.* 7.224–7; Sen. *Med.* 707–9, 720–2; Luc. 6.438–9.
83 Compare *HP* 2.3, where Theophrastus expressly disassociates himself from the magical and superstitious beliefs of his day.
84 Tupet (1986), 2635–6.
85 On the magically coloured reasons for this see Watson (2003) on Hor. *Epod.* 5.17. On account of the practice witches came to be known as *tumbades* or *bustuariae*, 'tomb-haunters'.
86 Magical aspects of mandrake Riddle (2010), 55–77; of henbane Ducourthial (2003), 331–2; of belladonna *Orphic Argonautika* 916.
87 Dioscor. *MM* 4.75, Plin *HN* 25.147.
88 Dioscor. *MM* 4.75 'some call <the mandrake> Circe's plant, because it appears to be good for making love-philtres', Theophr. *HP* 9.9.1, the root and the juice of mandrake are useful for love potions.
89 The four aorist participles that convey instructions to the addressee of the recipe are all in the masculine gender. For botanical and other difficulties in the interpretation of this spell, see LiDonnici (2002), 365–6.
90 The nasal mucus/slime of a cow, the deerskin, the choice of barley grains, the release of the frog at the place where it was found. Eitrem (1925a) ad loc. cites multiple parallels for the use of these ingredients in magic rituals, but does not succeed in tying them to the kind of procedure in question here.
91 *Cyranides* 1.3 (p. 35 Kaimakis), if a woman wishes not to conceive, she should bind about her lower abdomen the opened fruit of the peony along with dirt from the ear of a mule. On the *Cyranides* see Brill's *NP* vol. 4 (2004), 1–2, especially p. 1 on the amuletic properties of plant and animal substances in both physical and pictorial (engraved) form, as recommended in the *Cyranides*.
92 *RE* IIA.1.1136–44 s.v. 'Selene' at 1139.
93 References in *RE* 6.1.556–61 s.v. 'Erve'.
94 E.g. hellebore, *sikuos agrios* (wild cucumber), the two types of *struchnos* (deadly nightshade), *chamaileōn* (white pine thistle), the *skorpios* plant.
95 On Theophrastus and the rootcutters see Lloyd (1983), 119–35; Scarborough (2006); on the rhizotomists more generally Gordon (2015), 143–52. For Theophrastus' other sources see Scarborough (1978), 355–7.
96 See Tobyn et al. (2011), 67–78.
97 Dioscor. *MM* 4.60 'the harvesting of specifically the third joint of the plant from the ground along with its surrounding leaves is helpful for treating tertian fever, as is the fourth joint for quartan fever'.
98 Tobyn et al. (2011), 327–36.
99 He and Dai (2011).
100 See Brill's *NP* vol. 8 (2006) pp. 558–68 s.vv. 'medicinal plants'; D'Angelo (2017), 197–201.

5

Animals in Magic

Patricia Watson

A wide variety of animals were employed in magic: larger mammals, both domesticated (e.g. donkeys, goats, cows and dogs) and wild (e.g. hyenas, wolves), birds such as roosters and doves as well as the more sinister owls and bats,[1] reptiles (e.g. snakes, lizards[2] and tortoises), amphibians (especially frogs[3]), insects (e.g. bugs, worms and beetles) and aquatic creatures such as the salpe and silurus fishes[4] or the crab. The Egyptian provenance of the *Greek Magical Papyri* explains the frequency in these of animals and birds such as the crocodile, cat, ibis, falcon and scarab beetle, which were native to the country and/or held in special veneration.[5] Where more exotic animals are mentioned, however, the names may in some cases have been codes for more readily available ingredients, devised by temple scribes in Egypt to keep their secrets hidden from the masses, thus deterring them from practising magic (for example, 'baboon's tears,'[6] or 'lion's semen' stand for dill juice and human semen respectively).[7]

Although animals were used in all the major types of magic – love spells, divination, apotropaic magic, curses/*defixiones* – our largest body of evidence is for their employment in healing, contained above all in the *Natural History* of Pliny the Elder, who offers a mind-boggling range of medical cures derived from animals and animal products. In their simplest form – by far the most common in Pliny's compendium – these remedies consisted of applying a substance derived from an animal to the affected part of the body (e.g. smearing mouse dung on the belly for stones in the bladder Plin. *HN* 30.65) or the ingesting of various animals or their parts (e.g. cures for stomach troubles include eating snails or taking a drink of roasted sheep's spleen mixed in wine Plin. *HN* 30.61).

A second type of cure encompassed principles that we would associate with magic, such as similarity (like curing like: an example would be the use of animal heads or brains to treat headaches, or eyes for eye disease),[8] or transference via contiguity, whereby an illness is passed on from the patient to an animal; this is seen for instance in a remedy for intestinal disease involving the placing of puppies on the sufferer's stomach and chest for three days and having the puppies suck milk from the patient's mouth (Plin. *HN* 30.64): the disease is transferred to the puppies, which sicken and die.[9]

Third, there are remedies involving overtly magic practices such as incantations, amulets, the use of magic numbers, astrology and so on. Although Pliny attacks magic at length (*HN* 30.1–18), calling it 'the most fraudulent of arts', he includes, for instance, among remedies for fever, an amulet made from a caterpillar in a linen cloth around which the healer must tie a thread three times with three knots, pronouncing the reason for the spell as he ties each knot (*HN* 30.101). And a treatment for boils (Plin. *HN* 30.108) consists of killing a shrew mouse and hanging it up so that the body does not touch the earth, then passing it three times round the boil while both the healer and the patient spit the same number of times. The two examples just cited include a number of characteristically magical features: the making of amulets, the use of linen, in Egypt a symbol of purity,[10] the magical number three,[11] the use of knots,[12] the accompaniment of spoken words, the injunction that the magic material should not touch the ground,[13] the magic circle[14] and apotropaic spitting.[15]

Of the various types of animal-based remedies recounted by Pliny, the first in particular (simple cures involving the application of animal products or ingesting animals or their parts) might seem to belong to the sphere of folk-medicine rather than magic proper, and it will be worthwhile, before proceeding further, to consider briefly the distinction between the two: a distinction notoriously difficult to draw (cf. e.g. Nutton (1992), 55–7) and one that is complicated by the fact that ancient concepts of magic were different from those of modern theorists.

The latter, for instance, would certainly class among magical cures those based on accepted magic principles such as similarity and transference, while Gordon (2010, 256–7) has extended this classification to include even the ingesting of creatures such as mice, snails or millipedes on the basis of the underlying magical assumption that disease, being an infraction of natural rules, could be counterbalanced by the deliberate overturning of normal alimentary practice. Ancient writers, by contrast, tended to regard as belonging to the realm of magic (as opposed to medicine) only those remedies involving more complex ritual or the use of exotic ingredients. This is demonstrated by the fact that collections of medical remedies[16] frequently record procedures in our second category, that is, which utilise what modern theorists would regard as magic principles without any accompanying magic ritual. The concept of *similia similibus* (like curing like) for instance, underlies prescriptions given by

Scribonius Largus, court physician to the emperor Claudius, in which the liver of a wolf is dried by immersion in boiling water and then given in hot water to a sufferer from liver problems[17] or Sextus Placitus 9 (a treatment for eye pain is to shred a wolf's eye and smear it on the afflicted eye);[18] a variant, whereby the sex of the animal corresponds to the sex of the patient, is seen in Sextus Placitus' prescription for a fertility drug (4.14: for conception a hare's rennet is taken in wine – that of a male hare by the husband and that of a female hare by the wife).[19] An instance of magic transference appears in Serenus Sammonicus' didactic medical poem (*Liber Medicinalis* 439–41), where disease of the upper abdomen is treated by placing a puppy on the patient's body and the disease transferred to it, causing the pup to die.

Attempts were made by Pliny and others to distinguish medicinal from what they regarded as magical cures. In citing the two magic remedies described earlier (*HN* 30.101, 30.108), for instance, Pliny attributes them to others, implying that he does not necessarily believe them himself. Dioscorides prefaced anything exotic with 'they say that …' (cf. Riddle (1985), 82–88), while Serenus Sammonicus, in his puppy remedy cited above, is careful to distance himself from the belief that the disease is actually transferred to the animal ('the whole of the illness *is said to be* transferred to the puppy'); similarly Pliny qualifies his remedies involving transference (30.61, 64)[20] by representing each as marvels.[21] A more overt separation between (folk) medicine and magic is seen in Pliny's constant attacks on the Magi, to whom he attributes remedies involving magic practices such as the use of astrology (e.g. *HN* 30.96–7, holding this up to ridicule at length), fantastic beliefs (e.g. that persons anointed with lion fat more easily attain popularity with 'peoples or kings' *HN* 28.89), or the use of uncanny or unpleasant ingredients (e.g. he scoffs at the Magi's use in an amulet of a *bubo*, an uncanny bird,[22] or their belief in the magic potency of the mole[23]).

Sometimes a distinction between the medical and the magical is made less explicitly, as for instance when Pliny juxtaposes folk-cures with others involving magic ritual, recording a potion made of vinegar with the spleen of a puppy or a hedgehog as a remedy for diseases of the spleen alongside a Magian cure that similarly uses an animal spleen to cure splenic complaints but also involves a complex magical procedure: the spleen of a sheep is placed over the spleen of the patient, accompanied by a spoken statement of intent; the spleen is then plastered into the bedroom wall, sealed with a ring thrice nine times and the same words repeated (*HN* 30.51).[24] By attributing the latter remedy to the Magi, Pliny is making an implicit distinction between what he would view as simple folk-medicine and a similar treatment employing overtly magical practices.

He is not, however, so discriminating[25] on other occasions. For example, at 29.112–14, a list of cures for headaches is a mixed bag of the non-magical (e.g. applying crushed snails or the ash of a mouse's skin in vinegar) and the magical (e.g. the head of a snail cut off with a reed as it feeds in the morning, preferably at the time of the full moon,[26] attached in a linen cloth by a thread to the head of the sufferer); in one case Pliny even voices his approval for the latter ('the small bone of a slug found between two wheel ruts, passed through gold, silver and ivory and attached as an amulet in the skin of a dog, *a remedy that is always generally beneficial*'). Similarly inconsistent is Serenus, who scathingly dismisses magic incantations as monstrous words, the mark of empty superstition,[27] yet it is in his work that we encounter the first instance of the best-known magic word of all: 'abracadabra'.[28] Incantations are also found in the fourth-century CE medical writer Marcellus Empiricus, one of which, for toothache, also utilises astrology.[29] Marcellus is in fact given to including magical cures. A remedy based on transference, for instance, contains many more overtly magical elements than the instances from Pliny and Serenus cited earlier:

> Take a green lizard and with the sharp point of a reed remove its liver and wrap it in a piece of cloth that is red or naturally black and hang it from the right part of the side or the arm of a sufferer from liver disease when he is in pain, then release the lizard alive and say to it: 'Look, I release you alive; see to it that his liver causes no pain to whomsoever I touch with this' (22.41).[30]

The examples just cited demonstrate the slenderness of the dividing line between folk-medicine and magic, and the futility of attempts to draw a firm distinction, regardless of whether magic is defined on modern or ancient lines. I conclude this section with an interesting example of a remedy with a decidedly magical character[31] which is reported as effective ('I know that …') by the physician Scribonius Largus: note that it is attributed, not to a sorcerer or elderly wise-woman, but to a respectable married woman (*honesta matrona*):

> I know that at Rome a certain respectable woman cured several persons of epilepsy with the following medication: half a pint of ivory shavings and a pound of Attic honey; these are mixed together, after that there is added, if the patient is a boy, all the blood that flows from a male tortoise and a male dove, each wild, i.e. only recently caught, making sure to release alive each of the animals: but if the patient is a girl, the animals should be female and captured in the same way and released after their blood has been drained. (You must drive a sharp nail of Cyprian bronze into the neck of the tortoise and cut with sharp bronze the veins of the dove which are under the wings.) This medication is sealed up in a wooden

vessel and stored away. When needed, there are given from it at the time of the waning moon for thirty days in a row first three spoonfuls, then five, then seven, then nine, finally eleven, and again nine, then seven, then five, after that three and a second time spoonfuls are given in increasing and diminishing numbers, until the aforementioned thirty days are used up. Afterwards the person afflicted will have to swallow half a pint of ivory shavings over two months, receiving three spoonfuls a day in three ladlefuls of water. The person using this medication must abstain from wine and pork and must also wear an ivory bracelet on their arm.

Scribonius Largus, *Compositiones* 16

Both animals and their by-products were employed in magic. The latter included wool,[32] milk, eggs,[33] feathers and especially dung.[34] Excrement from a variety of animals and birds was used in cures, ranging from simple folk-medicinal remedies such as the mouse dung referred to above, to more complex magical cures. An example from the so-called eighth book of Moses (*PGM* 13.245–6) combines the application of crocodile dung with the pronunciation of a holy name, in a remedy for erysipelas. Among the treatments of the Magi for quartan fever (Plin. *HN* 28.228) was the wearing as an amulet of cat's dung, along with the claw of an owl. Excrement might even be swallowed, e.g. for inflammation of the eyes, the dung of she-goats or gazelles coated with wax was to be eaten at the new moon (Plin. *HN* 28.170). It had other uses as well, for instance a way of making a woman repulsive to a man or vice versa was to put dog's excrement in the post-hole of their door, while pronouncing a ritual formula (*PGM* 13.240–2); in *PGM* 4.1390–1495, an offering of cow's dung is used to compel a variety of chthonic deities in cases where the initial fetching spell fails to work.

Many of the remedies and spells which we have touched on called for animal parts, the collection of which necessitated the killing of the animals in question: unremarkable in an ancient context where ritual slaughter of animals for religious purposes was an everyday occurrence.[35] More repulsive – at least to modern eyes – is magic requiring the mutilation of a living creature, such as Magian cures for quartan fever in which a viper's heart or a lizard's right eye were to be extracted while the animals were still alive (Plin. *HN* 30.98–9), a curse involving the ripping out of a rooster's tongue,[36] or an erotic spell (*PGM* 4.2943–66) in which the eyes are removed from a bat, which is then released,[37] and placed in the figurine of a dog.[38] A particularly cruel instance is found in Marc. Empir. 29.52: this involves thrusting a silver needle through the eyes of a newborn puppy in such a way that it exits via the anus and finally tossing the still-living puppy into a river.

Though it was most frequently animal parts that were employed in magic, whole animals were also used. For medical purposes, these were most often small creatures such as insects or lizards (e.g. Plin. *HN* 29.61–64, 29.138, 30.100; *Cyranides* 2.14, pp. 139–40 Kaimakis). Lizards, in general regarded as uncanny or noxious creatures,[39] also feature in love magic (e.g. Marcell. Empir. 33.64; cf. Theocritus, *Id*. 2.58) and could be used against an enemy for malicious purposes: according to Pliny (*HN* 29.73), an evil drug is made from the spotted lizard (*stelio*) which if drowned in wine and drunk, afflicts [by magical transference] the face of the drinker with an outbreak of freckly spots – for this reason, he adds, courtesans try to ruin a rival's complexion by killing a gecko in her face cream.[40]

In more complicated rituals involving sacrifice, birds, especially roosters (see below), were the main victims. *PGM* 12.14–95, for example, involves the sacrifice of various birds to obtain Eros as an assistant.[41] Common in the magical papyri, and especially Egyptian in character, is the drowning of animals in order to make them into a divine assistant (Esies). The most striking example is the very complex 'cat spell' (*PGM* 3.1–164), in which a cat is drowned in water and its deified spirit used to effect a variety of malicious purposes, such as to hex your opponent's charioteers and horses, send dreams, or for binding or separation in an erotic context.

Finally, *defixiones* were sometimes accompanied by the bodies of creatures such as a rooster (Audollent 222 and 241 from Carthage, second century CE) or a puppy (Audollent 111–12, second century CE in Latin, from Aquitania). In the latter case, the intention was that the men who were the subject of the curse might not be able to be defended by their advocates in court nor get up to defend themselves, just as the puppy's mother had been unable to defend it, and the animal itself, transfixed as it was, could not rise up. Faraone[42] comments that we can assume the puppy was 'brutally transfixed at the scene of the ritual'.

In the majority of instances it is difficult to discern a reason for the use of a particular animal, but this is not always so. Some animals, for example, were thought to possess innate magical powers. The mole is an interesting case in point, especially since belief in its power continued to be widespread throughout Europe and North America up until the twentieth century.[43] Pliny[44] comments that the most cogent demonstration of the vacuous folly of the Magi is that they attribute the highest magical potency to the mole, even though it is one of the most ill-favoured of creatures, being blind and living in darkness under the earth 'like the buried dead'. No doubt, it was the very fact that the mole was seen as having a close association with the realm of the dead that caused magical powers

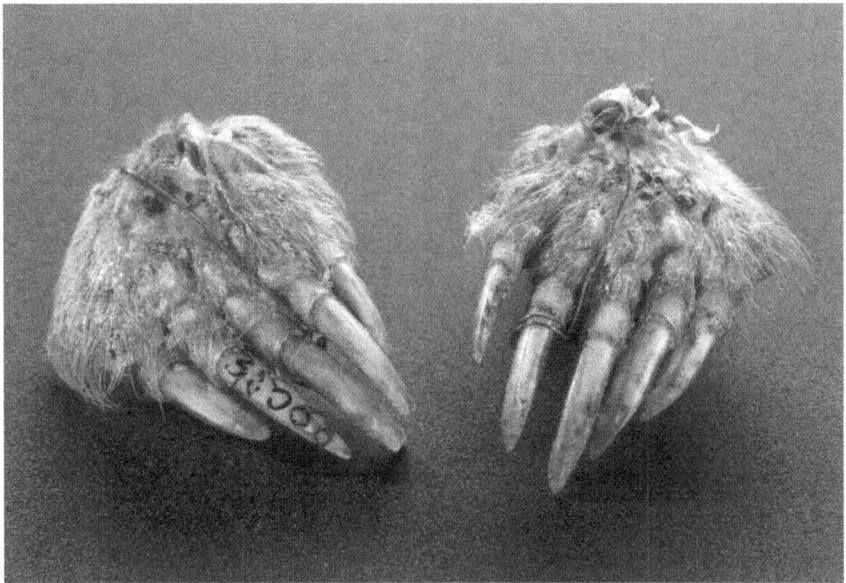

Fig. 7 Mole's foot amulet, Norfolk, England, 1890–1910. Science Museum, London (Wellcome Images / CC-BY 4.0).

to be assigned to it.[45] In any case, the Magi, according to Pliny, believed that the ability to foresee the future could be acquired by eating the heart of a mole extracted while it was still beating (*HN* 30.19);[46] its tooth, likewise taken from the living animal, could be worn as an effective amulet against toothache (*HN* 30.20). Interestingly, a similar analogical use of a mole's tooth finds a parallel in Kentucky until at least the 1930s,[47] while amulets consisting of a mole's foot were commonly employed as a cure for toothache, among other conditions, in Europe and in England: examples of these, collected from Norfolk (late nineteenth to early twentieth century), are held by both the London Museum of Science and the Pitt Rivers Museum in Oxford. Remedies from moles feature in Pliny's list (*HN* 30.38) of treatments for scrofula: the ash mixed with honey, the liver crushed and made into ointment, or the right foot. Finally, moles were thought efficacious in curing insanity, either by sprinkling the afflicted with their blood (Plin. *HN* 30.84, attributing the belief to the Magi) or by wearing the heart in a deer skin (*Cyranides* 2.3, p. 117 Kaimakis).[48]

The choice of a particular animal for magical purposes may also have been related to its habits or peculiar qualities. For example, the right foot of the proverbially slow tortoise if carried on board a ship was believed by some to cause the ship to move more slowly (Plin. *HN* 32.41). Conversely, since gout slowed down the sufferer's walk (hence the ironic title of the pseudo-Lucianic work on gout, 'Swiftfoot'), a foot of the famously nimble hare was a specific against the disease (Plin. *HN* 28.220; Marcell. Empir. 36.26).[49] The use of goat dung to cure eye inflammation, mentioned earlier, is connected by Pliny to the belief that the animals graze on certain herbs that afford them immunity to the condition; likewise the blood, liver and gall of goats is recommended to treat night-blindness because goats see well in the dark (Plin. *HN* 28.170; cf. id. 8.203, Dioscor. *MM* 2.47).[50] Another factor was the relationship, sympathetic or antipathetic,[51] between animals. Pliny, for instance, associates the use of deer in the avoidance and treatment of snake bites with the well-known 'fact' (*nemo ignorat*) that deer kill and eat snakes:[52] an enmity that extends to deer's body parts when killed and dismembered. Thus snakes can be driven away by the smell of burning antlers, by sleeping on a deer skin, by having a stag's tooth, or by rubbing on the marrow or suet, while the best remedy for snake bite is the rennet of a fawn cut out from its mother's uterus (Plin. *HN* 28.150; cf. 8.118).[53]

In the case of erotic magic the rationale for the use of certain animals and birds is obvious.[54] Not surprisingly, this kind of magic made use of creatures associated with heightened sexual activity, especially the dog[55] and the ass.[56] Two lists of animal-based aphrodisiacs given by Pliny (*HN* 28.261-2 and 30.141) feature mares,[57] doves,[58] cocks,[59] rams[60] and in particular, donkeys, of which the parts used include the right[61] testicle consumed in wine or worn as an amulet,[62] the seminal fluid from copulation collected in a red[63] cloth and enclosed in silver, or the penis, submerged seven[64] times in hot oil and rubbed on the appropriate parts. The ass could also be aphrodisiac for women (*Cyranides* 2.31.18-19, p. 164 Kaimakis). Conversely, a contraceptive amulet could be made of a bean tied up in the hide of a mule (*PGM* 63.26-8).[65] Being an ithyphallic animal, the ass was also used in apotropaic magic:[66] to sleep on its hide could protect you from nocturnal demons (*Cyranides* 2.31.20-1, p. 164 Kaimakis), while ass's hide was laid on babies to keep them free from fear (Plin. *HN* 28. 258).

A further important determining factor in the choice of animals was their connection with a particular deity.[67] The prominence of the ass, for instance, in the magical papyri in erotic and other contexts is due not so much to the animal's hyper-sexed nature as to its close association with the Egyptian god Seth,[68] who was identified with the Greek Typhon; indeed the blood of a donkey, commonly used as a form of ink in which spells were to be written, is frequently referred to as 'Typhon's blood'. In his manifestation as the animal of Seth, the donkey is a much more sinister, demonic creature, the god being the incarnation of evil.[69] Hence spells that utilise destructive chthonic powers make use of the donkey, for instance *PGM* 4.2006–125, in which the hide of an ass, inscribed in ass's blood with a spell invoking the aid of 'the powerful and inexorable god' (Seth) is placed under the body of a dead man who is called upon to appear as a supernatural assistant for carrying out various purposes which include causing illness, sending dreams, and restraining, as well as erotic attraction.[70]

Other animals and birds whose use in rites is determined by their relationship to deities include white cocks, sacred to the sun and moon[71] white doves, the birds of Aphrodite,[72] and dogs, associated with Hecate, Selene and Anubis.[73] In these cases, the aim is to gain the cooperation of the deity in effecting the spell by sacrificing to them animals that they favour.[74]

In the cases just discussed, a reason for the choice of a specific animal is easily found. A variety of factors, however, could come into play that were dependent not so much on the animal used as on the part chosen. This may involve the magical principle of similarity e.g. wearing the tooth of a hyena or a mole as an amulet to cure toothache (Plin. *HN* 28.95, 30.20).[75] Other considerations that played a role in determining the choice of animal were sex, colour and the side from which the organ was taken. The sex of the animal tended to correspond to that of the individual upon whom it was used; Pliny, for example, records that bladder stones could be relieved by boiling and eating the bladder of a wild boar: a male animal for men and a sow for women.[76]

In the case of colour, similarity is sometimes the important element, as with cures for jaundice, where the choice of a yellow, or yellow-footed, animal needs no explanation.[77] According to Pliny (*HN* 30.93–4) after purifying with water a hen's feet, which must be yellow, these are washed with wine, which the sufferer drinks. Pliny (*HN* 30.94) also reports a belief that if a person afflicted with jaundice happens to see a 'jaundice' bird,[78] they will be instantly cured, but the bird will die. Two magical principles are at work here: the analogous colour of the bird and the idea of transference whereby the disease is passed from the sufferer to the animal.[79]

Colour may also be important because of its symbolic associations.[80] The connection of black with death and evil, for instance, explains why animals of this colour are frequently employed in what we would nowadays call 'black' magic. A particularly nasty *defixio*, for instance, involves inscribing a spell and a figure on a lead tablet, smearing it with the blood of a bat, rolling it up and putting it in the opened stomach of a frog; this is then strung up with hairs from the tail of a black ox (*PGM* 36.231–55).[81] Alternatively, the same colour might have an apotropaic function, as in the belief, attributed by Pliny to the Magi (*HN* 30.82), that a house can be protected from sorcerers' potions by fumigating it with the gall of a black male dog, sprinkling the walls with its blood, or burying its genital organ under the threshold.[82]

Being associated with the Underworld, black was also the appropriate colour for various types of magic that called on the dead, such as necromancy, where a black sheep was the usual victim (in contrast to the sacrifice of a white animal to the Olympian gods in conventional Graeco-Roman religious practice),[83] or love spells where deities of the Underworld were invoked for their aid, as in a spell of compulsion (*PGM* 4.1440–95) in which an offering of the dung of a black cow accompanies a prayer to a lengthy list of chthonic powers.[84]

Black animals also feature in less sinister types of magic. Sometimes an explanation can be offered: for instance, amulets to cure quartan fever making use of the wool of black sheep (Plin. *HN* 28.82 and 111) might be related to the belief ([Hippocrates], *Nature of Man* 15) that these fevers were caused by black bile. Less clear, on the other hand, is the reason for the 'donkey sandwich' (the heart of a *black* jackass taken with bread in the open air on the first or second day of the moon) cited by Pliny (*HN* 28.225) as a cure for epilepsy.[85]

The colour white is most prominent in the sacrificial employment of white roosters or white doves. In these cases, the important factor is the connection of birds of this colour with specific deities (see above).[86]

It is often specified that an organ must come from a particular side of the animal. Again, the reason may be straightforward analogy, as where an eagle's right foot is attached as an amulet for pains in the right side, while left side pains are treated by the left foot of the bird (Plin. *HN* 30.54; cf. 29.117), or where the right eye of a frog worn as an amulet cures inflammation in the right eye, the left eye in the left (Plin. *HN* 32.74). But right and left also have symbolic meaning, at least in Greek thought, which may have influenced the use of the relevant animal parts, the right being commonly connected with the male, masculine strength, good fortune, light and life, the left with the female, weakness, bad luck, death and so on.[87] We have already noted the use in aphrodisiac amulets of the right testicles of asses and roosters;[88] similarly, a hyena's tooth from the upper right side tied to a man's arm ensures that his javelin will never miss its mark, according to the Magi (Plin. *HN* 28.100), while an amulet could be made from the right foot of a gecko to bring favour and victory (*PGM* 7.186–90). The right/left distinction is very clear in another Magian prescription from Pliny involving the hyena, whereby the left foot of the animal, if drawn across a woman in labour, causes death, whereas the right foot effects an easy delivery (*HN* 28.103).

We have examined uses of specific animals or animal parts where the reason for their selection can be easily discerned. Very often, however, there is no obvious explanation, and here it might have been the unusual circumstances in which an animal was used which was thought to bestow magical potency rather than the animal itself. Thus Gordon (2010, 254-7) argues, on the assumption that magic involves the unnatural / out of the ordinary, that an animal could be removed 'from the status of normal' by specifying rules for its collection (e.g. where toothache is cured by scraping teeth with bones extracted from the forehead of a lizard *when the moon is full and so that they do not touch the ground* Plin. *HN* 30.22), or by the breaking of normal alimentary or hygienic rules (e.g. ingesting snails or millipedes).[89]

Because of the essentially secretive, private nature of magic rituals, details of actual practice are not easy to find: nevertheless questions such as how animals were obtained, where ingredients were prepared and rituals carried out and by whom (client or magician) are worthy of speculation. In what follows, I will pose, and attempt to answer, several questions.

1. How were animal ingredients obtained?

   When small creatures such as insects, lizards or roosters were required, ready availability would not have presented a problem; the same would have applied if one needed animal products such as eggs, or dung from donkeys, dogs and so on. Where animals were eaten as meat, parts could be bought from a butcher: for instance, Pliny (*HN* 28.201) reports a Magian remedy which involves buying a calf's spleen for the price asked, as haggling might affect the efficacy of the cure. Other types of domesticated animal were valuable, and the killing of a donkey, for example, each time an organ was required would have been beyond the resources of most magicians and all but the wealthiest of their clients. In such cases it is likely that body parts, including blood, were collected and stored for future use (see below). The same would go for more unusual creatures such as the mole – notoriously difficult to catch (Borrell (2017)) – or the wolf, though spells involving animals like the *bubo*[90] may belong to the realm of fantasy.[91] On occasion, however, an exotic animal such as a lion might have been able to be acquired by a sorcerer after a wild beast show in the arena in the course of which large numbers of such animals perished and may have been made available as meat.[92] And it is of course highly probable that charlatans resorted to everyday substitutes for less easily obtainable animal parts, for example, offal bought from a butcher might have been paraded before the gullible as 'hyena's liver' or 'camel's heart'.

One of the most common animal substances used in magic is blood,[93] and it is worth considering how this would have been obtained. It might be imagined that the animal in question had to be killed (e.g. *PGM* 4.2100–01 specifies that ass blood used as writing ink must be taken from the heart of a sacrificial victim), but this was not necessarily always the case. Blood could be drained from a living animal: Pliny, for instance, mentions the cutting of the vein under a pigeon's wing to extract blood (29.126),[94] while a cure for quartan fever prescribed the blood of a living ass (*Cyranides* 2.31.15–16, p. 163 Kaimakis). Additionally, there is evidence that blood was sometimes extracted and then laid aside, being mixed with a liquid to reconstitute it when needed. The blood of Pontic ducks, for instance, used as an antidote to sorcerers' poisons, was stored away when it became thick and later diluted with wine (Plin. *HN* 29.104). Preserved blood was also employed in dried or congealed form, e.g. Pliny (*HN* 30.112) says that haemorrhages from the skull are treated with the congealed blood of a dove which is stored for this purpose, while anal abscesses could be cured by dried and powdered bull's blood (id. *HN* 28.217).[95]

2. What use was made of preserved animal ingredients?

In general, it is clear that magicians made frequent use of preserved animals or their parts. We have already suggested that this would have been expedient in cases where an animal was not readily available and/or expensive, and there is in fact extensive evidence that this was a regular procedure. Pliny, for instance, often refers to the preserving of animals, such as the pickling of shrew mice in oil to cure the bite of the same creatures (29.89) or the keeping in horn boxes of hen dung (it must be white) in old oil as a remedy for white ulcers on the pupil (29.124): both of which remedies follow magical principles.[96] Simple amulets consisting of an animal part (e.g. a hyena's tooth worn as an amulet to cure toothache (Plin. *HN* 28.95) would also have been prepared in advance).

Ready-to-use preparations included not just individual animals and their parts but pastes and pills manufactured from a combination of animal and vegetable ingredients. The magical papyri offer an insight into the process. One instance involves a powerful spell of attraction featuring a burnt offering which was said to have been taught by an Egyptian prophet to the emperor Hadrian who, on testing it out, was so impressed that he paid double the usual fee (*PGM* 4.2441–621). The ingredients for the offering included a deified mouse and two moon beetles, a crab, the fat of a virgin goat, the dung of a baboon, and ibis eggs, as well as various spices and plants.

These were ground together and placed in a lead box, from which a little of the mixture could be taken out and used whenever the ritual was performed. Similarly, several recipes are found for making pills or pellets that included animal parts, for instance in a love spell of attraction (*PGM* 4.2891–942) an offering is made to the star of Aphrodite (the planet Venus) consisting of a white dove's blood and fat, together with myrrh and wormwood, made into pellets. As Johnston (2002, 349 and n.13) comments, 'once he had manufactured them, the practitioner could store these pellets away until a client asked him to perform a love spell'.[97]

3. Who supplied the animals or their products for use in magic rites: the magician or the client?

    Itinerant magicians working in public places would presumably have carried around with them a bag of supplies,[98] which might have included animal parts. Likewise an old wise-woman (*saga*) called out in the case of illness[99] might carry on her person pre-made remedies that could be prescribed and handed over, with instructions on how to use them.

    Where magic workers came to a client's house to perform a purificatory rite, they may have brought with them inexpensive ingredients, like the old *saga* called in to purify the bedchamber of a sick girlfriend who carries eggs as well as sulphur in her trembling hand (Ovid, *Ars* 2.329–30). Presumably the cost of these ingredients would be factored into the charge for the *saga*'s services. An epigram of Martial and a passage from Lucian suggest that the situation might have been different where sacrifice was carried out. The former (Mart. 7.54) is an attack on a man who is constantly reporting disturbing dreams about the poet, necessitating Martial's bringing in of a *saga* to expiate them, with the consequent sacrifice of many of his lambs and the complete loss of his pigs, poultry and eggs.[100] In Lucian (*Philops.* 14) we find a story about elaborate necromantic rites performed by a *magos* in a client's house with much ceremony including drawing down the moon, the client being required to pay four *minae* in advance towards the cost of the victims. Even allowing for satiric hyperbole in both these passages, the underlying assumption is that the magic workers made use of sacrificial animals supplied by, or at least paid for, by the client.

4. Does the fact that some animals prescribed were exotic or difficult to obtain provide evidence about the socio-economic status of the persons using these forms of magic?

    Exploring this question in relation to plants, Lynn LiDonnici (2001) finds that the recipes in *PGM* often call for relatively expensive ingredients such as the costlier varieties of frankincense or myrrh. These are often, however, a part of more elaborate spells, especially of a divinatory character, in contrast to the many less complex spells for healing, or for success in business or love, which made use of readily available and relatively cheap ingredients. LiDonnici persuasively argues that it is mistaken to assume a single audience for the *PGM* collections; rather, they are drawn from magic rites intended for a variety of social groups – the urban elite, as well as poorer urban or rural dwellers. A similar claim could be made for magic requiring the use of animals: spells involving easily obtainable creatures, such as writing words on a seashell to induce sleeplessness in a desired woman (*PGM* 7.374–76) or sacrificing a rooster to obtain success in business (*PGM* 4.2359–72) could be employed by people of virtually any class, while recipes that are more elaborate and make use of exotic animals would have been available only to the wealthier:[101] this would include those requiring animals used as meat – a rare item in the diet of the poor (Garnsey (1999), 34).

The same could also be said of magic remedies attested in Pliny and elsewhere. In some cases, a number of alternatives are offered. For instance, treatments for splenic disease include a complex ritual using a sheep's spleen (described earlier), but also the consuming of a puppy's or a hedgehog's spleen in vinegar (Plin. *HN* 30.51–2), while pains in the side could be treated using a hoopoe's heart or eagle's feet, but also by the more everyday snails and millipedes (Plin. *HN* 30. 53–4). While the more unusual or costlier ingredients such as eagles or sheep would have been out of the reach of the urban poor, they had other less expensive options.[102]

In the context of attacking foreign medicine, the arrival of which at Rome he associates with moral degeneracy, Pliny (*HN* 24.4–5) contrasts the cheap (herbal) remedies provided by Nature and featuring on the dinner tables of even the poorest with the exotic medicines, deriving from the East, with which profit-seeking charlatans exploit those gullible enough to be impressed by them.[103] The principle could easily be applied to magic, and it is highly likely that some wealthy people[104] became the targets of such charlatans: we could imagine, in fact, magicians tailoring prescriptions to the financial circumstances of their customers (an eagle for a rich client, snails and insects for a poor one…).[105]

5. Where magic involved ritual practices, who performed them: the magician or the client? At what stage was the magic performed: in the presence of the client or beforehand? Where was the magic performed?

Many rituals would have been carried out by the magic workers, for example the *sagae* referred to earlier who performed simple rites of purification. Sometimes a ritual also involved the active participation of the client/patient, as for instance in the healing of boils mentioned by Pliny which required both healer and patient to spit three times (Plin. *HN* 30.108 discussed earlier in this chapter). In the case of very elaborate spells such as we find in the *Greek Magical Papyri*, magic workers may have carried out rituals on behalf of clients, as reflected perhaps in Lucian's story (*Philops.* 14) of a magician performing necromantic rites in order to bring his client Glaucias' *inamorata* to him, or the (frustrated) attempts of Aglaidas to seduce the virtuous Justina by paying a magician to force her by magic means.[106]

On some occasions, though, the person benefiting from the magic would have carried out the rites themselves. A passage from Philostratus' *Life of Apollonius of Tyana* (7.39.2) is enlightening in this connection, as it describes a scenario in which users of magic acquired spells from professionals which they then performed for themselves. So for instance, while inveighing against the propensity of lovers to resort to practitioners of magic for help, the comment is made that a lover will sing the praises of magic in cases where the love spell works, but if it fails to have the desired effect *'he will blame some omission, saying that there was something or other which he failed to burn or sacrifice or melt, and this is something crucial but unobtainable'*.

The magical papyri also offer evidence of situations where a person wishing to employ magic was expected to perform it himself. For example at *PGM* 7.186–90, instructions are given for a rite to bring favour and victory: you make an amulet by taking a gecko, cutting off its right foot (the animal must be released alive), and fastening the foot to your garment. In this case, it would have been a simple matter for a magician to pass this on to a client, who later carried out the ritual as instructed. More complex is the fetching spell recorded at *PGM* 4.1390–1495, which begins 'leave a little of the bread which you eat … say the spell to the pieces of bread and throw them. And pick up some polluted dirt from the place where you perform the ritual and throw it inside the house of the woman *whom you desire*, go home and go to sleep'. If after three days of trying the magic has not worked, the lover is advised to attempt a more coercive prayer to the chthonic powers, adding an offering of dung from a black cow and again throwing the polluted dirt 'as you have learned'. Clearly, the magic is here to be carried out by the person who hopes to be benefited by the spell rather than the magic worker.[107] On the other hand, although the magician could provide his client with instructions on how to carry out the ritual acts, the spells and prayers which here accompany them are lengthy, elaborate and partly in verse form: hardly the sort of thing that could easily be memorised.[108] Yet the formula[109] (e.g. 'come today, Moirai and Destiny; accomplish the purpose with the help of the love spell of attraction, that you may attract **to me** her, NN whose mother is NN, **to me NN**, whose mother is NN... because **I am calling**...) implies that the words must be spoken by the lover rather than the magician. Did the latter dictate the words while the client repeated them? Or did he provide a written copy for the client, who then read them out as he performed the ritual?

The answers to the second question – at what stage the magic was performed – are again various. Rituals attendant on the making of an amulet, for instance, might be performed in advance. In his book on amulets, Bonner (1950, 69–71) described a type made of jasper or onyx with the image of a gecko; on some there were also words referring to blindness or the restoration of sight, or an image of a crescent moon. These artefacts offer an intriguing confirmation of descriptions in several authors of a procedure for making magical amulets that involved the blinding of a green lizard which was then shut in a container together with ring stones carved with a lizard design; after a period of time the lizard supposedly regained its sight and was set free, the stones being retained and used as amulets for treating diseases of the eye.[110] Since the lizard had to be caught at a specific time: the time of the waning moon in September,[111] this was clearly the sort of magic object which needed to be pre-manufactured.

Conversely, there were amulets that would have been made in the client's presence, especially those like Pliny's magical cures for quartan fever which included amulets made from the snout and ears of a mouse t hat was afterwards released, and a viper's heart or lizard's right eye extracted while the animals were still alive (Plin. *HN* 30.98–9). In such cases, since the living animal was assumed to take away the disease with them,[112] the ritual would need to be performed on each occasion when the healing act was performed.

Spells in the magical papyri are very often formularies, the name of the user and the target or beneficiary of the spell being written as NN, leaving the practitioner to substitute the appropriate names when the spell is performed (cf. Chapter 1). An example is the love spell of attraction mentioned earlier (*PGM* 4.2943–66) in which the eyes of a bat, released alive, are inserted into the wax figure of a dog. This figurine then has to be sealed up in a vessel with a papyrus strip attached, on which a formulaic spell is written: 'I adjure you three times by Hekatē PHORPHORBA BAIBO PHORBORBA, that she, NN, lose the fire in her eye or even lie awake with nothing on her mind except me, NN, alone' etc. Clearly in a case like this the magician cannot make use of ready-prepared materials, and must perform the rite afresh for each new client.

As regards the venues in which magic was performed, there is abundant evidence from various locations and periods for itinerant magic workers who practised their trade in public places such as market places or temples, as well as for healers and exorcists who attended the houses of clients.[113] In the magical papyri, it is sometimes specified that a ritual is to be carried out in a particular place, either in various locations within the home of the person performing the magic (e.g. the rooftop, *PGM* 1.56f., 4.171, 2441, 2708–84, *PDM* 14.295, 875;[114] a room on the ground floor *PGM* 2.22, 6.1–47, 13.1–343; a bedroom *PGM* 2.150, 7.628; a dark room *PDM* 14.17–49, 282) or outdoors (e.g. in the open air *PGM* 3.420, 4.580, 785, 900, 11a 1–40; in a deserted place *PGM* 3.612–32, 633–71; at a tomb *PGM* 3.26, 12.201–69).

It is worth considering whether some magic workers also had a home workshop in which they stored their apparatus (potions, ingredients, magic books, etc.), prepared ingredients and carried out rites, rather like a medieval alchemist. Hard evidence is thin on the ground and reliant to a large extent on literary representations of witchcraft, which may or may not reflect real-life practice. Two passages in Apuleius' novel *The Golden Ass* (*Metamorphoses*) are of greatest relevance in this connection.[115] In the third book (3.17), the hero of the story, Lucius, is staying as a guest in the house of Milo, whose wife Pamphile ('Mrs Loveall') is a renowned witch specialising in the use of magic to secure the affections of attractive young men. One evening the maid Photis describes to Lucius how her mistress engaged in a fetching spell to entice the latest object of her fancy. Going up to a rooftop room where she practises her secret arts, Pamphile, in preparation for a ritual, sets out in her *officina* ('workshop') spices, metal plaques with strange magic writing on them, the remains of ill-omened birds, and various body parts from human corpses including the preserved blood (*seruatus cruor*) of murder victims. She then recites a charm over pulsating entrails (of a sacrificed animal?) and makes a liquid offering which includes cow's milk. On a second occasion (*Met.* 3.21), Lucius, who is desperately eager to learn about the magic arts, persuades Photis to let him watch through a crack in the door of Pamphile's workshop as she engages in a ritual. This time, she opens a chest and removes several small jars (*pyxides*) containing a magic ointment which when smeared over her body will transform her into a bird.

The Apuleius passages encompass the sort of fantastical elements that we see in other literary accounts of magic. Nevertheless, there may be some basis in actuality. As we saw, the use of a room at the top of the house has parallels in the *PGM*, though in the latter the rooftop is the location for the carrying out of rites rather than the storage of ingredients: the person performing the magic is instructed to go up there for the ritual after getting the offering ready earlier, suggesting that the preparation is done elsewhere (in a workshop?).[116] Magic laboratories are in fact attested in two magic texts: a *defixio* from Africa dating to the third century CE (Kropp 11.2.2/1), which refers to an *officina magica* and *PGM* 95.1–6 ('take the skin of a mouse .../ and have in the workshop, beneath ...'), which despite the fragmentary nature of the text, certainly offers evidence for a magic ritual, or at least preparations for one, being carried out in a workshop.[117] And given, as we have seen, that animal parts such as blood were frequently preserved and potions and amulets prepared in advance, it is a reasonable assumption that a magic worker would need a place in which to store and prepare ingredients (not to mention books of spells).

None of the evidence assembled, however, helps with the question of whether magic workers received clients in their workshops as well preparing magic there. In discussing the practice of doctors, Nutton (1995, 15 and n.66) suggests that *ergastēria* (Latin *officinae*) may on occasion refer to surgeries where doctors were consulted, and though it was the usual practice in Greece and Rome for patients to call doctors to their homes, he thinks that doctors would have rooms in their houses to treat the (less numerous) sick patients who could not be treated in their own homes (Nutton (1992), 49).[118] Whether any inferences can be drawn from this which might be applied by extension to magic healers is a moot point: in any case the attractive idea of a magician being consulted in his home workshop in which were prominently displayed jars labelled 'bat's eyes', 'crocodile's blood' or the like which were designed to impress an overly-trusting client must be relegated to the realms of speculation.

Fig. 8 David Teniers the Younger, *An Alchemist in His Laboratory*, c. 1650. Wellcome images via Wikimedia Commons Wellcome L0049848.

Fig. 9 Joan's Cottage. © The Museum of Witchcraft and Magic, Boscastle, Cornwall.

I pass now to a consideration of the role played by animals and animal parts in literary accounts of magic, and the extent to which such accounts may have a basis in real-life magic practice. Witches such as Circe and Medea are portrayed in early Greek literature (Homer, Greek tragedy) as relying solely on *pharmaka*, plant-based drugs. In the third century BCE Theocritus has his Simaitha include powdered lizard among her ingredients,[119] but it is not till the Roman writers that we get descriptions of witches making comprehensive use of animals in their rites. Canidia, for instance, a sorceress who features in poems of Horace from the 30s BCE,[120] is seen engaging in nocturnal rituals that involve the sacrifice of a dark lamb for purposes of necromancy,[121] as well as the burying of a wolf's beard and a snake's tooth (*Sat.* 1.8.42–3), while in the fifth *Epode* the magical ingredients in her love potion include the eggs and feathers of a nocturnal screech-owl (*strix*) smeared with the blood of an ugly toad (19–20). Erotic magic is also a feature of Roman love elegy, where there are allusions to the use of toads, snakes (Prop. 3.6.27–8), crows (Prop. 4.5.15–16) and the infamous *hippomanes*, a love-charm derived from horses (see below).[122] Some of the most striking Latin descriptions of the operations of sorceresses involve Medea. In surviving texts, her transformation into a full-blown witch begins in Apollonius' epic *Argonautika*,[123] where her character oscillates between that of a young virgin in love and a skilled sorceress, a priestess of Hecate. Though Medea's magical apparatus consists mainly of herbs, an animal victim appears on one occasion, when she instructs Jason, in preparation for making his body invulnerable with the magic ointment she has given him, to perform an invocatory ritual to Hecate, which includes the sacrifice of a ewe (Apollon. *Arg.* 3.1032–6). But it is in Ovid, and later Seneca, that animals feature as ingredients in Medea's magic rites. In *Metamorphoses* 7, Ovid presents a Medea who, like her Greek literary predecessors, employs her expertise in the use of powerful (herbal) drugs to assist Jason, but when the poet turns to a less familiar story in which Medea demonstrates her magical prowess by rejuvenating Jason's aged father Aesōn, she becomes a formidable sorceress, offering prayers for help to the Night, Hecate and the Earth, scouring the earth in her dragon-drawn chariot for special herbs, and engaging in an elaborate ritual that involves, among other things, appeasing chthonic deities with the sacrifice of a black sheep, purification of the old man and finally cutting his throat and replacing his blood with a magic brew prepared in a bronze pot. What is interesting is that the brew contains animal, as well as herbal ingredients: the wings and flesh of a screech-owl (*strix*), a werewolf's entrails, the skin of a water-snake, the liver of a stag and the eggs and head of a crow (Ov. *Met.* 7.269–74). Likewise in Seneca's tragedy *Medea*, the protagonist's preparation of the poisoned robe and necklace to be sent as deadly gifts to Jason's new wife Creusa, merely alluded to in Euripides' version, is described in mind-boggling detail. To a potion containing snake venom and poisonous herbs obtained from every possible source, Medea adds the heart of a *bubo* (horned owl) and the entrails cut out from a living *strix* (733–4). Last but not least is Lucan's Erictho, a Thessalian witch of hyperbolic potency and malevolence[124] who revives a corpse for the purpose of revealing the future, pouring into the body a potion that incorporates a variety of animal ingredients: the foam of rabid dogs, parts obtained from a lynx, a hyena, a stag that has fed on snakes, an *echenēis*-fish, dragons' eyes, serpents from Arabia and Libya, and last but not least, a phoenix (Lucan, *De bello ciuili* 6.671–80).

The vast majority of animals or animal substances that recur in these literary representations of magic are sinister, exotic or fabulous.[125] Take for instance the commonly mentioned *hippomanes* (lit. 'horse madness'), which was believed to be employed by witches to drive men mad with love, thereby transferring the notorious[126] sexual lust of mares to a human target. Usually defined as an excrescence on the forehead of newborn foals that must be gathered before the mother eats it,[127] or as the fluid exuded by mares on heat, after intercourse or during pregnancy,[128] it was especially sinister because it was extremely dangerous, an overdose capable of inducing insanity or even death[129] (Lucan, *De bello ciuili* 6.453–6: part of the repertoire of Thessalian witches, Juv. 6.615–17; cf. Plin. *HN* 28.180 [*hippomanes* will be omitted because it is *noxium*]).[130]

Equally macabre, as well as belonging to the realm of folklore and fantasy, is the *strix* – a sort of owl[131] that was said to suck the blood of infants left unattended at night.[132] Although owls in general were regarded as inauspicious creatures,[133] the *strix* was especially so because of its uncanny high-pitched cry (*strix* is derived from Latin *stridere*, to screech[134]), its nocturnal habits and its association with *strigae* (witches): Ovid (*Fasti* 6.141f.) expresses uncertainty as to whether the *striges* who attack a sleeping child are actual birds or old women transformed into owls by magic spells.

The frequently sinister nature of the animals appearing in Roman poetical descriptions of magic is closely related to the context: so in *Epode* 5, the rite in which Horace's Canidia is seen engaging involves murdering a child in order to turn his liver and marrow into a love-charm. In Ovid's *Metamorphoses* Medea employs magic to deadly effect, and though in the case of Aesōn there are happy consequences, the episode foreshadows Medea's malevolent tricking of the daughters of Pēlias into murdering their own father in the mistaken belief that the sorceress will pour the same rejuvenating substance into his opened veins.

Likewise *hippomanes* is employed in a variety of contexts where magic is depicted in negative and sinister terms: it is often used by the *lena*/witch, the elegiac poet's arch-enemy; Juvenal's misogynistic satire on the vices of married women rises to a crescendo with the employment against their husbands of erotic magic, exemplified by the notorious case of the emperor Caligula, whose madness was reputedly caused by an overdose of *hippomanes* administered by his wife Caesonia; in the *Georgics*, a didactic poem on agriculture, the section on breeding of cattle and horses concludes with a tirade against the pervasive and destructive power of sex, culminating in the hypersexuality of mares which has as its climax an allusion to *hippomanes*, gathered by wicked stepmothers[135] for purposes of erotic magic.[136]

But though there is an emphasis in these literary portrayals of witches on the dark and fantastic side of magic, they are not entirely divorced from reality. Thus, the practices described are often based on sound magical principles: for instance, in her ritual to prolong Aesōn's life, Medea uses a stag and a crow, both of which were renowned for longevity (Plin. *HN* 7.153), while in *Epode* 5 the smearing of blood and the use of eggs and feathers are all commonly attested in the magical papyri and elsewhere (see Watson (2003) *ad loc.*) The same link with actual magic practice applies as well to many of the animals chosen. Thus the use in magic/folk-medicine of the owl known as a *bubo* is mentioned several times by Pliny,[137] while the hyena was regarded by the Magi as the animal with the most intrinsic magical powers (see n.48 above). Toads, too, had various magic uses (Plin. *HN* 32.49–52); the liver and heart of the animal could be worn as an amulet against quartans (Plin. id. 114) or (as in *Epode* 5) they could be used in love magic (Plin. *HN* 32.52, 139; see also Watson (2003), on *Epode* 5.19). And according to Pliny (*HN* 29.99) the saliva of a mad dog is used to combat hydrophobia, while the Magi burned the heads of dogs which had died from rabies as a cure for toothache (*HN* 30.21) and pains in the side (*HN* 30.53: it is unclear whether this remedy is Magian). Notwithstanding these parallels between literature and actual magic practice, however, the poets single out and concentrate on those ill-omened animals that are best suited to the literary context, ignoring the more mundane or humble creatures such as donkeys, goats or insects that populate the pages of Pliny and the magical texts. One example will clarify this point: a list given by Pliny (*HN* 30.98–101) of animals worn in magical amulets to ward off quartan fevers includes vipers and snakes, but it also mentions hawks, (not rabid) dogs, wasps, mice, lizards, flies, beetles, scorpions, caterpillars, slugs and so on: most of these not exactly poetical and/or sinister in nature.

What distinguishes poetic accounts of animals in magic, then, is not so much that these are entirely fantastical, though there are such elements, e.g. the *strix*, as well as the phoenix and werewolf. Rather, we could say that they are based on the principles and practices of actual magic, but with an overlay of fantasy and a decided bias towards the macabre.[138]

Appendix: amulets

As there has been frequent occasion in this chapter to instance the use of animal derivatives in amulets, it is appropriate to speak more generally here of such artefacts.[139] Amulets (Gk. *phulaktēria*, 'protectives', *periammata*, *periapta*, 'things attached to, things hung about the body', Latin *amuleta*), are defined by Bonner (1946), 26 thus: 'in the broadest sense of the word, an amulet is any object which by its contact or its close proximity to the person who owns it, or to any possession of his, exerts power for his good, either by keeping evil from him and his property, or by endowing him with positive advantages'.[140] These, if not as important for the student of Graeco-Roman magic as the *PGM* and the *defixiones*, nonetheless represent a rich trove of material that involves magic of a profoundly practical type that was practised at every level of society.[141] This is the case for the very simple reason that amulets tap into the deepest of human anxieties, such as the fear of illness, of being unloved, of being overwhelmed by some crisis or other, or falling victim to the Evil Eye: this last was a cause of particular unease in the ancient world and one reason why Roman children wore a particular kind of phallic amulet known as the *bulla*. The use of amulets goes back a long way. There are a few allusions in Greek comic poets of the fifth–fourth centuries BCE to magic rings with apotropaic powers, and to a protective formula suspended about the neck or shoulders in a little leather pouch.[142] Other (scanty) references to the early but undoubtedly widespread employment in ancient Greece of protective amulets, generally in combination with an incantation, as equally happened in later times, are surveyed by Kotansky (1991), 108–12. But by far the bulk of our evidence for the amuletic arm of magic comes from the Empire period, much of it from Graeco-Roman Egypt.

In discussing amulets, a couple of initial distinctions must be made: first, between those that employed perishable material and those were durable, and second, between amulets that were inscribed and those containing no text, for example a number of the magic gems studied by Bonner (1950), which merely have figures. Materials that were perishable i.e. organic in nature, included leaves and plants,[143] animal skins[144] and papyrus. Naturally amulets fashioned from the first two substances have not survived – although as we have seen in Chapter 4 and this chapter there is extensive textual evidence for them – but because of the exceptionally dry climate of Egypt, many phylacteries written in Greek on papyrus, or formulas for fashioning amulets made of papyrus, have been preserved; they are amply represented in the corpus of the *PGM*, for example 7.218–21:

> **Phylactery for daily fever with attacks of shivering.** Write on a clean sheet of papyrus the following and wear it as an amulet
>
> > Iaō Sabaōth Adōnai akrammachammarei
> > aō Sabaōth Adōnai akrammachammarei
> > ō Sabaōth Adōnai akrammachammarei
> > Abrasax

Imperishable materials are represented by gems, usually with intaglios cut upon them, and by rings, and *lamellae*, little plates of metal foil engraved by a stylus,[145] as in the opening lines of a prescription for fashioning an amulet at *PGM* 7.580–90,

> **A Phylactery**. A protector of the body against daimons, against phantasms, against every disease and affliction. Written upon a leaf of gold or silver or tin or upon hieratic papyrus, when worn it works like a seal. For it is the name of power of the great god and his seal, which is as follows.

The text continues with a string of unintelligible magic words that represent the god's name of power and mystic seal, harnessed for protection by the amulet-bearer. Lastly it prescribes the inscribing of a circle in the shape of the *ouroboros*, the snake swallowing its tail, inside which are to be written the abovementioned names and other magic symbols, and, above the base of the circle, this formula 'protect my body and the entire soul of me, NN'.

As noted, amulets might bear writing, or they might not. Uninscribed amulets depended for efficacy on some occult power or association intrinsic to the material of which they were composed. Stones were widely credited with magical efficacy, as we see from the *Cyranides* and the *Orphic Lithika*, a versified treatise on the power of these. Hence a phylactery made of red or reddish-brown haematite, a semi-precious stone, might in view of its colour be thought effective in stopping bleeding (a further factor was the formation of its name from Greek *haima*, 'blood'): so Pliny *HN* 36.145. By a similar process of reasoning galactite, 'the milk stone' was held to promote the flow of milk in women and animals

(*Orphic Lithika*, 201–23). The skin or hoof of a mule, attached as an amulet, drew on the association of the animal with sterility to act as a contraceptive (*PGM* 36. 329; Dioscor. *MM* 3.134). The prominent eyes of the gecko, in conjunction with the inference that the creature accordingly had excellent powers of sight, seems to be the rationale underlying amulets to counter eye disease which have been inscribed with the image of a lizard.[146] In a refinement of this, some specimens of the type additionally sport the Greek word *pēra*, 'maimed, mutilated': the thinking upon which these specimens draw is explained by a gruesome curative rite described in Pliny's *Natural History* 29.130, Aelian's *On the Nature of Animals* 5.47 and the late medico-magical writer Marcellus Empiricus 8.49. A green lizard is blinded with a bronze needle and shut up in a vessel of glass or earthenware along with a ring or rings. After nine days the lizard supposedly recovers its sight and is released, while the rings which had been sealed up along with it, worn on the finger, now serve as a prophylactic against *lippitudo*,[147] bleariness of sight, having somehow absorbed the powers of ocular recuperation manifested by the animal.

In other instances it is the shape of the amulet that endows it with power. This is particularly the case with amulets of the type to which Faraone (2012) has applied the label 'vanishing acts', that is specimens in the form of a right-angled or isosceles triangle from which the initial, or the initial and terminal letters, are successively removed until all that remains is a single character (the identical process of letter-subtraction obtains with amulets inscribed with the famous *abracadabra* formula, Serenus Sammonicus 935–40). Examples of the second type are *PGM* 18b.1–7, 33.1–25, 88.1–19 and 91.1–14. Examples of the first type are *PGM* 120.1–13 and 43.1–27, of which only the portion containing the shape is reproduced here:

ablanathanalba
blanathanalba
lanathanalba
anathanalba
nathanalba
athanalba
thanalba
analba
alba
lba
ba
a

The thought-process behind the above instances, all of which are phylacteries against illness, is straightforwardly analogical, as with many spells in the *PGM* and *defixiones*: the disease should mimic the progressive vanishing of the letters by gradually abating until it disappears entirely.[148]

It is not however to be supposed that the protective or apotropaic effect of the above instances depend solely on the pictogram. On the contrary, each design is supplemented by a formula that explicitly conjures away the disease (e.g. *PGM* 18b 'I adjure you [the sacred appellation at the bottom left of the spell] ... to heal Dionysius or Anys, whom Heraklia bore, from every attack of shivering and fever ... immediately immediately, quickly quickly'). In addition, words of arcane power (*akrammachammarei, ablanathanalba* etc.) or divine names (*Iaō Sabaōth Adōnai*; *PGM* 18b) are enlisted to work against the illness: such cryptic magical language is a ubiquitous feature of the spells in the *PGM*, not merely the amuletic ones. Here then we encounter once more an instance of magic's pronounced tendency to operate on several fronts at once, on the basis that the more armaments are brought into play, the more likely a spell is to be successful.

We noted above that stones were thought to be invested per se with magic powers (something not generally true of papyrus or *lamellae*). From the first century CE onwards, in a supplementation of their lapidary powers, amulets often took the form of gems – usually semi-precious[149] – incised with figures of various deities, sometimes Greek, but more often, in a sign of the Egyptianisation or internationalisation of Graeco-Roman magic in the Empire period, Egyptian or Oriental. Very commonly too, in a further sign of the influence of Egypt, with its theriomorphic divinities, monstrous shapes such as the cockerel-headed demon with snake legs seen in many amulets of the period, the so-called anguipede, were carved on the stones.[150] The figures might or might not be accompanied by inscriptions such as 'protect me' or 'give me charm' (Bonner (1950), 48–50), but in view of the miniaturised form of the medium, these were necessarily brief, so that the apotropaic emphasis falls predominantly upon the figurines.

For more extended inscriptions upon amulets we must look beyond the magic gems which were the primary focus of the book-length study by Bonner (1950) to the very thin plates of metal, *lamellae* – usually of gold and silver but not excluding copper and bronze – incised with a stylus, and usually rolled up and worn as an amulet. The text upon these can at times run to surprising length. A case in point is a hundred or so line inscription of the fourth century CE, number 52 in Kotansky's 1994 study of these artefacts, which near the beginning features the appeal 'protect Alexandra whom Zoe bore from every demon and from every compulsion of demons and from sorceries and binding spell' before proceeding at the close to spell out with remarkable specificity the extent of Alexandra's sorcery-inspired fears, 'in order that you [viz. hostile forces] may not hurt or defile or bewitch / use magic drugs upon her, either via a kiss or osculation,[151] or a chance meeting, or through food or drink[152] or in bed or via intercourse nor by a glance / the Evil Eye nor [by magical use of] her clothing'.[153]

Thus far we have spoken of amulets with an exclusively prophylactic function, and it is true that they are employed predominantly for such ends, in particular to repel illnesses presently afflicting an individual or thought likely to do so in future. The number of diseases that the medico-magical amulets seek to ward off is legion: it includes gout (which like other ailments may be addressed in amuletic texts as a living entity),[154] sciatica, migraine headache, stomach disorders, epilepsy, eye problems, 'wandering womb'[155] or other uterine problems, elephantiasis, hydrophobia and above all fever, that is malaria. At other times the amulet simply states, in a catch-all or 'global' formula, 'protect the wearer from all harm'.[156] It is interesting too how often the purpose of an amulet is specified as the aversion of sorcerous attacks upon the person, a testament to a deep-seated belief both in the prevalence of malign magic[157] and in the capacity of phylactery-based counter-magic to negate it, an idea also visible in the *PGM* (4.2176–8, 8.32–5, 36.221–3). Even the rationalist physician Galen grudgingly concedes on the basis of empirical evidence (12.207 Kühn) the worth of an amuletic green jasper in countering stomach ache, while the specialist in women's medicine Soranus (*Gynaeceia* 3.42) recognised the psychologically comforting effect of amulets, even while dismissing any other claims made for their curative powers (Aristotle's successor Theophrastus in his book on medical botany is similarly dismissive (*HP* 9.19.2)).

But what of amulets that sought to inflict harm, or to grab some questionable advantage for the bearer, belying the nomenclature *phylaktēria*, 'protectives' or the widely touted, if unsubstantiated derivation of Latin *amuleta* from the verb *amoliri*, 'to get rid of?' Instances of these two dubious types, though much less common than prophylactic amulets, are not far to seek. Item no. 151 in Bonner (1950) carries the message 'as the [mythical] Memnon, son of the goddess of the Dawn lies dead, so may also Antipater, son of Philippa'. Bonner with some justice labels this amulet a *defixio*, 'curse', since as we have seen *defixiones* often sought to inflict death upon their targets. In Kotansky Amulets no. 24, a Romanian *lamella* of the second century CE, a demon is sent to menace the house of one Julia Cyrilla. More graphically still, some magical gems show figures either undergoing mutilation (e.g. with blood jetting from neck and wrists), or being mutilated by some demonic figure – evidently a pictorial conjuration of what the amulet-wearer desires for an enemy or an antagonist, such as a rival charioteer.[158] Exactly the same type of figurines can be found accompanying *defixiones* and the more aggressive spells of the *PGM*, notably in *PGM* 36.

In other instances, also like the immediately preceding ones case-specific, an amulet is designed to manipulate for the benefit of the wearer circumstances where the outcome is uncertain, such as a trial or a chariot race. The most prominent category here, however, involves the vicissitudes of love. Amulets with this theme may involve the wished-for bestowal of 'charm' in the eyes of all or the more focused 'charm … especially in regard to him before whom she herself desires this' (Kotansky Amulets no. 40). But amatory amulets can also be physical equivalents of the *diakopoi*, separation spells and *agōgai*, amatory fetching spells, of the *PGM*. In a celebrated case, several intaglios on surviving gems replicate the erotically themed schemata involving Aphrodite and the mythical lovers Cupid and Psyche, which are to be engraved on a magnetic stone according to the procedure for an erotic fetching spell at *PGM* 4.1716–1870, the 'Sword of Dardanos'.[159] The purpose of the preserved intaglios, as in the images prescribed in the 'Sword', was to draw a female love-object to the male wearer, just as Psyche was drawn to Cupid.

To sum up this brief survey, amulets are of considerable importance – not least in view of the current interest in the physicality of magic[160] – and the fact that, in terms of quality, amulets interestingly ranged from simple types, such as homespun phylacteries bound about bodily parts afflicted by illness, to elaborate artefacts requiring considerable expertise for their production. However, rather than opening up fresh avenues of investigation or theoretical pathways, they instead supplement and corroborate the evidence of the *PGM* and the *defixiones*. Some instances of this overlap, such as their featuring or copying the same types of figures as we find in the papyrus spells and curse tablets, or the basing of their presumptive powers on analogical reasoning, have been noted above. In addition, the international syncretism and Egyptianising flavour of the amulets, coming as they do mostly from the Empire period, mirrors that of the *PGM* and the later, highly complex *defixiones*: likewise the incorporation in amuletic ideograms of magic signs (*charaktēres*), series of vowels and 'words of power'. Further, quite apart from the appearance in some amulets of 'NN', which as we saw represents a kind of blank space to be filled in with the name of an individual when he or she commissions a spell, it is clear that many *phylaktēria* were composed using formularies, which is what the *PGM* by and large are (see Chapter 1 on the distinction between formulaic and applied spells). It would be possible to pursue at length further commonalities between magical amulets and the *PGM* in particular, for example their joint use of *historiolae*, brief allusions to mythical episodes, such as that of Memnon mentioned above, in order to underscore and give precedent to the desired outcome of a spell.[161] But enough has hopefully been said to establish the evidential value of amulets – important, but in the end ancillary to more substantial sources.

Notes

1. The bat was regarded by the ancients as a type of bird: see Oliphant (1913), 134 n.4. On the use of birds in magic, see Pollard (1977), 130–4.
2. See Nock (1972c).
3. On frogs, see Plin. *HN* 32.48–52; *PGM* 10.36–50, 36.231–55, 320–32; Deonna (1950), Weber (1970).
4. For fish in erotic magic, see Dosoo and Galoppin (forthcoming), n.57.
5. For the sacredness of the ibis, see Smelik (1979), 225–43; for the falcon, id. 226, 240; for the cat, Delvaux and Warmenbol (1991); for the crocodile, Zecchi (2010).
6. The baboon was extinct in Egypt in the later period (Smelik (1979), 226).
7. *PGM* 12.413, 416 with Betz's n.95 (p. 167f.). See Ogden (2014), 300. On the difficulties of interpreting such lists see LiDonnici (2002).
8. Plin. *HN* 29.112–13, 32.74–5. Cf. id. 29.98–100, 30.20, 30.51–2; Beagon (1992), 232; Gilhus (2006), 20–21; and discussion in Chapter 4. The medical cures from animals treated by Dioscorides in his second book include several based on the principle of similarity e.g. patients bitten by a mad dog could lessen their hydrophobia by eating a rabid dog's liver (*MM* 2.47); cf. Sextus Placitus 2.66 (a lizard was eaten as a remedy for lizard bite); Riddle (1985), 138.
9. Cf. *HN* 30.61 (stomach troubles are cured by placing a duck on the belly, which takes the illness away with it and subsequently dies). For transference in magic, cf. Chapter 4 and Plin. *HN* 30.99, *HN* 32.115 (the Magi used crab's eyes, attached as an amulet before sunrise, as a cure for tertian fever; the blinded crabs had to be released into the water, presumably to carry off the illness with them); *PGM* 36.320–32 (discussed in Chapter 4); Gilhus (2006), 21.
10. See Abt (1908), 289–90.
11. See Tupet (1976), 46–7; Gow (1965), on Theocr. *Id.* 2.43.
12. For magic knots see Ritner (1993), 142–4; Faraone (1999), 101–3.
13. This injunction, for purificatory purposes, is very common in magic, e.g. *PDM* 14.62ff.; cf. Plin. *HN* 28.226, 258, 29.131, 30.22, 123 and n.33 to Chapter 4.
14. On circles cf. Chapter 4.
15. Dickie (2001), 109; Ritner (1993), 74ff.; Chapter 4. n.15.

16 Such compendia include works by Dioscorides and Scribonius Largus (first century CE), Quintus Serenus [Sammonicus] (late second to early third century CE) and Marcellus Empiricus and Sextus Placitus (fourth century CE). Harris (2016a) has recently presented a case for drawing a distinction between rational medicine (as practised e.g. by Hippocrates or Galen) and folk-medicine, the latter overlapping with other popular forms of healing, including magic. Thus, when medical writers like those listed above include folk remedies they are temporarily straying outside their field.

17 *Compositiones* 123. Cf. Sextus Placitus 8.11 (eating a boar's bladder cures bladder pain).

18 For further examples, see n.8 above.

19 Cf. n.76 below.

20 See n.9 above.

21 30.61 *quod ... traditur in torminibus mirum est* 'what is handed down concerning gripings is of a miraculous character'; 64 *sunt occulti interaneorum morbi de quibus mirum proditur* 'there are obscure illnesses of the gut concerning which a marvellous cure is prescribed'. Cf. *HN* 28.155 (if you whisper in an ass's ear that you have been stung by a scorpion you will be cured, the injury being passed on to the ass; this essentially magical cure is also recorded in the magico-medical treatise *Cyranides* (2.31.27–9, p. 164 Kaimakis), which adds that the ass will die). Pliny qualifies it with *tradunt*, 'they say that'.

22 *HN* 28.228–9; cf. 30.95: the ash from a *bubo*'s incinerated eyes is regarded as *inter ea quibus prodigiose uitam ludificantur* 'amongst those things with which in an unnatural way they (magicians) mock mankind'. For the uncanniness of the *bubo* see n.133 below.

23 See nn.43–45 below.

24 The accompaniment of spoken words and the number three are both magical elements. The magic idea behind the plastering and sealing with a ring is to confine the spleen so that the disease transferred to it cannot escape back to the patient.

25 On Pliny's occasional lack of discrimination between magic and medicine, cf. Beagon (1992), 111, 216.

26 A good example of Pliny's inconsistency: while here observing lunar cycles, he elsewhere attacks the Magi at length for using astrology (30.96) and often Magian remedies which he records involve the phases of the moon (e.g. 30.22).

27 *Lib. Med.* 929–31 'I'll pass over in silence many monstrosities of words (monstrous words) for it is empty superstition and trembling mothers that believe fever can be expelled by various incantations'.

28 *Lib. Med.* 935–40. Charms were, in fact, commonly used in popular Greek and Roman healing, from the time of Homer on (see Plin. *HN* 28.21); Pliny touches on them when dealing with the superstitiousness of the Romans, but refuses to record any because of the controversy they arouse.

29 'A marvellous charm for toothache of proven efficacy. At the waning of the moon on either the day of Mars (a Tuesday) or the day of Jupiter (a Thursday) repeat the following words seven times: "Argidam margidam sturgidam"' (12.24).
30 The recipe is a somewhat confused mélange of similarity (an animal liver used as a cure for liver disease) and transference (the disease passed to the animal which is released alive: except that a lizard without a liver is hardly likely to be still living!), with the addition of a cloth of magically significant colour and the magical formula addressed to the lizard.
31 Matching the sex of the patient to the sex of the animal (cf. n.19 above), the use of Cyprian bronze, the astrological detail, the odd (magical) numbers, the decreasing numbers suggesting analogically the diminution of the disease, the ivory bracelet worn as a prophylactic (i.e. to protect the person administering it from harm (common in *PGM* (e.g. 4.2622–707)); cf. Chapter 4 with n.21).
32 Plin. *HN* 29.30 says the Romans of old assigned to wool an *auctoritas religiosa* ('supernatural power').
33 See Watson and Watson (2014), on Juvenal 6.518; Watson (2003), on *Epode* 5.19.
34 See also Chapter 6 n.59. Animal products like dung as well as milk, fat, blood etc. were also used in (folk) medicine: see Riddle (1985), 138–41 for these in Dioscorides; and Gourevitch (2016), 256–9 and Nutton (2016), 275f. for Galen's use of dung.
35 On animal sacrifice in religion see Gilhus (2006), 114–37. For the sacrifice of animals in magic and its close relationship with religious sacrificial rites, see Johnston (2002).
36 Kropp 11/.1/1/8 = Audollent 222 (cf. n.42 below and Chapter 3 n.145): the tongue is used by analogy to silence the tongues of one's enemies.
37 Cf. Marcell. Empir. 29.45 and n.9 above for further examples of releasing a mutilated animal in the context of transference.
38 See further Chapter 2 n.43. For the mutilation of animals in love magic see also Faraone (1999), 66–8.
39 Nock (1972c), esp. 272–4; Waegeman (1984), 220.
40 The text says 'women' but one assumes these are courtesans. On the close connection between this profession and the use of magic, see Chapter 2 *ad fin.*
41 Johnston (2008), 146, 154 suggests that small creatures like a rooster were sacrificed in magic ceremonies (as opposed to larger animals such as sheep in religious rituals) because it was more convenient for magicians practising in their own or client's houses. The black sheep, though, was the regular victim in rites of necromancy: see further below.
42 (1999), 67. Faraone also discusses the two examples involving a rooster, in the second of which the bird is, like the puppy, transfixed. Cf. also Ogden (2014), 301; and Faraone (1991), 21–2.
43 See Hand (1980), 201–13. So potent was the animal considered that there was a common belief that by crushing a mole in one's hand the magical healing power of the mole could be transferred to the killer (id. 202–4).

44 *HN* 30.19; so too in the *Cyranides* (2.3.13, p. 117 Kaimakis), a fourth(?)-century compilation of folk-magic/medicine, the mole is said to have divine powers.
45 Cf. Hand (1980), 202. He connects its alleged powers of divination to its blindness and acute sense of hearing. Gordon (2010), 263, on the other hand, argues that the mole is a unique creature (cf. n.48 below) because it is the only sightless quadruped.
46 The *Cyranides* (2.3.9–11, p. 117 Kaimakis) goes further, saying that in addition the heart has to be worn in hoopoe's skin with two hoopoe's eyes.
47 Hand (1980), 207: the tooth from a living mole was to be rubbed over an aching tooth.
48 Other animals thought to have intrinsic magical powers include the wolf (Plin. *HN* 28.157), the owl (Aelian, *NA* 1.29 says the owl is like a witch), the hoopoe (cf. *Cyranides* 1.7.49–102, pp. 52–4 Kaimakis; Waegeman (1984), 221; Pollard (1977), 132), the cricket (Plin. *HN* 29.138), the tick (Plin. *HN* 30.82–3), and especially the hyena, to which Pliny gives a lengthy treatment (see Ogden (2014), 296–9; cf. Solinus 27.23–5, Aelian, *NA* 6.14). In the case of the last three, along with the chameleon and the mole, Gordon (2010), 257–65 argues that Magi exploited popular beliefs about them to show that they were unique creatures (e.g. the tick is the only animal to have no anus, the hyena to change sex each year, etc.) thereby rationalising the employment of these in magic.
49 For tortoises and hares as exemplars respectively of slowness and speed, cf. the Aesopian fable of the Tortoise and the Hare.
50 Cf. Aristotle, *History of Animals* 8.4 (the most acute vision is found in eyes which are the colour of a goat's).
51 On sympathy (similarity)/antipathy as a magical principle, see Chapter 4 and n.8 above.
52 Cf. Isid. *Orig.* 12.1.18 (deer are the enemy of snakes). Stags were thought to draw snakes out of their lairs by the breath of their nostrils (cf. Lucretius, 6.766); in fact deer are normally herbivores, though they do occasionally kill snakes in self-defence (or in defence of their fawns: see Tupet (1976), 72 n.1).
53 In the same way, carrying hyena's leather protects against the attacks of panthers because panthers are the special enemies of hyenas, or geckos left to rot in oil are applied to scorpion wounds because scorpions are said to be terrified of geckos (Plin. *HN* 29.90; cf. Waegeman (1984), 222).
54 In general, see Villalobos and Barrientos (2015).
55 E.g. *PGM* 4.2943–66, 19b.4–18, 36.370–1; see Scholz (1937), 24 for the use of dogs in love magic.
56 Cf. Apuleius *Met.* 7.21; Schlam (1992), 40 n.1; Griffith (2006) 224. It is relevant that the animal was associated with such phallic deities as Dionysus, Silenus, the Satyrs, Pan and Priapus (Deonna (1956), 630–7).
57 Cf. nn.126–8 below.
58 Doves, famous for their kissing (cf. Plin. *HN* 10.32, Mart. 11.104.9 with Kay (1985) *ad loc.*), were sacred to the love-goddess Aphrodite (n.72 below).

59 For the sexual prowess of cocks, see Csapo (1993), 11–16.
60 For the ram as a hyper-sexed animal see Davies (1990), esp. 173 n.12.
61 Cf. n.88 below.
62 A cock's right testicle was used for the same purpose: see Plin. *HN* 30.141; cf. Csapo (1993), 15 n.73 (citing also the *Cyranides*). Cf. Sextus Placitus 11.14 (bulls' testicles as an aphrodisiac).
63 Red, symbolising life, is commonly mentioned in magic, often in the form of materials of a red colour (see Pinch (2001); Rowe (1972), 357f.).
64 A magical number.
65 The mule, the offspring of a jackass and a mare, is infertile. See also the discussion of *PGM* 36.320–32 in Chapter 4.
66 The phallus was apotropaic: cf. the *bulla* (an amulet in the shape of a phallus) worn by Roman children to protect them from harmful things such as the evil eye; see Watson (2003), 195–6. For the image of an ithyphallic ass on amulets, see Deonna (1956), 637–8, 647.
67 See Dosoo and Galoppin (forthcoming).
68 The sexual nature of the ass is also relevant insofar as Seth is a god who represents violent, irresponsible sexuality (not fertility): see Te Velde (1967), 32–59, esp. 55, 58.
69 Sicherl (1937), 47–59; Deonna (1956), 649; Te Velde (1967), 149.
70 Cf. *PGM* 4.3255–74, where a brick on which is drawn a picture of an ass is smeared with 'Typhon's blood' in a violent erotic spell invoking Typhon/Seth. See Winkler (1991), 231 on the close relationship between binding spells and erotic spells of attraction, both using chthonic powers / the untimely dead as agents.
71 Cf. Aelian, *NA* 4.17; Paus. 5.25.9; D'Arcy Thompson (1936), 40; Gilhus (2006), 132.
72 Aelian, *NA* 10.33; Plut. *De Iside et Osiride* 379d; D'Arcy Thompson (1936), 292.
73 See Scholz (1937).
74 Cf. Johnston (2002), 349. For the sacrifice of a white rooster in rites invoking the sun god Apollo or Helios (and also the moon, Selene) cf. *PGM* 2.74–9, 3.633–731; *PGM* 12.307–16.
75 In these cases, the intrinsic magic potency attributed to the animals in question enhanced the effect. For other examples of similarity see n.8 above.
76 Plin. *HN* 28.212. Cf. Plin. *HN* 28.232 (for dropsy, cow dung is used for female patients and bull dung for males) and the examples from Sextus Placitus (4.14) and Scribonius Largus (*Compositiones* 16) discussed earlier in this chapter.
77 In the same way, plants with yellow flowers were often used: cf. Ducourthial (2003), 247. For the analogical use of colour, cf. also Plin. *HN* 29.132 (white ulcers are treated with an ointment of pounded white spider in oil) and the discussion in Chapter 4.
78 Latin *icterus* ('jaundice'), according to Pliny a nickname given to the *galgulus* (the golden oriole?) because of its colour. See D'Arcy Thompson (1936), 119; Capponi (1979), 304f.
79 See n.9 above.

80 On the symbolism of black, see André (1949), 46–57; Rowe (1972), 355–6; Watson and Watson (2014), 263. For red, cf. n.63 above. Red animals are occasionally specified e.g. Plin. *HN* 28.170, but the reason is unclear.

81 Cf. *PGM* 12.107–21, a ritual to send dreams, in which a papyrus with writing on it is put in the mouth of a black cat that has died violently.

82 For the black dog as a chthonic animal, see Scholz (1937), 24; André (1949), 46; cf. Ter. *Phorm.* 706 (a black dog is a bad omen).

83 Ogden (2014), 300, (2001), 171–4; Rowe (1972), 355. Conversely, Johnston (2002), 350 n.16 mentions the offering of the brains of a black ram as part of a compulsive procedure addressed to the sun god (*PGM* 2.1–64, 4.1275–1322, 7.528–39). She suggests that, since the normal sacrifice to this god was a white animal, the magician offers the god something he would not like, to make him uncomfortable and so more ready to obey.

84 Cf. *PGM* 11a1–40 (the blood of a black dog is used as writing ink in an invocation to Nephthys, wife of Seth); *PGM* 4.1331–89, 4.1390, 7.300a–310.

85 Unless the use of a black ass was connected to the belief of magicians ([Hipp.] *On the Sacred Disease* 4) that night terrors in epileptics were inflicted by the chthonic goddess Hecate.

86 Contrast the use in later magic, in America for instance, of *black* hens and cocks (Hand (1980), 192, 196).

87 See Rowe (1972), 354; Lloyd (1962). Pliny (*HN* 28.93) says that a hyena swerving to the left is considered a sign of its failing strength.

88 Cf. n.62 above. Lloyd (1962), 60 notes that right testicles were believed by some to produce male children, or that a foetus on the right side of the womb was male.

89 Gordon suggests that by specifying such conditions, magicians were implicitly rationalising (offering a reason for) the use of such animals in magic.

90 Dickie (2001), 122, citing Pliny (*HN* 29.82) on the rarity of the *bubo*, suggests that where recipes involving such ingredients appear in collections of magical lore such as that of Bolus (the source of the magic attributed by Pliny to the Magi, according to Dickie, 120) the function might be literary rather than practical, and that if they were included in the books of practising magicians, they might have been designed simply to impress. But Pliny sometimes gives medicinal uses of the *bubo* which are not attributed to the Magi (e.g. 29.81, 30.52,121).

91 And in some cases (e.g. the lion or the baboon) they may be pseudonyms for plants: see above with n.7.

92 Either in the form of mass handouts, or as items for sale in butcher's shops. Some of the animals killed in the arena might also have been fed to animals in *uiuaria* (private zoos or holding places for animals intended for the arena: see Epplett (2003), 88f.): another possible source of lion parts for an enterprising magician. See Kyle (1998), 184–212. That lion's fat was available is suggested by casual references to it, e.g. Pliny, *HN* 28.89 (as a cosmetic); Serenus Sammonicus, *Lib. Med.* 941 (as a cure for fever).

93 Cf. Gordon (2010), 260 n.42.
94 Cf. Scribonius Largus, *Compositiones* 16, discussed earlier in this chapter, where blood is extracted by driving a nail of Cyprian bronze into the neck of a tortoise and cutting the veins of a dove which are under the wings; the animals had to be released alive afterwards.
95 Cf. *HN* 32.135; Apuleius, *Met.* 3.17 *seruatus cruor*. For dried blood cf. Scribonius Largus, *Compositiones* 177.
96 Cf. also *HN* 29.135–6. Pliny even sometimes prefers old ingredients to fresh: e.g. *HN* 28.95 (a hyena preparation works best if kept in a box of Cyprian copper), 28.163, 172.
97 Cf. Plin. *HN* 32.33: the blood of a tortoise was preserved in flour, made into pills and administered as needed in wine as an antidote to poisons, Scribonius Largus, *Compositiones* 16 (cited earlier), 175.
98 Cf. Dickie (2001), 116.
99 See Dickie (2001), 165 on Roman women calling on wise-women to treat their children in preference to doctors.
100 On eggs in purifications see Watson and Watson (2014), on Juvenal 6.518.
101 Sometimes this included even the Roman emperor himself: according to Dio 69.22, for instance, Hadrian resorted to magic when suffering from a severe illness.
102 For variations in the price of ingredients and the social classes of clients in popular medicine see Harris (2016a), 53–6.
103 *Postea fraudes hominum et ingeniorum capturae officinas inuenere istas in quibus sua cuique homini uenalis promittitur uita* 'afterwards the deceits of men and cunning profiteering invented those workshops in which every man is promised his life at a price'. Cf. *HN* 29.28 'the crazy convictions of some who consider no substance beneficial unless it costs a lot'; Harris (2016a), 54 and following note.
104 And not only the wealthy: cf. Colum. 1.8.6: the overseer of the country estate (*uilicus*) is advised not to admit soothsayers and *sagae* (witches) who 'through empty superstition drive unformed minds to expenses and then to shameful practices'; Philostr. *Vit. Apollon. Tyan.* 7.39 on lovers who will accept from magicians 'a magic girdle to wear, as well as precious stones, ... all the spices which the gardens of India yield; and the cheats exact vast sums of money from them for all this, and yet do nothing to help them at all'. Cf. Lucian, *Philops.*: a parody of the gullibility of those who use magic (see n.138 below).
105 This practice would not have been confined to charlatans: Galen advised doctors to pad out simple remedies with expensive additives in the case of wealthy patients, since these did not believe that a cheap drug could be effective (cf. Nutton (2016), 275 n.14).
106 Recorded in the *Lives of Saints Cyprian and Justina*, mid-fourth century. See Ogden (2008), 87f. (for Lucian), 120f. (for Justina).

107 Cf. Lucian, *Dial. of the Courtesans* 4 *ad fin.*, where a witch teaches a courtesan how to perform rites (not in this case involving animals).
108 In Lucian, *Philops.* 17, Eukratēs declares that an Arab taught him 'the spell of many names'. Magic workers may have taught shorter spells to clients: cf. Clem. *Homilies* 5.3 (Appiōn relates how as a young man he sought the help of an Egyptian magician who taught him an incantation by means of which he attained the woman he desired); Dickie (2000), 579f.
109 On spells in the shape of formularies see below on *PGM* 4.2943-66.
110 Gaillard-Seux (1998) suggests several rationales for the use of a green lizard in procedures to cure ocular disease: the lizard was valued in magic for its regenerative powers; its large eyes suggested the idea of keen sight; the animal's connection with the sun; the supposedly beneficial effect of the colour green on the eyes. On lizard amulets of the type under discussion see also appendix to this chapter.
111 Marcell. Empir. 8.9, a detail confirmed by the image on some amulets of a crescent waning moon (Bonner *loc. cit.*). See also appendix to this chapter.
112 Cf. n.9 above.
113 Dickie (2001), 93, 108f., 116f., 133, 233f., 246, 311.
114 In such cases, the location of the ritual is clearly associated with the deity invoked (the moon goddess), communication with whom is enhanced by proximity.
115 Compare Phaedra's nurse who has love philtres in the house (Eur. *Hipp.* 478-82, 509-15), while Simaitha keeps in a box deadly *pharmaka* learnt from an Assyrian stranger (Theocritus, *Id.* 2.161-2); Dickie (2001), 88-9, 100-04.
116 *PGM* 4.2708-84 for instance begins: 'Take some Ethiopian cumin and fat of a dappled virgin goat and after putting the offering together, offer it to Selene on the 13th, 14th, on an earthen censer, on a lofty housetop'. Similarly, the spell allegedly employed by the emperor Hadrian (4.2441), mentioned earlier, involves the preliminary manufacture of a mixture to be used as a burnt offering: when the rite is performed, it must be done 'on a lofty roof' accompanied by an invocation to the moon goddess.
117 Cf. also Hor. *Epod.* 17.35 where Canidia is described as 'a workshop (*officina*) aglow with magic spells'.
118 Cf. a story in Galen (Kühn 8.197-8) about a country man who was accustomed to consult a doctor in the city. The passage from Pliny cited above (n.103) might also suggest that doctors prescribed medications in their workshops.
119 Simaitha also employs a *iunx* (literally 'wryneck'), a magic wheel spun to attract a lover, which may have originally had the actual bird attached. The twisting dance of the wryneck (a type of woodpecker) was mistakenly believed to be a mating dance; evidence for the magical exploitation, literally or figuratively, of its supposed erotic power goes back to the eighth century BCE: see Ogden (2014), 295-6; also Pollard (1977), 130-1; and Chapter 6 n.9.

120 *Sat.* 1.8, *Epode* 5 and 17.
121 *Sat.* 1.8.27–29; a black sheep was the usual victim in necromantic rites (see n.83 above).
122 The association between the *lena*/prostitute and erotic magic may reflect reality: cf. n.40 above.
123 But see Gordon (1987a), 81 for atrocities perpetrated by her in lost fifth-century tragedies.
124 Ogden (2014), 299–300 calls it 'parody' but I would question whether this concept would be appropriate in a serious epic poem.
125 Lucan in fact specifies that the ingredients employed by Erictho are sinister/ill-omened (*huc quidquid fetu genuit natura sinistro / miscetur* 670-1).
126 See Aristotle, *Hist. An.* 572a 8–12; Verg. *Georg.* 3.266–83.
127 Aristot. *Hist. An.* 577a 7–10; Plin. *HN* 8.165; cf. Verg. *Aen.* 4.515-6; Ov. *Ars* 2.100; Juv. 6.616-17. Tupet (1976), 81 points out that this has no basis in fact, but that the belief could have arisen from the presence in mares' amniotic fluid of brown fibrous egg-like substances which end up on various parts of the foal when it is expelled and often on the head, as well as the habit of mares of licking their foals as soon as they are born.
128 Aristot. *Hist. An.* 572a 19–21; Pausanias 5.27.3; Verg. *Georg.* 3.280–1; Tib. 2.4.58; Ov. *Am.* 1.8.8; Prop. 4.5.17–18; Plin. *HN* 28.261. In Theocritus it is a type of plant (Theocr. *Id.* 2.48–51; cf. Servius on *Georg.* 3.280).
129 Ogden (2014), 300; Tupet (1976), 2653.
130 Toads were likewise sinister because they were thought (erroneously) to be extremely poisonous (e.g. Aelian, *NA* 17.12; Plin. *HN* 32.50); they also had infernal associations (Watson (2003), on *Epode* 5.19).
131 Pliny *HN* 11.232 rejects the story that *striges* feed babies from their teats and says that even in ancient times the *strix* was regarded as a sinister/ill-omened creature, but he does not think there is agreement as to which bird it is.
132 Ovid, *Fasti* 6.131–140; Scobie (1978); Oliphant (1913) is useful for source material but argues improbably that the *strix* is a bat rather than an owl.
133 See Aelian, *NA* 10.37 (the owl is a bad omen), Pliny (*HN* 10.34) finds the *bubo* especially sinister and ill-omened; cf. Apuleius, *Met.* 3.23: owls (*bubones*) which got into houses were nailed to the doorpost to expiate the misfortune they were thought to bring on the family by their ill-omened flight.
134 Cf. Ovid, *Fasti* 6.139–40 'the reason for this name is that they are accustomed to screech (*stridere*) horribly at night'.
135 *Hippomanes quod saepe legere malae nouercae / miscueruntque herbas et non innoxia uerba* ('*hippomanes*, which often evil stepmothers gather, and they mix in herbs and malignant spells'). Stepmothers were frequently depicted as attempting to seduce their stepsons (or else to poison them, though this is not the point here).

The sinister character of *hippomanes* is reinforced by the allusion to the proverbially malevolent stepmothers, here identified as witches. See further Watson (1993), 842–7.

136 In the same way Pliny, when attacking or ridiculing the Magi, often focuses on the macabre or disgusting: e.g. he comments on the Magi's use of the tick, 'a most disgusting creature' (*HN* 30.82). See also Chapter 6 n.59.

137 E.g. *HN* 28.228–9, 29.81–2, 30.95, 110. Owls also appear several times in *PGM*, though the exact species is unclear.

138 A similar bias is seen in other literary portrayals of magic, e.g. in a dialogue of Lucian (*Philops.* 7–8), a character describes a magic cure for rheumatic pain in the foot, in which the tooth of a weasel is wrapped in the skin of a recently flayed lion. One of the audience, Deinomachus the Stoic, comments that Asclepius, god of medicine, used healing drugs, not amulets made of lions' skins and weasels.

139 What follows mostly formed part of the penultimate draft of this book, but was excised because I felt that I had nothing original to contribute on the subject of amulets, and because anything I did say would surely be overtaken by the ongoing work of Christopher Faraone on various aspects of the topic. I have, however, restored these pages following a suggestion of the expert reader, who felt that for the sake of completeness something should be included on the topic.

140 In general on amulets see Bonner (1946 and 1950); Delatte and Derchain (1964); Kotansky (1991) and Kotansky *Amulets*; Michel (2001 and 2004, both with excellent drawings and photographs of amuletic gems); Mastrocinque (2003 and 2007); Faraone (2012); Bohak (2015); Nagy (2015); also Ogden (2002a), 261–74 for a convenient selection of amulets. I have been unable to consult Mastrocinque (2014b).

141 For prominent Romans using amulets cf. Plin. *HN* 28.29 and 39, Plut. *Sull.* 29.6, and n.144 infra.

142 Bonner (1946), 28–30.

143 E. g. centaury (Kotansky *Amulets* no. 8), or 'a herb accustomed to grow on the head of a statue' (Marcell. Empir. 1.43), pennywort (id. 14.65), artemisia (id. 26.41). See further Chapter 4 with n. 91.

144 E.g. the seal-skin carried by Augustus as a protection against lightning (Suet. *Aug.* 90), on the grounds that seals are never struck by lightning (Plin. *HN* 2.146).

145 For a possible prototype in the so-called Orphic *lamellae*, see Kotansky (1991), 114–15.

146 On these amulets see Bonner (1950), 69–71.

147 A blanket term covering all kinds of eye diseases, serious or otherwise.

148 It is important however to note that not all the pictographic 'vanishing acts' are conjurations against illness: *PGM* 19a and 36.102–33 for example, which both feature such diagrams, are amatory fetching spells.

149 Bonner (1946), 35 lists the most commonly used stones.
150 See Bonner (1950), descriptions 162–76 for instances, also *PGM* vol. 2 Abbildung 18 for a good representation in a papyrus spell. In general on the iconography, origins and protective capacity of the anguipede, see Mastrocinque (2003), 84–90.
151 Both nouns refer to kissing as a form of social greeting.
152 '<A reference> to poisoning, erotic love-potions, or both' Kotansky.
153 A sorcerer, by getting hold of an item of clothing used by Alexandra, could use it to harm her, since it was still mysteriously invested, it was thought, with the essence of its one-time wearer and thus a stand-in for Alexandra herself.
154 Bonner (1950), 76 refers to an amulet that shows on the obverse Perseus flying, holding the head of Medusa, while the reverse is inscribed 'flee, Gout, Perseus is pursuing you'.
155 See Bonner (1950), 81 for a gem carved in the shape of a uterus – a common type of amulet – with the inscription 'put the womb of NN in its proper place'.
156 Cf. Bonner (1946), 29.
157 See e.g. Graf (2007).
158 Nagy (2015), 215–16 seems to understate the malign dimension of amulets when he proclaims 'among the few thousand known magical gems, only a couple can be securely identified as a harmful', especially since he does not include under the category of 'harmful' those which seek to coerce another to love, such as the 'Sword of Dardanos' (see the text immediately below).
159 A full discussion in Mouterde (1930). The text which accompanies Kotansky Amulets, no. 62, a tiny gold *lamella* featuring the image of a sword, invokes erotic madness on a female target, an idea amply paralleled in the *PGM*.
160 See notably the essays in Boschung and Bremmer (2015).
161 For *historiolae* incorporated in amulets see Kotansky (1991), 112–13.

6

Fictional Witches

A subject of perennial fascination, the witches of ancient Greece and Rome, both fictional and real, have been the recipient of much attention lately, with a volume of essays on the typology of the sorceress-figure (Stratton and Kalleres (2014)), a monograph on 'Rome's First Witch' (Paule (2017)), and a study examining perceptions of the witch-figure across different eras, continents and cultures, including those of Greece and Rome (Hutton (2017)). The present chapter directs its attention to the witch as a literary construct; however, mentions of witchcraft as actually employed in Greece and Rome will inevitably occur in the discussion that follows, given that at times the boundary between the procedures adopted by the literary witch and the ritual practices recorded in the handbooks of practising magicians is gossamer-thin. At the outset I should make it clear that, in keeping with accepted English usage, the term 'witch' is understood in what follows to refer exclusively to a *female* practitioner of magic, a sorceress.

Fictional witches are a creation primarily of poetry, but also have a significant presence in the novelistic prose of the Roman Empire. While male sorcerers are by no means lacking in fictional prose writings at least,[1] the most substantial accounts of magicians in the imaginative literature of Greece and Rome almost invariably make them female; in particular, they often represent them as motivated to use sorcery by some form of amatory passion, be this the agonies of rejected love, high-octane lust or overwhelming sexual jealousy. That said, literary witches appear in a wide variety of guises, both physical and emotional. Among other possibilities, they may be young and sympathetic, old and grotesque, risible inepts, vainglorious charlatans, symbols of alterity in ethnic terms and, in extreme cases, embodiments of monstrous evil.

The study of the literary witch prompts a number of questions. To what extent do the verbal and ritual procedures in which literary witches engage reflect the actual protocols of authentic magical spells, in particular those of the *PGM*? What is the aim of authors of fiction in populating their pages with such figures? How does the figure of the witch evolve and develop over time? How effective are witches in literature perceived to be? How seriously are we meant to take the various accounts of witches in imaginative literature? What factors propel the gendered presentation of them as typically female?

As the profile of the literary witch, as we will see, changes over the centuries, the discussion will proceed in roughly diachronic order. The story of Greek and Roman witchcraft begins with the 'fair-tressed, dread goddess' Circe of Homer's *Odyssey*, an epic poem that probably attained its final, that is to say written as opposed to oral, form early in the seventh century BCE. In book ten of the work, Odysseus and his companions fetch up at the island of Circe, Aeaea. Odysseus sends off a scouting party to Circe's palace, where his men are met with wolves and lions, which fawn upon them instead of attacking. Circe entertains the men with a pottage of cheese, meal, honey and wine, mixing into this 'baneful drugs', *pharmaka lugra*, 'so that they might utterly forget their native land', and strikes them with her wand, turning them into swine (in later versions her victims are transformed into a variety of animals). No reason for this action on Circe's part is given. One of the party, having held back from the entertainment because he suspected a snare, reports to Odysseus what has happened. The hero sets off for Circe's palace, but is met on the way by the god Hermes, who gives him a flower, *mōlu*, whose identity has been the subject of endless discussion (Stannard (1962)), which will protect him from the effects of Circe's magic potion. Circe

Fig. 10 Kylix showing Odysseus' men turned into animals by Circe (sixth century BCE). Wikimedia Commons / CC-BY 2.0.

serves Odysseus the same enchanted meal as his men, but to no effect, because of the *mōlu*. As instructed by Hermes, Odysseus draws his sword as though meaning to kill Circe, and when invited to have sex with her, extracts from Circe an oath that she will not make Odysseus 'weak and unmanned' when she has him naked. The promise duly given, the two retire to Circe's bed, initiating a pleasurable stay in Aeaea which will last for a year.

It is important to register the sequel to these events. Circe now reveals a more benign aspect. At Odysseus' solicitation, she retransforms Odysseus' men into humans, making them more youthful and more handsome than before. When Odysseus and his men prepare finally to leave, she gives Odysseus precise instructions on how to conjure up from Hades, at the edge of the world, the shade of the dead seer Tiresias, whom Odysseus must consult about a return to his homeland of Ithaca. The necromantic conversation with Tiresias once accomplished, Odysseus returns to Aeaea, where Circe provides him with a stratagem to escape the Sirens, Lorelei-like sea-spirits who, by the beauty of their songs, detained passing sailors until they rotted away to shrivelled corpses. Circe also advises Odysseus how to navigate past the fearsome monsters Scylla and Charybdis. In sum, Circe is by no means all bad, but has a benign side to her character.

It has been argued, most forcibly by Matthew Dickie,[2] that because the idea of magic as a distinct category of thought supposedly did not crystallise until the fifth century BCE, there is no indication in the Homeric text that Circe was thought of as a sorceress. This line of reasoning seems fallacious. Circe can metamorphose men into animals, make them forget ties to family and homeland, move swiftly and invisibly (*Ody.* 10.571–4), understands necromancy, practises sex-magic, and, above all, is a mistress of herbs and drugs (there was even a magical plant known as 'Circe's root' named after her). In other words, she prefigures so markedly the doings and capacities of later witches, that notwithstanding the absence of any label in the text explicitly identifying her as such, it is hard to believe that she did not occupy de facto the category 'witch', even if the theoretical framework for defining such persons, and the concept 'magic' more generally, had yet to be worked out.[3] What is beyond doubt is that the Homeric Circe was powerfully influential in fashioning the later paradigm of the witch.

The next witch to call for attention is like Circe a goddess (Pind. *Pyth.* 4.9–11), her close relative Medea, an altogether more fearsome figure than the former. Also like Circe however, she has her positive side too; this, Martin (2005, 129–34) has argued, may indeed have predominated in her earliest realisation:

on the other hand already in various, mostly lost tragedies of the fifth century BCE she is credited with a variety of atrocities (Gordon (1987a), 81–2). Among surviving Greek texts we meet her in Pindar's fourth *Pythian Ode* (fifth century BCE), in Apollonius of Rhodes' third-century BCE epic *Argonautika* ('Voyage of the Argonauts') and the eponymous fifth-century BCE tragedy *Medea* of Euripides. Initially she appears as an innocent young girl constrained by the gods to fall helplessly in love with Jason, the leader of the quest to return the Golden Fleece to Greece. The immortals' purpose is that the lovesick Medea should use her magical powers to let Jason effect two seemingly impossible trials, the overcoming of which her father Aiētes makes a precondition for getting the Golden Fleece. Medea duly provides Jason with a magic salve that shields him from the flames of the fire-breathing bulls which he must yoke and use to plough the plain of Ares: it equally protects him from the spear points of the earthborn men who spring from the serpent's teeth which he is to sow in the freshly turned furrows. She also tells Jason how to direct the martial rage of the earthborn men away from himself onto each other, and finally lulls to sleep by means of a spell and a magical drug the dragon that guards the Golden Fleece. Prior to the ordeals, Jason performs, as instructed by Medea, an elaborate rite to Hecate, the goddess of witches,[4] of whom Medea is a priestess (Ap. Rhod. 3.252); this will secure him from danger in the coming trials.

The primary source for the above is book three and the opening of book four of Apollonius' *Argonautika*. But in the rest of book four Medea, who has by now eloped with Jason from her homeland of Colchis, reveals a far more dangerous side; critics have often remarked the striking difference between the Medeas of the respective books (however, it should be noted that her witchy credentials are firmly established in book three, so that her more sinister aspects hardly come out of nowhere). In book four she connives at the treacherous murder of her brother Apsyrtus, for which appalling crime she must be purified by Circe, and employs the Evil Eye to kill the bronze giant Talos, who is barring the Argonauts' passage. The same lethal traits are on display in Euripides' *Medea*, where, having been thrown over by a self-serving Jason in favour of an advantageous marriage to the Corinthian princess Creusa, she sends the new bride gifts imbued with a sort of magical napalm which horribly consumes not only the princess, but also the bride's father Kreon. It is notable that, in contrast to later accounts, little detail is given of the concoction of this incendiary substance. At the conclusion of the play, Medea avenges herself for Jason's treachery by killing her own children by him, before fleeing in a chariot drawn by flying dragons.[5]

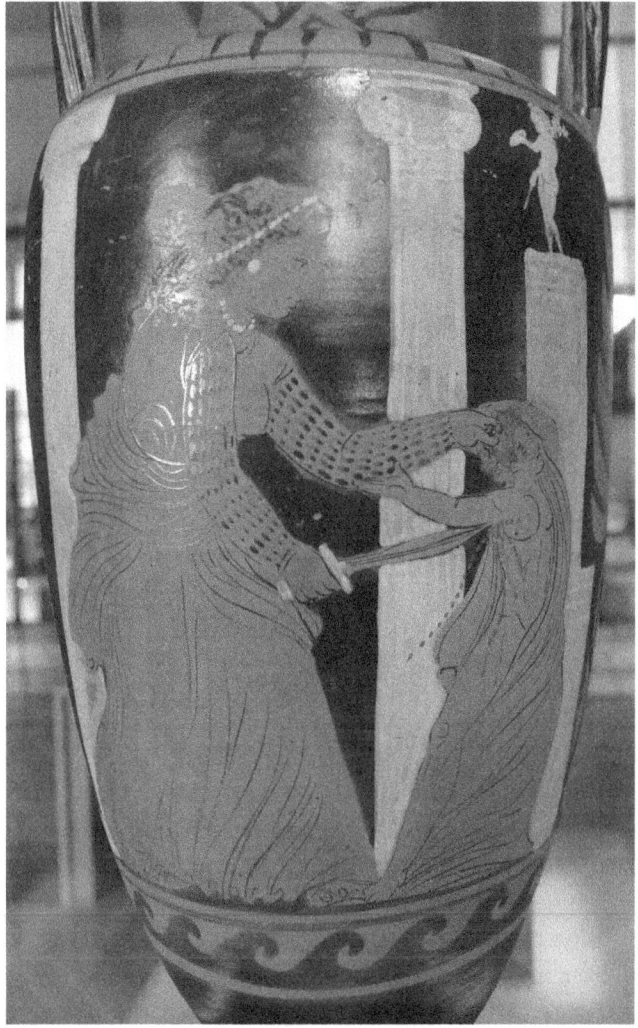

Fig. 11 Medea murdering one of her sons (Ixion painter, Cumae, *c.* 330 BCE).

Both before and after the events at Corinth, Medea perpetrates a number of miracles and atrocities – the rejuvenation of Jason's father Aesōn by means of magical herbs, the tricking of the daughters of Pēlias into murdering their father in the belief that he would be similarly restored by her to youth, and the attempted murder of her stepson Theseus using the hellish plant aconite. The main Greek sources for these events having been almost completely lost,[6] we must wait until book seven of Ovid's *Metamorphoses* (opening decade of the first century CE) for a full account of them. In Ovid's treatment the two aspects of Medea, insecure amatory novice and terrifying witch, are so starkly juxtaposed that, Carole Newlands (1997) has plausibly argued, a key purpose of the poet was to highlight the fundamental irreconcilability of these radically different features of the Medea legend. Of Ovid's Medea, more below.

Besides Medea, there are several Greek witch-figures of lesser importance who occur in fifth–fourth century BCE literature, as well as passing references to Thessalian women having the capacity to draw down the moon (Ar. *Clouds* 749–50, Plat. *Gorg.* 513a), a procedure which becomes over time a virtuoso demonstration of *art pour l'art* only rarely having a practical purpose;[7] it is captured in a line drawing of a now lost vase where two naked witches are shown performing this feat while appealing to the goddess 'hear me, Lady Moon' (Ogden (2002a), Fig. 11.1). But it is not until the second *Idyll* of the influential Greek poet Theocritus of Syracuse (*floruit* approximately 280–70 BCE), that we encounter the first really detailed portrait of a fictional witch conducting a magic rite.[8] In the *Idyll*'s first section (1–63), the protagonist Simaitha, aided by her maid Thestylis, attempts by means of a magic rite and incantation to recover the affections of her faithless lover Delphis. The lines read:

> Where are my bay leaves? Bring them, Thestylis. And where are my magic stuffs (*philtra*)? Wreathe the bowl with the finest quality red wool, so that I can bind the man I love, who is being hard to me, who – the wretch! – has not even come to me for eleven days now, nor does he know whether I am dead or alive, nor, in his cruelty, has he even knocked at my door. Assuredly Love and Aphrodite have gone off, taking his fickle heart elsewhere. Tomorrow I will go to the wrestling school of Timagētos to see him and I'll reproach him for how he is treating me. But for now I will bind him with burnt offerings. But, Moon, shine bright. For to you I will chant softly, goddess, and to Hekate of the Underworld, at whom even the dogs tremble, as she passes through the tombs and the dark blood. Hail, fearsome Hekate, and accompany us to the end, making these drugs of mine in no way inferior to those of Circe or Medea or golden-haired Perimēdē.
>
> *Iunx*,[9] drag that lover of mine to my house.
>
> First, barley groats are consumed in the fire. Come on, sprinkle them, Thestylis. Wretched girl, where have your wits flown? Have I really become a subject of mockery to you as well, you foul creature? Strew them and say 'I sprinkle the bones of Delphis'.
>
> *Iunx*, drag that lover of mine to my house.
>
> Delphis has caused me pain. And I, to get at Delphis, burn this bay. And as it, catching fire, crackles loudly and suddenly is aflame, and we see not even the ashes of it, so may Delphis's flesh waste in the flame.
>
> *Iunx*, drag that lover of mine to my house.

Now I will burn the bran. And you, Artemis, can move even the adamant in Hades and anything else that is stubborn – Thestylis, the dogs are howling in the city; the goddess is at the crossroads. Sound the gong at once!

Iunx, drag that lover of mine to my house.

Look, the sea is still, the breezes are still. But the pain I feel within my breast is not stilled, but I am all afire for him who made me, poor thing, wretched and a virgin no longer, instead of a wife.

Iunx, drag that lover of mine to my house.

As I, with the goddess's help, melt this wax, so may Delphis of Myndos straightaway melt with love. And as this *rhombus* of bronze whirls by Aphrodite's power,[10] so may he whirl at my door.

Iunx, drag that lover of mine to my house.

Three times do I make a libation and three times, lady, do I say the following. Whether it is a woman who lies beside him, or whether it is a man, may he experience as much forgetfulness of them as once, they say, Theseus did when he forget fair-tressed Ariadne on Dia.

Iunx, drag that lover of mine to my house.

Hippomanes is a plant in Arcadia, for which all the foals and the swift mares go mad upon the mountains. Even so may I see Delphis, and may he, leaving the sleek wrestling school, come to this house of mine like one who is mad.

Iunx, drag that lover of mine to my house.

This fringe from his cloak Delphis lost, which I now shred and cast in the fierce flames. Alas, cruel Love, why have you attached yourself to me like a leech from a marsh and drunk up all the dark blood from my flesh?

Iunx, drag that lover of mine to my house.

Tomorrow I will pulverise a lizard and bring you a dangerous potion. Thestylis, now you take these magic herbs and knead them surreptitiously above his threshold while it is still night and say, muttering, 'I knead the bones of Delphis'.

Iunx, drag that lover of mine to my house.

For present purposes the key point to note is that virtually every detail of Simaitha's procedures can *either* be readily paralleled in verbal and ritual protocols which are attested in magical operations of the Classical and pre-Classical periods,[11] *or else* closely shadow those of the erotic spells in the *PGM*, which have a textual history going back hundreds of years,[12] and seem to speak to a continuous tradition of Greek erotic magic which commenced soon after the advent of literacy.[13] For reasons of space the resemblances can only be noted summarily here.

Simaitha's rite is what is known, in *PGM* parlance, as a fire-spell (*empuron*); that is, she burns various substances, barley, bay leaves, bran, a fringe from

Delphis's cloak, above all a piece of wax which she melts – probably an image of her lover, a magical procedure already found in Sophocles.[14] The purpose of her fire-spell is induce by analogy a comparable erotic flame in Delphis.[15] There are several overlaps here with the 'love-spell of attraction over myrrh which is offered' of *PGM* 4.1496–595: in particular we may compare 'as I ... melt this wax, so may Delphis of Myndos straightaway melt with love' with the 'as I burn you <the incense> and you are potent, even so burn the brain of her, NN, whom I love, inflame her' of the myrrh-spell. Procedurally speaking, Simaitha's operation is an *agōgē*, a fetching spell – the commonest type of love-spell in the *PGM* – her purpose being to restore Delphis to her house and bed. The insistence on the part of Simaitha that her magic should take effect immediately ('so may Delphis of Myndos *straightaway* melt with love') is mirrored in the demand for instant fulfilment of the charm in the formulaic 'now, now, immediately, quickly, quickly' which is found at the close of the myrrh-spell and is pervasive in the grimoires of the *PGM* and *defixiones*. Simaitha's request that Delphis 'forget' all lovers, male or female, other than herself mirrors the demand to the same effect that is a constant in amatory *defixiones* and erotic spells on papyrus[16] and already features in a fourth-century BCE Attic *defixio*, Audollent 68A–B, where one Charias, evidently the rival of the person responsible for the *defixio*, is enjoined to 'forget' (*epilathesthai*) sex with Theodora, 'the woman he loves';[17] it is also an idea more than once foreshadowed in Homer.[18] Similarly the desire for exclusivity in coitus articulated in the balancing clauses 'whether it is a woman who lies beside him, or whether it is a man, let them be forgotten', has ample precedent in documentary spells. It is found for example in two early amatory *defixiones*, both of the fourth century BCE; *DTA* 78, '(I bind) Aristokydes and the women who will present themselves to him. Let him not ever "marry" [i.e. have sex with] another woman or youth' and a *defixio* from Pella in Macedonia, where the female operative states 'may he not take any other woman than me'.[19]

Simaitha is equally au fait with the verbal dimension of real love spells. She states three times (3, 10, 159) that she will *katadein* Delphis, a technical term for 'binding' someone magically, already applied to amatory constraint as early as the fourth century BCE.[20] In seeking to recover Delphis's love, Simaitha uses the balancing clauses 'as X is the case, so may Y likewise take place' four times in all. In availing herself of this *similia similibus* formula,[21] first met in an oath ceremony at Hom. *Il.* 3.298–301, Simaitha once more draws on a pattern with an established precedent in erotic magic, seen in early *defixiones* with an amatory colour such as Audollent 68 and 85, and other *defixiones* of that period besides (Eidinow

(2007), 150). Similarly in her appeal to Hecate (14) to 'accompany me to the end', the noun for 'end', *telos*, echoes the parlance of actual love spells (Faraone (1992)), as does the imperative verb in the refrain '*iunx*, drag (*helke*) that lover of mine to my house'; the same forceful term is used in the fetching spells of the amatory papyri in expressions like *PGM* 4.377–8 'drag her (*helke*) by the hair, guts, soul' to me, *SM* 46.22–3, 47.23 and 50.62–5.[22]

Simaitha's mastery of the rituals and the specialised lexicon of amatory magic is noteworthy and could be pursued at considerably greater length.[23] I emphasise the point partly because the commonalities that Theocritus has been so careful to establish between Simaitha's versified *agōgē* and actual love spells must surely call into question the currently fashionable reading of *Idyll* 2, according to which the poet has deliberately constructed Simaitha as a bumbling amateur at the magic art, or even as a risible inept.[24] The wrongheadedness of the latter approach in particular should become obvious if one compares Simaitha with the self-delusional, lovesick Polyphemus of Theocritus *Idylls* 6 and 11, who *is* genuinely absurd, or later Roman witches who *are* sometimes presented as manifestly ridiculous, as we shall see. In the present writer's view most of the arguments advanced in favour of the above reading are ill-founded, that is, they cannot withstand judicious scrutiny of documentary magical texts both amatory and non-amatory (space prohibits him from going into detail here),[25] and in general smack of over-interpretation. It is significant that in the latter half of Virgil *Eclogue* 8, which is very closely modelled on *Idyll* 2, the fetching spell conducted against Daphnis by an unnamed sorceress proves successful; in other words, Virgil apparently saw no reason to question Simaitha's magical competence. Furthermore, if, as many believe, Simaitha is a prostitute,[26] mastery of erotic magic will have been part of her professional repertoire – and this included magic to recover, as here, the affections of a party who had thrown a woman over.[27] All in all, it seems better to suppose that Theocritus' interest in *Idyll* 2 lay, not in painting Simaitha as a hopeless incompetent, but, as Pliny *HN* 28.19 suggests, in exploring in the person of his fictional protagonist, a belief system – belief in the efficacy of amatory magic included – which had taken firm root in the intellectual substratum of his day and would immediately strike a responsive and sympathetic chord in the mind of his readers.

If I have lingered over the issue of the youthful Simaitha's magical competence, I have done so in part because it serves as a lead-in to the next topic, the multiple ways in which the sorceresses of Latin literature differ from their earlier Greek counterparts (Stratton (2007), 69; Spaeth (2014), 46–56). For one thing, Roman witches, in contrast to the canonical embodiments of Greek witchcraft, Circe and

Medea – goddesses both and hence by definition beautiful – are frequently mocked as old and ugly. *And in an important corollary of this sneering ageism*, they are often also portrayed as feckless or ineffectual at magic, in marked contrast to Simaitha, as I believe; a tendency to catastrophic failure that, as we will see, is repeated in the witches of later Greek fiction. Second, witches in Roman literature generally use magic for purely selfish, mostly harmful ends; by contrast Circe and Medea are, as noted, a mix of good and evil. Third, many of the witches in Latin literature, Horace's Canidia, Apuleius' tavern-keeper Meroe, Propertius' procuress Acanthis, the equally bibulous Dipsas ('Thirsty') of Ovid *Amores* 1.8, to name some instances, are of markedly low standing, in contrast to the high-status Greek figures just mentioned. Fourth, the witches of Greek imaginative literature operate mostly in mythical contexts, Latin witches largely in a contemporary framework.[28]

Of these four points, the first and second will be pursued in some detail below, while the third and fourth will emerge tangentially in the discussion of selected passages. There is however a fifth difference between Greek and Roman witches, and this is the most important of all. It involves the powers that they respectively arrogate to themselves. The witches of Greek literature are generally circumscribed in their aims, tend to focus on a single outcome, and are versed primarily in herbs and potions,[29] as in a fragment of Sophocles' lost fifth-century BCE tragedy *The Root-Cutters* (*Rhizitomoi*), which describes Medea gathering magical herbs and their sap; 'she, keeping her gaze averted behind her hand, received in bronze casks the cloudy juice that dripped from the cutting ... and the covered baskets concealed the roots' cuttings' (frg. 534 Radt). In stark contrast to this Roman witches, including Latin poetic realisations of the Greek figures Circe and Medea, are malignantly polyvalent, mistresses of all the black arts, possessing a whole gamut of supernatural abilities that often go far beyond the immediate needs of the spell in which they are engaged. For example, in addition to the familiar feat of pulling the moon from the heavens, the loathsome Canidia of Horace's *Epodes* and *Satires* (late first century BCE) essays child-murder as part of a love-spell to recover the affections of the faithless Varus, but equally has expertise in herbs and poisons, induces illness in others (in technical parlance a *kataklitikon*), inflicts madness, pillages graves to get *materia magica*, practises necromancy, engages in 'a ritual puppet show' (Oliensis (1991), 112) involving 'voodoo dolls', and boasts hubristically that she can make the world bow to her will. The *copa* (female innkeeper, a low-status profession) Meroe, of Apuleius' *Metamorphoses* (second century CE), similarly has at her command a whole repertoire of magical effects. Although the primary context in which we encounter her is that of erotic magic,[30] she by no means restricts her activities to the amatory sphere: she also possesses the standard capacity to interfere with the laws of nature (cf. *PGM* 1.119–25, 4.2674), to metamorphose individuals into animal shape, to close up for many years the womb of a pregnant rival, to call up the dead, to work doormagic, to relocate far away the home of an enemy, to utilise the blood and body parts of the dead for sorcerous ends, and lastly (Watson 2004) to use binding magic to prevent an enemy from escaping her vengeance.

Of a piece with the above are the fantastical, hyperbolical claims for their powers made by witches in Latin literature, that they can pervert or overturn the rhythms of nature, control the universe, interfere with the weather,[31] and engage in paranormal feats such as flying through the air[32] or walking on water.[33] Beginning with Apollonius of Rhodes' brief account of Medea's occult powers (3.531–3) – still at this point based on herbal expertise – a distinct miraculous typology, involving proverbial impossibilities executed by sorceresses,[34] develops, which may be illustrated by two instances, the first a verse insert in Petronius' prosimetric Latin novel the *Satyricon* (first century CE) Chapter 134, in which the aged priestess Oenothea asserts her magical control of all nature:[35]

> Whatever you see in the world, obeys me. The flowering earth, when I wish, languishes and grows parched, its vital juices dried up. When I wish, it pours forth its riches, and crags and bristling rocks jet forth Nile-like waters. For me the sea lowers its waves so that they lie inert, and the winds lay down their blasts in silence at my feet. The rivers obey me, as do Hyrcanian tigers and snakes whom I make to stay still. But why do I speak of trifles? The face of the moon descends, drawn down by my spells, and Phoebus [the Sun] is compelled in fear to turn back his raging steeds, retracing his course. So great is the power of words ... by my cunning in these arts I will set the bushes of Mount Ida in the sea and, reversing the process, set rivers on mountain tops.

Next, a very similar passage from Ovid's *Metamorphoses*, where Medea, in preparation for the magic rejuvenation of her husband Jason's father Aesōn, appeals for the aid of various infernal and terrestrial powers by reminding them of supernatural services previously rendered, and the success of her own magical feats in the past.

> With your help, when I have so wished, rivers have returned to their sources, as their banks look on in wonder; by my spells I check the waves when roused up, and rouse them up when calm, I drive away the clouds and bring on the clouds, I drive away and summon the winds, I make to burst the jaws of snakes by words and incantations. Living rocks and oaks torn up from their soil and woods I make to move; I bid the mountains quake, the earth to groan and ghosts to exit

from their graves. You too, Moon, I draw down from the sky, though the bronze of Temesa tries to lessen your throes.[36] Even the chariot of my grandfather [the Sun] grows pale at our spells, the goddess of the dawn pales at my magic stuffs.

Ov. *Met.* 7.199–209

Here, because it bears directly on the conceptualisation of the Roman, as opposed to the Greek witch, we must address the recent claim by Paule (2014; 2017) that the magical activities in which the sorceresses of Latin literature engage are so disparate that they have at best a tenuous similarity based on the loose idea of a female with wide-ranging supernatural powers; each individual Latin sorceress, he proposes, is essentially *sui generis* and must be viewed as an artistic creation in her own right, having minimal overlap with her witchy sisters. Thus, Paule contends, the Canidias of Horace *Satires* 1.8, *Epode* 5 and *Epode* 17 are all quite different individuals; the Canidia of the fifth *Epode*, for example, is reminiscent of child-killing demons, such as the Sumerian Lilith, which have been studied by Johnston (1995b) while that of *Epode* 17 is allegedly like the Greek Empousa, a murderous, seductive figure who preys on young men, reducing them to skin and bone.

These arguments are ill-founded: Paule confuses terminological disparity – there is, as he says, no single generic label for 'witch' in Latin – with conceptual disparity. In the first place, the frequency of what Ogden (2002a, 124–5) has called stock 'thumbnail sketches' of the witch's paranormal powers (drawing down the moon, interfering with the weather, controlling or harming people against their will etc.) gives a degree of typological homogeneity to the figure of the sorceress. Thus Apuleius' Meroe, wrongly labelled 'unique' by Paule (2014, 753),[37] in fact possesses precisely such paranormal capacities (Apul. *Met.* 1.8). More importantly, the sheer multifariousness, the great diversity of the feats imputed to Roman sorceresses point to an overarching concept that gives unity to the figure of the witch, namely the conviction – shared by people at large (Plin. *HN* 25.10) – that her potency is expressed precisely in a sensational capacity to interfere with natural processes, and *in an almost innumerable range of ways*, as we saw in the case of Horace's Canidia and Apuleius' Meroe; an idea encapsulated in a remark of the nurse-witch in [Sen.] *HO* 463 'in the face of my incantations nothing retains its nature,[38] and the similar claim of Petronius Trimalchio, undoubtedly reflecting the conception of the witch in popular imagination, 'there are midnight hags who can turn everything upside down' (*Sat.* 63). This virtuosity in diversity represents the same kind of thinking that routinely sees ascribed to individual spells in the *PGM* a whole range of different and entirely unconnected functions, for example restraining charioteers in a race, sending revelatory dreams, erotic binding, separation of friends or lovers, and sowing enmity (*PGM* 3.162–4).[39] And the polyvalence of magic spells is equally in evidence when the authors of the *PGM* also employ introductory lemmata like '<a rite> for all purposes'[40] or conclude the magical recipes with remarks like 'or use it for whatever end you wish' (*PGM* 1.328ff., 5.489).

In view of the immense, frequently cosmos-altering powers either attributed to or claimed for themselves by witches in the later tradition, it comes as something of a surprise that they are as often as not unsuccessful at the magic to which they ardently devote themselves, and which indeed defines their very being. This is particularly (though not exclusively) the case if the witches are elderly or of humble status. On one level the authors of accounts of witchcraft are plainly here debunking magic as an illusory, corrosive superstition which has widespread currency among the common people, but is seen for what it is, mere *uanitas*, empty nonsense, by the more educated. Let us consider two instances, both of the later Greek period, where magic fails or falls unexpectedly short.

The first comes from one of the fables (no. 56 Perry) attributed to the semi-legendary figure Aesop (sixth century BCE), recorded in a manuscript of the later Roman empire, but quite possibly in its essence belonging to an earlier period. It tells of a female mage who claimed the ability to defuse divine anger with incantations. On account of this she was charged with making religious innovations and condemned to death. As she was led away from the courtroom, a bystander sneered 'Poor woman. You claimed that you could turn aside the anger of the gods, so how come that you were unable to persuade mere mortals?'[41] The tale, states the moralising conclusion, shows up the pretensions of 'a fantasising woman who promises great achievements, but is shown to be incapable of even moderate ones,' a charge, as we shall see, that is often levelled against literary witches, whose failures are usually, however, allowed to speak for themselves, rather than pinpointed as in the fable.

Even more spectacular is the fall from magical grace in the necromancy performed by an old woman in the Greek novel *An Ethiopian Tale* (6.14–15) of Heliodorus (third or fourth century CE). Here the scene is set on a battlefield littered with corpses, and the dead party to whom the old woman addresses her necromantic enquiries is her own son. The corpse initially proves reluctant to be revived and a second, compulsive spell has to be resorted to by the witch, who wants to know whether her other son will survive the fighting. Once reanimated, the corpse rounds on his mother for engaging in the black art of necromancy and tells her that not only will her other son not survive, but that she will die too. Informed in addition that there are two witnesses to her sacrilegious rites, she launches herself in pursuit of the spies – and ends by accidentally and fatally impaling herself through the groin on a broken spear shaft that stood upright from the ground. So in a sense the witch's sorcery works, in that the resultant disclosures prove true: but this is counterbalanced by her grisly end, and by the fact that the information gleaned from the necromancy is the direct cause of her death, since it prompts her headlong rush to uncover the witnesses to her secret doings. In an oblique way, then, the question is posed, 'just how efficacious is magic?', or, as Richard Gordon (1987a, 70) puts it apropos another necromantic conjuration, from the Latin poet Lucan's *De bello ciuili* (first century CE), which also ends on a note of bathos, 'the validity of the scene is suddenly doubtful ... the power of magic simultaneously unlimited and null'.

Both the preceding examples are taken from later Greek literature, but the pattern of ineffectuality is also, as already noted, amply represented in Latin fictional texts. Here it is in the arena of love and sex – so often the dominant motivation of literary witches – that magic most commonly proves ineffectual or goes awry. Even goddesses in Latin poetry are not immune from such failure. The arch-witch Circe, 'more susceptible than any other woman to the flames of love' (Ov. *Met.* 14.25-6), notwithstanding the vaunted power of her charms (ibid. 34, 355-7) twice fails in Ovid *Metamorphoses* book 14 to capture the object of her desires[42] and must content herself with exacting frightful vengeance for the rejection of her overtures (thereby making her a far more sinister figure than in Homer). Perhaps the best encapsulation of the incapacity of erotic spells to work their magic, in literary texts at least, comes in what appears as *PGM* 34 in Preisendanz's edition, but has come to be recognised as a fragment of a Greek novel.[43] The text reads

> <the sun> will stand still, and if I so bid the moon, it will come down from the sky, and if I wish to check the day, night will remain for me, and if we conversely require day, the light will not depart; and if I wish to sail the sea, I do not need a ship, and if I want to go through the air, I will be lifted up. It is only for love that I cannot find the appropriate drug, neither one that can cause it, nor one that can stop it. For the earth, fearing the god, does not produce it. But if anyone has such a thing, and is prepared to give it, I beg, I beseech him 'give it to me, I wish to drink it, I wish to anoint myself....'

Love, it appears, is not amenable to sorcerous manipulation in the same way as the Sun and the Moon.[44]

Very often failure such as this has a comic overtone to it; spells of an amatory sort rarely prove successful, in literary texts at least. For example, at the conclusion of Horace *Satires* 1.8, where the sorceresses Canidia and Sagana engage in a rite that combines erotic domination of a lover with conjuration of the dead for necromantic purposes, their ghastly procedure is cut short by an explosive fig-wood fart from an adjacent statue of Priapus, which terrifies them into flight, shedding false teeth and wig in the process – a combination of the sinister with the humorous which will come to characterise many Roman depictions of magic (cf. Ogden (2008), 66). As I have argued elsewhere (Watson (2003), 187–9), the intention of Canidia and her henchwomen in Horace *Epode* 5 to starve a boy to death and excise his liver to make a love philtre is more than likely aborted in deflationary panic by the fearsome curses that the intended victim hurls at them. In Apuleius *Metamorphoses* books 2–3, an *agōgē* to fetch a handsome young Boeotian to the nymphomaniac witch Pamphile goes laughably wrong, when, instead of the human target, three inflated goatskins arrive at her door, striving to force their way into the premises.[45]

The tone of risibility struck here is part of a broader pattern whereby the sinister art of witchcraft is regularly debunked by presenting its practitioners in an absurd or ridiculous light. This result may be effected in a number of ways. One method is by an ironic expression of belief in a sorceress's phantasmagorical powers, as in Ovid, *Amores* 1.8, where the poet states of his witch-bawd Dipsas 'I suspect that she flies through the night-time shadows in changed form and that her old woman's body is covered with feathers', before appending the slyly insinuating 'I suspect <that she does this>, and so the rumour goes'. This makes clear how much credence Ovid attaches to the report, as well as the immediately preceding catalogue of the standard miracles that Dipsas can supposedly perform (reversing the course of rivers, clouding over the sky etc.). Not dissimilar is Tibullus 1.2.61; here, after listing with seeming faith in their veracity a number of stock feats performed by a 'truth-telling witch', who has given him a spell to blind his mistress's man to her infidelity, even should he catch the two of them in bed together, the poet proceeds to cast doubt on the reliability of the witch's undertaking (and by extension the preceding clutch of miracles) with the question 'but can I credit it?'

A second procedure is to unmask magic as mere persiflage by pointing up a yawning gap between the fantastical powers attributed to witches and the mean, sordid reality of their daily existence. For example, Ovid's witch-bawd Dipsas ingenuously confesses to the latter when she says to the girl whom she is instructing in the ways of the courtesan 'if you become rich by taking a wealthy lover, I shall not be poor' – as she evidently is now (*Am.* 1.8.27–8). The conclusion of Propertius' poem on Acanthis exposes another witch-bawd's grinding poverty in the most lurid colours:

> I saw the phlegm clot in her wrinkled throat and the bloodstained spittle trickle through the gaps in her teeth. I saw her breathe out her rotten spirit on the [pauper's] mat inherited from her father: her sagging hovel shivered with the fire gone out. For her funeral she had stolen bands that bound her sparse hair and a cap with colour dimmed by foul neglect.
>
> Prop. 4.5.67–72

The (somewhat grisly) jest here is that the abject poverty of the witch-*lenae* sits very oddly indeed with the immense magical powers with which they are credited by the poets. After all, magicians were supposed to be able to discover buried treasure (Lucian *Alexander* 5, 24) and were known for extracting fat fees from gullible clients,[46] while one of the spells in the *PGM* (4.2440) promises to bring the practitioner 'silver, gold … much wealth'. Surely the procuresses, had they been the authentic article, could have used their sorcerous expertise to improve their material circumstances, to translate their wretched existence into one of at least moderate comfort?[47] The implication must be that the powers in question are more froth than substance, and affiliate the witch-*lenae* to the classical type of the *alazōn*, an individual who brings down mockery on his own head by making grandiose claims that he is unable to substantiate.

A third possibility is to turn the sorceress into an outright figure of fun. Various approaches are taken here. One is the humorously telling detail, for example the grotesque likening of the witch Sagana's bristling hair to the spines of a sea urchin, as she engages in ritual preparations for the murder of an innocent child (Hor. *Epod.* 5.25–8), and the groans emitted by her fellow-sorceress Veia as she laboriously excavates the pit in which the boy-victim is to be deposited (ibid. 29–34); or the mainly liquid fee, a bowl of wine all to herself, exacted by a bibulous Syrian woman for magically restoring the passion of a disaffected lover in Lucian's *Dialogues of the Courtesans* 4 (second century CE).[48] Another tactic is the jarringly inappropriate comparison. One instance is the old witch Meroe's laughable description of her feckless, sadly diminished lover Socrates as 'her Endymion, her Ganymede', youths of such transcendent beauty as to attract the sexual attentions of deities (Apul. *Met.* 1.12), inhabitants of a mythical world as far removed as possible from Meroe's ageing, sordid existence. Another example is

Horace's transparently disingenuous and parodic assimilation of Canidia in *Epod.* 17.39–44 to the fabled mythic beauty Helen of Troy: an assimilation so spectacularly inappropriate as to throw markedly into relief the essential ludicrousness of Canidia; that is, an elderly, unlovely female pursuing her desires at a time of life when such behaviour was deemed immodest and unseasonable (Watson (1994)), and attempting to compensate for the loss of physical charms by resort to erotic magic. But this was a tactic inevitably doomed to fail, according to a widely canvassed view expressed by Afranius *Com.* 378–82 Ribb., who proclaims that no sorcery can compensate for a woman's loss of physical attractiveness: 'if men could be ensnared by blandishments, all old women would now have lovers. Youth and a tender body and obedience, these are the love charms of beautiful women. Senescence can discover no such blandishments'.[49] A final tactic to make a witch look absurd is simply to place her in an intrinsically preposterous situation, as with the flight-inducing fart of Horace *Satire* 1.8 noted above (the fart was itself a well-established comic routine); or when two old witches stagger in a condition of drunken passion after Petronius' Encolpius, having failed to cure his impotence by a virility-restoring rite of which great things were promised ('I am the only woman who knows how to remedy that disease'), but which served mainly to gratify their lust (*Sat.* 134–8).

It is not to be supposed that all witches in later literature are figures of fun. Far from it. There is in Latin poetry a whole phalanx of genuinely frightening or horrific beings. They include the terrifyingly malicious Medea and Circe of Ovid's *Metamorphoses*, the vampiric *striges*, half-bird, half-human of Ovid, *Fasti* 6.131–68, who tear the flesh and suck the blood of infants, the uncanny sounding *strigae*, witches, of Petronius, *Satyricon* 63, who steal a child and leave in his place a baby made of straw and the Medea of Seneca's play of that name, a vastly more fearsome figure than her Euripidean counterpart;[50] her inflammable bridal gifts, containing a host of fantastic mythical substances imbued with the seeds of fire (822–30, 775–80) will not only 'cause crawling flames to burn its way deep into <Creusa's> bones' but will combust the regal palace as well. But none of these can equal for extremity of horror Lucan's superwitch Erictho, a monstrous being to whom the impressive magical feats of the notorious Thessalian witches, her countrywomen, are as mere bagatelles.[51] In her magic, Erictho employs a ghastly and seemingly improbable assemblage of human body parts and funereal relics tainted with the most sinister associations, which she garners with manic zeal in a repulsive *mélange* of vivisection, cannibalism and corpse-violation. Here is the passage in question:

The smoking ashes and the burning bones of persons who die young she snatches from the heart of the funeral pyre, and grabs the very torch which the parents held, and gathers up the pieces of the bier that flutter in black smoke and the burial-clothes that are disintegrating into ashes and the cinders that reek of the corpse's limbs. But when bodies are confined in stone by which the inner moisture is drained off, and become desiccated by absorption of the decay of the inmost parts, then she greedily vents her savagery on all the limbs and plunges her hands into the eyes and gleefully gouges out the stiffened eyeballs and gnaws the yellowed nails on the withered hand. The noose and its fatal knots she ruptures with her own teeth, she tears pieces off the hanging corpses [of suicides], and scrapes clean crosses, wrenching away the entrails battered by rain-clouds and the innards parched by exposure to the sun. She steals the nails driven into the hands and the black ichor of corruption that drips all over the limbs and the clotted putrefaction and hangs suspended by her teeth if a tendon resists her bite. And whenever a corpse lies exposed on the ground, she settles before the wild beasts and birds arrive; but she is not prepared to harvest the limbs with the blade or her own hands, but waits for wolves to bite them so that she can snatch the flesh from their hungry jaws. Nor do her hands hold back from murder, if she needs fresh blood, such as spurts forth immediately a throat is slit, and her deadly offering-tables require still palpitating flesh. In like fashion, by piercing a pregnant womb, she extracts a foetus, but not via the opening designed by nature, to offer it on a burning altar. And as often as she requires savage, bold ghosts, she personally creates them. Every human death she puts to use. She tears off the bloom on the cheeks of a young man, she cuts with her left hand a lock of hair from a dying youth. Often too, at a relative's funeral, the dreadful witch stoops over the dear body and, planting kisses on it, mangles the head and with her teeth opens the closed mouth and, biting the tip of the tongue lodged in the dry throat, pours whispered sounds into the chill lips and sends a secret message of horror down to the shades of Styx.

Luc. De bello ciuili 6.533–68

So far, so horrible. But there is more. The Erictho episode climaxes in an eerie necromantic scene, which sees her pour into the breast of the dead soldier whom she wishes to reanimate warm blood from post-mortem wounds inflicted on his corpse, as well as a range of esoteric substances such as the innards of a lynx, the froth of rabid dogs, the stones in an eagle's nest, the tiny ship-retarding *echenēis*-fish, the eyes of dragons and the ashes of the fabled, self-immolating phoenix (6.667–80).

Unsurprisingly, given the unsurpassable evil of her doings, Lucan's Erictho has been invested by scholars with all kinds of symbolic associations: she is an *altera ego* for the sacrilegious Caesar of the poem, an icon of a world morally unhinged by civil war and feeding on its own vitals,[52] the inverse of the sacrificant Emperor who embodied the piety of the Principate and its correct standing with the gods.[53] What is indisputable is that, by ratcheting up the horror of Erictho's doings to unendurable levels, by making her focused exclusively on doing evil,[54] Lucan has created 'the first recognisably modern witch in European literature' (Johnson (1987), 19), an embodiment of pure wickedness, a monster of alterity and liminality:[55] liminality in the sense that, upon our first sight of her – 'the face of the impious creature is emaciated, repulsive with decay: her features, never seen by a clear sky, fearsome because of their Styx-like pallor, are oppressed and weighed down by uncombed locks' (6.515–18) – she seems to exist in the pallid interstices between life and death; an impression reinforced by her deliberate choice to live on the fringes of society, in a hinterland of 'deserted graves and tombs whose ghost occupants she has expelled' (511–12). As for her alterity, this effect comes partly from her Thessalian ethnicity – Thessalians and other races who lived on the fringes of the civilised world were routinely associated with dubious magical practices,[56] as a marker of their cultural otherness – but mainly from her complete abnegation of all prevailing moral standards, her wanton embrace of the most perversely antisocial behaviour. She engages in human sacrifice, defilement of tombs and corpses, necromancy, murder and other abominations besides.[57] She is also resolutely 'other' in being a terrifyingly all-powerful woman, moreover precisely at that time of life, old age, when female standing was conventionally thought to be diminished (Bremmer (1987)). In short, she is a conceptual nightmare in the patriarchal society of ancient Rome. She is also, it appears, curiously sexless,[58] and in this she seems to anticipate the weird sisters of Shakespeare's *Macbeth*.

Let us return to the battery of exotic and hard-to-procure substances that are employed by Erictho for the physical constituents of her spells. In regard to the gradual intensification of the macabre in Latin scenes of sorcery which reaches its apogee in Lucan's Erictho and depends in large measure on the utilisation of loathsome, repulsive and outré ingredients, critics have rightly spoken of an incremental 'bizarreification' (Pollard (2013), 22) of the witch-figure and of 'Gothic fantasy' (Ogden (2008), Chapter 2). Now it is unquestionably the case that the incorporation in these fictional rituals of revolting, frequently arcane *materia magica* serves the purpose of reinforcing the sinister, other-worldly aura attaching to literary witches. Yet we must be careful not to uncouple such substances too far from the material reality of magic as actually practised, to isolate them artificially in a matrix of purely literary invention.

If we consider the categories of materials typically used in magic, they may be summarised under the following (slightly overlapping) heads (1) parts or organs of the body – skulls, eyes, liver, marrow, fingers, noses etc.; (2) anything associated with death, whether organic or inorganic; (3) so-called *excrementa* (literally 'outgrowths') of the body, viz. hair and nails, likewise its so-called *Ausscheidungen* (Muth, 1954), that is matter emitted from it, blood, urine, spittle, faeces; (4) animals or animal parts; (5) herbs and plants; (6) ingredients especially difficult to obtain and accordingly regarded as particularly potent; (7) the disgusting.[59]

All seven categories are present in the stomach-churning constellation of bodily fragments amassed by Erictho in lines 533–68 and the ritual preliminaries to her necromantic revivification of the corpse (667–718). But the individual components, including the most outré-seeming ones, it is important to note, have a grounding in actual magical praxis, so that for an ancient reader, the macabre and phantasmagorical feel of the scene may have depended not so much on the nature per se of the materials harvested by Erictho, as on an authorial gaze which lingers sadistically and with repulsive fullness of detail over grisly vignettes of bodily depredation.

Considerations of space do not permit me to dilate at any length upon this topic. I content myself by noting *exempli gratia* a number of unlikely-sounding and improbably sinister details in Erictho's witchy procedures that nonetheless have their imprimatur in documentary magical texts describing spells of different kinds. The 'burial-clothes that are disintegrating into ashes' are mirrored in the employment of a funeral shroud at *PGM* 12.1[60] and 'a piece of clothing from one who died violently' in a compulsive spell at *PGM* 2.49.[61] 'The cinders that reek of the corpse's limbs' have a parallel in the 'half-consumed ashes smeared with human gore' unearthed along with *defixiones* inscribed with the prince's name during Germanicus' final illness (Tac. *Ann.* 2.69); 'the lock of hair' from a dying youth in the multipurpose employment of human hair in magic (a spell to make someone mad *PDM* 14.1182–7, the burial of a lock of the victim's hair along with a *defixio*, the hair of a man torn from a cross supposedly good for quartan fever, Plin. *HN* 28.41). As for 'the noose and fatal knots <which> she ruptures with her own teeth' we can appeal to the tralaticious advice of Marcellus Empiricus 29.13 to apply 'the rope with which someone has ended his life' as a specific against intestinal pain, for the 'nails driven into the hands <of a crucified person>' stolen by Erictho, to Pliny *HN* 28.46 'a piece of nail taken from a cross'. Erictho's gathering of fresh warm blood by committing murder (554–5) or by stabbing the flesh of the dead soldier (667–8) has its documentary correlate in *PGM* 4.79–80 and 2209 ('the blood of someone who has died by violence') as well as Plin. *HN* 28.4 and 43. As for such animal exotica as the froth of a rabid dog (671), or 'the hump of a dread hyena' (672), we learn from Pliny (*HN* 29.99) that the slime under an infected dog's tongue prevents hydrophobia,[62] and from Pliny (*HN* 28.92–106), Solinus 27.23–5 and Aelian (*NA* 6.14) that the hyena has a host of magical powers, which helps to explains why parts of it are used in various procedures from the magical papyri (*PGM* 7. 203–5, 206–7; *PDM* 14.83–4, 1194–5).

It is not to be supposed, then, that the employment of recherché, exotic and repulsive stuffs in their conjurations by the dedicated practitioners of the magic art whom we meet in the imaginative literature of the first century BCE onwards is simply an alluring fiction, a belletristic flourish designed to make the flesh creep agreeably. The opposite is the case. I have sought to demonstrate this point at some length elsewhere in connection with Horace's *bête noire* Canidia.[63] A further instance of the overlap between fiction and actual magical practice is Apuleius' polyamorous witch Pamphile, who at *Metamorphoses* 3.17–18 engages in an *agōgē*, a fetching spell, and to this and other sinister ends keeps in her magical workshop (*officina*) human hairs (as she supposes them),

> aromatic plants of every kind, metal plates inscribed with mysterious characters, the surviving remains of ill-omened birds, a good number of limbs from corpses earlier mourned by relatives and in some cases even buried, noses and fingers, nails used in crucifixions with flesh still clinging to them, the preserved gore of murder victims and mangled skulls wrenched from the jaws of wild beasts.

As John Winkler (1991, 224) pointed out, 'before the recovery of the rituals in *Papyri Graecae Magicae* one might have thought that Apuleius' picture was so much fantasy. But everything in it [i.e. the physical objects listed and the ritual performed by Pamphile] belongs to the regular procedures for drawing a person helplessly out of her house and into one's bed'.

One final point of importance on his topic. It has been noted by LiDonnici (2002) that, of four categories of ingredient prescribed in the recipe sections of the *PGM*, the fourth involves materials of such remarkable specificity as to make them seem not a little bizarre or exotic. Instances include 'the blood of a dog-faced baboon', 'the little nail of the right forefoot of a black ram' and 'the severed right foot of a tomb-inhabiting, blood eating gecko'.[64] Such ingredients are evidently not in everyday use, albeit impressively outlandish or mysterious-sounding substances may be aliases for more easily procurable materials, as we learn from *PGM* 12.401–44, which purports to decode a series of outré-sounding ingredients whose identity had been concealed by temple scribes to preserve them from the curiosity of the masses. But, as LiDonnici shows, all sorts of problems attend the proper understanding of this list: further, even if the objects thus decoded were in reality common or garden items, the fashioning of aliases may well represent a deliberate, self-promoting 'bizarreification' of these components by the spells' authors, so as to make them seem as weird as possible – with the unintended consequence that they begin to sound not a little like the fantastic compounds utilised by fictional sorceresses in their conjurations. In sum, once more we see a degree of coalescence between the figure of the witch in literature and the real-life expert, a foreshortening of the ritual distance between the two. This represents a further reason to treat with caution the general position of Graf and others that literary accounts of witchcraft do not point to the reality of magical practice and are primarily good for showing how the Greeks and Romans thought about the cognitive category 'witch',[65] or the approach that sees the doings of Canidia, Meroe and co. as no more than baseless male fantasies aimed at denigrating women as irrational, self-centred and over-sexed.[66]

The witches of literature, we have seen, can be a fusion of good and bad, can be ridiculous, unrelentingly evil, or extravagantly overdrawn like Seneca's Medea. They are also at times sympathetic figures. A case in point is the Simaitha of Theocritus *Idyll* 2, where sympathy for her intrinsically pitiable situation, abandonment and betrayal by a practised seducer, is enhanced by judicious use of literary allusion (Segal (1984); Goldhill (1991), 261–72). So also is the Medea of Apollonius' *Argonautika*, who, thanks to divine machinations, must endure an unwinnable tug of war between passion for Jason and filial piety. Above all, one thinks of the Dido of Virgil *Aeneid* book 4, who, faced with the departure of Aeneas, to whom she is helplessly in thrall, contemplates – though in the end she does not use – amatory magic 'either to give him back in love to me or to release me from my love for him' (*Aen.* 4.479).[67] In such cases magic is something of a last resort, a final court of appeal, when all other possibilities of success appear foreclosed;[68] as Dido says to Anna, 'dear one, I make the gods and you, my sister, and your sweet person my witnesses that I do not willingly arm myself with magic arts' (492–3). Magic for women in their circumstances offers the possibility (or the illusion) of agency, a feeling of control in an otherwise erotically desperate situation;[69] it is powered by a sense of emotional maltreatment or betrayal on the part of the beloved, flagged in adjectives like *anarsios*, 'cruel', *tachinos*, 'fickle' and *astorgos*, 'incapable of love' (Theocr. *Id.* 2) or *perfidus*, 'traitor' (Verg. *Aen.* 4.305, *Ecl.* 8.91) hurled at the offending male. In the sense that it is emotion-driven, reactive and infused with authentic feelings of despair, it is radically different from the calculating carnality of the spells to induce *erōs* in the *PGM* and *defixiones*, discussed at length in Chapter 2. It is also in consequence much better positioned to evoke a quantum of readerly sympathy.

According to Richard Gordon (2009, 214) 'it is not ... easy to go beyond the thought that the Augustan poets in some sense took magic seriously'. While Gordon goes on to qualify his 'seriously' from various standpoints, his remark does invite the question: why did Greek and Roman writers of fiction – above all the Augustan poets – show such a fascination with the figure of the witch? A traditional answer, pointing to the evidence for magical practice in Rome's very earliest, fragmentarily preserved legal codes, the Twelve Tables, has been that the poets were simply reflecting things that actually went on, fuelled by a deep vein of superstitious belief on the part of the uneducated, humblest strata of society.[70] This approach needs to be tempered with caution. It may be the case that large swathes of society believed in things like the efficacy of amulets in protecting against disease and misfortune, in the capacity of *defixiones* to harm or even kill an enemy, the magical transference of crops, the need for elaborate sacro-magical rituals in culling medicinal plants, the ability of erotic spells such as are met in the *PGM* to induce a person to fall irresistibly in love with one, or even (Plin. *HN* 25.10) that eclipses of the sun and moon were caused by the 'charms and magic herbs' of sorceresses. But the fact remains that many of the feats attributed to witches in Augustan and later poetry – metamorphosing themselves into birds, summoning legions of the dead from Hades, forcing rivers to flow backwards, turning an aged ram into a newborn lamb, taming the hounds of Hecate and so on – are so fantastical, so extravagant as to lack any connection to empirical reality: they belong solely to the realm of literature, not life. A more nuanced explanation than the traditional one is therefore a desideratum.

A more promising line of attack perhaps is that the poets distilled into verse, for the delectation alike of themselves and their upper-class readers, the fascination that the arcane topic of magic has always had for intellectuals:[71] a fascination that is surely attested by the profound and detailed overlaps between the descriptions of sorcerous rites as recounted in fictional texts and the real-life spells of the *PGM*:[72] for irrespective of whether one chooses with Graf and others to regard literary accounts of magic rituals as a jumble of ritually ineffective acts or as something closer to reality, it is hard to account for the similarities of detail between the two classes of text other than by the supposition that the poets had first-hand knowledge of the books of magic which we know to have circulated widely in the Roman world.[73]

A further approach to the question posed above would see the modish fascination with magic and witchcraft in Roman literature as a specialised instance of the increasing taste for creating scenes of horror, suspense and black humour that so stamps the poetry of the late Republic and the first century CE, reaching its apogee in Lucan,[74] and, in the particular case of sorcery, in his Erictho scene with its welter of repulsive details. In this sense the progression would be broadly akin to the arc of increasingly bloody, visually confronting effects traced by the cinematic horror genre as it moved from, say, the relatively tame Hammer classics of the 1960s to the so-called 'slasher movies' of later years. Certainly the subject of witchcraft, with its intrinsic eeriness and other-worldliness, as captured for example by Goya, gave ample scope for indulging the fundamental human taste for being agreeably scared and shocked.

It has been often argued that exponents of magic in literature are typically female, but in documentary magical texts typically male; the claim is advanced with particular reference to love-magic, so often the focus of fictional accounts of sorcery, and a class of magic abundantly represented in the *PGM* and *defixiones*. The first part of the equation is essentially correct – there are relatively few well-developed sorcerer-figures in either Greek or Latin literature – the second far from accurate, in relation to amatory magic at least, as we have argued in Chapter 2. This prompts the question: why do the writers of fiction almost invariably represent practitioners of magic as female,[75] and to what end? One answer is that they are reflecting the fact that women were in reality the domestic inheritors of medico-magical knowledge involving plants, potions, salves and foodstuffs: hence it was easy to extrapolate from this fact to impute to fabulous female figures such as Medea, or their more quotidian congeners like Canidia, expertise in all kinds of baneful, sinister and exotic herbs and plants; especially since there existed an early prototype for such a personage in the shape of Homer's Circe, who served a meal infused with 'baneful drugs' (*Ody.* 10.236) which turned Odysseus' men into swine. It helped here that plants often had an intrinsically supernatural aura,[76] mandating all kinds of magical precautions and ritual procedures for the gathering of them (see Chapter 4).

A second answer to the gendered construction of fictional mages as female, starting from the observation that literary sorceresses are mostly engaged with love-magic, posits that in actuality it was men who used this type of magic, but, since such behaviour was perceived as deeply unmasculine, recourse to these underhand devices was projected in literature onto the other sex (Graf (1997), 189–90). A third approach to the question, likewise pointing to the fact that sorceresses in imaginative fiction are often seen deploying amatory magic,[77]

Fig. 12 Goya, *The Witches' Sabbath*, 1798.

would see such depictions as premised on a number of male preconceptions about the nature of women which helps to explain this thematic focus; the idea that women were more body-directed than males (Spelman (1982)); that women as a species were obsessed with sex;[78] that they were physiologically programmed for unbridled sexuality (Carson (1990)); that they required regular intercourse for the maintenance of bodily and mental equilibrium;[79] that they had a deep emotional and also pragmatic need to feel loved and desired, which often expressed itself as sexual jealousy or insecurity;[80] that they were wily and thus predisposed to make a sneak attack in the shape of love-magic.[81] A related procedure in the case of literary sorceresses was to marry these preconceptions with the stock figure of the *graus kaprōsa*, sex-crazed old woman, who in this particular realisation of the witch – in Antiquity, as later, often pictured as elderly and decrepit[82] – becomes a would-be enchantress who seeks to compensate for the diminution of her physical charms by engaging in compulsive love-magic. The main representatives of the type, as noted above, are Apuleius' Meroe, Petronius' Oenothea, and Horace's Canidia and her helper Sagana, whose name derives from Latin *saga*, 'witch, wise woman' – a noun which the lexicographer Nonius 23M claims can also signify a woman who hunts down men to gratify her lust.[83]

It is possible to approach the gendered construction of the witch in literature from a more theoretical perspective, if we start from the fact that the sorceresses in Roman literature of the first century BCE to the second CE are immeasurably more sinister and powerful than their major Greek counterparts, Homer's Circe, Euripides' and Apollonius' Medea (at least the Medea of book 3) – not to mention Theocritus' more down-market Simaitha. This development is true not only of divine beings like Ovid's Circe, the Medea of Ovid and Seneca, as well as the fabled sorceresses of Thessaly (Luc. 6.434–506) and the supreme representative of these, Erictho, who views it as a matter of honour to trump her countrywomen's fearsome doings (Luc. 6.507–9) and is a macabre distillation of all sorcerous evil.[84] It is, importantly, also true of their more mundane, domesticated congeners like Canidia, Meroe and Pamphile.[85] As we have seen, these are credited with the same powers to wreak havoc, even disrupt the cosmos, as the more stellar representatives of the sisterhood. It is on the latter figures that we will concentrate here. Among them, Horace's Canidia, an authentically Italic creation, calls for especial attention.

In *Epode* 17 Canidia claims, or has credited to her all kinds of magical feats – the capacity to 'dislodge' i.e. draw down the stars and moon from the sky, to reduce Horace to skin and bone while closing off the possibility of an end to his suffering by death, to bring back the dead to life, to brew poisons or love potions and, startlingly, to 'make the earth give way to her triumphant pride' (75), a rodomontade which in effect arrogates to herself divine powers.[86] Significantly too in Horace *Satire* 1.8, abetted by Sagana, Canidia manipulates two effigies, 'one of wool, the other of wax, the woollen one larger, so as to control the lesser by punishing it. The waxen effigy stood in a suppliant pose, as if about to perish in the manner of a slave'. The procedure here closely shadows that in 'the wondrous spell for binding a lover' of *PGM* 4.296–466, which opens with the instruction: 'take wax or clay from a potter's wheel and make two figures, a male and a female. Make the male in the form of Ares fully armed, holding a sword in his left hand and threatening to plunge it into the right side of her neck. And make her with her arms behind her back and down on her knees'. But there is a crucial difference between the two rituals. In the *PGM*, Ares, symbolising the male operator, dominates and threatens the submissive female figure, a surrogate for the target of the spell. In Horace the roles are inverted: the larger image, evidently representing Canidia, 'controls' and inflicts punishments on the lesser one, presumably a male upon whom she has set her amatory sights (Faraone (1989), 298).

In view of these and other disquieting expressions of female agency, especially in the amatory arena, and the venomous, antisocial polyvalence of Roman witches more generally, it has been suggested (Stratton (2007), 73–105) that Canidia and her ilk operate as a kind of trope for the independently wealthy, sexually rapacious women like Sallust's Sempronia or the Clodia of Cicero's *pro Caelio* who came to the fore in the late Republic. In other words, the long-established figure of the witch is conflated with the contemporary stereotype of the 'wicked woman' who so troubled Roman moralists as an intolerable threat to patriarchal authority and traditional moral canons; whose supposedly rampant impudicity was the trigger for Augustus' marital legislation of 18 BCE and 9 CE, which criminalised adultery and a range of erotic offences going under the heading of *stuprum*, loosely speaking 'fornication'.[87] This reading has its attractions because it sees the sorceress, in particular the erotically inclined sorceress, as drawing together and embodying in a single bogey-figure several deep-seated anxieties of the Roman male: the perception of women as an unfathomable 'other' whose lives were more intimately linked to nature than men's could ever be; the contemporary fear of independent female agency which is so vividly refracted in Livy's account (34.1–7) of the debate over the repeal of the Oppian Law;[88] the perception of women's sexuality as a kind of caged beast constantly striving to break free from the trammels of conventional morality;[89] and the stereotypical perception that women lacked emotional self-control, so as to pose a risk to the patriarchal social fabric which must be constantly guarded against (e.g. Livy 34.2.2).

The reading under discussion is open to one obvious objection. If Roman writers took magic seriously, why did Propertius and Ovid in their elegies, Apuleius, and above all Horace regularly present their female witches as figures of fun?[90] It is not enough to say that there is a tradition, stretching back to the Hippocratic author of *On the Sacred Disease*, of debunking magicians as frauds and charlatans.[91] Nevertheless an accommodation between the idea of social criticism and holding sorceresses up to ridicule can be reached. By subjecting magic to a sustained campaign of mockery, Roman writers paradoxically pay it the compliment of regarding it a serious light: whether because the kind of amatory magic imputed to Canidia in particular was genuinely cruel and malevolent, as we have seen from our discussion of the *PGM* and the *defixiones*, or because writers thought, with Pliny the Elder, that magic needed to be shown in its true light as a vain and idle superstition[92] by holding it up to ridicule and mocking some of its more absurd and far-reaching claims. In either event, the writers are operating with the principle known in Greek as *to spoudaiogeloion*, saying serious things in a humorous way, a concept encapsulated by Horace in a famous dictum, 'humour is often more forceful and effective than hostile abuse when it comes to cutting through important issues' (*Sat.* 1.10.14–15).

In the cases of Canidia it is also possible to delve beneath the surface humour to unearth a more serious message. The *Epodes* of Horace, in which she stars, were written in the turbulent decade leading up to the outbreak of civil war between Mark Antony and Octavian, the later Augustus, and Horace's patron at one remove. Not only does Canidia share a name with P. Canidius Crassus, a prominent adherent of Antony and hence an enemy of Octavian, but, more important, Octavianic propaganda of the time alleged that Antony's wits had been turned by witchcraft worked upon him by Cleopatra; also, attempts were also made to taint the Pompeian faction[93] – still potent enemies of Octavian in the 30s BCE – with the charge of practising necromancy, which was also a speciality of Canidia.[94] In other words, the attack on Canidia, the sorcerous antiheroine of the *Epodes*, encodes an oblique political message and, if the critics are to be believed, a powerfully symbolic one as well.[95] In somewhat similar fashion, the mock-horrific story of Thelyphron in Apuleius *Met.* 2.20–31, who loses his ears and nose to shape-shifting, predatory witches, may have a more serious import: in this case to contrast the malign, destructive magic of the female witches with the benign, salvific magic of the goddess Isis.[96] It is she who restores Lucius, the hero of the tale, to human shape in the final book of the novel, she whose devotee Apuleius himself likely was,[97] and whose priest Zatchlas is presented in a largely or entirely positive light at the close of book 2, where he revives a corpse and unmasks a murderess.

It is difficult to draw together the threads of the foregoing discussion into a cohesive picture, given that the sorceresses of Graeco-Roman literature in their terrifying polyvalence embody so many different physical and psychic types. Yet some generalisations do seem possible. The Erictho of Lucan, and the likes of Horace's Canidia and Sagana, 'ugly/uncanny old women' (*Epod.* 5.98), bent wholly on evil, clearly foreshadow the aged, unnatural hags who will become so important a stereotype in European artistic, literary, and diabolical accounts of the witch; indeed even the most passing mentions of witches in Greek and Latin literature routinely envisage them as old women.[98] The magical horizons of witches in Latin literature expand enormously by comparison with their Greek compeers, to embrace thaumaturgical powers scarcely known to the latter. The magic of Roman and to a lesser extent Greek witches is generally malign or antisocial, the benign or protective dimension of the art being largely elided. It is pragmatic, goal-directed, usually aimed at solving some personal crisis of one kind or another (often an amatory one), a feature that it shares with the real-life (if more complex) love-magic of the documentary spells; in this regard, the transformation by Homer's Circe of visitors into a variety of wild beasts appears highly anomalous, because merely gratuitous. The magic of sorceresses as represented in literature poses in a particularly acute form the question 'does magic actually work, does it generate the desired outcomes?' It is, paradoxically, both horrific in its details and subject to authorial ridicule, scepticism and disbelief. It is a troubling assertion of female agency, hinting at the subversive possibilities of renegotiating the boundaries of women's existence in a world dominated by men, yet doing so in the comforting security of a fictional crucible. It is the product of reductive male constructions of the female and shibboleths about her nature. Further, the predominance of witches over sorcerers in the imaginative literature of Greece and Rome is surely a product of the enticing possibility of conflating a figure of great intrinsic interest with a palette of male-authored prejudices about the second sex. Above all, the magic of the sorceress is the vehicle for conjuring into being an alternative mode of existence, a world in which all things are notionally possible, untrammelled by the dictates of patriarchal reality or the mundane exigencies of interpersonal relations.

Notes

1 Notably the Kalasiris of Heliodorus' *An Ethiopian Tale*, the Nectanebo of Pseudo-Callisthenes' *Alexander Romance* 1–7, 12 (see Ogden (2002a), no.55), both however of Egyptian ethnicity.
2 See Dickie (2001), 5, 25–7 and his Chapter 1 in general, rebutted by Ogden (2008), 21–7.
3 I am grateful to the anonymous reader of this volume for alerting me to the forthcoming piece by Gregory, which takes the opposite view of Circe's witchy status to the one espoused here.

4 A role with which Hecate was not originally associated, but which, for reasons that are not entirely clear, she has assumed well before the end of the fifth century BCE. Possible factors: she was never without her uncanny side; she had marked ties to the processes of birth and death, and in the latter capacity, with the *aōroi* and *biaiothanatoi*, disembodied souls plucked prematurely from life who, the classic tool of magicians, were ultimately under the control of Hecate; Hecate was the keeper of the gates to the Underworld and in that sense the deity through whom access was gained to the infernal beings whose aid is harnessed by magicians; she was closely associated with dogs, infernal creatures par excellence and had herself canine characteristics; she had well-established connections with crossroads, places viewed in Antiquity as sinister and magical. On all this, see Johnston (1999) and Bortolani (2016), 224–8.
5 Noting in addition to the above atrocities Medea's betrayal of her natal family, Baertschi and Fögen (2006), 233 aptly describe her as 'a serial offender against her own flesh and blood'.
6 For the scanty surviving literary evidence and the more substantial visual evidence for these activities, see Gordon (1987a); 81–2, Watson (1995), 225; Ogden (2008), 30–3.
7 Exceptions: Ap. Rhod. 4.57–61 (to produce nocturnal darkness suitable for practising sorcerous rites), Luc. *De bello ciuili* 6. 505–6, 669 (gathering the moon's froth for use in malign magic).
8 The piece appears to be based – to what extent is disputed – on a much briefer description of an exorcism by the fifth-century BCE mimographer Sōphrōn: see Gow (1965), vol. 2.34–5 and Hordern (2002) for details.
9 Originally a bird spreadeagled about a wheel (Pind. *Pyth.* 4.213–19), by Theocritus' day *iunx* – the origin of our term 'jinx', to cast a spell on someone – apparently signified 'a small wheel, perhaps usually made of metal, through which a loop of thread was passed so that it could be made to spin vertically between the hands, with the magical effect of attracting a lover' Ogden (2014), 295. On the *iunx* and erotic fetching see further Pirenne-Delforge (1993); Johnston (1995a); Turner (2005), 74–82.
10 The *rhombus* here is probably a 'bullroarer', 'an instrument of attractive magic' (Gow (1965), 44), which was whirled about the head to produce a whirring noise, but ancient authorities are divided as to what this implement was, so the meaning of the term varies from passage to passage.
11 See e.g. Petropoulos (1988).
12 See Chapter 1. It is hard to fault the remarks of Gow (1965), 35–6, 'the details of Simaitha's magic have every appearance of being true to contemporary practice ... the numerous points of agreement <between the *PGM* and> Theocritus <*Idyll* 2> and the Latin poets from Virgil onward show that much of the material which they systematise is far older than themselves, and some of it must be of immemorial antiquity'.

13 See Faraone (1999).
14 Sophocles *The Root-Cutters* frg. 536 Radt.
15 Analogical burning of so-called 'voodoo dolls' or substances otherwise symbolising the target of a love-spell: Sophocles (prev. n.); *P. Oxy.* 5304 col. 2.35-8; Kuhnert (1894); Tavenner (1942).
16 Cf. *PGM* 4.2756-61 'may she come maddened to my doors in extreme haste, forgetting her children and life with her parents and loathing all the race of men and women except me, but having me alone in her thoughts' and 61.28-31 'so that she may love me and do all I wish and forget her father and mother, brothers, husband, male friend, so that, except for me alone, she may forget all these', further Watson (2003) on Hor. *Epod.* 5.69-70, and, for an interesting variation on the theme, Jordan (2003).
17 Discussion of Audollent 68 in Eidinow (2007), 218 (text and translation 396-7).
18 Petropoulos (1988), 218-20.
19 Voutiras (1998); text and translation in Eidinow (2007), 452-3.
20 Jordan (1999b), 120-3. A later term for a binding spell with specifically amatory intent is *philtrokatadesmos* (cf. *P. Oxy.* 5304 col 2.28 with the other occurrences listed by Maltomini ad loc.).
21 See Heim (1893), 484-91.
22 Cf. *AP* 5.205.1-2, a *iunx* 'which can haul (*helkein*) a man from across the sea and girls from their chambers' and the equally violent *P. Oxy.* 4674.13-15 'haul her forcibly (*ekspason*) out of her house, enflamed in her guts, her entrails'. Accompanying the two fetching spells *PGM* 36 69-101 and 102-33 are images of demons dragging away the intended targets, apparently by the hair of their heads (reproduced in Betz ad loc.).
23 Further resemblances include: Simaitha's appeal for help to the triple deity Selene-Artemis-Hecate and evocation of Hecate's canine associations in an erotic spell (Petrovic (2004), 424; Colomo, 2007); employment of the technical term *philtron* (ll. 1, 159); her use (45-6) of a mythological allusion (*historiola*) to give force and precedent to the wish being conjured (Ritner (1993), 76; Frankfurter (1995); Brashear (1995), 3438-40; *PGM* 12.373-5, 32a 1-12, 36.287-91, 68.5-10; Audollent 188.10-13; Bonner (1950), 44; Kotansky Amulets no. 13); the demand that Delphis arrive at her door in a condition of mad lust (cf. *SM* 45.6-7, *SM* 72 col. 1.10-11 with Brashear (1979), 268); *PGM* 4.2756 (n.14) and 2908-10 '<make her>, coming at top speed, to appear before my door ... for love and sex, driven by frenzy'; Watson (2003), on Hor. *Epod.* 5.75-6); the pronouncement of her own and Thestylis' magical incantations in hushed tones (11, 62): cf. *PGM* 4.746, Val. Flacc. 7.488-9; Abt (1908), 211-13; Baldini Moscadi (1976b); van der Horst (1994); Brashear (1995), 3431 n.242; the tenfold refrain '*iunx*, drag that lover of mine to my house', which mimics the intensifying repetitiveness characteristic of Greek spells, the amatory

spells of the *PGM* and erotic *defixiones* prominently included: cf. Dover (1971), xlix–l; García Teijeiro (1999), 80; *DTA* 68 (translation in Eidinow (2007), 363–4); *PGM* 16.

24 Hordern (2002), 164; Lambert (2002); Gordon (2009), 226, (1987a), 68; Domány (2013); and especially Graf (1997), 176–85, who concludes with the claim '<Theocritus> constructs a mosaic, a kind of superritual capable of activating in its readers all sorts of associations connected with magic . . . but, taken as a whole, <it> would not work'. Conversely, drawing on folkloric evidence, Curtis (2015), 647 has recently asserted 'each spell or act of magic <on Simaitha's part> is an authentic one'.

25 For example, scholars instance Simaitha's intention of renewing her magical attack on Delphis the following day as a sign of amateurism and well-founded distrust in the efficacy of her rituals. This will not do. Spells in the *PGM* often allow for the possibility of failure (or delay in fulfilment) – in which case it will be necessary to begin again with an alternative or more potent rite.

26 The status of Simaitha is contested: a convenient summary of the issue in Dover (1971), 95–6; Faraone (1999), 153–6; Lambert (2002), 82–4. Dickie (2001), 102–4 offers a forceful defence of the case that Simaitha is a prostitute. Ogden (2008), 43 disagrees.

27 Dickie (1994), (2000), 577–82; Faraone (1999).

28 Though this is to a large extent a function of the respective genres, epic and tragedy as opposed to humbler modes like iambic, satire and the novel, in which the two classes appear.

29 See Chapter 4.

30 Viz. binding Socrates to her by a single act of sexual congress (*Met.* 1.7), causing the farthest-flung to love her (*Met.* 1.8), and ritually murdering her lover for attempting to flee her clutches.

31 A particularly good example of such claims in Sen. *Med.* 752–69, summed up in the phrase *lege confusa*, 'confounding the laws <of nature>'. Other instances of the Latin Medea's facility in this regard in Fiedler (1931), 9.

32 Other instances of this feat in Lucian, *Philops.* 13; ps.-Lucian *Lucius or the Ass*, 4; Hull (1974), 52, 53. Females summoned by an erotic fetching spell are sometimes said to fly through the air (*SM* 38.11 with Daniel and Maltomini ad loc.).

33 For walking on water compare Lucian *Philops.* 13; *PGM* 1.121.

34 The typology of such feats is established in the fifth-century BCE Hippocratic treatise *On the Sacred Disease*, where male charlatans are attacked for claiming to be able to draw down the moon, eclipse the sun and interfere with the weather and so on (Collins (2008), 35). But from Hellenistic times onwards it is to females that such magical doings are typically ascribed.

35 For other instances of this magical *topos* see Pease on Verg. *Aen.* 4.489–91; Ogden (2002a), 124–5.

36 The banging of bronze was believed to drive off the malign influences responsible for lunar eclipses, which were popularly attributed to the action of witches in drawing the moon down from the sky (Hill (1973)).
37 Paule bases this claim on the idea that the doings of Meroe are very different from those of other witches in Latin literature. In fact a number of these are readily paralleled in other literary accounts of witchcraft. In addition, like nearly all witches in literature, she is characterised by an aggressive libido: see n.58 infra.
38 And given its fullest expression in Lucan *De bello ciuili* 6.452-91 on the thaumaturgical powers of the Thessalian witches.
39 Other multipurpose charms: *PGM* 4.2441-5, 7.429-31, 10.24-5, 12.15-17, 13.235-340.
40 *PGM* 4.1595, 3.494 'a procedure for every rite, for all things', 4.1167, 4.1275 'Bear charm which accomplishes everything', 12.201.
41 One is inevitably reminded of the taunts levelled at Jesus on the Cross, 'he saved others, but he cannot save himself' (Mt. 27.42; Mk. 15.31; Lk. 24.35).
42 Glaucus (*Met.* 14.1-67) and Picus (*Met.* 14.320-415).
43 Dodds (1952). One of the factors that clearly identifies this piece as belonging to a fictional text is the abject confession of incapacity in the face of love. By contrast the spells both amatory and non-amatory in the *PMG* are, in a variety of ways, highly aggressive in asserting their efficacy.
44 Similar in spirit to *PGM* 34 is the complaint of Valerius Flaccus' Medea that her magic can control wild bulls and dragons, but is ineffectual in the face of Jason's amatory betrayal.
45 Pamphile's maid Fotis had been instructed by her mistress to procure some hairs belonging to the Boeotian, so that she could fetch him to herself, using a fire-spell; but, having been detected in the act of purloining these, Fotis substituted some hairs of a similar colour which had been trimmed from goatskin bags, with the result that these, rather than the Boeotian, were summoned to Pamphile's door (Apul. *Met.* 2.2, 3.16-18).
46 E.g. Hor. *Epod.* 17.60 'what is the point of my having enriched old Paeliginian women' (i.e. wise women) in pursuit of magical expertise?, Lucian *Philops.* 16, *Alexander* 23, 49; Philostr. *Vita Apollon. Tyan.* 8.7.10.
47 The undercutting of the witches' powers here is of a piece with the sneers against religious charlatans of various types, 'driven by destitution', 'who ask for small change from the very people to whom they promise riches' in some lines of Ennius quoted by Cic. *Div.* 1.132.
48 As noted by Paule (2014), 748 n.11, drunkenness is not a defining characteristic of the witch – but it does help to fix her in a low-life ambience by bringing her into association with the stock type of the bibulous old woman familiar from art and literature.

49 See Plut. *Coniug. Praecept.* 139a; Fauth (1980) for further expressions of the view that love-magic is of no avail and that by contrast 'beauty has no need of assistance from magic' (Tib. 1.8.24).
50 The process by which Medea evolves from a figure who was in the beginning largely benign to the frightful sorceress that she has become in Ovid and Seneca is well traced by Martin (2005), 129-42.
51 Use of magical herbs, compulsion of the gods by means of spells, creation of sexual passion where none naturally exists, weather magic and interference with the rhythms of nature, subjugation of fierce wild animals (Luc. 6.438-505).
52 The first part of her name could suggest Greek *eris*, 'strife'.
53 For this last view see Gordon (1987b), 241.
54 A defining characteristic of the witch across different cultures and historical periods (Hutton (2017), 21-3 etc.).
55 For this as a characteristic of the Roman witch, see Spaeth (2010).
56 See Nisbet-Hubbard on Hor. *Carm.* 1.27.21; Phillips (2002).
57 On the marginality and otherness of Erictho, see further Graf (1997), 190-1.
58 This said, Baertschi and Fögen (2006), 246, arguing that an unifying feature of the literary witch is her aggressive sexuality, include Erictho under that rubric on account of her mangling of corpses, which, they suggest, has 'a perverse-libidinous dimension'.
59 'With regard to animal products used in magic, it is safe to say that that the more disgusting a thing was, the more likely it was to be used and the greater the virtues ascribed to it by magicians' J.J. Mooney ap. Lowe (1929), 28 n.2. Even though Galen 12.249 Kühn rejects as 'loathsome' the use of multiple parts of the human body and its various excreta in medicinal magic, and labels *goētes* ('magicians/charlatans') those who prescribe the ingestion of stork dung, owl's blood, human urine and the like (12.305-6 Kühn), his stance is revealingly inconsistent in regard to such treatments: he equally admits to having used or even positively recommends remedies based on dung (Muth (1954), 230-40). For the use of human semen in magic of an unspecified kind see *PGM* 12.416; cf. also Apollod. *Bibl.* 2.7.6. Cf. additionally *P. Oxy.* 5315 for a list of magico-medical recipes involving the dung of various flying creatures. A particularly egregious example of a disgusting magical concoction is *PGM* 36.320-32, quoted in Chapter 4.
60 Cf. *SM* 44, a love-spell possibly written on part of a mummy-shroud.
61 Similarly *PGM* 2.145 and 170-2. The late medical writer Alexander of Tralles 1.15 recommends 'a piece of bloodied clothing from a slain gladiator'.
62 It does not signify that this substance is here used for beneficial, rather than malign effects, as it is by Erictho. What matters is the magical power attributed to such an animal.
63 Introduction and commentary on Horace *Epodes* 5 and 17 in Watson (2003).
64 *PGM* 13.316, 2.46, 7.186-90.

65 Graf (1997), 175–6; Paule (2014), 757 n.39; Spaeth (2014), 43.
66 For advocates of this view see Ripat (2014), 363 n.90.
67 See Eitrem (1933), who argues p. 34 that Dido (and Virgil) leave her intentions unclear; Kraggerud (1999) critiques Eitrem's reading.
68 Frankfurter (2014), 325; Briggs (1996), 285 'ultimately witchcraft was a theory of power; it attributed secret and unnatural power to those who were formally powerless'.
69 As it also does in real-life domestic impasses where a wife is driven to use a *defixio* against a slave-girl to whom her husband has become so emotionally attached as to threaten the stability of their marriage: Ripat (2014); also Frankfurter (2014), 325.
70 Gordon (2009), 209–10 and Ripat (2014), 353 list some exponents of this view, espoused in particular by Eitrem (1941), 63–8. For claims by elite writers that the masses were sunk in a morass of superstition, cf. Colum. 1.8.6 'soothsayers and witches, two classes of people who through empty superstition drive unformed minds to expenses and then to shameful practices'; Plin. *HN* 25.10; Origen *c. Celsum* 6.41, 7.4; Philostr. *Vit. Apollon. Tyan.* 7.39.1; Gordon (2009), 218 with. n.37.
71 Such as – to cite a notable instance from a later period – the Renaissance figure Henry Cornelius Agrippa, who wrote extensively on occultism.
72 For Theocritus see the discussion above. For Lucan see Fahz (1904), *passim*; Nock (1972b), 184–7; Baldini Moscadi (1976a). For Apuleius the remarks of Winkler quoted supra, as well as the rich collection of parallels from the *PGM* assembled in Molt (1938). For Horace's *Epodes* see Watson (2003) on *Epodes* 5 and 17. For Verg. *Ecl.* 8, see Faraone (1989).
73 See Chapter 1.
74 Some representative bibliography in Watson (1991), 179–87.
75 See e.g. Eur. *Hipp.* 478–81 (her nurse speaks to the lovesick Phaedra) 'there are incantations and words that can enchant. A drug/remedy [*pharmakon*] will be discovered for this disease of yours. I tell you that men would be slow to find such solutions, if we women don't', Plin. *HN* 25.10, the long-standing conviction that eclipses are brought about by a magic which is the specialised preserve of women and women only.
76 See e.g. Laevius frg. 27 Courtney.
77 To the cases already mentioned add the wife of Hipparchus in ps.-Lucian *Lucius or the Ass* 4 who is 'a clever, lustful witch, who ogles every young man'.
78 Watson (2008), 275 n.43 has assembled examples of such allegations.
79 See Kay on Martial 11.71.1; Stratton (2007), 59.
80 Cf. Watson (2008), 274 n.35.
81 Cf. Watson (2008), 274 nn.37 and 40; Stratton (2007), 25, 67–9. Note in this connection that the name of the archetypal witch-figure Medea is connected with the Greek verb *mēdomai*, 'plan, plot, contrive'.
82 For example, the name of Horace's Canidia plays on Latin *canus*, 'grey-haired'.

83 *Sagae mulieres dicuntur feminae ad lubidinem uirorum indagatrices.*
84 The name 'night-witch' is often given to such hellish creations (Gordon (1987b), 239–40).
85 Canidia: Hor. *Epod.* 17 *passim*; Meroe: Apul. *Met.* 1.8–10; Pamphile: Apul. *Met.* 2.5, 3.15–18.
86 It is also important for Canidia's self-construction that the immediately preceding line 'then I shall be carried along, riding on the shoulders of my enemy' adapts a well-known visual schema in which the goddess Aphrodite, for whom the witch here substitutes herself, sits astride the shoulders of her enemy Psyche. Cf. *PGM* 4.1722–6; Mouterde (1930); Ogden (2002a), no 249.
87 For Augustus' marital legislation see Treggiari (1991), 60–80, 277–98 (adultery). For libertine sexual behaviour as the target of the legislation see Dio 54.16 and a host of supportive, pro-regime voices assembled by Williams (1962).
88 The Oppian Law, imposed during the dark days of the Second Punic War, inter alia limited women's possession of gold to an ounce or less, and forbade females to ride in a carriage within the walls of the city or an adjacent town.
89 Cf. Watson (2003), 385–6. The Elder Cato, in his speech opposing the abrogation of the Oppian Law, characterises women as an *indomitum animale*, 'an uncontrollable beast' (Liv. 34.2.13).
90 Horace's Canidia is of especial importance here: see Watson (2003), on *Epode* 5 passim and on *Epode* 17; Gordon (2009).
91 A practice enshrined lexically in the alternative meaning 'charlatan' for one of the main Greek terms for magician, *goes* (Collins (2008), 61). For the attack on magicians in *On the Sacred Disease*, see Collins (2008), 33–42.
92 *Vanitas* Plin. *HN* 28.89, 94, 29.81, 30.1 etc.
93 Led by Sextus Pompey, son of Pompey the Great, the defeated enemy of Julius Caesar, whose inheritor Octavian became.
94 For the charge of necromancy see Ogden (2002b).
95 See conveniently Gowers (2012) on Hor. *Sat.* 1.8.24.
96 For Isis as a goddess of magic, see *PDM* 14.257, 561; Lucian *Philops.* 34; Ritner (1993), 31–5.
97 So e.g. Harrison (2000), 226, 243.
98 For the witch in the first and last of these sources as a repulsive hag see Petherbridge (2013), whose volume in addition illustrates the bifurcation of the witch-figure in the European artistic tradition into grotesque elderly females and comely young seductresses.

7

Human Sacrifice in Ancient Magic?

On 17 March 1990, under the heading 'Ritual killing fears in child sex rings', the quality British paper *The Independent* published a lengthy piece which contained, among other details, the following:

> foetuses are being killed by paedophiles during satanic rites, senior social workers believe. Evidence from children has convinced them that sophisticated child sex rings are involved in this ritual murder. Under age girls are impregnated, the foetuses aborted after several months and sacrificed on an altar, according to the report. The suspected practice is so fraught with imponderables that the National Society for the Prevention of Cruelty to Children (NSPCC), which this week broke the silence among social workers by disclosing a growth in ritual sexual abuse, has made no public mention of its suspicions. Social workers are concerned that child sexual abuse work could be discredited if the suspected killings were disproved, but believe that the killings have happened in exceptional circumstances. Social workers and police are liaising to gather information on the suspected killings. Jan Van Wagtendonk, consultant in child sexual abuse work with the National Children's Home, said yesterday 'I believe that this does happen. Children are telling us about seeing babies killed, of killing animals, drinking urine and eating human flesh. Kids who at the time of the abuse were only eight years old are saying that they have been involved in the killing of babies, but we have no physical proof. I don't know of any bodies having been dug up. I don't know if dolls are being used and the children are being confused. We just don't have the proof that these things have happened but I believe that killings have taken place.' ... a woman ... <supposedly> introduced to satanism at a party in Surrey ... said 'when a girl is 13, if both her parents are in the coven, she will be presented so that she can be initiated by the high priest who ritually rapes her. The foetus is allowed to grow until it is four or five months old and is aborted.[1] I saw one foetus having its throat cut. The blood was collected for drinking and the body was burned. Sometimes killing will be done by stabbing through the heart. Bits of the body are taken out. The liver and the heart are important. They are eaten or stored

in a freezer until the next time around. Sometimes they will melt down the fat for candles and bones are used as aphrodisiacs. Babies are important because it is believed that Satan likes something that is pure[2] so that it can be defiled. Children are considered pure, so to defile them and drink their blood is seen as enhancing a person's power. The girls are kept through blackmail. It is very hard to get them to talk. A girl of 13 may have killed a baby. That is murder. People will tell them that they can't go to anyone because they have killed as well'.[3]

On the same page, by way of reaffirmation, the paper carried a report on the so-called 'Oude Pekela affair', which took place in a small Dutch town in the spring of 1987. At the time more than a hundred children from this village in north-east Netherlands were allegedly subjected to sadistic sexual abuse, often in the context of satanic rituals. Among the reports of victims assembled by two local doctors, themselves the parents of three children, Fred Jonker and his wife Ietze, who instigated an official investigation of the scandal, was the following:

the children speak of being in church, of having to lie down on a table naked ... they also mention the presence of babies ... of them being 'strapped up in candles', of having to cut the babies loose, and of having to cut crosses in their backs. There was also a baby put in a plastic bag. They spoke of a black baby which they were forced to hit with sticks, but they told us that this wasn't bad because black babies don't have a heart or blood anyway. We asked them 'was the black baby a doll then?' The children told us that dolls don't cry or crawl. A number of children spoke of 'a brown-coloured, deformed child. A yellow cross was placed on its chest. Its chest was cut open, and something reddish-brown was taken out and placed in a box'. The older children spoke most often of events where they were forced to wear long white robes, Dr [Fred] Jonker said. They mentioned animals being present. The acts took place in a candle-lit shed. 'The children were forced to assist the killings by beating the victims with shovels on these occasions', he added. The children said that adults, who spoke a queer-sounding language, told them that they must not speak about the events at home. If they did, their parents would be killed, their houses would be set on fire, and 'what had been done to the kitten would be done to them'. Some of the children then described how they saw a kitten killed with a circular saw.

What has all this to do with the issue of human sacrifice in ancient magic? Simply that there is a quite remarkable number of homologies between the above reports, as well as their aftermath, and the numerous flesh-creeping accounts of human sacrifice preserved from Antiquity in the context of magical or parareligious rites allegedly practised by both pagans and Christians. The homologies between the two sets of data are, as we shall see, fourfold.

Obsequio á el maestro.

Fig. 13 Goya, *Wizards and Witches Offering a New-Born Baby to Their Master*, 1796–8. Wellcome Library, London.

At the most basic, level there is a remarkable similarity of detail between ancient tales of human sacrifice for magic or ritual purposes and modern stories of perverted satanic rites, which have surfaced again very recently.[4] The similarities include: ritual murder, in particular of children, the drinking of human blood, the eating of sacrificial human flesh, the blackmail of participants by making them complicit in murder or other crimes, the abortion of foetuses, promiscuous and indiscriminate sexual activity in ceremonial contexts, and finally the notion that the purity of children made them peculiarly suitable victims of ritual murder, in ancient times often in the context of extispicy – for the Romans a long-standing, religiously sanctioned method of divining the future, but using animal entrails, not human ones, as in the tales of magical atrocities.[5] All these motifs will feature in passages to be discussed below, some arguably factual, some indubitably fictional, but all illuminating for the issue of whether ritual murder really did occur in ancient magic, the question which the present chapter sets itself to investigate.

Most of the above themes appear in a particularly lurid example of such reports that I quote here as a preliminary sample of the ancient material, with its striking pre-echoes of modern atrocity stories of the particular type under consideration. It comes from the *Panarion* of Epiphanius, bishop of Salamis in Cyprus, who is attacking a Christian (Gnostic) splinter group, the Phibionites. Although Epiphanius himself lived in the fourth century CE, his charges reflect a long-established paradigm. The early Christians levelled accusations of child sacrifice and other abominations such as are tabulated by Epiphanius against heretical Christian sects. This had the unintended consequence that already by the beginning of the second century CE pagans came to suspect Christians as a whole – *whose unsanctioned religious practices they aligned with magic* – of the ritual slaughter of children and related atrocities (Dölger (1934), 219, 223, 227). Indeed most of the evidence for the pagan conviction that Christians practised child sacrifice comes from fathers of the Church who repeat such charges in some detail before addressing them by way of refutation (Lanzillotta 2007). Here is what Epiphanius has to say.[6]

> Their very liturgy they defile with the shame of promiscuity, consuming and contaminating themselves with human and unclean flesh ... [At their feasts], they serve rich food, meat and wine even if they are poor. When they have thus eaten together and so to speak filled their veins to excess they turn to passion. The man, leaving his wife, says to her, 'Stand up and make love with your brother'.
>
> Then the unfortunates make love with each other ... After they have had intercourse in the passion of fornication they raise their blasphemy toward heaven. The woman and the man take the fluid of emission from the man into their hands; then, standing, turn toward heaven, the hands besmeared with uncleanness, and pray ... and then they eat it, their own ugliness, and they say, 'This is the body of Christ and this is the Passover for the sake of which our bodies suffer and are forced to confess the suffering of Christ'. They do the same with what is of the woman, when she has the flow of blood: collecting the monthly blood of impurity from her, they take it and consume it in the same way.

They have intercourse with each other but they teach that one may not beget children ... and if someone among them is detected to have let the natural emission of semen go in deeper and the woman becomes pregnant, then hear, what even worse they do: they pull out the embryo once they can reach it with the hand. They take out this unborn child and in a mortar pound it with a pestle and into this mix honey and pepper and certain other spices and myrrh, in order that it may not nauseate them, and then they come together, all this company of swine and dogs, and each partakes with his finger of the crushed up child. After they have finished this cannibalism finally they pray to God.

Many other horrible things are done by them ... they smear their hands with their own emissions. They stretch them out and pray with besmirched hands stark naked.

The density of the typological similarities between this representative sample of the material from Antiquity and the sensational reports spawned by the satanic panic of the 1980s and 1990s – the deviant sexuality, the misuse of human bodily secretions, the ingestion of human flesh, the blood-motif, the aborting of foetuses and, above all, the killing of a child – permits us to answer in the affirmative the question put by David Frankfurter (2006, xii) 'can one legitimately draw comparisons between satanic ritual abuse charges of the late twentieth century and the atrocity accusations of the Roman era, given their widely different cultural and historical contexts?' Frankfurter, who devoted a lengthy article and a monograph to just this question, came down firmly on the side of 'yes'. In his opinion, the glue that holds together the two sets of data is compounded primarily of two things: the deliberate overturning or reversal of moral and religious protocols *in a consciously ritual framework*,[7] and a universal human fascination with the horrific, the shocking and the sexually antinomian as well as a craving for the rhetoric of evil that can be seen for example in the voyeuristic, quasi-pornographic account of Epiphanius quoted above.[8] There is more, however, to be said on the matter of connections than this, as I shall now attempt to show.

A further similarity between ancient and modern reports of ritual sacrifice is the way in which charges and countercharges are exchanged between the respective sides. As we noted (see further below), pagans accused Christians of ritual atrocities, in particular levelling against them allegations of human sacrifice – supposedly a classic practice of magic or perverted religious usage. Christian polemic responded in kind, using the so-called 'retorsion' technique, whereby one seeks to prove one's accusers guilty of the very crimes with which they charge you.[9] Should the mention of Christians in connection with such accusations surprise, it is crucial to note that according to a view pervasive in

Antiquity and influential among modern theorists, magic, especially magic of a questionable character, may be defined as *any religious practice not officially sanctioned, or deemed illegal by the state*[10] – most particularly if this took the form of gatherings with an 'underground' or secret profile such as characterised early Christianity; groups of this sort were typically suspected of using that secrecy as a cloak for the perpetration of unmentionable rites.[11] Given this well-established presupposition of abominations performed clandestinely by groups that refused to subscribe to the dominant religious mores of the state, Christians, from the perspective of Roman pagans, could easily be construed as practitioners of human sacrifice, especially in view of the ease with which the nature of the Christian Eucharist, with its mystic mention of drinking blood and eating flesh,[12] could be misunderstood (Dölger (1934), 223–8). Nor, as noted, was the traffic in atrocity accusations all one way. Charges of unspeakable rituals involving human sacrifice were hurled in turn by Christians against the adherents of the despised polytheism that their own religion was in the process of supplanting:[13] it was in just such a context that Tertullian (*Apol.* 23.1) charges that 'magicians ... put children to death in order to get a response from the oracle'.

The just-noted pattern of mutual recriminations was in a sense mirrored in what could without exaggeration be described as the war which broke out in the late 1980s and 1990s between those who believed in the allegations of satanic abuse and ritual murder mentioned at the beginning of the chapter, and those who dismissed them as the product of childish fantasy, of watching video nasties at an inappropriate age, of leading questions put to malleable young persons by over-zealous investigators[14] and, in sum, an overheated atmosphere of unsubstantiated paranoia. On one side were ranged the NSPCC, which circulated internally a catalogue of alleged satanic abuses which it believed it had uncovered (Boyd (1991), 29–30), before toning the document down for public consumption on account of the explosive nature of its contents, social workers who interviewed and oversaw the young individuals involved, and lastly temporary foster parents to the children, who were shocked by the tales which their young wards recounted.[15] On the other side of the fence were the police, to an extent the judiciary, and the newspapers, especially the sensationalist tabloid *The Mail on Sunday*, which printed a series of pieces attacking the social services for totalitarianism, and for breaking up innocent families by taking children into care without due process. Essentially the same attitude of official disbelief and accusations in the press of mass hysteria and overactive childish imaginations put an end to the campaign initiated by the Jonkers to have their findings taken seriously – though here too, it is important to note, opinions were split. The Jonkers won the support of Mek Gerret, a professor of child psychiatry at the University of Groningen, and Prof. Gerret and Fred Jonker presented at the Third International Conference on Incest and Related Problems (London, August 1989) a joint paper on the Oude Pekela affair which was subsequently published in a reputable academic journal.[16]

A third point of overlap between the ancient and modern testimonies is the extreme tendentiousness, innate bias and tendency to rush to judgement which infuse the so-called evidence. Those who dismissed the notion of satanic gatherings in the Nottingham and Rochdale cases as a tissue of obscene fantasy were quick to assume that the social workers and carers involved had become too emotionally invested in the individuals under their care and were besides excessively credulous in accepting at face value the fantastic tales of young children (Boyd (1991), 7–22). In addition, the believers' case was notable for (and indeed tainted by) the involvement of Christian fundamentalists, who were intrinsically predisposed to believe in the reality of Satan as a metaphysical or physical entity.[17] Again, what has been called the epidemic of sensational accusations of satanic abuse in the Britain of the late 1980s and early 1990s, an outbreak of satanic panic, rapidly issued in a number of potboilers on the topic; the authors of these might reasonably be thought to have had a vested interest in presenting the shocking charges as true, and indeed in actively promoting them.[18] It is indeed difficult to navigate one's way through such a welter of conflicting and partisan data. But things are no better with the evidence of ritual sacrifice from Roman times. Indeed, in the context of ancient society, saturated as it was with the rhetoric of outrageous slander and over-the-top invective, the sheer extremity of the charges can often per se serve as grounds for suspicion. As we will see below, Christian apologists were fond of reporting in lurid detail accusations of human sacrifice and cannibalism levelled against them by pagans, charges which they simultaneously denied and flung back upon their accusers. But in some respects the most outrageous and illuminating denunciations in this field issued from the Christians themselves against heretical sects, or against those who in their view had deviated shockingly from the true faith. One such case involves the Emperor Julian, the so-called Apostate, who reigned briefly as Roman emperor from 361–3 CE. As an occupant of the imperial throne who threw over his early training under an Arian bishop in favour of pagan Neoplatonism and theurgy, he was naturally a target for savage Christian polemic. Suspected of having conducted divination using a human liver[19] – a frequently alleged rationale for the practice of human sacrifice, possessed of a superficial degree of plausibility since it was primarily this organ which was scrutinised in the religious practice of extispicy using animal victims[20] – he supposedly maintained a sacred precinct (*sēkos*) which, when opened after his death, was found to contain 'a poor woman [victim of Julian's purported liver-divination] suspended by her hair, and with her hands cut off'. Thus Theodoret, *History of the Church*, 3.26. Theodoret's final, designedly telling detail closely mirrors the key datum in a notorious tale from the First World War. A correspondent for *The Times* reported that he had seen 'German soldiery cut off the arms of a baby which clung to its mother's skirts'. The French government's propaganda organ subsequently published a photograph of the handless baby. To top it off, the newspaper *La rive rouge* later featured a drawing that showed the German troops eating the hands. The whole thing was a total fabrication, yet at the same time one of the most successful pieces of British-French propaganda in the First World War.[21] And these two touchstone instances serve as a powerful caution that ultra-gruesome stories of any era, whether involving human sacrifice or, as here, attendant mutilation of the human body, must be treated with an extreme degree of caution, to be viewed perhaps as a particularly lurid form of black propaganda.

The fourth and final factor to link ancient and modern instances of purported human sacrifice in magical or religiously deviant contexts, one which is intimately linked to the preceding point, is the sheer difficulty of establishing the veracity of such accusations, of weighing how much credence to award them. The police in the two main British cases, at Nottingham and Rochdale,[22] complained of the lack of physical evidence for the alleged satanic rites,[23] and of unwarranted credulity and zealotry on the part of the social services. The ancient evidence in turn is, as already hinted, overlarded with atrocity propaganda, religious vitriol, a taste for sensationalism, deliberate distortion or lies in the interest of character assassination, and indulgence of cultural prejudices.

It is the primary task of this chapter to sift the ancient testimonia and to pose pertinent questions. Are accusations of human sacrifice in the service of magic or perverted religious usage likely true?[24] Occasionally true, a possibility with which some specialists flirt?[25] True in essence but imaginatively embellished? Driven to a notable degree by a morbid fascination with the titillating and the macabre, a feature that certainly marked the literature of the Roman Empire? Or to be dismissed, with David Frankfurter, as completely false[26] (as the notorious Cleveland child sex abuse case in the UK in 1987 seems to have been)?[27] All these shades of possibility will crop up in the ensuing discussion.

Broadly speaking, I will concentrate initially, in what follows, on cases where scepticism seems in order, before proceeding at the close of the chapter to adduce evidence that may possibly suggest that ancient sorcerers were not on occasion averse to murder or child sacrifice in pursuit of their magical aims. Two preliminary words of caution are in order here. The first is that I focus exclusively on the Roman period; there does not seem to be any evidence of human sacrifice being performed in ancient Greece in a context specifically denoted as magical,[28] whereas that label is explicitly and opprobriously attached to the many purported instances of ritual sacrifice in the Roman late Republican and Imperial eras. Second, I will not go into the historical reality of human sacrifice in cultures other than Rome (or Greece). This was practised by various German tribes, probably some Celtic tribes, and certainly the Punic cities of the western Mediterranean, but the topic lies outwith my brief here, which is to investigate whether there is any truth to the allegations, widely touted in literary and documentary texts written in both Greek and Latin, that magicians engaged in human sacrifice. I do, however, broach by way of comparison at the close of the chapter the issue of Carthaginian child sacrifice.

Whenever the subject of human sacrifice in Classical and post-Classical times comes up, one of the first texts to be invoked is a famous passage of the Christian apologist Minucius Felix (early third century CE), who reports the vile slanders aimed against his fellow-believers:

> I turn now to that well known report about the initiation of newcomers <to the Christian religion>, a report as loathsome as it is notorious. An infant covered with sacrificial meal, so as to deceive the unwary, is placed before the person who is experiencing the sacrament for the first time. That infant is killed by the newcomer with unperceived and undetected wounds, for he is induced by the covering of meal to administer as it were guiltless <sc. because unwitting> blows. They thirstily drink his blood – oh horrible! – vie in dividing up his limbs, seal their religious compact with their victim, by this complicity in crime are pledged to mutual silence. These rites are more foul than any act of sacrilege.
>
> Minucius Felix, *Octavius* 9.5

Returning to the topic in Chapters 30–1, Minucius rehearses the same fiction of initiation into Christianity via infant sacrifice, adducing a host of examples, many of them non-Roman or mythical and thus hardly relevant,[29] to prove that it is instead pagans who indulge in human sacrifice: he then appends a further anti-Christian slander, that, following the sacrament, incestuous intercourse takes place.

Minucius Felix's rebuttals are generally thought to depend on the defence against the accusation of sacramental baby killing, *sacramentum infanticidii*, on the part of the Christians issued by his second-century predecessor Tertullian in his *Apologeticus* 7–9. Tertullian (Chapter 9) adduces the same instances as Minucius to prove that it is pagans, not Christians, who are guilty of human sacrifice, and three times rehearses in almost identical terms, and with his trademark sarcasm, the charge of ritual murder which Minucius was at pains to deny. I quote one instance, from *Apologeticus* 8.7:

> and yet, it is customary for those wishing to be initiated, I suppose, first to approach that 'father' of the ritual, to map out what is to be prepared. Then he says 'You must have a baby still of tender years, such as knows nothing of death, that can smile under your knife. Likewise you must have bread, with which to collect its bloody juice. Besides there are to be lampstands and lamps, some dogs and scraps of food, to set the dogs to overturning the lights. Above all else you will have to come with your mother and sister' (i.e. so as to have incestuous intercourse with these).

If we sum up the allegations tabulated by Minucius and Tertullian they amount to this: above all, the ritual sacrifice of newborn infants, the perversion of the Eucharist, the drinking of the victim's blood (either directly, or by consumption of bread steeped in this),[30] the entrapment of initiands by making them unwittingly guilty of murder, and finally, incest crossing generational boundaries.

In a classic article of 1934 addressed to the question of human sacrifice in late Republican and Imperial times, and in particular to the issue that formed the subtitle of his piece, 'the killing of a child and the enjoyment of his flesh and blood as a supposed initiatory act in the earliest days of Christianity', F.J. Dölger asked why accusations of ritual killing came to be spawned so profusely under the early Empire. Among the factors that he highlighted was the practice of the blood-oath in political conspiracies, that is the communal drinking of human blood as a ritual gesture designed to seal each individual's participation in the secret undertaking. Dölger was thinking particularly of the Catilinarian conspiracy of 63 BCE, which he regarded as having a powerful formative influence on later accounts of alleged cultic or magical atrocities.[31] In the earliest, near contemporary, account of the conspiracy, the Roman historian Sallust's *Bellum Catilinae*, the sealing of the compact is described as follows:

> there were at that time people who claimed that Catiline, after making his speech, when he came to impose an oath on the associates in his crime, circulated in bowls blood from a human body mixed with wine; and that when all had tasted of it, after invoking a curse on themselves, as has become the usual practice in solemn ceremonies,[32] he revealed the details of his plans; and that he repeatedly said that he had done this (viz. administered the blood-oath) so that they might be more faithful to each other due to being mutually complicit in so great an abomination. Some regarded both these

details, and many others besides, as invented by persons who believed that the ill-feeling which subsequently arose against Cicero[33] could be moderated by the atrocious nature of the crime perpetrated by those who had been executed. In proportion to its importance the matter is not sufficiently known to me to make a statement on it.

Sall. *Cat.* 22

If the story is true, as Henrichs for one believes,[34] citing Greek parallels for the mixing of blood and wine, then it seems likely that murder *was* perpetrated to get the blood. But the circumspection with which Sallust expresses himself is noteworthy ('there were ... people who claimed ... some regarded these details ... as invented ... in proportion to its importance the matter is not sufficiently known to me to make a statement on it'). Such caution was soon thrown to the winds, as supposition became fact and atrocity was piled on atrocity. Plutarch (*c.* 50–120 CE), replacing vampirism with cannibalism, baldly asserts 'the conspirators both made other pledges to each other and, after sacrificing a man, tasted of his flesh' (*Life of Cicero* 10.4), while Dio Cassius, writing in the early third century CE, ratchets up the horror still further, 'for having sacrificed a child and having made oaths over his entrails, they then ate these in company with the others' (Dio 37.30). A clear instance of how charges of human sacrifice and the like can take on a life of their own.

There may just, as noted, be a kernel of truth in the accusations concerning blood-sacrifice at the swearing-in ceremony of the Catilinarian conspiracy. Let us look now at some cases where such charges are manifestly untrue, factitious, vexatious or quite simply fictional, because these can prove illuminating notwithstanding their tenuousness or falsity. For instance, exploiting the reputation of Pythagoreans for practising magic, Cicero attacked his arch-enemy Vatinius in the following terms,

> you are in the habit of calling yourself a Pythagorean and using the name of a most learned individual as a screen for your monstrous and barbarous practices.[35] I would like you then to explain to me what utter perversity of mind, what sheer madness, possessed you – *after undertaking unheard of and unspeakable rites, even though you are in the habit of evoking the spirits of the Underworld, in the habit of appeasing the ghosts of the dead with the entrails of boys*[36] – to show contempt for the auspices under which this city was founded.

Cic. *in Vat.* 14

This passage tells us more about the impunity of Roman orators to trade in the most extreme slanders than anything Vatinius actually did. It is essentially of the same order as what the satirist Juvenal later charged foreign soothsayers with: 'he will rummage through the breasts of chickens, the entrails of a puppy – sometimes even a child's' (*Sat.* 6.551–2). The passage from Cicero's *against Vatinius* is routinely cited in connexion with allegations of human sacrifice in Antiquity. It is less often noticed that a mere two years later, when forced by powerful individuals to defend Vatinius, Cicero recanted entirely the accusations of murderous witchcraft quoted above (*scholia Bobiensia* to Cic. *in Vatin.* 14). The conclusion to be drawn from all this is that charges of this order were essentially a means to an end – in the case of Vatinius to blacken his character by accusing him of a crime so atrocious as to stamp him more broadly as unfit to hold public office.[37] In no sense can they be regarded as objective evidence.

No more credible were the accusations of child sacrifice laid against Apollonius of Tyana, a Neopythagorean holy man of the first century CE, branded a magician and a sorcerer by hostile sources, who ran foul of Domitian on account of his philosophical opposition to tyranny, which led him to criticise the emperor publicly. These accusations are recorded several times in the novelistic, hagiographic biography of Apollonius penned by the third-century CE sophist Philostratus.[38] The key points of the charges were these: enlisted by Nerva and his followers, who hoped to supplant Domitian, Apollonius cut the throat of an Arcadian boy in the countryside, in order to inspect his young entrails for divinatory signs that might encourage Nerva in his planned coup. The sacrifice took place at night when the moon was already setting, Apollonius, in the characteristic fashion of sorcerers, cloaking his acts in darkness, when nothing can be seen. Playing on the stereotype of the sorcerer, Apollonius, in his defence, sarcastically conceded that he *had* sacrificed the boy and indeed compounded this by eating the child's flesh.[39] Various points emerge from the above. First, that the charges were politically motivated, like some of the instances already discussed. Second, that the accusations were both tenuous and tendentious. Third, and most important, the assumption that human and especially child sacrifice is the sort of thing that magicians *do*, their stock in trade, as it were.

This last point can conveniently be illustrated by looking at two indubitably fictional accounts of witchy or similar activities, one poetic, one in prose. The superwitch Erictho of Lucan's first-century CE epic *De bello ciuili* has at her command a whole repertoire of sorcerous atrocities, but for present purposes these are the most pertinent:

> nor are her hands slow to commit murder, if she needs the blood of a living creature, to burst forth immediately the throat is cut, and her deadly feasts demand still quivering entrails. In the same way, by piercing the womb, a foetus

is extracted – but not via the passage nature intended – to be placed on the fiery altar. And as often as she requires a savage, bold spirit, she personally creates the ghost in question ... 'if I summon you <the powers of Hades> with a tongue that is adequately abominable and polluted, if I never chant these spells without having feasted on human innards, if I have often chopped up and washed with warm brains human breasts filled with divinity, if any infant, after placing his head and guts on your platters would have lived <sc. without my ministrations>, comply with my petition'.

Luc. 6.554–60, 706–11

Our second, unquestionably fictional atrocity story comes from a second-century CE papyrus containing limited, occasionally illegible fragments of Lollianos' picaresque novel *A Phoenician Story*. Fragments B1 recto 9ff. and B1 verso 7ff. read

> meanwhile there came along another naked man with a deep red girdle about his loins. Throwing the body of the boy on its back, he dealt him a blow, cut open his body, and took out the heart and put it on the fire. Then removing the roasted heart from the fire he cut it up into two halves. The surface of it he sprinkled with barley meal and wet it with oil,[40] and when it had been sufficiently got ready <in the fire> he gave a share of it to the initiands, and, as they held this in their hands, bade them swear by the blood of the heart ... neither to leave their companions in the lurch nor betray them, not even if they should be led off to prison, or tortured, or had their eyes gouged out.
>
> The half of the heart which remained (?was eaten).
>
> The heart of the boy ... to drink and lick up the vomit that lay on the table. They again tried to make tender <the boy's flesh> by cooking it, but Androtimos cried loudly 'Blast it! My food is still raw ... damn this girl (boy?) ... stop emitting a foul stench through your mouth and from your rear end as well. For a long time I have endured the unpleasant smell. But pour the boy's blood into the biggest possible wine-cup'. They called it ...
>
> And there was no one left outside. The doors ... they had intercourse with the women in view of Androtimos ... they went to sleep exhausted.

While the second passage concerns an initiatory rite of a secret band (such as featured in the sacrificial rites of the Egyptian *Boukoloi*)[41] rather than magic per se, a clear typology in regard to acts of human sacrifice and attendant ritual begins to emerge from the two texts. At the centre of such acts is the killing of a boy or foetus. Then there is a focus on the victim's internal organs (usually heart and liver), which are excised and feasted upon. Likewise integral is the drinking of the corpse's blood, rounded off, as in Lollianos, by a sexual free-for-all.

There is thus a clearly established template for the representation of ritual murder in forensic rhetoric, poetry, sub-literary prose and religious polemic. The examples that we have examined so far are almost without exception improbable, tendentious, fictional and consciously sensationalist. But if we now look beyond such highly embellished and stereotypical material, is there any evidence that human sacrifice, especially in a magical setting, did actually take place? The evidence is more piecemeal, certainly less lurid, but the answer may be a very cautious 'yes'. Some of the passages cited below do appear distinctly suggestive.

In a context *which explicitly deals with magic and its pernicious influence*,[42] the Elder Pliny states: 'it was not until the 657th year of the City <97 BCE> that in the consulship of Gnaeus Cornelius Lentulus and Publius Licinius Crassus there was passed a resolution of the senate forbidding human sacrifice, so that down to that date it is clear that such monstrous rites were practised' (*HN* 30.12). Nor was the usage, it seems, thereby stamped out: according to Porphyr. *de Abst.* 2.56.3, the Emperor Hadrian (117–38 CE) had to reaffirm the ban[43] – although, oddly, the historian Dio Cassius (69.11) asserts it as a fact (*hōs hē alētheia echei*) that Hadrian's favourite Antinous voluntarily submitted to being sacrificed in order to indulge the emperor's passion for divination. Most importantly, ritual murder was expressly prohibited in the Roman legal codes. In the *Sententiae* of Paulus (a late third century CE text),[44] under the rubric of the *lex Cornelia de sicariis et ueneficis*, 'the Cornelian law regarding assassins and magicians/poisoners'[45] which was first promulgated in 81 BCE and served as basis for all subsequent Roman anti-magic legislation,[46] we read 'whoever sacrifices a man or makes an offering with his blood ... is to be thrown to the beasts, or if they are of more elevated status, they are subject to capital punishment'. These prohibitions are duly echoed, always under the rubric of the *lex Cornelia*, in later legal enactments,[47] one of which states, 'if anyone commits the crime of killing an infant, let him know that he is to suffer capital punishment',[48] which prompts a learned commentator to speculate that the reference may be to human sacrifice.[49] At the very minimum, these legal provisions serve notice of an official conviction that human sacrifice and related atrocities really did take place.

I turn now to a number of passages that, although not *stricto sensu* concerned with human sacrifice, raise the closely related possibility that magicians were prepared to commit murder in order to acquire human organs for malevolent purposes (it is important to remember here that one of the primary rationales alleged for human sacrifice was to get the victim's liver for divinatory purposes). In two parallel passages at *PGM* 4.2574–9 and 2642–8 we read: 'some woman is burning for you, goddess, some dreadful incense, dappled goat's fat, blood and filth, the bloody discharge of a dead virgin, the heart of one untimely dead, the magical material of a dead dog, and a woman's embryo' and 'some woman is burning for you, goddess, some hostile incense, dappled goat's fat, blood and filth, the embryo of a dog, the bloody discharge of a prematurely dead virgin, and the heart of a young boy'. These passages derive from slander spells, whereby an operative tries to enlist a deity's cooperation against the target of the spell by accusing the latter of sacral abominations (see Chapter 2 n.20), so one must tread with great care in unpicking them. This said, mention in the context of two distinctly malign spells[50] of 'the heart of one untimely dead', 'the heart of a young boy', 'a woman's embryo' and 'the bloody discharge of a dead/prematurely dead virgin' squares neatly with what we read in literary texts about sorceresses' supposed, sometimes murderous expropriation and use of human body parts in harmful magic. We have already noted the case of Lucan's Erictho and her magic-motivated killings to get fresh blood and bodily organs. Another well-known instance, which equally involves intended murder (as opposed, say, to raiding graveyards to get human remains) comes from Horace's fifth *Epode*, according to which the arch-witch Canidia and her cronies kidnap a boy, meaning to bury him up to the neck in a pit and starve him to death, 'in order that the boy's dried-out liver and marrow, cut out, might serve as a love potion' (*Epod.* 5.37–8).[51] As Dölger (1934, 212) judiciously observed of the two *PGM* texts, they reflect the kind of abominations that people readily imputed to black magic – and they certainly invite speculation as to how the organs in question might be procured by the user.[52] Certainly the charge of using human organs in sorcerous contexts is not without an evidential basis. In a passage of his *Natural History* which, like book 30, expressly treats of magic, Pliny the Elder affirms that individuals seek 'to secure the leg-marrow and brain of infants' for curative purposes,[53] before going on to remark 'to look upon human entrails is considered a sin: how much worse is it to eat them?', a practice that he accuses the Persian magician Osthanes of introducing (*HN* 28.4–6). Later too in the same book (28.70), and still in the context of magic, he speaks of 'aborted foetuses cut up limb by limb for criminal purposes' (cf. 'the woman's embryo' of the slander spell quoted above). At the very least, it does not seem excessively rash to suspect from the above that murder, whether ritual or not, might occasionally have been committed to acquire the desired organs; nor should it be forgotten that the widespread practice of child-exposure[54] facilitated the procuring of young bodies – dead or alive – which might be turned to sorcerous ends (Aubert (1989), 436). That witches did not baulk – or were thought not to baulk – at child-killing emerges from a famous verse text (*CIL* 6.19747 = *CLE* 987) where, in the manner of many funerary inscriptions, the dead person is made to speak from the tomb. This is what he says:

> I was just approaching my fourth year when I was seized and my life snuffed out, although I could have been dear to my mother and father. I was carried off by a witch's hand (*saga manus*) that practises cruelty everywhere, remaining upon the earth and doing harm with its evil art. You parents, guard well your children, lest anguish, becoming implanted, take over your hearts.[55]

This is but one of a number of inscriptions where the premature death of a young person is ascribed to black magic.[56] The context in which the young victim was 'carried off' is unclear (the Latin verb in question, *eripuit*, is susceptible of more than one interpretation); but it is noteworthy that, according to a spooky tale recounted in Petronius' *Satyricon* Chapter 63, some witches substituted for the dead body of a young child 'a handful of straw. It had no heart, no intestines, no anything. Clearly the witches had stolen the boy and put a straw baby in his place' – evidence of a folk-belief that the internal organs of children might be harvested for sorcerous ends.[57]

I have deliberately postponed till last what is surely the most notorious accusation of human sacrifice to issue from Antiquity. It comes from that part of Tertullian's *Apologeticus* mentioned earlier where he seeks to establish that Christians do not practise human sacrifice – but that pagans unquestionably do. The awkwardly phrased passage reads

> in Africa infants used to be sacrificed quite openly to Saturn right up to the proconsulship of Tiberius,[58] who, using the same trees as belonged to their temple and had served to shade their crimes, hung the priests themselves alive on votive crosses.[59] So testified the soldiers of my father, who executed that selfsame task for that proconsul. But even now this accursed crime persists in secret.
>
> *Apol.* 9.2–3

As Rives has shown, Tertullian slants his facts here to make it appear that they are entirely contemporary, which does not seem to be the case. But that the Punic cities of the western Mediterranean did practise child sacrifice over an extended period seems settled almost beyond question by the archaeological evidence,[60] which has confirmed various ancient assertions – revealingly, often dismissed by scholars as black propaganda – to that effect.[61] Nor is there any reason to doubt the statement of Pliny *HN* 28.12, reaffirmed by Plutarch *Roman Questions* 283f., that once 'the Romans had buried alive in the Forum Boarium a Greek man and woman and victims from other peoples with whom we were then at war'. But in the first instance we are dealing with a specifically Carthaginian cultic usage, in the second with acting on a recommendation by the Sibylline books made under stress of war, which leads to a pointed disclaimer by Livy 22.57 that the Romans normally engaged in such rites.[62]

The just-cited examples of human sacrifice are mentioned here because, among instances of human sacrifice in a religious or parareligious framework, they stand out as exceptional precisely because they appear in a specifically defined and verifiable context. In other words, they are in pointed contrast to the extreme slipperiness of the accusations of ritual murder in magical, religiously deviant or allegedly satanic contexts with which this chapter has been primarily concerned. The latter exist in a twilight world where atrocity accusations are traded in an atmosphere of mutual hostility and ideological dogma, an intellectual matrix where grotesque exaggeration, cynical distortion of the facts, a highly focused type of slander and outright sensationalism reign, and truth is generally at a discount. Yet the evidence mustered towards the conclusion of the chapter appears to suggest that human sacrifice did on occasion occur in magical or related contexts – or at the very least was believed at the official level to do so. And for what it is worth, there are clear indications that child sacrifice was practised in older civilisations other than those of Greece and Rome.[63] In sum, I would go slightly further than some other writers on the topic in believing in the possible reality of ritual murder under the mantle of magic or deviant religious practice, and would therefore regard as unwarranted the summary dismissal of such charges in some quarters as pure fiction.[64]

Notes

1   The women in question were designated 'brood mares'. The idea apparently originated in a book by Lauren Stratford, *Satan's Underground* (Oregon, 1988), which was almost immediately exposed as a fake, but seems to have been powerfully influential in the early stages of the British epidemic of fears about ritual killings in satanic contexts (La Fontaine (1998), 39, 56, 137).

2   An idea that has a close correlate in ancient thinking. Prepubertal boys were thought appropriate for use in magical rites because their chastity was guaranteed: see Chapter 4 with n.60. Another form of purity involved the use in magical and religious ritual of children whose parents were both still alive, in other words, children untainted by death (cf. Watson (2003) on Hor. *Epod.* 5. 101). It was this rationale, rather than the sadistic one imputed to him, that determined the choice of victim in the murderous divinatory rites allegedly performed by Elagabalus at the instigation of his court magicians:

> he also killed human victims, choosing for this purpose noble and comely boys throughout Italy, who still had their father and mother alive, no doubt so that the pain, if suffered by two parents, should be the greater. In sum, every kind of magician was in attendance on him, and they performed their rites daily, as he urged them on and gave thanks to the gods, because he had found the latter friends of those men, while he inspected the entrails of the boys and tortured his victims after the religious form of his race
>
> <div align="right">SHA <i>Elagab.</i> 8</div>

Cf. also Dio Cassius 79.11.

3 Further details of this 'Pandora's box of horrors' in La Fontaine (1998), 76–7; also Boyd (1991), 54.

4 See Chris French, addressing in *The Guardian* of 18 November 2014 claims by two charities that satanic abuse is rife in Scotland and has been for decades. French abruptly dismisses these claims on the grounds that the alleged cases involve false memories of satanic abuse in childhood elicited by over-zealous psychiatrists. It is important to note that the satanic activities alleged to have taken place in the 1980s and 1990s and subsequent years are, as reported, in part a cloak for paedophilia and the sexual abuse of children – something that is not part of the ancient narrative (but an issue very much in the public consciousness following the Jimmy Savile and Rolf Harris affairs). The peer reviewer draws my attention to an article on the mutilated torso of a West African boy found floating in the Thames in late 2001, apparently the victim of a magical or perverted ritual sacrifice (https://www.theguardian.com/uk/2002/jun/02/ukcrime.paulharris).

5 It is not of course suggested that there are deliberately contrived continuities between ancient magic and premodern or modern witchcraft or satanism, an idea long discredited among specialists on the topic. The social anthropologist La Fontaine (1998), 22–35 does, however, argue that consideration of the witch-hunts of early modern Europe can help to explain the mindset of those who believe in the reality of satanic masses in the present day. Cf. also Frankfurter (2001), 372.

6 The translation of *Panarion* 26.4–5 which follows is a truncated form of that provided by Benko (1985) 65–6.

7 'A bricolage of inversions' Frankfurter (2006), 85.

8 The psychosexual thrill of vicarious immersion in transgressive delights is one of the main factors which Frankfurter (2006) sees as responsible for the proliferation of reports of satanic ritual abuse – which, he asserts, 'never took place' (Frankfurter (2006), xiii).

9 On the retorsion technique see Rives (1994), 61–2 and (1995), 74–7.

10 For the view of magic as a set of beliefs and practices operating outside the religious collectivity and hence unacceptable to the person doing the labelling, see Aune

(1980), 1514–16 and Rives (2006), 48, both with further references. A specifically Roman version of this formulation in Gordon (1987a), 60.

11 For such suppositions in regard to groups which operated in secret, see Schwenn (1915), 193. For the Romans, the pattern of such suspicions began with the Bacchanalia scandal of 186 BCE, on which see Livy 39.8–18, especially Chapters 8 and 13 for an account of alleged atrocities.

12 Jn 6.53, in the King James version, 'Verily, verily, I say into you, Except you eat the flesh of the Son of man, and drink his blood, ye have no life in you'.

13 Along the same lines, religious usages stemming from the East, such as the cult of the sun imported by the early third-century CE emperor Elagabalus, could likewise be damned as a form of peculiarly pernicious magic which sanctioned the ritual sacrifice of young persons (see n.2 supra). Such charges served the purpose of distinguishing the Romans from the barbarian Other.

14 Cf. Frankfurter (2006), 57–9.

15 In addition, the columnist for *The Independent* who was responsible for the report excerpted at the beginning of this chapter was also prepared to allow that the accusations might be true. By contrast, the columnist for *The Guardian*, *The Independent*'s broadsheet rival, dismissed the allegations out of hand.

16 *The American Journal of Child Abuse and Neglect*, 1990 (*non uidi*).

17 Cf. La Fontaine (1998), 5–6, 38–40, 65, 80–2, 92, 121, 140, 160, 171–2; Frankfurter (2006), 65–8. Boyd (1991), 19 disputes claims that a prominent Christian counsellor and consultant, Maureen Davies, did anything to propagate the idea of satanic ritual abuse in the Rochdale case. On the other hand, as La Fontaine (1998), 171–2 notes, two senior social workers in the Nottingham case had gone out of their way 'to disassociate themselves from the evangelical ReachOut and its spokesperson Maureen Davies', in order to counter criticism that their team was influenced by Christian beliefs.

18 E.g. Boyd (1991); Tate (1991). This is not to say that such writers were being disingenuous: on the contrary, to a man or woman they made the telling point that child 'victims' who had had absolutely no contact with each other independently came up with the same stories and rightly questioned how this could have come about in the absence of some factual underpinning. La Fontaine (1998), who takes an exceptionally sceptical position towards the whole issue, rather begs the question in his Chapter 5 (76–93) of where the allegations of ritual abuse came from.

19 For charges of this sort levelled against Julian by Christian writers, see Hopfner OZ 1.§638.

20 Bouché-Leclercq (1882), 61–74.

21 Knightley (1975), 107; Ponsonby (1980), 78–82.

22 Boyd (1991), 9–22.

23 Cf. Frankfurter (2006), 124.

24 Frey (1989), 34–42 believes that claims that Elagabalus sacrificed children in magical rites (cf. n.2) are based in fact. Benko (1985), 64–8 holds that libertine heresies of the Phibionite type, with their attendant excesses, did exist: he notes Epiphanius' admission that he was speaking from personal experience of the sect. For other scholars who embrace a position broadly similar to Benko's on antinomian Christian heresies, see Frankfurter (2001), 370–1. See also following n.

25 Hubert (1904), 1520 (imprudent to discount a priori stories of human sacrifice, but caution is in order), Henrichs (1970), 33 and 35; Schwenn (1915), 188 and Henrichs (1972), 33 (Catilinarian conspiracy); Schwenn 195 (secret bands); Henrichs (1972), 32, Lanzillotta (2007), 81 n.3 (the Egyptian *Boukoloi*); Henrichs (1972) 36, Dölger (1934), 220, Hopfner OZ 1.§638, Lanzillotta (2007), 99 (Gnostic sects).

26 Frankfurter (2006), 118 'fantastic constructions'; id. (2001), 380 'heresiographical fantasies'.

27 At least, the judicial enquiry into the case, led by Elizabeth Butler-Sloss, was highly critical of the social workers and child protection agencies involved (La Fontaine (1998), 57 and 103).

28 Indeed Hughes (1991), the standard work on the topic, is deeply sceptical of the *historical* reality of the various reports of human sacrifice issuing from ancient Greece, going so far as to deny (96–107) the historicity of the best attested instance, the supposed sacrifice of a human being on Mount Lykaion in Arcadia, which was allegedly still going on the fourth century BCE and even in the time of the geographer Pausanias (*floruit c.* 150 CE). The recent publication of a sacred law (*c.* 500 BCE) from the Lykaion, prescribing the sacrifice of a *korwos*, i.e. a *kouros*, a boy or youth, every ninth year, along with various animal sacrifices (Heinrichs (2015)) has however called Hughes's position into question.

29 The Carthaginians, the Pontic Tauri, the Egyptian Busiris, the Gauls i.e. the Druids.

30 It is undoubtedly to rumours of this sort that Pliny *Ep.* 10.96.7 is referring when he reports to the Emperor Trajan that ex-Christians whom he interviewed in Bithynia stated that it had been their custom, as part of their worship, 'to take food – but of an ordinary and harmless kind'.

31 Dölger (1934), 207–210. Other precipitating factors that he singled out were the transference to the Christians of the accusation of ritual killings allegedly perpetrated by the Jews, the misunderstanding of the nature of the Eucharist (see above), and the attaching to mainstream Christians of the accusations of child sacrifice levelled by them against various heresies.

32 The reference here is to the provisional self-imprecation (*Selbstverwünschung*) involving all kinds of misfortunes which parties to an oath of loyalty called down upon their own heads, to be activated in the event that they subsequently betrayed this oath. See Watson (1991), index s.v. 'self-imprecation'.

33 The political machinations behind this were complex, but in essence the charge was that Cicero had had the Catilinarian conspirators put to death without a proper

trial. The clouds around his head took some time to gather, but eventually led to Cicero's exile in 58 BCE.

34   See n.25 supra.
35   Apparently a reference to the erudite Publius Nigidius Figulus, a professed Pythagorean and, some said, a magician (Watson (2003), 179–80). In general on Pythagoreanism and magic, see Kingsley (1995).
36   Mention of boy's entrails used to appease the ghosts of the dead indicates a divinatory purpose to Vatinius' alleged human sacrifices. According to Servius on Verg. *Aen*. 6.107, 'necromancy or divination using the shades of the dead never took place without the killing of a human being'. Seneca *Epigram* 16 (see Watson (2003), 180 n.39) similarly associates necromancy with human sacrifice and perverted magic ritual.
37   For the widespread rhetorical tactic of accusing a politician of some act so heinous or perverted as to legitimise the inference that such an individual was unfitted for public office see e.g. Corbeill (1996).
38   Philostr. *Vit. Apollon. Tyan.* 5.12 magicians resort to barbarous sacrifices. Also 7.11.3, 7.12.2, 7.20.1–2, 7.33.2, 8.5.2–3, 8.7.30, 8.7.35, 8.7.39–40, 8.7.42–3 (entrails), 8.7.45 and following n.
39   Philostr. *Vit. Apollon. Tyan.* 8.5.2–3. This represented Apollonius' ironic (and slightly bemusing) response to a leading question of the same overall type as the familiar 'when did you start beating your wife?' put to him by Domitian's prosecutor. The prosecutor's words, as reported by Philostratus, were 'tell me, having gone forth from your house on such-and-such a day, and having travelled to the countryside, to whom did you sacrifice the boy?'
40   For seasoning the flesh of the sacrificial victim to make it more palatable; cf. Epiphanius *Panarion* quoted above.
41   Cf. Lanzillotta (2007), 81 n.3, who refers to Achilles Tatius' novel *Leukippē and Kleitophōn* 3.15 for the apparent sacrifice of Leukippē, involving the extraction of her entrails and communal feasting thereon by the *Boukoloi*, a robber band which operated in the north-west part of the Nile delta, in the vicinity of Alexandria.
42   Book 30 of Pliny's *Natural History* is specifically devoted to the subject of magic and the Persian Magi.
43   So the passage of Porphyry is understood by Schwenn (1915), 187 and Hopfner OZ 1.§637, and a remark of Lactantius *Div. Inst.* 1.21 that a Cypriot human sacrifice 'was recently abolished during the time of Hadrian' lends support to this interpretation. But this understanding of Porphyry's remark is contentious. See Hughes (1991), 124 and 129 and *RE* 18.3.239–44 s.v. 'Pallas'.
44   Paulus *Sententiae* 5.23.16 ed. Krueger (1878).
45   *Veneficis* can signify both poisoners and practitioners of magic of a sinister kind. The combination of the word in the title of the law with *sicariis*, 'assassins', is suggestive of the kinds of things *uenefici* were thought to do.

46 This law is generally agreed to have laid the foundation for the treatment of antisocial magic as illegal (Watson (2003), 178–9; Rives (2006), 48), but it underwent modifications and accretions over the years. Certainly the distinction made by Paulus in the matter of punishment between persons of higher and lower status belongs to the Empire period.
47 Justinian *Institutes* 4.18.5 ed. Thomas (1975), Justinian *Digest* 48.8.13, prescribing condemnation for anyone who practises *mala sacrificia*, 'evil sacrifices', and the further provision quoted immediately below in the text.
48 *Codex Iustinianus* 9.16.7 (8) ed. Krueger (1877), a provision of 374 CE.
49 Pharr (1932), 288 n.68.
50 Respectively a love spell of attraction (*agōgē*), which can also be used to cause illness or to destroy; and a compendious spell that 'attracts in the same hour, sends dreams, causes sickness, produces dream visions and kills enemies if you alter the wording'.
51 For the rationale behind this procedure, see Watson (2003) ad loc.
52 Since the two just-quoted slander spells of the *PMG* feature parts of a dead dog, and dogs were sacrificed to Hecate, who is the addressee of the spells in her manifestation as the triple goddess (Selene, Artemis, Hecate), there might be an implication that the human body parts mentioned in the spells were also acquired by ritual sacrifice.
53 The same passage also attests to a superstitious belief in the capacity of human blood to cure epilepsy when drained directly from the wounds of gladiators. Marcellus Empiricus 19.18 records the Egyptian custom of 'bathing in a tub filled with human blood' as a cure for elephantiasis, without mentioning whence this was derived.
54 See Watson and Watson (2014) on Juv. *Sat.* 6.592–609.
55 I.e. lest your offspring suffer a like fate. For the prosopographical background to this inscription, see Ogden (2008), 48.
56 Graf (2007).
57 Smith ad loc. remarks 'in other tales the victim's skin is left as an empty shell after his flesh and blood have been removed from within'.
58 The identity of this Tiberius, and hence the date when the attempt was made to put a stop to the practice of infant sacrifice, has long been contentious: see conveniently Rives (1994), 54 n.2. The issue is not of primary concern here.
59 I.e. the trees served as improvised crosses.
60 E.g. excavations at Carthage which have uncovered about 20,000 urns, deposited between 400 and 200 BCE, mostly containing the charred remains of humans a few months to three years old (Henrichs (1972), 14). See Brown (1991) and in particular the paired 2013 contributions by Smith, Stager et al. and Xella, Quinn et al. which, to my mind at least, have decisively settled in the affirmative the deeply contested issue of whether the Carthaginians practised infant sacrifice, or whether this was a libel occasioned in particular by the desire of the Romans to blacken the reputation of their old adversaries. In addition to this physical evidence, Rives (1994), 63 makes

the telling point that Tertullian – who himself came from Carthage or the vicinity – could easily have been confuted if his claims regarding child sacrifice at Carthage were a slanderous fiction.

61 Literary evidence: Rives (1995), 68–9.
62 *Hostiis humanis, minime Romano sacro*, 'human sacrificial victims, a rite by no means Roman'. As Weissenborn and Müller (1962) observe ad loc., by using the phrase 'a rite by no means Roman' Livy diverts the blame for the extraordinary measure onto the Sibylline books, which were of foreign origin.
63 See in particular the report by Kristin Romey in the *National Geographic* for 26 April 2018, which presents evidence for the mass sacrifice of more than 140 children in Peru some 550 years ago.
64 Janowitz (2001), 1 and 3; Frankfurter (2001), 372, (2006), 122–3 et passim.

Bibliography

Abt, A. 1908. *Die Apologie des Apuleius von Madaura und die antike Zauberei*. Giessen (repr. Berlin 1967).
André, J. 1949. *Études sur les termes de couleur dans la langue latine*. Paris.
André, J. 1985. *Les noms de plantes dans la Rome antique*. Paris.
Aubert, J.J. 1989. 'Threatened Wombs: Aspects of Ancient Uterine Magic'. *GRBS* 30: 421–49.
Aune, D.E. 1980. 'Magic in Early Christianity'. *ANRW* 23.2: 1507–57.
Baertschi, A.M. and Th. Fögen. 2006. 'Zauberinnen und Hexen in der antiken Literatur'. *Gymnasium* 113: 223–51.
Baills-Talbi, N. and V. Dasen. 2008. 'Rites funéraires et pratiques magiques'. In F. Gusi, S. Muriel and C. Olária, eds. *Nasciturus, infans, puerulus, uobis mater terrae: La muerta en la infancia*, 595–618. Castellon.
Bain, D. 1991. 'Six Greek Verbs of Sexual Congress'. *CQ* 41: 51–77.
Beagon, M. 1992. *Roman Nature: The Thought of Pliny the Elder*. Oxford.
Benko, S. 1985. *Pagan Rome and the Early Christians*. London.
Bernabé, A. 2013. 'The *Ephesia Grammata*: Genesis of a Magical Formula'. In C. Faraone and D. Obbink, eds. *The Getty Hexameters: Poetry, Magic and Mystery in Ancient Selinous*, 71–95. Oxford.
Bernand, A. 1991. *Sorciers grecs*. Paris.
Bevilacqua, G. 1997. 'Un incantesimo per l'odio in una *defixio* di Roma'. *ZPE* 117: 291–3.
Bevilacqua, G. 2006-7. 'Una nuova *defixio* latina dalla via Ostiense'. *NSA*⁹ 17/18: 303–29.
Bevilacqua, G. 2009. 'Aurora, Orchi Soror'. *PP* 64: 47–70.
Bevilacqua, G. 2010. 'Esseri rapitori e divinità femminili vendicatrici: Nuovi aspetti del mondo infero dal pantheon delle *defixiones*'. *SMSR* 76.1: 77–99.
Blänsdorf, J. 2007. '"Würmer und Krebs sollen ihn befallen": Eine neue Fluchtafel aus Groß-Gerau'. *ZPE* 161: 61–5.
Blänsdorf, J. 2008a. 'Die *Defixiones* des Mainzer Isis und Mater-Magna Heiligtums'. In M. Hainzmann and R. Wedenig, eds. *Instrumenta Inscripta Latina II*, 47–70. Klagenfurt.
Blänsdorf, J. 2008b. 'Die Verfluchungstäfelchen des Mainzer Isis-und Mater-Magna Heiligtums'. *Der altsprachliche Unterricht* 51.2: 68–70.
Blänsdorf, J. 2010a. 'The Texts from the Fons Annae Perennae'. In Gordon and Simón, 215–44.

Blänsdorf, J. 2010b. 'Dal segno al scrittura: Le *Defixiones* della fontana di Anna Perenna (Roma, Piazza Euclide)'. *SMSR* 76.1: 35–64.

Blänsdorf, J. 2010c. 'The *Defixionum Tabellae* from the Sanctuary of Isis and Mater Magna in Mainz'. In Gordon and Simón, 141–89.

Bohak, G. 2015. 'Amulets'. In R. Raja and J. Rüpke, eds. *A Companion to the Archaeology of Religion in the Ancient World*, 83–95. Malden, Massachusetts/Oxford.

Bonner, C. 1932. 'Witchcraft in the Lecture Room of Libanius'. *TAPA* 63: 34–44.

Bonner, C. 1946. 'Magical Amulets'. *HTR* 39: 25–53.

Bonner, C. 1950. *Studies in Magical Amulets Chiefly Graeco-Egyptian*. Ann Arbor, Michigan.

Bonnet, C. 2002. Review of Faraone 1999. *LEC* 70: 395–6.

Borrell, B. 2017. 'Going Underground: Inside the World of the Mole-Catchers'. *The Guardian*, 8 March. Available online: https://www.theguardian.com/world/2017/mar/08/mole-catchers-britain.

Bortolani, L.M. 2016. *Magical Hymns from Roman Egypt: A Study of Greek and Egyptian Traditions of Divinity*. Cambridge.

Boschung, D. and J.N. Bremmer, eds. 2015. *The Materiality of Magic*. Paderborn.

Bouché-Leclercq, A. 1882. *Histoire de la divination dans l'Antiquité*, Vol. 4. Paris.

Bounegru, G.V. and G. Németh. 2013. 'Cursing the *nomen*'. *ZPE* 184: 238–42.

Boyd, A. 1991. *Blasphemous Rumours: Is Satanic Ritual Abuse Fact or Fiction? An Investigation*. Glasgow.

Brakke, D. 2000. Review of Faraone 1999. *Journal of Interdisciplinary History* 31.2: 250–1.

Brashear, W. 1979. 'Ein Berliner Zauberpapyrus'. *ZPE* 33: 261–78.

Brashear, W. 1991. *Magica Varia*. Brussels.

Brashear, W. 1992. 'Ein neues Zauberensemble in München'. *SAK* 19: 79–109.

Brashear, W. 1995. 'The Greek Magical Papyri: An Introduction and Survey; annotated Bibliography (1928–1994)'. *ANRW* 18.5: 3380–684.

Bravo, B. 1987. 'Une tablette magique d'Olbia Pontique, les morts, les héros et démons'. In *Poikilia: Études offertes à Jean-Pierre Vernant*, 185–218. EHESS, Paris.

Bremmer, J.N. 1987. 'The Old Women of Ancient Greece'. In J. Blok and P. Mason, eds. *Sexual Asymmetry: Studies in Ancient Society*, 191–215. Amsterdam.

Bremmer, J.N. 1999. 'The Birth of the Term "Magus"'. *ZPE* 126: 1–12.

Bremmer, J.N. 2015. 'From Books with Magic to Magical Books in Ancient Greece and Rome'. In Boschung and Bremmer, 241–70.

Briggs, R. 1996. *Witches and Neighbours: The Social and Cultural Context of European Witchcraft*. London.

Brooten, B.J. 1996. *Love Between Women: Early Christian Responses to Female Homoeroticism*. Chicago/London.

Brown, P. 1970. 'Sorcery, Demons, and the Rise of Christianity from Late Antiquity into the Middle Ages'. In M. Douglas, ed. *Witchcraft Confessions and Accusations*, 17–45. London.

Brown, S. 1991. *Late Carthaginian Child Sacrifice and Sacrificial Monuments in Their Mediterranean Context*. Sheffield.

Burriss, E.E. 1935. 'The Place of the Dog in Superstition as Revealed in Latin Literature'. *CPh* 30.1: 32–42.

Cameron, A. 1939. 'Sappho's Prayer to Aphrodite'. *HTR* 32: 1–18.

Capponi, F. 1979. *Ornithologia Latina*. Genova.

Carson, A. 1990. 'Putting Her in Her Place: Woman, Dirt, and Desire'. In D.M. Halperin, J.J. Winkler and F. Zeitlin, eds. *Before Sexuality: The Construction of Erotic Experience in the Ancient Greek World*, 135–169. Princeton.

Collins, D. 2008. *Magic in the Ancient Greek World*. Malden, Massachusetts/Oxford.

Colomo, D. 2007. 'Ecate, Anubi e i cani negli incantesimi erotici su papiro'. In B. Palma, ed. *Akten des 23. internationalen Papyrologenkongresses, Wien, 22-28 Juli 2001*, 117–24. Vienna.

Corbeill, A. 1996. *Controlling Laughter: Political Humor in the Late Roman Republic*. Princeton.

Corell, J. 2000. 'Invocada la intervención de Iau en una *defixio* de Sagunto (Valencia)'. *ZPE* 130: 241–7.

Csapo, E. 1993. 'Deep Ambivalence: Notes on a Greek Cockfight (part 1)'. *Phoenix* 47.1: 1–28.

Curbera, J. 1999. 'Maternal Lineage in Greek Magical Texts'. In Jordan, Montgomery and Thomassen, 195–203.

Curbera, J. 2012. 'The Curse Tablets of Richard Wünsch Today'. In Piranomonte and Simón, 193–4.

Curbera, J. 2015a. 'Seven Curse Tablets from the Collection of Richard Wünsch'. *ZPE* 195: 143–56.

Curbera, J. 2015b 'From the Magician's Workshop. Notes on the Materiality of Curse Tablets'. In Boschung and Bremmer, 97–122.

Curbera, J. 2016. 'Five Curse Tablets from the Athenian Kerameikos'. *ZPE* 199: 109–18.

Curtis, P. 2015. 'The *Pharmakeutria* of Theokritos: A Charming Story' *Mnemosyne* 68: 641–8.

D'Angelo, T. 2017. 'Medicine, Religion and Magic in Two Inscribed Bronze Tablets from Ticinum (*CIL* V 6414-6415)'. *ZPE* 202: 189–207.

Dasen, V. 2015. '*Probaskania*: Amulets and Magic in Antiquity'. In Boschung and Bremmer, 177–203.

Davies, M. and P.J. Finglass. 2014. *Stesichorus: The Poems*. Cambridge.

Davies, M.I. 1990. 'Asses and Rams: Dionysiac Release in Aristophanes' *Wasps* and Attic Vase-Painting'. *Mètis* 5: 169–83.

Dawson, W.R. 1949. 'Anastasi, Sallier, and Harris and Their Papyri'. *JEA* 35: 158–66.

Dedo, R. 1904. *De antiquorum superstitione amatoria*. Greifswald.

Delatte, A. 1961. *Herbarius: Recherches sur le cérémonial usité chez les anciens pour la cueillette des simples et des plantes magiques*. 3rd edn. Brussels.

Delatte, A. and Ph. Derchain. 1964. *Les intailles magiques gréco-égyptiennes de la Bibliothèque Nationale*. Paris.

Delvaux, L. and E. Warmenbol, eds. 1991. *Les divins chats d'Egypte: Un air subtil, un dangereux parfum*. Leuven.

Deonna, W. 1939. 'La soif des morts'. *RHR* 119: 53–77.

Deonna, W. 1950. 'La grenouille et le lion'. *BCH* 74: 1–9.

Deonna, W. 1956. '*Laus Asini*: L'âne, le serpent, l'eau et l'immortalité'. *RBPH* 34.3: 623–58.

Dickie, M.W. 1994. 'The Identity of Philinna in the Philinna Papyrus'. *ZPE* 100: 119–22.

Dickie, M.W. 2000. 'Who Practised Love-Magic in Classical Antiquity and in the Late Roman World?'. *CQ* 50.2: 563–83.

Dickie, M.W. 2001. *Magic and Magicians in the Greco-Roman World*. London/New York.

Dodds, E.R. 1952. 'A Fragment of a Greek Novel'. In M.E. White, ed. *Studies in Honour of Gilbert Norwood, Phoenix Suppl. 1*, 133–7. Toronto.

Dölger, F.J. 1934. '*Sacramentum Infanticidii*: Die Schlachtung eines Kindes und der Genuss seines Fleisches und Blutes als vermeintlicher Einweihungsakt im ältesten Christentum'. *Antike und Christentum* 4.3: 188–228.

Domány, J. 2013. 'Magic and Irony in Theocritus "Idyll 2"'. *Hermes* 141: 58–64.

Dosoo, K. 2016. 'A History of the Theban Magical Papyri'. *BASP* 53: 251–74.

Dosoo, K. and T. Galoppin. Forthcoming. 'The Animal in Graeco-Egyptian Magical Practice'. In J.-C. Coulon and K. Dosoo, *Magikon Zoon: Animal et magie dans l'Antiquité et au Moyen Âge/Animals and Magic in the Ancient and Medieval World*. Paris.

Dover, K.J. 1971. *Theocritus: Select Poems*. London.

Dreher, M. 2012. '"Prayers for Justice" and the Categorisation of Curse Tablets'. In Piranomonte and Simón, 29–32.

Ducourthial, G. 2003. *Flore magique et astrologique de l'Antiquité*. Paris.

Edelstein, L. 1967. 'Greek Medicine in Its Relation to Religion and Magic'. In O. Temkin and C.L. Temkin, eds. *Ancient Medicine: Selected Papers of Ludwig Edelstein*, 205–46. Baltimore.

Edmonds, R. 2012. 'Magic in the Greco-Roman World'. *Oxford Bibliographies Online* (useful survey of the field, with handy summaries of some of the more important contributions on various aspects of the subject).

Egger, R. 1962. *Römische Antike und frühe Christentum I*. Klagenfurt.

Egger, R. 1963. 'Zu einem Fluchtäfelchen aus Blei'. In id. *Ausgewählte Schriften t. 2*, 247–53. Klagenfurt.

Eidinow, E. 2007. *Oracles, Curses and Risk Among the Ancient Greeks*. Oxford.

Eidinow, E. 2012. 'Risk and The Greeks: A New Approach to Understanding Binding Curses'. In Piranomonte and Simón, 13–21.

Eitrem, S. 1925a. *Papyri Osloenses Fasc. 1: Magical Papyri*. Oslo.

Eitrem, S. 1925b. 'Die rituelle *Diabolē*'. *SO* 2: 43–61.

Eitrem, S. 1933. 'Das Ende Didos in Vergils Aeneis'. In *Festkrift til Halvdan Koht* (no editor given), 29–41. Oslo.

Eitrem, S. 1941. 'La Magie comme motif littéraire chez les grecs et les romains'. *SO* 21: 39–83.

Elderkin, G.W. 1936. 'Two Curse Inscriptions'. *Hesperia* 5: 43–9.

Epplett, C. 2003. 'The Preparation of Animals for Roman *spectacula*: *Vivaria* and Their Administration'. *Ludica* 9: 76–92.

Evans-Grubbs, J. 1989. 'Abduction Marriage in Antiquity: A Law of Constantine (*CTh* IX.24.1) and Its Social Context'. *JRS* 79: 59–83.

Fahz, L. 1904. *De poetarum Romanorum doctrina magica quaestiones selectae*. Giessen.

Faraone, C.A. 1989. 'Clay Hardens and Wax Melts: Magical Role-Reversal in Vergil's Eighth Eclogue'. *CPh* 84.4: 294–300.

Faraone, C.A. 1991. 'The Agonistic Context of Early Greek Binding Spells'. In Faraone and Obbink, 1–32.

Faraone, C.A. 1992. 'Aristophanes, *Amphiaraus*, Fr. 29 (Kassel-Austin): Oracular Response or Erotic Incantation?'. *CQ* 42.2: 320–7.

Faraone, C.A. 1999. *Ancient Greek Love Magic*. Cambridge, Massachusetts.

Faraone, C.A. 2000. 'Handbooks and Anthologies: The Collection of Greek and Egyptian Incantations in Late Hellenistic Egypt'. *ARG* 2: 195–214.

Faraone, C.A. 2009. 'Does Tantalus Drink the Blood, or Not? An Enigmatic Series of Inscribed Hematite Gemstones'. In C. Walde and U. Dill, eds. *Antike Mythen: Medien, Transformationen and Konstruktionen*, 203–28. Berlin/New York.

Faraone, C.A. 2010. 'A Blinding Curse from the Fountain of Anna Perenna in Rome'. *SMSR* 76.1: 65–76.

Faraone, C.A. 2012. *Vanishing Acts on Ancient Greek Amulets: From Oral Performance to Visual Design* (*BICS* Supplement 115). London.

Faraone, C.A. and A. Kropp. 2010. 'Inversion, Adversion and Perversion as Strategies in Latin Curse-Tablets'. In Gordon and Simón, 381–98.

Faraone, C.A. and D. Obbink, eds. 1991. *Magika Hiera: Ancient Greek Magic and Religion*. New York/Oxford.

Fauth, W. 1980. '*Venena Amoris*: die Motive des Liebeszaubers und der erotischen Verzauberung in der augusteischen Dichtung'. *Maia* 32: 265–82.

Fehrle, E. 1910. *Die kultische Keuschheit im Altertum*. Giessen.

Ficheux, G. 2006. 'La magie amoureuse et l'anatomie du tendre'. In F. Prost and J. Wilgaux, eds. *Penser et représenter le corps dans l'Antiquité: Actes du colloque international de Rennes, 1–4 Septembre 2004*, 289–303. Rennes.

Fiedler, W. 1931. *Antiker Wetterzauber*. Stuttgart.

Forest-Hill, L. and M. Horton. 2014. 'The Inspiration for Tolkien's Ring'. *History Today* 64.1. Available online: https://www.historytoday.com/lynn-forest-hill/inspiration-tolkiens-ring.

Fountoulakis, A. 1999. 'Οὐσία in Euripides, Hippolytus 514 and the Greek Magical Papyri'. *Maia* 51.2: 193–204.

Fowler, R.L. 1995. 'Greek Magic, Greek Religion'. *ICS* 20: 1–22.
Fox, W. Sherwood. 1912. *The Johns Hopkins Tabellae Defixionum* (*AJPh* supplement 33.1). Baltimore.
Frankfurter, D. 1994. 'The Magic of Writing and the Writing of Magic: The Power of the Word in Egyptian and Greek Traditions'. *Helios* 21.2: 189–221.
Frankfurter, D. 1995. 'Narrating Power: The Theory and Practice of the Magical *Historiola* in Ritual Spells'. In Mirecki and Meyer, 457–76.
Frankfurter, D. 1997. 'Ritual Expertise in Roman Egypt and the Problem of the Category "Magician"'. In P. Schäfer and H.G. Kippenberg, eds. *Envisioning Magic: A Princeton Seminar and Symposium*, 115–35. Leiden.
Frankfurter, D. 1998. *Religion in Roman Egypt: Assimilation and Resistance*. Princeton.
Frankfurter, D. 2000. Review of Faraone 1999. *Phoenix* 54: 165–8.
Frankfurter, D. 2001. 'Ritual as Accusation and Atrocity: Satanic Ritual Abuse, Gnostic Libertinism, and Primal Murders'. *History of Religions* 40.4: 352–80.
Frankfurter, D. 2006. *Evil Incarnate: Rumors of Demonic Conspiracy and Satanic Abuse in History*. Princeton/Oxford.
Frankfurter, D. 2014. 'The Social Context of Women's Erotic Magic in Antiquity'. In Stratton and Kalleres, 319–39.
Frazer, J.G. 1917. *The Golden Bough*. 3rd edn. London.
Frey, M. 1989. *Untersuchungen zur Religion und zur Religionspolitik des Kaisers Elagabal*. Stuttgart.
Gaffino, S. 2002. 'Une nouvelle tablette de défixion: *Kataklitikon*'. *ZPE* 140: 185–94.
Gaillard-Seux, P. 1998. 'Les maladies des yeux et lézard vert'. In A. Debru and G. Sabbah, eds. *Nommer la maladie: Recherches sur la lexique gréco-latin de la pathologie*, 93–105. Saint-Etienne.
Garnsey, P. 1999. *Food and Society in Classical Antiquity*. Cambridge.
Gilhus, I.S. 2006. *Animals, Gods and Humans: Changing Attitudes to Animals in Greek, Roman and Early Christian Thought*. London.
Goldhill, S. 1991. *The Poet's Voice: Essays on Poetics and Greek Literature*. Cambridge.
Goodchild, R.G. 1953. 'The Curse and the Ring'. *Antiquity* 27: 100–2.
Goold, G.P. 1970. 'Servius and the Helen Episode'. *HSCP* 74: 101–68.
Gordon, R. 1987a. 'Aelian's Peony: The Location of Magic in Graeco-Roman Tradition'. *Comparative Criticism* 9: 59–95.
Gordon, R. 1987b. 'Lucan's Erictho'. In M. Whitby, P. Hardie and M. Whitby, eds. *Homo Viator: Classical Essays for John Bramble*, 231–41, Bristol/Oak Park, Illinois.
Gordon, R. 1999. '"What's in a List?" Listing in Greek and Graeco-Roman Malign Magical Texts'. In Jordan, Montgomery and Thomassen, 239–77.
Gordon, R. 2009. 'Magic as a Topos in Augustan Poetry: Discourse, Reality and Distance'. *ARG* 11.1: 209–28.
Gordon, R. 2010. 'Magian Lessons in Natural History: Unique Animals in Graeco-Roman Natural Magic'. In J. Dijkstra, J. Kroesen and Y. Kuiper, eds. *Myths, Martyrs*

and Modernity: Studies in the History of Religions in Honour of Jan N. Bremmer, 249-70. Leiden.

Gordon, R. 2013. 'Gods, Guilt and Suffering: Psychological Aspects of Cursing in the North-Western Provinces of the Roman Empire'. *ACD* 49: 255-81.

Gordon, R. 2014. 'Queering Their Pitch: The Curse Tablets from Mainz, with Some Thoughts on Practising "Magic"'. *JRA* 27: 774-84.

Gordon, R. 2015. 'From Substance to Text: Three Materialities of "Magic" in the Roman Imperial Period'. In Boschung and Bremmer, 133-76.

Gordon, R. and F. Marco Simón, eds. 2010. *Magical Practice in the Latin West*. Leiden/Boston.

Gourevitch, D. 2016. 'Popular Medicines and Practices in Galen'. In Harris 2016b, 251-71.

Gow, A.S.F. 1965. *Theocritus: Edited with a Translation and Commentary*. 2nd edn. Cambridge.

Gowers, E. 2012. *Horace: Satires Book 1*. Cambridge.

Graf, F. 1997. *Magic in the Ancient World*, transl. F. Philip. Cambridge, Massachusetts/London.

Graf, F. 2007. 'Untimely Death, Witchcraft and Divine Vengeance: A Reasoned Epigraphic Collection'. *ZPE* 162: 139-50.

Gregory, A. Forthcoming. 'Was Homer's Circe a Witch'? In J. Decker and D. Layne eds. *Otherwise than the Binary: Towards Feminist Rereadings of Ancient Greek Philosophy, Magic and Mystery Traditions*.

Griffith, M. 2006. 'Horsepower and Donkeywork: Equids and the Ancient Greek Imagination'. *CPh* 101.3: 185-246.

Hand, W.D. 1980. *Magical Medicine – The Folkloric Component of Medicine in the Folk Belief, Custom, and Ritual of the Peoples of Europe and America: Selected Essays of Wayland D. Hand*, foreword by L.G. Stevenson. Berkeley.

Hardy, G. and L. Totelin. 2016. *Ancient Botany*. London/New York.

Harris, W.V. 2016a. 'Popular Medicine in the Classical World'. In Harris 2016b, 1-64.

Harris, W.V., ed. 2016b. *Popular Medicine in Graeco-Roman Antiquity: Explorations*. Leiden.

Harrison, S.J. 2000. *Apuleius: A Latin Sophist*. Oxford.

He, D.-Y. and S.-M. Dai. 2011. 'Anti-inflammatory and Immunomodulatory Effects of *Paeonia lactiflora* Pall., a Traditional Chinese Herbal Medicine'. *Frontiers in Pharmacology* 2: art. 10.

Heckenbach, J. 1911. *De nuditate sacra sacrisque uinculis*. Giessen.

Heim, R. 1893. 'Incantamenta magica Graeca et Latina'. *Neue Jahrb. Supptbd.* 19: 465-576. Leipzig.

Heinrichs, J. 2015 'Military Integration in Late Archaic Arcadia: New Evidence from a Bronze Pinax (ca. 500 BC) of the Lykaion'. In W. Heckel, S. Müller and G. Wrightson, eds. *The Many Faces of War in the Ancient World*, 1-89. Cambridge.

Heitsch, E. 1964. *Die griechischen Dichterfragmente der römischen Kaiserzeit*, Vol. 2. Göttingen.
Henrichs, A. 1970. 'Pagan Ritual and the Alleged Crimes of the Early Christians'. In P. Granfield and J.A. Jungmann, eds. *Kyriakon: Festschrift Johannes Quasten*, 18–35. Münster.
Henrichs, A. 1972. *Die Phoinikika des Lollianos: Fragmente eines neuen griechischen Romans*. Bonn.
Hill, D.E. 1973. 'The Thessalian Trick'. *RhM* 116: 221–38.
Hoffman, C.A. 2002. 'Fiat Magia'. In Mirecki and Meyer, 179–94.
Hopfner, Th. 1928. 'Mageia'. *RE* 14.1.301–93.
Hordern, J.H. 2002. 'Love Magic and Purification in Sophron, *PSI* 1214a, and Theocritus' *Pharmakeutria*'. *CQ* 52.1: 164–73.
Hubbard, T.K. 2001. Review of Faraone 1999. *Journal of the History of Sexuality* 10.3/4: 542–5.
Hubert, H. 1904. 'Magie'. In Ch. Daremberg and E. Saglio, *Dictionnaire des antiquités grecques et romains* III.2, 1494–1521. Paris.
Hughes, D.D. 1991. *Human Sacrifice in Ancient Greece*. London.
Hull, J.M. 1974. *Hellenistic Magic and the Synoptic Tradition*. London.
Hutton, R. 2017. *The Witch: A History of Fear from Ancient Times to the Present*. New Haven, Connecticut/London.
Jahn, O. 1855. 'Über den Aberglauben des bösen Blicks bei den Alten'. *Berichte über die Verhandlungen der königlich sächsischen Gesellschaft der Wissenschaften zu Leipzig, philologisch-historische Klasse* 7: 28–110.
Janowitz, N. 2001. *Magic in the Roman World: Pagans, Jews and Christians*. London/New York.
Jeanneret, M. 1916–17. 'La langue des tablettes d'exécrations latines'. *RPh* 40: 225–58 and 41: 5–99, 126–53, 249–57.
Jendza, C. 2013. 'Supplemental Persuasive Analogies in *PGM* V 70–95'. *ARG* 15.1: 247–68.
Johnson, J.H. 1992. 'Introduction to the Demotic Magical Papyri', in Betz (for whom see List of Abbreviations), lv–vii.
Johnson, W.R. 1987. *Momentary Monsters: Lucan and His Heroes*. New York/London.
Johnston, S.I. 1995a. 'The Song of the *Iunx*: Magic and Rhetoric in *Pythian* 4'. *TAPA* 125: 177–206.
Johnston, S.I. 1995b. 'Defining the Dreadful: Remarks on the Greek Child-Killing Demon'. In Meyer and Mirecki, 361–87.
Johnston, S.I. 1999. *Restless Dead. Encounters between the Living and the Dead in Ancient Greece*. Berkeley.
Johnston, S.I. 2002. 'Sacrifice in the Greek Magical Papyri'. In Meyer and Mirecki, 344–58.
Johnston, S.I. 2008. *Ancient Greek Divination*. Maldon, Massachusetts/Oxford.
Jordan, D.R. 1980. 'Hekatika'. *Glotta* 58.1/2: 62–5.

Jordan, D.R. 1981. 'Magical Inscriptions on Talc Tablets from Amathous'. *AJA* 85.2: 184.
Jordan, D.R. 1985. '*Defixiones* from a Well Near the Southwest Corner of the Athenian Agora'. *Hesperia* 54.3: 205–55.
Jordan, D.R. 1988. 'A Love Charm with Verses'. *ZPE* 72: 245–59.
Jordan, D.R. 1996. 'Notes from Carthage'. *ZPE* 111: 115–29.
Jordan, D.R. 1997. 'An Address to a Ghost at Olbia'. *Mnemosyne* 50: 212–19.
Jordan, D.R. 1999a [2001]. 'P.Duk.inv. 230, an Erotic Spell'. *GRBS* 40: 159–70.
Jordan, D.R. 1999b. 'Three Curse Tablets'. In Jordan, Montgomery and Thomassen, 115–24.
Jordan, D.R. 2003. '*Remedium Amoris*: A Curse from Cumae'. *Mnemosyne* 56: 666–79.
Jordan, D.R. 2006. 'P.Duk.inv. 729, Magical Formulae'. *GRBS* 46: 159–73.
Jordan, D.R., H. Montgomery and E. Thomassen, eds. 1999. *The World of Ancient Magic: Papers from the First International Samson Eitrem Seminar at the Norwegian Institute at Athens, 4–8 May 1997*. Bergen.
Kambitsis, S. 1976. 'Une nouvelle tablette magique d'Égypte'. *BIFAO* 76: 213–23.
Kay, N.M. 1985. *Martial Book XI: A Commentary*. London.
Kedletz, E. 2000. Review of Faraone 1999. *BMCR*: 2000.02.19.
Keyser, P.T. 1997. 'Science and Magic in Galen's Recipes (Sympathy and Efficacy)'. In A. Debru, ed. *Galen on Pharmacology, Philosophy, History and Medicine*, 175–98. Leiden.
Kiernan, P. 2003. 'Did Curse Tablets Work?'. In B. Croxford, H. Eckardt, J. Meade and J. Weekes, eds. *Proceedings of the Thirteenth Annual Theoretical Roman Archaeology Conference*, 123–34. Leicester.
Kingsley, P. 1995. *Ancient Philosophy, Mystery, and Magic: Empedocles and the Pythagorean Tradition*. Oxford.
Knightley, P. 1975. *The First Casualty. The War Correspondent as Hero, Propagandist and Myth Maker from the Crimea to Vietnam*. London.
Kotansky, R. 1991. 'Incantations and Prayers for Salvation on Inscribed Greek Amulets'. In Faraone and Obbink, 107–37.
Kraemer, R.S. 2011. *Unreliable Witnesses: Religion, Gender, and History in the Greco-Roman Mediterranean*. Oxford/New York.
Kraggerud, E. 1999. 'Samson Eitrem and the Death of Dido: A Literary Reappraisal of a Magical Scene'. In Jordan, Montgomery and Thomassen, 103–13.
Krenkel, W. 2006. *Naturalia non turpia: Sex and Gender in Ancient Greece and Rome*. Hildesheim.
Kropp, A. 2010. 'How Does Magical Language Work? The Spells and Formulae of the Latin *Defixionum Tabellae*'. In Gordon and Simón, 357–80.
Krueger, P., ed. 1877. *Codex Iustinianus*. Berlin.
Krueger, P., ed. 1878. *Ulpiani Liber singularis Regularum: Pauli Libri quinque Sententiarum*. Berlin.
Kruschwitz, P. 2016. 'A Frog in the Throat: À propos *AE* 2012.740 = *ZPE* 181 (2012), 150'. *ZPE* 198: 162–3.
Kuhnert, E. 1894. 'Feuerzauber'. *RhM* 49: 37–58.

Kyle, D.G. 1998. *Spectacles of Death in Ancient Rome*. London.
La Fontaine, J.S. 1998. *Speak of the Devil: Tales of Satanic Abuse in Contemporary England*. Cambridge.
Lambert, M. 2002. 'Desperate Simaetha: Gender and Power in Theocritus, *Idyll 2*'. *Acta Classica* 45: 71–88.
Lamont, J.L. 2015. 'A New Commercial Curse Tablet from Classical Athens'. *ZPE* 196: 159–74.
Lanzillotta, L.R. 2007. 'The Early Christians and Human Sacrifice'. In J.N. Bremmer, ed. *The Strange World of Human Sacrifice*, 81–102. Leuven/Paris/Dudley MA.
Lebedev, A. 1996. 'Pharnabazos, the Diviner of Hermes: Two Ostraka with Curse Letters from Olbia'. *ZPE* 112: 268–78.
Lennon, J. 2010. 'Menstrual Blood in Ancient Rome: An Unspeakable Impurity?'. *CM* 61: 71–87.
LiDonnici, L.R. 1998 [2000]. 'Burning for It: Erotic Spells for Fever and Compulsion in the Ancient Mediterranean World'. *GRBS* 39: 63–98.
LiDonnici, L.R. 2001. 'Single-Stemmed Wormwood, Pinecones and Myrrh: Expense and Availability of Recipe Ingredients in the *Greek Magical Papyri*'. *Kernos* 14: 61–91.
LiDonnici, L.R. 2002. 'Beans, Fleawort, and the Blood of a Hamadryas Baboon: Recipe Ingredients in Greco-Roman Magical Materials'. In Mirecki and Meyer, 359–77.
LiDonnici, L.R. 2003. 'Compositional Patterns in *PGM* IV'. *BASP* 40: 141–78.
Lifshitz, B. 1970. 'Notes d' épigraphique grecque'. *RBibl* 77: 76–83.
Lloyd, G.E.R. 1962. 'Right and Left in Greek Philosophy'. *JHS* 82: 56–66.
Lloyd, G.E.R. 1983. *Science, Folklore and Ideology*. Cambridge.
Lowe, J.E. 1929. *Magic in Greek and Latin Literature*. Oxford.
MacMullen, R. 1986. 'Judicial Savagery in the Roman Empire'. *Chiron* 16: 147–66.
Malinowski, B. 1935. *Coral Gardens and Their Magic, Volume II: The Language of Magic and Gardens*. London.
Malinowski, B. 1974. *Magic, Science and Religion and Other Essays*. London.
Malinowski, B. 2002. *Argonauts of the Western Pacific*. London.
Markwald, G. 1986. *Die homerische Epigramme: Sprachliche und inhaltliche Untersuchungen*. Meisenheim.
Martin, M. 2005. *Magie et magiciens dans le monde gréco-romain*. Paris.
Martin, M. 2007. 'Monde aquatique et tablette de défixion'. *Études Magiques* 1 www.etudesmagiques.info/2007/EG_2007-03.pdf.
Martin, M. 2010. *Sois maudit! Malédictions et envoûtements dans l'Antiquité*. Paris.
Martin, S. 2010. *The Gnostics: The First Christian Heretics*. Harpenden, Herts.
Martinez, D. 1991. *P. Michigan XVI: A Greek Love Charm from Egypt (P. Mich. 757)*. Atlanta.
Martinez, D. 1995. '"May She Neither Eat nor Drink": Love Magic and Vows of Abstinence'. In Meyer and Mirecki, 335–59.
Mastrocinque, A. 2003 and 2007. *Sylloge Gemmarum Gnosticarum*, Bolletino di Numismatica Monografia, 2 vols. Rome.

Mastrocinque, A. 2014a. 'Acanto e spade nella magia amorosa'. *MHNH* 14: 25-38.
Mastrocinque, A. ed. 2014b. *Les intailles magiques du département des Monnaies, Médailles et Antiques*. Paris.
Mauss, M. 1972. *A General Theory of Magic*, transl. Robert Brain. London.
McCown, C.C. 1923. 'The *Ephesia Grammata* in Popular Belief'. *TAPA* 54: 128-40.
McDonald, K. 2016. Review of Faraone 2012. *BMCR* 2016.02.44.
McEnerney, J.I. 1983. '*Precatio Terrae* and *Precatio Omnium Herbarum*'. *RhM* 126: 175-87.
Merkelbach, R. and M.L. West. 1967. *Fragmenta Hesiodea*. Oxford.
Meyer, M. and P. Mirecki, eds. 1995. *Ancient Magic and Ritual Power*. Leiden.
Meyer, M. and R. Smith. 1999. *Ancient Christian Magic: Coptic Texts of Ritual Power*. Princeton.
Michel, S. 2001. *Die magischen Gemmen im Britischen Museum*, 2 vols. London.
Michel, S. 2004. *Die magischen Gemmen: Zu Bildern und Zauberformeln auf geschnittenen Steinen der Antike und Neuzeit*. Berlin.
Mirecki, P. and M. Meyer, eds. 2002. *Magic and Ritual in the Ancient World*. Leiden.
Molt, M. 1938. *Ad Apulei Madaurensis Metamorphoseon Librum Primum Commentarius Exegeticus*. Groningen.
Moscadi, L. Baldini. 1976a. 'Osservazioni sull' episodio magico del libro VI della *Farsaglia* di Lucano'. *SIFC* 48: 140-99.
Moscadi, L. Baldini. 1976b. '"Murmur" nella terminologia magica'. *SIFC* 48: 254-62.
Mouterde, P.R. 1930. 'La glaive de Dardanos'. *Mélanges de L'Université de Saint Joseph* (Beyrouth) 15.3: 53-64.
Mura, M.I. 1994. 'Le *tabellae defixionum* africane come fonte di storia sociale: nota preliminare'. In *L'Africa romana: atti dell'XI convegno di studio, Cartagine, 15-18 dicembre 1994*, 1535-45. Sassari.
Murano, F. 2012. 'The Oscan Cursing Tablets: Binding Formulae, Cursing Typologies and Thematic Classification'. *AJPh* 133: 629-55.
Muth, R. 1954. *Träger der Lebenskraft: Die Ausscheidungen des Organismus im Volksglauben der Antike*. Wien.
Muth, R. 1968. 'Urin'. *RE* Supptbd. 11.1292-1303.
Nagy, A.M. 2015. 'Engineering Ancient Amulets: Magical Gems of the Roman Imperial Period'. In Boschung and Bremmer, 205-40.
Németh, G. 2013. 'Curses in the Box'. *MHNH* 13: 201-6.
Newlands, C. 1997. 'The Metamorphosis of Ovid's Medea'. In J.J. Clauss and S.I. Johnston, eds. *Medea: Essays on Medea in Myth, Literature, Philosophy, and Art*, 178-208. Princeton.
Nicholson, F.W. 1897. 'The Saliva Superstition in Classical Literature'. *HSCP* 8: 23-40.
Nisbet, R.G.M. and M. Hubbard. 1970. *A Commentary on Horace: Odes Book 1*. Oxford.
Nock, A.D. 1972a. *Essays on Religion and the Ancient World*, ed. Z. Stewart, Oxford.
Nock, A.D. 1972b. 'Greek Magical Papyri'. In Nock, 176-94.
Nock, A.D. 1972c. 'The Lizard in Magic and Religion'. In Nock, 271-6.

Nutton, V. 1992. 'Healers in the Medical Market Place: Towards a Social History of Graeco-Roman Medicine'. In A. Wear, ed. *Medicine in Society: Historical Essays*, 15–58. Cambridge.

Nutton, V. 1995. 'The Medical Meeting Place'. In Ph. J. van der Eijk, H.F.J. Horstmanshoff and P.H. Schrijvers, eds. *Ancient Medicine in Its Socio-Cultural Context Volume 1*, 3–25. Amsterdam.

Nutton, V. 2016. 'Folk Medicine in the Galenic Corpus'. In Harris (2016b), 272–9.

O'Connell, P.A. 2017. 'New Evidence for Hexametric Incantations in Curse Rituals'. *ZPE* 201: 41–6.

Ogden, D. 1999. 'Binding Spells: Curse Tablets and Voodoo Dolls in the Greek and Roman Worlds'. In B. Ankarloo and S. Clark, eds. *Witchcraft and Magic in Europe: Ancient Greece and Rome*, 1–90. Philadelphia.

Ogden, D. 2000. Review of Faraone 1999. *CR* 50: 476–8.

Ogden, D. 2001. *Greek and Roman Necromancy*. Princeton.

Ogden, D. 2002a. *Magic, Witchcraft, and Ghosts in the Greek and Roman Worlds: A Sourcebook*. Oxford.

Ogden, D. 2002b. 'Lucan's Sextus Pompey Episode: Its Necromantic, Political and Literary Background'. In A. Powell and K. Welch, eds. *Sextus Pompeius*, 249–71. Swansea.

Ogden, D. 2008. *Night's Black Agents: Witches, Wizards and the Dead in the Ancient World*. London/New York.

Ogden, D. 2014. 'Animal Magic'. In G.L. Campbell, ed. *The Oxford Handbook of Animals in Classical Thought and Life*. Oxford.

Oliensis, E. 1991. 'Canidia, Canicula, and the Decorum of Horace's *Epodes*'. *Arethusa* 24.1: 107–38.

Oliphant, S.G. 1913. 'The Story of the Strix: Ancient'. *TAPA* 44: 133–49.

Pachoumi, E. 2012. 'Eros as Disease, Torture and Punishment in Magical Literature'. *SO* 86: 74–93.

Pachoumi, E. 2013. 'The Erotic and Separation Spells of the Magical Papyri and *Defixiones*'. *GRBS* 53: 294–325.

Pachoumi, E. 2017. *The Concept of the Divine in the Greek Magical Papyri*. Tübingen.

Parsons, P. 2007. *City of the Sharp-Nosed Fish: The Lives of the Greeks in Roman Egypt*. London.

Paule, M.T. 2014. '*QVAE SAGA, QVIS MAGVS*: On the Vocabulary of the Roman Witch'. *CQ* 64.2: 745–57.

Paule, M.T. 2017. *Canidia, Rome's First Witch*. London.

Pease, A.S. 1935. *P. Vergili Maronis Aeneidos Liber Quartus*. Harvard.

Petherbridge, D. 2013. *Witches and Wicked Bodies*. Edinburgh.

Petropoulos, J.C. 1988. 'The Erotic Magical Papyri'. In V.G. Mandēlaras, ed. *Proceedings of the XVIII International Congress of Papyrology, Athens 25–31 May 1986*, 215–22. Athens.

Petropoulos, J.C. 1993. 'Sappho the Sorceress – Another Look at fr.1 (LP)'. *ZPE* 97: 43–56.

Petrovic, I. 2004. 'ΦΑΡΜΑΚΕΥΤΡΙΑ ohne ΦΑΡΜΑΚΟΝ: Überlegungen zur Komposition des zweiten Idylls von Theokrit'. *Mnemosyne* 57.4: 421–44.

Pharr, C. 1932. 'The Interdiction of Magic in Roman Law'. *TAPA* 63: 269–95.

Phillips, C.R. 1986. 'The Sociology of Religious Knowledge in the Roman Empire'. *ANRW* 16.3: 2677–773.

Phillips, O. 2002. 'The Witches' Thessaly'. In Mirecki and Meyer, 378–86.

Phillips, R. 2003. Review of Faraone 1999. *AC* 72: 476–8.

Pichon, R. 1966. *Index verborum amatoriorum*. Hildesheim.

Pinch, G. 2001. 'Red Things: The Symbolism of Colour in Magic'. In W.V. Davies, ed. *Colour and Painting in Ancient Egypt*, 182–91. London.

Pinch, G. 2006. *Magic in Ancient Egypt*. Rev. edn. Austin, Texas.

Piranomonte, M. 2010. 'Religion and Magic at Rome'. In Gordon and Simón, 191–213.

Piranomonte, M. and F. Marco Simón, eds. 2012. *Contesti magici – Contextos magicos*. Rome.

Pirenne-Delforge, V. 1993. 'L'Iynge dans le discours mythique et les procédures magiques'. *Kernos* 6: 277–89.

Pollard, E.A. 2013. 'Indian Spices and Roman "Magic" in Imperial and Late Antique Indomediterranea'. *Journal of World History* 24.1: 1–23.

Pollard, J. 1977. *Birds in Greek Life and Myth*. London.

Pomeroy, S. 1986. 'Copronyms and the Exposure of Infants in Egypt'. In R.S. Bagnall and W.V. Harris, eds. *Studies in Roman Law in Memory of A. Arthur Schiller*, 147–62. Leiden.

Ponsonby, A. 1980. *Falsehood in Wartime: Containing an Assortment of Lies Circulated Throughout the Nations During the Great War*. Torrance, California.

Preisendanz, K. 1950. Zur Überlieferungsgeschichte der spätantiken Magie'. In *Festgabe Georg Leyh* (*Zentralblatt für Bibliothekswesen Beiheft 75*) (no editor given), 223–40. Leipzig.

Preus, A. 1988. 'Drugs and Psychic States in Theophrastus' *Historia Plantarum* 9.8-20'. In W.W. Fortenbaugh and R.W. Sharples, eds. *Theophrastean Studies on Natural Science, Physics and Metaphysics, Ethics, Religion, and Rhetoric*, 76–99. New Brunswick/Oxford.

Riddle, J.M. 1985. *Dioscorides on Pharmacy and Medicine*. Austin, Texas.

Riddle, J.M. 2010. *Goddesses, Elixirs, and Witches: Plants and Sexuality Throughout Human History*. New York.

Riess, W. 2012. *Performing Interpersonal Violence: Court, Curse, and Comedy in Fourth-Century BCE Athens*. Berlin.

Ripat, P. 2014. 'Cheating Women: Curse Tablets and Roman Wives'. In Stratton and Kalleres, 340–64.

Ritner, R.K. 1993. *The Mechanics of Ancient Egyptian Magical Practice*. Chicago.

Rives, J.B. 1994. 'Tertullian on Child Sacrifice'. *MH* 51.1: 54–63.

Rives, J.B. 1995. 'Human Sacrifice Among Pagans and Christians'. *JRS* 85: 65–85.

Rives, J.B. 2003. Review of Faraone 1999. *AJA* 107: 682–4.

Rives, J.B. 2006. 'Magic, Religion, and Law: The Case of the *Lex Cornelia de sicariis et veneficis*'. In C. Ando and J. Rüpke, eds. *Religion and Law in Classical and Christian Rome*, 47–67. Stuttgart.

Roesch, P. 1966–7. 'Une tablette de malédiction de Tebessa'. *BAA* 2: 231–7.

Romey, K. 2018. 'Exclusive: What May be World's Largest Ancient Mass Child Sacrifice Discovered in Peru'. *National Geographic*, 26 April. Available online: http://press.nationalgeographic.com/2018/04/26/exclusive-what-may-be-worlds-largest-ancient-mass-child-sacrifice-discovered-in-peru/.

Roscher, W.H. 1890. *Über Selene und Verwandtes*. Leipzig.

Rowe, C. 1972. 'Conceptions of Colour and Colour Symbolism in the Ancient World'. In A. Portmann and R. Ritsema, eds. *Eranos Yearbook* 41: 327–62.

Rynearson, N. 2009. 'A Callimachean Case of Lovesickness: Magic, Disease and Desire in *Aetia* Frr. 67–75 Pf.'. *AJPh* 130: 341–65.

Sánchez Natalías, C. 2012. '*Fistus Difloiscat Languat* . . . Re-Reading of *Defixio* Bologna 2'. *ZPE* 181: 140–8.

Sánchez Natalías, C. 2014. '". . . Ut illam ducas . . .": Una nueva interpretación de la *defixio* contra *Salpina*'. *ZPE* 191: 278–81.

Sánchez Natalías, C. 2016. 'A New *Defixio* from Verona'. *ZPE* 199: 119–22.

Scarborough, J. 1978. 'Theophrastus on Herbals and Herbal Remedies'. *Journal of the History of Biology* 11.2: 353–85.

Scarborough, J. 1991. 'The Pharmacology of Sacred Plants, Herbs and Roots'. In Faraone and Obbink, 138–74.

Scarborough, J. 2006. 'Drugs and Drug Lore in the Time of Theophrastus: Folklore. Magic, Botany, Philosophy and the Rootcutters'. *Acta Classica* 49: 1–29.

Schlam, C.C. 1992. *The Metamorphoses of Apuleius: On Making an Ass of Oneself*. Chapel Hill.

Scholz, H.H. 1937. 'Der Hund in der griechisch-römischen Magie und Religion'. Diss., Berlin.

Scholz, M. 2011. 'Verdammter Dieb. Kleinkriminalität im Spiegel von Fluchtafeln'. In M. Reuter and R. Schiavone, eds. *Gefährliches Pflaster: Kriminalität im Römischen Reich*, 88–105. Mainz.

Scholz, M. and A. Kropp. 2004. '"Priscilla, die Verräterin": Eine Fluchtafel aus Groß-Gerau'. In K. Brodersen and A. Kropp, eds. *Fluchtafeln: Neue Funde und neue Deutungen zum antiken Schadenzauber*, 33–40. Frankfurt am Main.

Schreckenberg, H. 1964. *Ananke: Untersuchungen zur Geschichte des Wortgebrauchs*. Munich.

Schwenn, F. 1915. *Die Menschenopfer bei den Griechen und Römern*. Giessen.

Scobie, A. 1978. 'Strigiform Witches in Roman and Other Cultures'. *Fabula* 19.1: 74–101.

Segal, C.P. 1984. 'Underreading and Intertextuality: Sappho, Simaetha, and Odysseus in Theocritus' Second Idyll'. *Arethusa* 17.2: 201–9.

Sicherl, M. 1937. 'Die Tiere in der griechisch-ägyptischen Zauberei: hauptsächlich nach den griechischen Zauberpapyri'. Diss., Prag.

Smelik, K.A.D. 1979. 'The Cult of the Ibis in the Graeco-Roman Period, with Special Attention to the Data from the Papyri'. In M.J. Vermaseren, ed. *Studies in Hellenistic Religions*, 225–43. Leiden.

Smith, G.A. 2004. 'The Myth of the Vaginal Soul'. *GRBS* 44: 199–225.

Smith, J.Z. 1995. 'Trading Places'. In Meyer and Mirecki, 13–27.

Smith, M.S., ed. 1975. *Petronii Arbitri Cena Trimalchionis*. Oxford.

Smith, P., L.E. Stager, J.A. Greene and G. Avishai. 2013. 'Age Estimations Attest to Infant Sacrifice at the Carthage Tophet'. *Antiquity* 87: 1191–9.

Sørensen, J. 2007. *A Cognitive Theory of Magic*. Lanham/New York.

Spaeth, B.S. 2010. 'The Terror that Comes in the Night: The Night Hag and Supernatural Assault in Latin Literature'. In E. Scioli and C. Walde, eds. *Sub Imagine Somni: Nighttime Phenomena in Greco-Roman Culture*, 231–58. Pisa.

Spaeth, B.S. 2014. 'From Goddess to Hag: The Greek and Roman Witch in Classical Literature'. In Stratton and Kalleres, 41–70.

Spelman, E.V. 1982. 'Woman as Body: Ancient and Contemporary Views'. *Feminist Studies* 8.1: 109–31.

Stannard, J. 1962. 'The Plant Called Moly'. *Osiris* 14: 254–307.

Stannard, J. 1982. 'Medicinal Plants and Folk Remedies in Pliny, *Historia Naturalis*'. *History and Philosophy of the Life Sciences* 4.1: 3–23.

Stratton, K.B. 2007. *Naming the Witch: Magic, Ideology, and Stereotype in the Ancient World*. New York.

Stratton, K.B. and D.S. Kalleres, eds. 2014. *Daughters of Hecate: Women and Magic in the Ancient World*. New York.

Stroud, R.S. 2013. *Corinth Volume XVIII.6: The Sanctuary of Demeter and Kore – The Inscriptions*. Princeton.

Stylow, A.U. 2012. 'Stumm wie ein Frosch ohne Zunge'. *ZPE* 181: 149–55.

Tambiah, S.J. 1968. 'The Magical Power of Words'. *Man* 3.2: 175–208.

Tambiah, S.J. 1990. *Magic, Science, Religion, and the Scope of Rationality*. Cambridge.

Tate, T. 1991. *Children for the Devil: Ritual Abuse and Satanic Crime*. London.

Tavenner, E. 1916. *Studies in Magic from Latin Literature*. New York.

Tavenner, E. 1942. 'The Use of Fire in Greek and Roman Love Magic'. In *Studies in Honor of Frederick W. Shipley* (no editor given), 17–37. St. Louis.

Te Velde, H. 1967. *Seth, God of Confusion: A Study of His Role in Egyptian Mythology and Religion*. Leiden.

Teijeiro, M. García. 1993. 'Religion and Magic'. *Kernos* 6: 123–38.

Teijeiro, M. García. 1999. 'Il secondo "Idillio" di Teocrito'. *QUCC* 61: 71–86.

Thesaurus Defixionum Magdeburgensis. Available online: http://www.thedema.ovgu.de/thedema.php.

Thomas, J.A.C. 1975. *The Institutes of Justinian: Text, Translation and Commentary*. Amsterdam/Oxford.

Thomas, K. 1971. *Religion and the Decline of Magic*. Middlesex/New York, 1971.

Thompson, D'Arcy W. 1936. *A Glossary of Greek Birds*. Oxford.

Tobyn, G., A. Denham and M. Whitelegg. 2011. *The Western Herbal Tradition: 2000 Years of Medicinal Plant Knowledge*. Edinburgh/London/New York.

Tomlin, R.S.O. 2010. 'Cursing a Thief in Iberia and Britain'. In Gordon and Simón, 245–73.

Tomlin, R.S.O. 2018. *Britannia Romana: Roman Inscriptions and Roman Britain*. Oxford/Philadelphia.

Treggiari, S. 1991. *Roman Marriage: Iusti Coniuges from the Time of Cicero to the Time of Ulpian*. Oxford.

Tremel, J. 2004. *Magica Agonistica: Fluchtafeln im antiken Sport*. Nikephoros Beiheft 10. Hildesheim.

Tupet, A.-M. 1976. *La magie dans la poésie latine*. Paris.

Tupet, A.-M. 1986. 'Rites magiques dans l'Antiquité romaine'. *ANRW* 16.3: 2591–675.

Turner, M. 2005. 'Aphrodite and Her Birds: The Iconography of Pagenstecher Lēkythoi'. *BICS* 48.1: 57–96.

Urbanová, D. 2018. *Latin Curse Tablets of the Roman Empire*, transl. Natália Gachallová. Innsbruck.

van der Horst, P.W. 1994. 'Silent Prayer in Antiquity'. *Numen* 41.1: 1–25.

Veenman, J. 2003. Review of Faraone 1999. *CW* 96.2: 219–21.

Vermaseren, M. 1977. *Cybele and Attis: The Myth and the Cult*. London.

Versnel, H.S. 1985. '"May He Not Be Able to Sacrifice . . .": Concerning a Curious Formula in Greek and Latin Curses'. *ZPE* 58: 247–69.

Versnel, H.S. 1991a. 'Beyond Cursing: The Appeal to Justice in Judicial Prayers'. In Faraone and Obbink, 60–106.

Versnel, H.S. 1991b. 'Some Reflections on the Relationship Magic-Religion'. *Numen* 38.2: 177–97.

Versnel, H.S. 1998. '"And Any Other Part of the Entire Body There May Be . . .": An Essay on Anatomical Curses'. In F. Graf, ed. *Ansichten griechischer Rituale: Geburtstag-Symposium für Walter Burkert*, 217–67. Stuttgart/Leipzig.

Versnel, H.S. 2002a. 'Writing Mortals and Reading Gods'. In D. Cohen, ed. *Demokratie, Recht und soziale Kontrolle im klassischen Athen*, 37–76. München.

Versnel, H.S. 2002b. 'The Poetics of the Magic Charm: An Essay on the Power of Words'. In Mirecki and Meyer, 105–58.

Villalobos, C.M. and A.C. Barrientos. 2015. 'Simbolismo Animal, Astrología y Sexualidad en los Textos Antiguos'. *MHNH* 15: 141–82.

Voutiras, E. 1998. *Dionysophōntos Gamoi: Marital Life and Magic in Fourth Century Pella*. Amsterdam.

Waegeman, M. 1984. 'The Gecko, the Hoopoe . . . and Lice'. *L'antiquité classique* 53: 218–25.

Watson, L. 1991. *Arae: The Curse Poetry of Antiquity*. Leeds.

Watson, L. 1994. 'Horace *Odes* 1.23 and 1.25: A Thematic Pairing?'. *AUMLA* 82.1: 67–84.

Watson, L. 2003. *A Commentary on Horace's Epodes*. Oxford.

Watson, L. 2004. 'Making Water Not Love: Apuleius, *Metamorphoses* 1.13–14'. *CQ* 54.2: 651–5.
Watson, L. 2008. 'Juvenal *Satire* 6: Misogyny or Misogamy? The Evidence of Protreptics on Marriage'. *PLLS* 13: 269–96.
Watson, L. and P. Watson. 2014. *Juvenal Satire 6*. Cambridge.
Watson, P.A. 1993. 'Stepmothers and *Hippomanes*: *Georgics* 3.282f.'. *Latomus* 52.4: 842–7.
Watson, P.A. 1995. *Ancient Stepmothers: Myth, Misogyny and Reality*. Leiden.
Weber, M. 1970. 'Frosch'. *RAC* 8: 524–38.
Weissenborn, W. and H.J. Müller. 1962. *Titi Liui ab Urbe Condita Libri, Band IV, Buch 21–3*. Berlin.
Williams, G. 1962. 'Poetry in the Moral Climate of Augustan Rome'. *JRS* 52: 28–46.
Winkler, J.J. 1991. 'The Constraints of Eros'. In Faraone and Obbink, 214–43.
Wortmann, D. 1968. 'Neue magische Texte'. *BJ* 168: 56–111.
Wünsch, R. 1909. 'Deisidaimoniaka'. *ARW* 12: 1–45.
Xella, P., J. Quinn, V. Melchiorri and P. van Dommelen. 2013. 'Phoenician Bones of Contention'. *Antiquity* 87: 1199–207. Published conjointly with Smith, Stager et al. under the heading 'Cemetery or Sacrifice? Infant Burials at the Carthage Tophet'.
Zecchi, M. 2010. *Sobek of Shedet: the Crocodile God in the Fayyum in the Dynastic Period*. Todi [Perugia].
Ziebarth, E. 1934. 'Neue Verfluchtungstafeln aus Attika, Boiotien, und Euboia'. *SB Berlin* 33: 1022–50.

Index

amatory spells
  explicitly sexual character of 33–4
  extreme violence of 24–33
  Faraone's *erōs* and *philia* spells 34–6
  gender of targets confused in formularies 36–7
  homoerotic 52 n.93
  male-authored spells aimed at sexually available women 41–3
  philtrokatadesmos thaumastos 26, 30, 192–3
  rationalisations of violence in 26–33
  'romantic' approach to 33
  sleep deprivation and fever invoked in 31
  solipsism of 33–4
  utilised by both sexes 36–41
amulets
  animal shapes carved on 152
  harmful 153–4
  healing 128, 130–1, 133, 135–6, 138, 142, 148, 150–1, 153–4, 189
  inscribed or uninscribed 149–50
  lamellae 152–3
  perishable or durable 149–50
  pictogrammatic 151–2
  prophylactic 153
  similarities to *PGM* 154–5
  stones, magical powers of 150–1
animals and magic
  blood, use of 138
  botanical aliases for animals 127, 187–8
  cost of animal ingredients 139–40
  divine assistants, animals used to create 132
  donkey-Seth connection utilised 134–5
  doves 130–1, 135–6, 138–9, 158 n.58
  fantastic creatures used by literary witches 146–9
  folk-medicine 128–31
  frogs and toads 118, 163 n.130
  gecko *under* 'lizards'
  hippomanes 146–8
  hyena 158 n.48
  libidinous animals used in erotic spells 134
  lizards 130–2, 136–7, 142, 146, 150–1, 162 n.110
  moles 129, 132–3, 137, 157 n.43, 158 nn.44–5, n.47
  mutilation of animals 85, 97 n.145, 131–2, 151
  preservation of animal ingredients 138–9
  procuring of animal ingredients 137–8
  right and left, significance of 136
  sex of animal corresponds to sex of beneficiary 135
  suppliers of animal parts 139

Belgian baby without hands 210
Betz, H.D. 8
botanēarsis under 'Herbal Magic'

D'Anastasi, J. 7–8
defixiones (curse tablets)
  agonistic 61–2
  anatomical *defixiones*, violence of 69–72
  Anna Perenna hoard 81–2
  Audollent, A. 63
  categories of 62–3
  charaktēres and *uoces magicae* in 59
  commissioned from professionals 59
  cursing formulae in 60, 85
  defined 57
  deposition sites for 59–60
  disproportion between crime and punishment in 72
  earliest instances 58, 89 n.56
  feelings of animus behind 74–5

illogicality in 80
infernal powers implement 60–1, 84
internationalisation of 58–9, 76
irony in 94 n.100, 96 n.126
lead used for tablets 57, 89 n.36
lethal intent of 73–4, 76, 78
listing of body parts for punishment in 72–3
Mainz *defixio*-cache, anomalous features of 76–9
nekudaimones, aōroi, biaiothanatoi invoked in 60
new discoveries necessitate expanded view of 63–4
'onomastic' 60
pictograms in 59
pierced with nails 30, 57, 81
'prayers for justice' 62–3, 84, 89 n.42
psychosomatic effects 85–6
retrograde writing in 85, 96 n.124, 97 n.141
rhetorical features 59
rites attendant on deposition of 84
social status of users 59, 61, 68–9
symbolic melting of 77
uia Ostiense defixio, unusual features 64–70
Wünsch's *Defixionum Tabellae Atticae* 61
Dieterich, A. 8

Ephesia grammata 59
Evil Eye 107, 149

Faraone, C. 13–15, 18 n.17, 28, 34–7, 39–42, 51 n.79, 54 n.115, 55 n.121, 61, 85, 89 n.43, 132, 151, 164 n.139, 175, 193
Frankfurter, D. 12, 207, 210

Germanicus 32, 69
Gordon, R. 18 n.9, 72, 90 n.46, 97 n.148, 128, 137, 158 n.48, 170, 180, 189
Greek Magical Papyri (*PGM*)
  discovery and publication 7–11
  Egyptian religious and cultural elements in 12, 127
  Greek elements 13
  Greek or Egyptian inspiration? 13, 17

love spells predominate in 11
polyglot 10
setbacks to publication 8–9
tralaticious character of 14–15
transmission history of 14
variety of spells in 11

Hecate 15, 60, 68, 103, 110, 135, 146, 170, 196 n.4, 197 n.23, 224 n.52
Henrichs, A. 9–10, 222 n.25
herbal magic
  bittervetch 118–19
  botanēarsis 101, 105–6, 113–15, 122 n.10
  dangers of 101–3, 122 n.14
  left hand used in 114
  protective measures during 102–3, 114
  protocols for 106, 114
divinity of plants 115
henbane 118–19
herbs, magical pedigree of 99–103
hupotamnon 100
katananke 109
mandrake 117, 122 n.20, fig. 6
moly 100, 168–9
peony 101–3
pharmacological potency of magical herbs 118–20
pharmaka, meaning of 100–1
rhizotomos 106, 112, 115, 117, 119
Solanaceae and witches 117
Sophocles *Rhizotomoi* 100, 176
human sacrifice in magic
  Apollonius of Tyana accused 214
  Carthaginian child sacrifice 218–19, 224 n.60
  Catilinarian conspiracy the template for such accusations 212–13
  Christian child sacrifice allegations rebutted 211–12
  Dölger, F.J. 212
  Elagabalus and ritual murder 219 n.2
  Epiphanius *Panarion* 206–7
  Eucharist misunderstood 208
  extispicy an alleged motive for 206, 209–10
  human body parts used in magical procedures 216–17

human sacrifice outlawed by Senate 216
inscriptional evidence of killing for
    magical ends 217–18
manifestly false accusations 213–15
perverted sacrifice, parallels between
    ancient and modern accounts of
    205–10
prohibited by Roman legal codes 216
'retorsion' technique 207–8
stereotyped nature of accusations 216
Vatinius accused of sacrificing children
    213–14

Lord of the Rings, The 82–3
Louvre poppet 26 and fig. 1

magic
    abracadabra 130
    antipathy 107, 121, 134
    belief in efficacy 1, 32–3, 84
    books, circulation of 15–16, 23
    circles 114, 117, 128
    colour of agent significant 107–8,
        135–6, 150, 159 nn.77–8
    contiguity 111–12, 127–8
    'doctrine of signatures' 103, 107
    dung, uses of 127, 131, 134, 136–9, 142,
        157 n.34, 200 n.59
    emic and etic approaches 1
    folk-medicine 5, 104, 106, 116–17, 120,
        129, 130, 156 n.16; *also* 'Animals
        and magic: folk medicine' and
        'Magic: medicine and'
    Isis and 194
    iunx 162 n.119, 196 n.9
    laws of 106–10
    magical materials, categories of 186
    medicine and 104–5
    On the Sacred Disease 193
    ousia 24
    Oxyrhynchus Papyri 11
    performance of 141–4
    performative utterance 2, 85, 96 n.129
    'persuasive analogy' 13, 28, 77–80, 85,
        108, 110–11, 174; *also* 'Magic:
        similia similibus formula'
    phylacteries against 32, 84, 149, 153
    'pluralising for power' 85, 113, 121
    religion and 1, 208

remote locales, a locus of 115
ritual nakedness 111
ritual purity in 125 n.60
similarity, law of 5, 106–7, 127–8, 135,
    155 n.8; *also* 'Magic: doctrine of
    signatures'
similia similibus formula 79, 85, 128–9,
    174
social status of users 41–2, 51 n.79,
    87 n.18, 130, 140
Supplementum Magicum 10
sympathy 4, 103, 105, 107–11, 114,
    122 n.13, 127–8, 134; *also*
    'Magic: similarity, law of'
transference 111–12, 118, 127–30, 132,
    135, 147, 155 n.9
urine and 112, 186
workshops 143–5
Malinowski, B. 1, 18 n.14, 113
Mauss, M. 1, 106–8, 111
medicine, herbs integral to 103–4
Moon 103, 113–14, 118

nomen omen 109

Ogden, D. 1–2, 18 n.9, 26, 49 n.62, 59, 62,
    75, 158 n.48, 164 n.140, 172, 178,
    185, 202 n.94

Pliny and the Magi 112–14, 129, 132–3,
    156 n.26
Preisendanz, K. 9

Satanic rituals, alleged 203–4
Seth 24, 134
spitting, apotropaic 102, 111, 128
strix 67, 70, 91 n.66, 146–7
'Sword of Dardanos' 37, 154

Tupet, A.-M. 117

'vaginal soul' 34, 50 n.70
Versnel, H.S. 27, 44 n.20, 46 n.30, 54 n.109,
    60, 62–3, 69–70, 72–3, 76
'voodoo dolls' 23, 81

Winkler, J. 26, 28
witches in literature
    aged 176, 179, 182–3

'black and midnight hags' 194–5
Canidia 16, 41, 146–7, 176, 178, 181,
    183, 187–8, 190, 192–4, 201 n.82,
    202 nn.86, 90, 217
Circe 6, 99–100, 146, 168–9, 175–6,
    180, 183, 190, 192
documentary spells, similarity with
    witches' procedures 172–5,
    186–8
Erictho, 'the witch's witch' 147, 184–7,
    192, 214–15
fail when put to the test 179–81
fantastic powers claimed by 177–8
gender of 167, 190–3

Greek and Roman fictional witches,
    differences between 175
horrific 183–6
Hecate, goddess of witches 196 n.4
Medea 99–100, 104, 146–8, 169–72,
    175–6, 183, 188, 192
natural processes overturned by 177
politico-moral dimension 193–4
polyvalence of Roman witches 176–7
profiles, various 167
risibility 181–3
Roman fascination with 189–90
Simaitha 99, 103, 146, 172–6
sympathetic figures 188–9

www.ingramcontent.com/pod-product-compliance
Lightning Source LLC
Chambersburg PA
CBHW050349230426
43663CB00010B/2047